DATE DUE

THE COMPUTER INVASION

THE COMPUTER INVASION

Craig T. Norback

VNR VAN NOSTRAND REINHOLD COMPANY
NEW YORK   CINCINNATI   ATLANTA   DALLAS   SAN FRANCISCO
LONDON   TORONTO   MELBOURNE

Van Nostrand Reinhold Company Regional Offices:
New York Cincinnati Atlanta Dallas San Francisco

Van Nostrand Reinhold Company International Offices:
London Toronto Melbourne

Copyright © 1981 by Litton Educational Publishing, Inc.

Library of Congress Catalog Card Number: 80-23902
ISBN: 0-442-26121-7

Manufactured in the United States of America

Published by Van Nostrand Reinhold Company
135 West 50th Street, New York, N.Y. 10020

Published simultaneously in Canada by Van Nostrand Reinhold Ltd.

15 14 13 12 11 10 9 8 7 6 5 4 3 2 1

Library of Congress Cataloging in Publication Data

Norback, Craig T
    The computer invasion.

    Includes index.
    1. Privacy, Right of—United States.   2. Records—
Law and legislation—United States.   3. Records—
United States—Data processing.   I. Title.
KF1262.N67   342.73′0854   80-23902
ISBN 0-442-26121-7

Foreword

The Computer Invasion was written to provide rudimentary information on most of the personal files to which an individual might desire access. *Rudimentary* is the correct word because, as an individual will quickly find out, there are no available guidelines that apply to every file.

The book is divided into three main sections. The section on files maintained by the federal government lists the name of the file, who has the right of access to that file, and any special instructions concerning how a request for information should be made. For an update on any files maintained by the federal government, the individual should refer to the current edition of the *Federal Register.*

The section on files maintained by state and local governments is less detailed than the section on the federal government. This is because each state is responsible for enacting its own "privacy law" and some states as yet have not passed such a law. Most states require that the individual contact the state department or agency involved. Note, however, that most governors' offices can provide the individual with information on which department or agency might be involved. In the case of local governments, the individual must go to the town, county, or township office and make inquiries.

Caveat emptor certainly applies to the consumer section. In some instances, there are laws to protect consumer rights, as is the case with the credit and insurance companies. For the most part, the individual must go to the source and make a request for a file or those portions needed for medical or personal reasons. Whether a file is released may depend upon the company or doctor involved.

The main point is that the individual must take the initiative and keep trying, particularly where large government agencies are involved. The individual must not be put off by anyone at any level of business or government; sometimes starting at the top is the best course of action. In some instances, a first request will bring results; more often, a third or fourth request will be needed. Legal action may be necessary as a last resort.

Introduction

Americans today are scrutinized, watched, counted, recorded, and questioned by more governmental agencies, social scientists, and law enforcement officials than at any other time in our history. Each trip on an airline, the simple reservation of a room at a hotel chain, and each car rental leave distinct tracks in the memory of a computer. Few of us are aware to what extent modern technology is capable of monitoring, centralizing, and evaluating these electronic entries, no matter how numerous or how scattered. When collated and analyzed, they tell a great deal about our activities, habits, and associations.

To an astounding degree, federal agencies and private companies are using computers and microfilm technology to collect, store, and exchange information about the activities of private citizens. Rarely does a week go by without the existence of a new data bank being disclosed; many more remain undercover.

By and large, these data-gathering activities are well-intended efforts to achieve socially desirable objectives, or at the very least they can be justified as such by the surveillance agency. But there is a negative side to these mushrooming data banks, both private and governmental. We know, for example, that army intelligence units have kept watch on the lawful public activities of certain groups and have prepared incident reports and dossiers on members of such nonviolent organizations as the NAACP, the ACLU, the Southern Christian Leadership Conference, and the Women's Strike for Peace.

Arthur Miller of Harvard Law School points out that many Americans, while recognizing the benefits of the computer in the twentieth century, are afraid that the computer may become the heart of a surveillance system in which their homes, finances, and associations are bared to even the most casual observer.

These fears arise primarily from five factors: (1) government demands for more information about individuals, with which to carry out its various responsibilities; (2) burgeoning private sector activities in research, market analysis, and procedures for handling economic transactions; (3) evidence that the Social Security number and other types of personal identifiers are used in ways unknown to their owners; (4) the inability of individuals to readily determine what records are kept about them, or who has access to the records and for what purposes; (5) the impact of modern data-processing technology on the handling of information at almost incomprehensible speeds.

While modern technology has made privacy a particularly pressing issue, it is scarcely a new concern. At the turn of the century, a new form of recordkeeping – photography – was seen as a possible invasion of privacy. In 1927, Justice Louis D. Brandeis wrote in a dissenting opinion in *Olmstead* v. *United States* that "every unjustifiable intrusion by the Government upon the privacy of the individual, whatever the means employed, must be deemed a violation of the Fourth Amendment."

The key word here is *unjustifiable*. Safeguards against privacy invasion have lagged behind mushrooming technological development, leaving major areas of recordkeeping altogether open to abuse by the recordkeepers. As noted, information-gathering and -retaining activities have touched upon almost all phases of our lives; those areas most vulnerable to invasion by computer fall primarily within four major categories: criminal justice information, employee records, data banks, and consumer privacy interests. Legislation dealing with possible invasions of privacy in these areas has been the subject of several commissions and panels since the signing into law of the Privacy Act of 1974, which pertains mainly to the practices of federal agencies.

State and local governments, as well as the private sector, remain relatively free of restraint; indeed, abuses at the federal level continue to occur either through failure to adhere to the principles of the Privacy Act or through loopholes in the legislation.

All citizens concerned with the possible invasion of their privacy have an obligation to consider the various means by which the computer may touch their lives in these four areas. They should also consider the legislation necessary to protect them.

Criminal Justice Information

While law enforcement agencies are the primary collectors of criminal justice information, they are not the sole users of it. Therefore, legislation dealing with such information is a fundamental issue in the protection of individual rights. Without exploring too deeply the enormously complicated issues involved in setting up such legislation (Should there be a single agency to administer and enforce the provisions of any bill? Is noncompliance with such a bill a proper subject for criminal penalties?), let us look into the major considerations affecting a possible invasion of personal privacy in regard to criminal justice information.

It seems to be generally agreed that individuals' access to their own records is an important aspect of any privacy legislation. With respect to criminal justice records, however, unique problems arise:

Rap sheet data. Should individuals have access to their own rap sheets? Should access be permitted wherever the information is located, or only at central repositories? Who has the responsibility to correct data? Should data be available only to the individual or also to others at his or her request or with his or her consent?

Correctional records. Should individuals have full access to correctional records or should they be restricted? How should records of other agencies in a correction file — presentence reports, psychiatric reports — be handled?

Intelligence and investigative records. Can access be permitted without jeopardizing law-enforcement interests? Is the granting of access consistent with the rules of discovery in criminal proceedings? If access to active files is denied, can access to closed files be authorized after a limited period?

Audit trails. Should an individual have access to the audit trail? Can distinctions properly be made among the various types of information regarding access to audit trails? Is there a proper distinction between records of criminal justice access in connection with permitting individuals access to audit trails?

Sealing and expungement. Should some or all criminal justice records be sealed or expunged after a period of time? Expungement admits of no exceptions; the record ceases to exist. Sealing, on the other hand, may permit exceptions; the seal on any record can be broken for specified reasons.

Which records should be subject to sealing or expungement? After what period of time?

Automated versus manual systems. Whether valid or not, there appears to be more public concern about automated criminal justice information systems than about manual ones. Should there be a total prohibition on patrol-car and other mobile terminals? Should automated centralized systems operate on a pointer system (that is, an index that merely indicates what agency, if any, has a record on an individual) rather than store information directly?

Noncriminal justice access. Should only conviction information be available, or may other rap-sheet information be provided? Under what circumstances, if any, should investigative or intelligence information be available for noncriminal justice purposes? Is it necessary to make some correctional information available in order to secure rehabilitation services?

Arrest records. What can we do about information that notes only an arrest and does not indicate any disposition of charges? Should dissemination of an arrest record outside the arresting agency be prohibited, thus denying the information to noncriminal justice agencies and to other criminal justice agencies as well? Or should access be permitted to current arrest information but not arrests for which no disposition is indicated within a specified reasonable time? Or should circumstances in which criminal and noncriminal justice agencies have access to arrest information be narrowly defined? Sealing and expungement are particularly relevant to these considerations.

Impact on the press. Impact on the press is one of the most troublesome aspects of any criminal justice information bill. If certain information is to be protected from public disclosure, then it must not be available to the press. On the other hand, the press can serve as a safeguard against abuses in the system, but only if it has access to information. If rap sheets, for instance, consist entirely of notations that were originally public information, can the compilation of that information be denied to the press? Is a distinction feasible between current information available to the press and past history that is not available?

To be sure, part of a citizen's right of privacy is lost through engagement in criminal activity. Nevertheless, it seems apparent that legislation must be developed that clearly defines the degree to which that loss is subject, especially when so many cases exist in which arrest does not lead to conviction.

Employee Records

Personnel records frequently contain collections of information acquired from many sources and unknown to the employee or applicant for employment. This information, often widely shared among officials of the employing organization and with other organizations, is used for a variety of personnel management purposes, as well as for answering inquiries from creditors, law enforcement agencies, private investigators, recruitment agencies, and other prospective employers. These varied uses can constitute a substantial threat to the personal privacy of the individuals about whom personnel records are maintained.

Personnel managers must ensure that the personnel management system contains the information needed to carry out their responsibilities effectively. They must also take all steps necessary to protect the privacy of employees and applicants.

Five fundamental principles for handling personal information in the files of any recordkeeping organization are gaining wide acceptance, although they are by no means universally followed:

1. There must be no personal-data recordkeeping operation whose very existence is secret.

2. There must be a way for individuals to find out what information about them is in a record and how it is used.

3. There must be a way for individuals to prevent information about them that was obtained for one purpose from being used or made available for other purposes.

4. There must be a way for individuals to amend or correct a record of identifiable information about themselves, at little or no expense.

5. Any organization involved with identifiable personal information must ensure the reliability of the data and take precautions to prevent its misuse.

An employee's privacy, however, cannot be guaranteed simply by proscribing the collection and dissemination of certain types of data. Detailed procedures must be developed for controlling the acquisition, retention, and dissemination of information concerning employees, and these procedures should be standardized.

Ideally, the detailed operating procedures should make clear which items of information individuals are required to provide about themselves and which they may refuse to provide. They should provide for a designated point at which user requests for information are received and processed. The procedures should specify how long information is to be retained and who is allowed to see it or change it and under what circumstances. Security procedures to be adopted to control access to the data, and methods for verifying their accuracy and timeliness, should be spelled out.

The matter of unqualified access to records by employees, or by candidates for employment, does indeed raise questions. Should they have full access to medical information or information supplied in confidence to the employer or prospective employer? Who else in the employing organization has the right of access to employee records? Who should be able to see whether an employee has taken out a loan or mortgage, has life insurance, or has had checks bounce? To whom are performance evaluations and efficiency reports relevant? Who needs to know an employee's outside activities and club or political affiliations?

These questions must be answered not only by the agencies and companies collecting and using the data, but on a more personal level, by the individual employees or job seekers. How much of their privacy, in short, are they willing to relinquish in order to earn a living?

Data Banks

The five fundamental principles listed previously for handling personal information about employees or candidates for employment are applicable in toto to *any* fair information practice, and should govern the acquisition and retention of information by data banks in any sector. General legislation on personal-data recordkeeping practices of governmental agencies, from the local to the federal level, can provide both the starting point for, and the backbone of, a comprehensive framework of safeguards for personal privacy. Once established in general legislation, basic individual rights as well as obligations of recordkeeping organizations can be reaffirmed, strengthened, extended, or modified in other statutes or in implementing regulations. Drafting such legislation, however, is not easy. There are no models to follow, and expert advice seems to be both hard to come by and extraordinarily diverse.

Most general data-bank legislation consists of five principal parts, each of which poses as many questions as it answers. The questions in themselves illustrate the enormous complexity of the privacy issue and the insidious and invasive paths that the recordkeeping process can take.

The first basic requirement of data-bank legislation establishes individuals' rights to see, copy, review, and challenge records about themselves. Conceptually, this section may seem the least complicated of all, its principal objectives being to guarantee individuals the right to establish that a recordkeeping organization does indeed maintain a record about them; to see and copy it in a form they can understand (i.e., decoded if the record is kept in machine-readable form); to challenge the accuracy, relevancy, timeliness, and completeness of the information; and to find out who has access to it and for what purposes.

Clear-cut requirement? Not exactly. How, for example, do people establish that records are being kept about them? Should they be able to see, copy, and challenge all information in that record, once they find it—for example, information about their health? information pertaining to others who are also named in the record? information provided by a third party, which would reveal the third party's identity?

And suppose an individual claims the information is inaccurate, outdated, irrelevant, or incomplete—whose judgment should prevail? Who should be required to verify what? If the differences cannot be resolved, what recourse does the individual have? What about the period during which the record is being contested? Should the individual be able to insert a statement in the record setting forth his or her version of the facts? Many other questions can be raised.

A second basic provision of data-bank legislation ought to impose certain minimum obligations on recordkeeping organizations. Recognizing that individuals cannot ask to see records they do not know exist, regulations for serving notice must be established. Individuals asked to provide information about themselves should be told why they are being asked, under what legal authority, whether they can refuse to answer, and what will happen if they do, and what uses will be made of the information. Assurances that information will be kept confidential are not reliable.

In addition to the notice served to the individual at the time of the inquiry, certainly the public is entitled to some form of general notice attesting to the existence of each personal-data recordkeeping system, describing its principal characteristics and outlining the steps individuals must take to find out if records are being kept about them, what information the records contain, and the procedures for challenge.

And what degree of accuracy can the public logically demand of the data bank? To expect the bank to meet some absolute standard of accuracy totally unrelated to the uses for which its records will be used is perhaps unduly demanding of time and money. But surely the citizenry is entitled to assurance, by legislation, that any information the data bank actually uses in making a decision about an individual is as accurate, relevant, timely, and complete as is necessary to insure that the information itself does not cause an unfair decision to be made.

Third, the principle that an individual's consent should be obtained before divulging information in a record about him or her is the backbone of a responsible transfer and disclosure policy. Obviously, however, if that principle had to be followed to the letter, most government organizations and many private ones would cease to function.

Generally, there are three reference points in drafting "conditions of disclosure" policy: (1) existing so-called confidentiality statutes that forbid or otherwise limit certain types of disclosures; (2) existing public-record statutes that mandate certain disclosures; (3) "threshold requirements" to be applied in cases where information transfers and disclosures are not covered by existing statutes or where existing statutes are being superseded.

The key point in the first two cases is that the decision to overturn or reaffirm existing law should not be made lightly lest a purported privacy statute turn out to be a substantial stimulant to the free (i.e., without consent) disclosure and circulation of personal information.

The third reference point, the threshold issue, is equally delicate because it involves the establishment of need-to-know policies. To what extent do we want extensive legislation to tie the hands of officers and employees of the data bank who need day-to-day access to the records? Do we want to impede unnecessarily the work of statisticians and researchers? How can we cope with emergency situations where the best interests of the record subject would be served by permitting some outside person access to a record about him or her? And what about a sizable class of disclosures for which there seems to be no reason to suspend the individual consent requirement except that not to do so would create an administrative nightmare? Would informing individuals of such "routine" uses at the time when they are asked to provide information about themselves constitute their explicit consent?

A fourth basic provision of any data-bank regulation must deal with which records or record systems ought to be exempted from privacy legislation. Should there be blanket statutory exemptions for certain categories of records, such as those maintained by criminal justice agencies? Should the rulemaking route to obtaining discretionary exemptions involve a public hearing and an opportunity for court review of the final determination? From which specific requirements should exemptions be permitted?

If we are to concede that some justification exists for the exemption of certain records from the controls we have been discussing, can we be absolutely assured that the exemption procedure would be one that modifies rights or permits deviations from organizational obligations only when it is clear that some significant individual *interest* will be served or that some paramount societal interest can be persuasively demonstrated?

Finally, the fifth requirement of any data-bank regulation must deal with remedies, either civil or criminal, to be taken when a recordkeeping organization is in contempt of legislation enacted to protect privacy. Should the data bank be vulnerable to civil suits for privacy safeguard violations that do not result in actual injury to the individual? For violations that do not result from arbitrary, willful, or capricious conduct? Of particular importance in fashioning a remedies provision will be the continuing existence of public-records statutes that penalize *withholding* rather than disclosure of personal information; the two requirements are not easily reconciled.

Control of data-bank recordkeeping is obviously of first priority in the battle to protect our privacy from computer invasion. Experience suggests that the government first put its own house in order, since that is the seat of the majority of recordkeeping organizations, before pressing the fight for privacy against giant credit bureaus, medical data banks, educational institutions, and all the rest of the private sector eager to commit our lives to tape.

Consumer Interests in Privacy

Consumer interests in privacy extend to records containing information on the acquisition of property, services, money, insurance, or credit for personal or family use. The breadth and diversity of consumer transactions and the variety of recordkeeping practices associated with them defy easy definition of personal privacy interests, specification of privacy abuses, or prescription of effective remedies against infringements of privacy.

The effective operation of the modern marketplace seems to require the collection and use of consumer-related data. Business decisions affecting consumers based on inaccurate, obsolete, irrelevant, and incomplete data can seriously jeopardize the reputation and economic interests of the individual. On the other hand, misuse of information can similarly produce adverse consequences for the individual. Certainly unrestrained access to records on consumers and linkages of these records have enormous privacy implications.

The Fair Credit Reporting Act of 1971 is limited to credit-reporting agencies and by no means covers the full scope of consumer transactions in the marketplace. What is vitally needed is a definition of intergovernmental roles and responsibilities for overseeing and regulating recordkeeping practices in the private sector.

Vast quantities of personally identifiable data on consumers are collected, maintained, and distributed in today's business world primarily by companies doing interstate and international business. Credit-reporting agencies, financial institutions, retailers, credit-card companies, and insurers make frequent use of data on individuals, data that are stored in and retrieved from computers. Individuals are thus susceptible to, even when they do not actually suffer from, invasions of personal privacy.

Again, there are more questions than answers. What rights should consumers have regarding the collection, maintenance, and distribution of information about their lives? How should those rights be protected? How should sensitive data — their sexual habits, emotional problems, use or abuse of drugs and alcohol — be treated? Are there special problems with special types of records — medical, long-distance telephone, travel, financial transactions?

Certain cable-television systems have the capacity to determine which program is being watched in which home. Individual sets can also be turned on and off from a central service. Should there be federal legislation monitoring cable television as it comes into the private home and forbidding disclosure of identifiable information about the viewing habits of subscribers?

Electronic funds-transfer systems are supposedly the wave of the future, allowing immediate point-of-sale transfer of payments from consumer to merchant accounts. The unauthorized disclosure, interception, or use of such data could result in a severe invasion of privacy if it revealed a clear picture of a consumer's movements, spending preferences, and personal habits. A national commission on electronic funds transfer has been created; what should its goals be?

What about unsolicited mail, which indicates that the recipient's name has turned up on yet another mailing list? Are the very real privacy interests to be protected? Are there indeed material privacy abuses in this area? What about "opt out" opportunities for removing one's name from lists — do they work? Are they worth the effort? Should lists developed by government agencies be treated differently from those developed by the private sector?

A framework for the protection of the public must be developed, and it must be superimposed on information practices to minimize the misuse of an otherwise socially desirable instrument. The problem of striking a balance between democracy and technology has been manageable in the past, and the nation's policymakers should not shrink from the task.

We must ask ourselves if privacy, instead of residing securely under the Fourth Amendment as an inalienable right of the people, has not become, like the bald eagle or the blue whale, an endangered species. Too easily taken for granted, privacy can be eroded to the degree that it can become a memory rather than a reality. Just as the eagle and the whale are integral parts of our natural ecology, privacy is an integral part of our social ecology. It is up to the people to make sure an assault on this endangered species is halted.

Contents

THE COMPUTER INVASION

Federal Government

Following is a partial list of agencies and subagencies in the federal government, with their abbreviations:

CPSC	Consumer Product Safety Commission
CWPS	Council on Wage and Price Stability
CEQ	Council on Environmental Quality
DMA	Defense Manpower Administration
ERDA	Energy Research and Development Administration
EEOC	Equal Employment Opportunity Commission
EIB	Export-Import Bank (Eximbank)
EPA	Environmental Protection Agency
FCA	Farm Credit Administration
FCC	Federal Communications Commission
FDIC	Federal Deposit Insurance Corporation
FEC	Federal Election Commission
FEA	Federal Energy Administration
FHLBB	Federal Home Loan Bank Board
FMC	Federal Maritime Commission
FMCS	Federal Mediation and Conciliation Service
FPC	Federal Power Commission
FRS	Federal Reserve System
FTC	Federal Trade Commission
FCSC	Foreign Claims Settlement Commission
GSA	General Services Administration
IAF	Inter-American Foundation
ITC	International Trade Commission or United States International Trade Commission
JBEA	Joint Board for the Enrollment of Actuaries
ICC	Interstate Commerce Commission
MMC	Marine Mammal Commission
NASA	National Aeronautics and Space Administration
NFAH	National Foundation on the Arts and the Humanities
NLRB	National Labor Relations Board
NSC	National Security Council
NTSB	National Transportation Safety Board
NRC	Nuclear Regulatory Commission
OSHRC	Occupational Safety and Health Review Commission
OMB	Office of Management and Budget

OTP	Office of Telecommunications Policy
OPIC	Overseas Private Investment Corporation
PCC	Panama Canal Company
PADC	Pennsylvania Avenue Development Corporation
PCWHF	President's Commission on White House Fellowships
PPSC	Privacy Protection Study Commission
RB	Renegotiation Board
RRB	Railroad Retirement Board
SEC	Securities and Exchange Commission
SSS	Selective Service System
SRTN	Office of the Special Representative for Trade Negotiation
TVA	Tennessee Valley Authority
USIA	United States Information Agency
USPS	United States Postal Service
USRA	United States Railway Association
VA	Veterans Administration
WRC	Water Resources Council

U.S. Department of Agriculture

Following is a list of the agencies and subagencies of the Department of Agriculture, with their abbreviations:

ASCS	Agricultural Stabilization and Conservation Service
APHIS	Animal and Plant Health Inspection Service
CCC	Commodity Credit Corporation
FmHA	Farmers Home Administration
FAA	Federal Aviation Administration
FCIC	Federal Crop Insurance Corporation
FNS	Food and Nutrition Service
OGC	Office of General Counsel
OMF	Office of Management and Finance
USDA	United States Department of Agriculture

ACCOUNTS RECEIVABLE (USDA/FCIC)

Individuals who are indebted to the Federal Crop Insurance Corporation.

Director, National Service Office, Federal Crop Insurance Corporation, 8930 Ward Parkway, Kansas City, MO 64114, (816) 926-6553.

Request for information should contain: Individual's name and address, state and county where he or she farms, and the individual policy number, if known.

ACKNOWLEDGMENT OF RESPONSIBILITY FOR DOCKET SECURITY (USDA/CCC)

Individuals who have responsibility for drafting, reviewing, approving or signing Commodity Credit Corporation Dockets.

Records and Communications Management Branch, Administrative Services Division, USDA/ASCS, Room 3116, Auditors Building, 14th & Independence Ave., SW, Washington, DC 20250, (202) 447-6763.

ADMINISTRATIVE BILLINGS AND COLLECTIONS (USDA/OMF)

Individuals (USDA, former USDA, or non-USDA employees) who are indebted to the department for any reason.

Director, National Finance center, Office of Management and Finance, USDA, New Orleans, LA 70160, (504) 255-5370.

ADMINISTRATIVE PROCEEDINGS BROUGHT BY THE DEPARTMENT PURSUANT TO THE PLANT VARIETY PROTECTION ACT, THE FEDERAL SEED ACT OR THE AGRICULTURAL MARKETING ACT OF 1946 (USDA/OGC)

Individuals who are regulated by the subject act and against whom the department recommends that an enforcement action be brought by the government.

Director, Marketing Division, USDA/OGC, 14th & Independence Ave., SW, Washington, DC 20250, (202) 447-5935.

ADMINISTRATIVE PROCEEDINGS BROUGHT BY INDIVIDUALS PURSUANT TO THE PLANT VARIETY PROTECTION ACT OR THE EGG PRODUCTS INSPECTION ACT, AS AMENDED (USDA/OGC)

Individuals regulated by the subject act who file a petition with the secretary pursuant to the authority of the subject act.

Director, Marketing Division, USDA/OGC, 14th & Independence Ave., SW, Washington, DC 20250, (202) 447-5935.

AGRICULTURAL STABILIZATION AND CONSERVATION SERVICE (ASCS), FOREIGN AGRICULTURAL SERVICE (FAS) AND COMMODITY CREDIT CORPORATION (CCC) CASES

Individuals who apply for and/or receive marketing quotas or acreage allotments from ASCS, or loans, payments, credits or indemnities from ASCS, FAS, or CCC; or who apply for and/or enter into contracts or agreements with ASCS, FAS, or CCC or participate in programs financed or administered by ASCS, FAS, or CCC, or who violate or may have violated ASCS, FAS, or CCC regulations, federal or state laws, or who may otherwise be involved in litigation with ASCS, FAS, or CCC.

Director, Foreign Agricultural and Commodity Stabilization Division, USDA/OGC, 14th & Independence Ave., SW, Washington, DC 20250, (202) 447-4600.

Request for information should contain: Individual's name, address, and particulars involved.

BIOGRAPHICAL BACKGROUND (USDA/ASCS)

Individuals who hold key positions in ASCS, guest speakers and recipients of ASCS awards.

Records and Communications Management Branch, Administrative Services Division, USDA/ASCS, Room 3116, Auditors Building, 14th & Independence Ave., SW, Washington, DC 20250, (202) 447-6763.

CASES AGAINST THE DEPARTMENT UNDER THE FEDERAL MEAT INSPECTION ACT, THE POULTRY PRODUCTS INSPECTION ACT, THE VOLUNTARY INSPECTION AND CERTIFICATION PROVISIONS OF THE AGRICULTURAL MARKETING ACT OF 1946 AND RELATED LAWS (USDA/OGC)

Individuals regulated or not regulated by the subject acts who bring suit against the government or a governmental official pursuant to, or as a consequence of the department's administration of, the subject act.

Director, APHIS Division, USDA/OGC, 14th & Independence Ave., SW, Washington, DC 20250, (202) 447-5550.

Request for information should contain: Individual's name, address, and particulars involved.

CASES AGAINST THE DEPARTMENT UNDER THE HORSE PROTECTION ACT OF 1970 (USDA/OGC)

Individuals regulated or not regulated by the subject act who bring suit against the government or a governmental official pursuant to, or as a consequence of the department's administration of, the subject act.

Director, APHIS Division, USDA/OGC, 14th & Independence Ave., SW, Washington, DC 20250, (202) 447-5550.

Request for information should contain: Individual's name, address, and particulars involved.

CASES AGAINST THE DEPARTMENT UNDER THE HUMANE METHODS OF LIVESTOCK SLAUGHTER LAW (i.e., The Act of August 27, 1958) (USDA/OGC)

Individuals regulated or not regulated by the subject act who bring suit against the government or a governmental official pursuant to, or as a consequence of the department's administration of the subject act.

Director, APHIS Division, USDA/OGC, 14th & Independence Ave., SW, Washington, DC 20250, (202) 447-5550.

Request for information should contain: Individual's name, address, and particulars involved.

CASES AGAINST THE DEPARTMENT UNDER THE LABORATORY ANIMAL WELFARE ACT, AS AMENDED (USDA/OGC)

Individuals regulated or not regulated by the subject act who bring suit against the government or a governmental official pursuant to, or as a consequence of the department's administration of, the subject act.

Director, APHIS Division, USDA/OGC, 14th & Independence Ave., SW, Washington, DC 20250, (202) 447-5550.

Request for information should contain: Individual's name, address, and particulars involved.

CASES AGAINST THE DEPARTMENT UNDER THE 28 HOUR LAW, AS AMENDED (USDA/OGC)

Individuals regulated or not regulated by the subject act who bring suit against the government or a governmental official pursuant to, or as a consequence of the department's administration of, the subject act.

Director, APHIS Division, USDA/OGC, 14th & Independence Ave., SW, Washington, DC 20250, (202) 447-5550.

CASES AGAINST THE DEPARTMENT UNDER THE VARIOUS ANIMAL QUARANTINE AND RELATED LAWS (USDA/OGC)

Individuals regulated or not regulated by the subject act who bring suit against the government or a governmental official pursuant to, or as a consequence of the department's administration of, the subject act.

Director, APHIS Division, USDA/OGC, 14th & Independence Ave., SW, Washington, DC 20250, (202) 447-5550.

Request for information should contain: Individual's name, address, and particulars involved.

CASES AGAINST THE DEPARTMENT UNDER THE VARIOUS PLANT PROTECTION AND QUARANTINE AND RELATED LAWS (USDA/OGC)

Individuals regulated or not regulated by the subject act who bring suit against the government or a governmental official pursuant to, or as a consequence of the department's administration of, the subject act.

Director, APHIS Division, USDA/OGC, 14th & Independence Ave., SW, Washington, DC 20250, (202) 447-5550.

Request for information should contain: Individual's name, address, and particulars involved.

CASES BROUGHT BY THE GOVERNMENT PURSUANT TO THE COTTON FUTURES PROVISIONS OF THE INTERNAL REVENUE CODE OF 1954 (USDA/OGC)

Individuals who are regulated by the subject act and against whom the department recommends that an enforcement action be brought by the government.

Director, Marketing Division, USDA/OGC, 14th & Independence Ave., SW, Washington, DC 20250, (202) 447-5935.

CASES BROUGHT PURSUANT TO THE UNITED STATES GRAIN STANDARDS ACT OR THE FEDERAL SEED ACT IN WHICH THE GOVERNMENT IS DEFENDANT (USDA/OGC)

Individuals regulated or not regulated by the subject act who bring suit against the government or a governmental official pursuant to, or as a consequence of the department's administration of, the subject act.

Director, Marketing Division, USDA/OGC, 14th & Independence Ave., SW, Washington, DC 20250, (202) 447-5935.

CASES BY THE DEPARTMENT UNDER THE FEDERAL MEAT INSPECTION ACT, THE POULTRY PRODUCTS INSPECTION ACT AND THE VOLUNTARY INSPECTION AND CERTIFICATION PROVISIONS OF THE AGRICULTURAL MARKETING ACT OF 1946 (USDA/OGC)

Individuals who are regulated by the subject acts and against whom the department recommends that an enforcement action be brought by the government.

Director, APHIS Division, USDA/OGC, 14th & Independence Ave., SW, Washington, DC 20250, (202) 447-5550.

CASES BY THE DEPARTMENT UNDER THE HORSE PROTECTION ACT OF 1970 (USDA/OGC)

Individuals who are regulated by the subject act and against whom the department recommends that an enforcement action be brought by the government.

Director, APHIS Division, USDA/OGC, 14th & Independence Ave., SW, Washington, DC 20250, (202) 447-5550.

CASES BY THE DEPARTMENT UNDER THE HUMANE METHODS OF LIVESTOCK SLAUGHTER LAW (USDA/OGC)

Individuals who are regulated by the subject act and against whom the department recommends that an enforcement action be brought by the government.

Director, APHIS Division, USDA/OGC, 14th & Independence Ave., SW, Washington, DC 20250, (202) 447-5550.

CASES BY THE DEPARTMENT UNDER THE LABORATORY ANIMAL WELFARE ACT, AS AMENDED (USDA/OGC)

Individuals who are regulated by the subject act and against whom the department recommends that an enforcement action be brought by the government.

Director, APHIS Division, USDA/OGC, 14th & Independence Ave., SW, Washington, DC 20250, (202) 447-5550.

CASES BY THE DEPARTMENT UNDER THE 28 HOUR LAW, AS AMENDED (USDA/OGC)

Individuals who are regulated by the subject act and against whom the department recommends that an enforcement action be brought by the government.

Director, APHIS Division, USDA/OGC, 14th & Independence Ave., SW, Washington, DC 20250, (202) 447-5550.

CASES BY THE DEPARTMENT UNDER THE VARIOUS ANIMAL QUARANTINE AND RELATED LAWS (USDA/OGC)

Individuals who are regulated by the subject act and against whom the department recommends that an enforcement action be brought by the government.

Director, APHIS Division, USDA/OGC, 14th & Independence Ave., SW, Washington, DC 20250, (202) 447-5550.

CHECK-BEFORE-USING PILOT LIST (USDA/FS)

Pilots who have performed unsatisfactorily while working under a contract for services.

Director, Aviation Management, Forest Service, USDA, 14th & Independence Ave., SW, Washington, DC 20250, (202) 447-3716.

Request for information should contain: Individual's name, FAA pilot license number, and information about previous employers while performing services for the agency.

CIVIL RIGHTS, ADMINISTRATIVE AND JUDICIAL ACTIONS (USDA/OGC)

Individuals who have brought suit or filed administrative complaints against USDA or USDA employees or recipients of USDA assistance alleging discrimination on the basis of race, color, or national origin by USDA, its employees, or recipients of assistance from USDA.

Director, Research and Operations Division, USDA/OGC, 14th & Independence Ave., SW, Washington, DC 20250, (202) 447-5565.

Request for information should contain: Individual's name, address, and particulars involved.

CIVIL RIGHTS COMPLAINTS AND INVESTIGATIONS (USDA/FNS)

Persons who have alleged discrimination of the type prohibited by Title VI of the Civil Rights Act of 1964 and subsequent regulations; files, names, case numbers and case file information regarding state or local agency compliance with Title VI (includes names and case numbers of individuals who have been contacted or whose case files have been reviewed to ascertain a state's compliance).

Director, Civil Rights Staff, USDA/FNS, 14th & Independence Ave., SW, Washington, DC 20250, (202) 447-8410.

Request for information should contain: Individual's name, and address and whether the records were compiled as a result of a complaint or an FNS compliance review.

CLAIMS AGAINST FOOD STAMP RECIPIENTS (USDA/FNS)

Individuals who have received food stamps to which they are not entitled due to excess income, excess resources, household size reported incorrectly, etc.

Director, Finance and Program Accounting Division, USDA/ FNS, 14th & Independence Ave., SW, Washington, DC 20250, (202) 447-6990.

CLAIMS BY AND AGAINST USDA (USDA/OGC)

Individuals who file or may file claims against USDA pursuant to the Federal Tort Claims Act and the Military Personnel and Civilian Employees Claims Act; claims against the forest service pursuant to 16 USC 502, 556c or 574; and tort suits against the United States or its officers or instrumentalities concerning USDA activities. Also, individuals against whom the department has a monetary claim arising out of USDA-provided services, their employment by USDA, or damages to USDA property.

Director, Research and Operations Division, USDA/OGC, 14th & Independence Ave., SW, Washington, DC 20250, (202) 447-5565.

Request for information should contain: Individual's name, address, and particulars involved.

CLAIMS BY AND AGAINST USDA UNDER THE FOOD ASSISTANCE LEGISLATION (USDA/OGC)

Individuals who seek to participate in the Food Stamp Act of 1964, National School Lunch Act or Child Nutrition Act of 1966. Also, individuals reported to be in violation of one or more of these acts.

Director, Food and Nutrition Division, USDA/OGC, 14th & Independence Ave., SW, Washington, DC 20250, (202) 447-4631.

CLAIMS, OTHER THAN TORT CLAIMS, BY OR AGAINST THE FOREST SERVICE (USDA/OGC)

Individuals who have filed appeals relating to the breach of terms or provisions of a contract with the United States Forest Service.

Director, Natural Resources Division, USDA/OGC, 14th & Independence Ave., SW, Washington, DC 20250, (202) 447-7121.

Request for information should contain: Individual's name, address, and particulars involved.

CONSULTANTS FILE

Individuals who perform consultant service for ASCS.

Deputy Administrator, Management Branch, USDA/ASCS, 14th & Independence Ave., SW, Washington, DC 20250, (202) 447-6763.

CONTRACT APPEALS – FOREST SERVICE (USDA/OGC)

Individuals who have filed appeals relating to the breach of terms or provisions of a contract with the United States Forest Service.

Director, Natural Resources Division, USDA/OGC, 14th & Independence Ave., SW, Washington, DC 20250, (202) 447-7121.

Request for information should contain: Individual's name, address, and particulars involved.

CONVEYANCES – FOREST SERVICE (USDA/OGC)

Parties or potential parties to transactions involving the conveyance, reconveyance, exchange, quitclaim or other disposal of lands or interests therein owned or claimed by the United States on behalf of USDA agencies; having boundary disputes with USDA agencies; or claiming title to lands also claimed by the United States for the use of USDA agencies.

Director, Natural Resources Division, USDA/OGC, 14th & Independence Ave., SW, Washington, DC 20250, (202) 447-7121.

Request for information should contain: Individual's name, address, and particulars involved.

COTTON LOAN CLERKS

Individuals who request permission to process loan documents.

Records and Communications Management Branch, Administrative Services Division, USDA/ASCS, Room 3116 Auditors Building, 14th & Independence Ave., SW, Washington, DC 20250, (202) 447-6763.

CASES BROUGHT BY THE GOVERNMENT PURSUANT TO THE AGRICULTURAL FAIR PRACTICES ACT (USDA/OGC)

Individuals against whom the department recommends that an enforcement action be brought by the government.

Director, Marketing Division, USDA/OGC, 14th & Independence Ave., SW, Washington, DC 20250, (202) 447-5935.

CASES BROUGHT PURSUANT TO THE AGRICULTURAL MARKETING ACT OF 1946 OR THE TOBACCO INSPECTION ACT IN WHICH THE GOVERNMENT IS DEFENDANT (USDA/OGC)

Individuals regulated or not regulated by the subject acts who bring suit against the government or a governmental official pursuant to, or as a consequence of the department's administration of, the subject acts.

Director, Marketing Division, USDA/OGC, 14th & Independence Ave., SW, Washington, DC 20250, (202) 447-5935.

CASES BROUGHT PURSUANT TO THE AUTHORITY OF AGRICULTURAL MARKETING AGREEMENT ACT OF 1937, AS AMENDED, OR THE ANTI-HOG CHOLERA SERUM AND HOG CHOLERA VIRUS ACT IN WHICH THE GOVERNMENT IS DEFENDANT (USDA/OGC)

Individuals regulated or not regulated by the subject acts who bring suit against the government or a governmental official pursuant to, or as a consequence of the department's administration of, the subject acts.

Director, Marketing Division, USDA/OGC, 14th & Independence Ave., SW, Washington, DC 20250, (202) 447-5935.

Request for information should contain: Individual's name, address, and particulars involved.

CASES BROUGHT BY THE GOVERNMENT PURSUANT TO EITHER THE AGRICULTURAL MARKETING AGREEMENT ACT OF 1937, AS AMENDED, OR THE ANTIHOG CHOLERA SERUM AND HOG CHOLERA VIRUS ACT (USDA/OGC)

Individuals who are regulated by the subject acts and against whom the department recommends that enforcement action be brought by the government.

Director, Marketing Division, USDA/OGC, 14th & Independence Ave., SW, Washington, DC 20250, (202) 447-5935.

CASES BROUGHT BY THE GOVERNMENT PURSUANT TO EITHER THE AGRICULTURAL MARKETING ACT OF 1946 OR THE TOBACCO INSPECTION ACT (USDA/OGC)

Individuals who are regulated by the subject acts and against whom the department recommends that enforcement action be brought by the government.

Director, Marketing Division, USDA/OGC, 14th & Independence Ave., SW, Washington, DC 20250, (202) 447-5935.

CASES BROUGHT BY THE GOVERNMENT PURSUANT TO EITHER THE COTTON RESEARCH AND PROMOTION ACT, POTATO RESEARCH AND PROMOTION ACT, OR THE EGG RESEARCH AND CONSUMER INFORMATION ACT (USDA/OGC)

Individuals who are regulated by the subject acts and against whom the department recommends that enforcement action be brought by the government.

Director, Marketing Division, USDA/OGC, 14th & Independence Ave., SW, Washington, DC 20250, (202) 447-5935.

COURT CASES BROUGHT BY THE GOVERNMENT PURSUANT TO EITHER THE COTTON STATISTICS AND ESTIMATES ACT OF 1927 OR THE UNITED STATES COTTON STANDARDS ACT (USDA/OGC)

Individuals who are regulated by the subject acts and against whom the department recommends that action be brought by the government.

Director, Marketing Division, USDA/OGC, 14th & Independence Ave., SW, Washington, DC 20250, (202) 447-5935.

COURT CASES BROUGHT BY THE GOVERNMENT PURSUANT TO EITHER THE EXPORT APPLE AND PEAR ACT OR THE EXPORT GRAPE AND PLUM ACT (USDA/OGC)

Individuals who are regulated by the subject acts and against whom the department recommends that enforcement action be brought by the government.

Director, Marketing Division, USDA/OGC, 14th & Independence Ave., SW, Washington, DC 20250, (202) 447-5935.

COURT CASES BROUGHT BY THE GOVERNMENT PURSUANT TO EITHER THE NAVAL STORES ACT, THE HONEYBEE ACT, THE VIRUS-SERUM-TOXIN ACT, OR THE TOBACCO SEED AND PLANT EXPORTATION ACT (USDA/OGC)

Individuals who are regulated by the subject acts and against whom the department recommends that enforcement action be brought by the government.

Director, Marketing Division, USDA/OGC, 14th & Independence Ave., SW, Washington, DC 20250, (202) 447-5935.

COURT CASES BROUGHT BY THE GOVERNMENT PURSUANT TO EITHER THE PEANUT STATISTICS ACT OR THE TOBACCO STATISTICS ACT (USDA/OGC)

Individuals who are regulated by the subject acts and against whom the department recommends that enforcement action be brought by the government.

Director, Marketing Division, USDA/OGC, 14th & Independence Ave., SW, Washington, DC 20250, (202) 447-5935.

COURT CASES BROUGHT BY THE GOVERNMENT PURSUANT TO EITHER THE PLANT VARIETY PROTECTION ACT OR THE EGG PRODUCTS INSPECTION ACT (USDA/OGC)

Individuals who are regulated by the subject acts and against whom the department recommends that enforcement action be brought by the government.

Director, Marketing Division, USDA/OGC, 14th & Independence Ave., SW, Washington, DC 20250, (202) 447-5935.

COURT CASES BROUGHT BY THE GOVERNMENT PURSUANT TO EITHER THE PRODUCE AGENCY ACT OR THE PROCESS OR RENOVATED BUTTER PROVISIONS OF THE INTERNAL REVENUE CODE OF 1954, USDA/OGC

Individuals who are regulated by the subject act and against whom the department recommends that enforcement action be brought by the government.

Director, Marketing Division, USDA/OGC, 14th & Independence Ave., SW, Washington, DC 20250, (202) 447-5935.

COURT CASES BROUGHT PURSUANT TO THE PACKERS AND STOCKYARDS ACT, AS AMENDED, IN WHICH THE GOVERNMENT IS DEFENDANT (USDA/OGC)

Individuals who bring suit against the government or a governmental official pursuant to, or as a consequence of the department's administration of, the subject act.

Director, Packers and Stockyards Division, USDA/OGC, 14th & Independence Ave., SW, Washington, DC 20250, (202) 447-5293.

COURT CASES BROUGHT PURSUANT TO THE PLANT VARIETY PROTECTION ACT OR THE EGG PRODUCTS INSPECTION ACT IN WHICH THE GOVERNMENT IS DEFENDANT (USDA/OGC)

Individuals regulated or not regulated by the subject acts who bring suit against the government or a governmental official pursuant to, or as a consequence of the department's administration of, the subject act.

Director, Marketing Division, USDA/OGC, 14th & Independence Ave., SW, Washington, DC 20250, (202) 447-5935.

DEBARRED, INELIGIBLE AND SUSPENDED BIDDERS (USDA/OO)

Individuals who, as principals or responsible employees of companies contracting with USDA or other federal agencies, have committed or are suspected of having comitted illegal or irresponsible acts in connection with the performance of those contracts.

Assistant Director, Office of Operations, Procurement, Grants and Agreements Management Staff, USDA, 14th & Independence Ave., SW, Washington, DC 20250, (202) 447-7527.

Request for information should contain: Individual's name, address, company name, date of debarment, ineligibility or suspension date, and date of last correspondence.

DISCRIMINATION COMPLAINTS UNDER TITLE VI OF THE CIVIL RIGHTS ACT OF 1964 (USDA/OEO)

Individuals who file complaints alleging discrimination or are recipients of USDA benefit programs.

Chief, Compliance and Enforcement Division, USDA/OEO, Room 4123, Auditors Building, 14th & Independence Ave., SW, Washington, DC 20250, (202) 447-4563.

EMPLOYEE ASSISTANCE PROGRAM CONCERN (USDA/FS)

Any employee with problems affecting his or her job performance.

CONCERN Program Administrator, Forest Service, USDA, 12th & Independence Ave., SW, Washington, DC 20250, (703) 235-8032.

FARMERS HOME ADMINISTRATION (FmHA) GENERAL CASE FILES (USDA/OGC)

Primarily applicants for FmHA financial assistance and FmHA borrowers and grantees; in some regional offices also parties to litigation, purchasers of FmHA security property, vendors to FmHA borrowers, contractors and builders of FmHA-financed projects, packagers of FmHA loan dockets, real estate salespeople and brokers dealing with FmHA property applicants or having a security interest in property owned or financed or to be financed by FmHA or to whom FmHA notes are assigned, present and former owners and holders of an interest in real property serving as security for FmHA loans, third-party converters, and individuals who file claims against FmHA.

Appropriate regional attorney or attorney-in-charge. (See local telephone directory, under "U.S. Government, Farmers Home Administration," for regional office addresses.)

FEDERAL CROP INSURANCE CORPORATION (FCIC) CASES (USDA/OGC)

Individuals who apply for and/or have insurance contracts with the FCIC; who have delinquent premiums or are otherwise indebted to FCIC; who have indemnity claims against FCIC; who are suspected of fraudulent dealings with FCIC;

who violate or may have violated FCIC regulations, federal, or state laws; or who may otherwise be involved in litigation with FCIC.

Director, Foreign Agricultural and Commodity Stabilization Division, USDA/OGC, 14th & Independence Ave., SW, Washington, DC 20250, (202) 447-4600.

Request for information should contain: Individual's name, address, and particulars involved.

FOOD STAMP PROGRAM INQUIRIES AND COMPLAINTS (USDA/FNS)

Recipients and other persons dissatisfied with or seeking information about local food stamp program policy and procedures.

Regional Food Stamp Program directors. (See local telephone book under U.S. Government USDA/FNS for regional office addresses.)

GENERAL CASE FILES – FOREST SERVICE (USDA/OGC)

Parties involved or expected to be involved in negotiations, administrative appeals, litigation or other attempts to resolve legal issues or disputes pertaining to those aspects of the organization, administration, regulations and other activities relating to the forestry and lands of the USDA not provided for under another system of OGC records. This includes but is not limited to land use planning, wilderness, forest practice, weather modification, and other environmental issues.

Director, Natural Resources Division, USDA/OGC, 14th & Independence Ave., SW, Washington, DC 20250, (202) 447-7121.

Request for information should contain: Individual's name, address, and particulars involved.

GRADUATION FILE (USDA/FmHA)

All FmHA borrowers whose loans are eligible for review, to determine whether the borrower should obtain credit from other sources. (All borrowers who have been in debt for at least two years on an emergency loan, three years on an operating loan, or five years on a real estate loan, are considered eligible for review.)

Freedom of Information Officer, USDA/FmHA, 14th & Independence Ave., SW, Washington, DC 20250, (202) 447-2211.

Request for information should contain: Individual's name, address, state and county where loan was applied for or approved, and particulars involved.

HOUSING CONTRACTOR COMPLAINT FILE (USDA/FmHA)

All housing contractors who have performed work for FmHA borrowers and about whom the borrower has seen

fit to file a complaint.

Freedom of Information Officer, USDA/FmHA, 14th & Independence Ave., SW, Washington, DC 20250, (202) 447-2211.

Request for information should contain: Individual's name, address, and location where work was performed.

INSECTICIDE, FUNGICIDE, HERBICIDE AND RODENTICIDE CASES – SOIL CONSERVATION SERVICE (USDA/OGC)

Persons claiming that certain existing or proposed United States Department of Agriculture activities involving the application of insecticides, pesticides, fungicides, rodenticides, herbicides, nematocides, defoliants, desiccants or plant regulators may be unlawful. Also, parties or potential parties to litigation or administrative hearings involving such activities.

Director, Natural Resources Division, USDA/OGC, 14th & Independence Ave., SW, Washington, DC 20250, (202) 447-7121.

Request for information should contain: Individual's name, address, and particulars involved.

INTELLIGENCE RECORDS (USDA/OI)

Suspects and unpaid informants.

Assistant Director for Information, Research and Development, Office of Investigation, USDA, 14th & Independence Ave., SW, Washington, DC 20250, (202) 447-6915.

INVESTIGATION AND AUDIT REPORTS (USDA/ASCS)

Individuals who are the subject of a formal investigation relating to alleged program or administrative irregularities.

Deputy Administrator, Management Branch, USDA/ASCS, 14th & Independence Ave., SW, Washington, DC 20250, (202) 447-3351.

INVESTIGATIONS OF FRAUD, THEFT OR OTHER UNLAWFUL ACTIVITIES OF INDIVIDUALS INVOLVING FOOD STAMPS (USDA/FNS)

Individuals who have been investigated for fraudulently obtaining food stamps or stealing food stamps.

Director, Food Stamp Division, Food and Nutrition Service, USDA, 14th & Independence Ave., SW, Washington, DC 20250, (202) 477-8982.

Request for information should contain: Individual's name, address, and whether requested information involves a complaint or refers to a compliance review which may have been conducted.

INVESTIGATIVE FILES AND SUBJECT/TITLE INDEX (USDA/OI)

The individual names of the Office of Investigation (OI)

index fall into one or more of the following categories:

Subjects. Individuals against whom allegations of wrong-doing have been made.

Principals. Individuals who are not named subjects of investigative inquiries, but who may be responsible for alleged violations.

Complainants. Individuals who allege wrongdoing, mis-management, or unfair treatment relating to USDA employees and/or programs.

Others. All other individuals closely connected with a matter of investigative interest or whose names have been checked through the index to determine whether they were on record. Among these names are those of people who are connected with a matter only in that they have shown unusual interest in having allegations investigated, or in learning the results of investigation. Also included in the index list are the names of persons on the Department of Justice crime list.

Assistant Director for Information, Research and Development, Office of Investigation, USDA, 14th & Independence Ave., SW, Washington, DC 20250, (202) 447-6915.

LEGISLATION—FOREST SERVICE (USDA/OGC)

Persons occupying USDA lands who are involved or ex-pected to be involved in disputes concerning the applica-bility of federal, state or local civil or criminal legislation or administrative regulations to their activities or possessory interests.

Director, Natural Resources Division, USDA/OGC, 14th & Independence Ave., SW, Washington, DC 20250, (202) 447-7121.

Request for information should contain: Individual's name, address, and particulars involved.

LISTS OF INELIGIBLE PRODUCERS (USDA/FCIC)

Individuals who have been determined as not eligible for Federal Crop Insurance on specific crops due to excessive losses or questionable farming practices. Also, individuals who have had contracts voided due to suspected or apparent fraud.

Manager, Federal Crop Insurance Corporation, USDA, 14th & Independence Ave., SW, Washington, DC 20250, (202) 447-6795.

Director, National Service Office, Federal Crop Insurance Corporation, USDA, 8930 Ward Parkway, Kansas City, MO 64114, (816) 926-6284.

Request for information should contain: Individual's name, address, state and county where farm is located, and the individual policy number, if known.

PACKERS AND STOCKYARDS ACT – ADMINISTRA-TIVE CASES (USDA/OGC)

Individuals who are regulated by the subject act and against whom the department recommends that an enforcement action be brought by the government.

Director, Packers and Stockyards Division, USDA/OGC, 14th & Independence Ave., SW, Washington, DC 20250, (202) 447-5293, or the appropriate regional attorney or attorney-in-charge.

PERISHABLE AGRICULTURAL COMMODITIES ACT (USDA/OGC) – DISCIPLINARY PROCEEDINGS TO DENY ISSUANCE OF A LICENSE TO AN APPLICANT THEREUNDER OR TO SUSPEND OR REVOKE A LICENSE ALREADY ISSUED OR TO PUBLISH THE FACTS AND CIRCUMSTANCES OF VIOLATIONS OF THE ACT

Individuals who apply for or hold licenses to do business in the perishable agricultural commodities industry in their individual capacities; partners of partnerships which apply for or hold licenses to do business in the perishable agri-cultural commodities industry; officers, directors, and holders of 10% or more of the stock of corporations which apply for or hold licenses to do business in the perishable agricultural commodities industry under the Perishable Agricultural Commodities Act of 1930, as amended.

Director, Food and Nutrition Division, USDA/OGC, 14th & Independence Ave., SW, Washington, DC 20250, (202) 447-4631, or the appropriate regional attorney or attorney-in-charge.

PERSONNEL SUITS (USDA/OGC)

Employees, former employees, and applicants for employ-ment with USDA who institute suits against USDA; officers or employees of USDA or the United States Government who allege that a wrongful personnel action was taken against them.

Director, Research and Operations Division, USDA/OGC, 14th & Independence Ave., SW, Washington, DC 20250, (202) 447-5565.

Request for information should contain: Individual's name, address, and particulars involved.

PLANT PROTECTION AND QUARANTINE PROGRAMS – REGULATORY ACTIONS (USDA/APHIS)

Violators and alleged violators of plant protection and plant quarantine laws and regulations.

Deputy Administrator, Plant Protection and Quarantine, USDA/APHIS, 14th & Independence Ave., SW, Washington, DC 20250, (202) 447-5601.

POWER OF ATTORNEY & DESIGNATED AGENTS (USDA/ASCS)

Individuals giving powers of attorney and individuals securing the powers to act as agent.

Records and Communications Management Branch, Administrative Services Division, USDA/ASCS, Room 3116, Auditors Building, 14th & Independence Ave., SW, Washington, DC 20250, (202) 447-6763.

QUALITY CONTROL SUBSAMPLE OF NONASSISTANCE HOUSEHOLDS PARTICIPATING IN THE FOOD STAMP PROGRAM (USDA/FNS)

Nonassistance households (those in which not all members are receiving public assistance) which are participating in the Food Stamp Program or those households which have been terminated from the program or denied benefits.

Director, Food Stamp Division, USDA/FNS, 14th & Independence Ave., SW, Washington, DC 20250, (202) 447-8982.

Request for information should contain: Individual's name, address, dates of participation in the Food Stamp Program, and date of contact by the federal reviewer, if available.

SUPERVISORS' NOTES ON EMPLOYEES (USDA/ASCS)

ASCS employees.

Services Division, USDA/ASCS, Room 3116, Auditors Building, 14th & Independence Ave., SW, Washington, DC 20250, (202) 447-6763.

TIMBER SALES – FOREST SERVICE (USDA/OGC)

Persons contracting to purchase timber from the Forest Service and persons whom the Forest Service seeks to debar from such contracting; unsuccessful bidders at such sales and persons protesting awards or proposed awards of same; individuals who have breached a provision of a timber contract or who have otherwise engaged in conduct which raises a legal question concerning timber sale administration.

Director, Natural Resources Division, USDA/OGC, 14th & Independence Ave., SW, Washington, DC 20250, (202) 447-7121.

Request for information should contain: Individual's name, address, invoice number and particulars involved.

TITLE CLAIMS AND OCCUPANCY AND USE CASES – FOREST SERVICE (USDA/OGC)

Individuals who file claims against USDA arising out of Forest Service land acquisitions under the Treaty of Paris, the Weeks Law, or the Uniform Relocation Assistance and Real Property Acquisition Policies Act; cases arising out of the occupancy and use of properties administered by the Forest Service in the Caribbean National Forest.

Director, Natural Resources Division, USDA/OGC, 14th & Independence Ave., SW, Washington, DC 20250, (202) 447-7121.

Request for information should contain: Individual's name, address, and particulars involved.

TORT CLAIMS FILE (USDA/FmHA)

All claimants who have filed civil suits against employees of FmHA or against the federal government, including those filed under the Tort Claims Act as a result of circumstances involving the Farmers Home Administration.

Freedom of Information Officer, USDA/FmHA, 14th & Independence Ave., SW, Washington, DC 20250, (202) 447-2211.

Request for information should contain: Individual's name, address, name of the defendant in the action, and date of the initiation of the action.

TORT, PROGRAM, AND CIVILIAN EMPLOYEE CLAIMS

Individual by whom or against whom a claim involving ASCS or CCC has been filed.

Records and Communications Management Branch, Administrative Services Division, ASCS/USDA, Room 3116, Auditors Building, 14th & Independence Ave., SW, Washington, DC 20250, (202) 447-6763.

TRESPASS AND CLAIMS (USDA/FS)

Individuals who have filed claims against the Forest Service pursuant to the Federal Tort Claims Act, the Military Personnel and Civilian Claims Act, or any of the various Forest Service claims acts; individuals against whom the Forest Service has filed claims pursuant to the Federal Claims Collection Act; individuals who claim title to National Forest System lands pursuant to the Adjustment of Land Titles Act, Quitclaim Act, Color of Title Act, Wisconsin Land Title Act or the Real Property-Quiet Title Act.

Director, Fiscal and Accounting Management, USDA/FS, 14th & Independence Ave., SW, Washington, DC 20250, (202) 235-8130, or the appropriate regional director of fiscal and accounting management.

TRESPASS AND CLAIMS CASES – FOREST SERVICE (USDA/OGC)

Persons who have or are suspected of having committed trespasses, other torts or breaches of contract on USDA lands involving unauthorized cutting of timber, occupancy and use, grazing, removal of minerals, the negligent or willful setting of fires, fire-suppression costs, breaches of timber sales agreements, or similar actions.

Director, Natural Resources Division, USDA/OGC, 14th & Independence Ave., SW, Washington, DC 20250, (202) 447-7121.

Request for information should contain: Individual's name, address, and particulars involved.

UNITED STATES MAGISTRATES – FOREST SERVICE (USDA/OGC)

Alleged and convicted violators of Forest Service petty offense regulations (36 CFR, Parts 211-95) and other minor offenses.

Director, Natural Resources Division, USDA/OGC, 14th & Independence Ave., SW, Washington, DC 20250, (202) 447-7121.

Request for information should contain: Individual's name, address, and particulars involved.

WATER CASES – FOREST SERVICE (USDA/OGC)

Persons claiming or believed to be claiming water rights, water-use privileges, or rights-of-way to transport water on land owned or leased by the United States and administered by USDA agencies; in conflict with or from the same sources as water rights claimed or reserved by the United States for the benefit of USDA agencies; or by reason of a permit from or agreement with USDA agencies.

Director, Natural Resources Division, USDA/OGC, 14th & Independence Ave., SW, Washington, DC 20250, (202) 447-7121.

Request for information should contain: Individual's name, address, and particulars involved.

Additional Files

Following is a list of the remaining files maintained by the USDA. Anyone interested in obtaining information from any of these files should contact the Secretary of Agriculture, Department of Agriculture, 14th & Independence Ave., SW, Washington, DC 20250, (202) 655-4000.

Acquisitions – Forest Service (USDA/OGC)
Adjuster's Report (USDA/FCIC)
Administrative Proceedings Brought Pursuant to the Authority of the Cotton Research and Promotion Act, the Potato Research and Promotion Act or the Egg Research and Consumer Information Act (USDA/OGC)
Administrative Proceedings Brought Pursuant to the Authority of Section 8c(15)(a) of the Agricultural Marketing Agreement Act of 1937, as amended, or the Anti-Hog Cholera Serum and Hog Cholera Virus Act (USDA/OGC)
Administrative Proceedings Brought Pursuant to the Tobacco Inspection Act or the United States Grain Standards Act (USDA/OGC)
Administrative Records System (USDA/SRS)

Advisory Committee Files
Appeals and Administrative Reviews (USDA/FS)
Applicant/Borrower or Grantee File (USDA/FmHA)
Applicant Files for Employment with International Organizations (USDA/FAS)
Biographical Information on McIntire-Stennis Advisory Board and Advisory Committee Members (USDA/CSRS)
Biographical Information – Office of Information (USDA/CSRS)
Biographical Material and Nominating Statements on ARS Employees Proposed for Major Awards (USDA/ARS)
Biographical Material on Persons Related to Science or Agriculture (USDA/ARS)
Biographical Sketch File (USDA/FmHA)
Blasters Certification Program (USDA/FS)
CCC Producer Loan Records
Casual Firefighter Data (USDA/FS)
Certification of Engineering Personnel (USDA/FS)
Certified Cost Collectors (USDA/FS)
Certified Scalers (USDA/FS)
Certified Silviculturists (USDA/FS)
Committee Management Records System (USDA/OMF)
Commodity Brokers
Community Development Division Litigation (USDA/OGC)
Contact Report File (USDA/FCIC)
Contract Cases (USDA/OGC)
Cooperative Extension Personnel Records System (USDA/ES)
Cooperative Employee Data (USDA/FAS)
County Office Employees Administrative Expense File
County Personnel Records
Credit Report File (USDA/FmHA)
Crop Insurance Actuarial Listing (USDA/FCIC)
Farmer's Name and Address Master File (Manual) USDA/ASCS
Fire Qualification and Experience Records (USDA/FS)
Food Stamp Recipient Refunds (USDA/FNS)
Forest Appeals – Forest Service (USDA/OGC)
Geometronics Skills Inventory (USDA/FS)
Grazing – Forest Service (USDA/OGC)
Grazing Permittees, Individual – National Forest System (USDA/FS)
High Liability Inspection Forms (FCIC 424) (USDA/FCIC)
Imprest Fund Payment System (USDA/OMF)
Indemnity and Incentive Programs (USDA/ASCS)
Insurance Contract Analysis (USDA/FCIC)
Insurance Contract Files (USDA/FCIC)
June Acreage, Livestock, and Labor Enumerative Survey (USDA/SRS)
Land Acquisitions – Forest Service (USDA/OGC)
Land Exchanges, General Exchange Act – Forest Service (USDA/OGC)
Land Exchanges, other than Exchange Act – Forest Service (USDA/OGC)
Leases – Forest Service (USDA/OGC)
Liaison Records (USDA/OI)
Listing of Indemnities Paid (USDA/FCIC)
Management Information System (USDA/OA)
Manpower File (USDA/ARS)

Manpower Programs (USDA/FS)

Maximum Payment Limitations (USDA/ASCS)

Meat and Poultry Inspection Programs — Slaughter, Processing, and Allied Industries Compliance Records System (USDA/APHIS)

Mineral Lessees and Permittees (USDA/FS)

Mineral Operators (USDA/FS)

Minerals and Mining Claims — Forest Service (USDA/OGC)

Mining Claimants (USDA/FS)

Non-Career Applicant File (USDA/SEC)

Ohio Livestock Producers Survey (USDA/FCS)

Packers and Stockyards Administration — Administrative Records (USDA/P&SA)

Patents and Inventions of Department Employees (USDA/OGC)

Perishable Agricultural Commodities Act (PACA) — History Files of Principals

Persons Interested in Forestry and Related Programs (USDA/FS)

Personnel Data Base (USDA/SRS)

Personnel Irregularities (USDA/OGC)

Personnel and Payroll System for USDA Employees (USDA/OP)

Personnel Security Clearance Status Files (USDA/FNS)

Persons Engaged in Business as Livestock Market Agents and Dealers under the Provisions of the Packers and Stockyards Act (USDA/P&SA)

Producer Appeals (USDA/ASCS)

Producer Payment Reporting File 365 and 368 (USDA/ASCS)

Producer Record for Pre-Pilot Counties (USDA/ASCS)

Program Cooperators — Soil Conservation Service (USDA/OGC)

Program Cooperators — Soil Conservation Service (USDA/SCS)

Public Correspondence Concerning Timber Management (USDA/FS)

Public Involvement Respondents on Forest Service Activities (USDA/FS)

Quarterly Agricultural Labor Survey (USDA/SRS)

Rappahannock Land Information System

Reserved Mineral Interests (USDA/FmHA)

Rice Cross-Compliance System (USDA/ASCS)

Rights-of-Way-Acquisition — Forest Service (USDA/OGC)

Sawtooth National Recreation Area Certifications (USDA/FS)

Security Records for USDA Employees (USDA/OP)

Shorn and Unshorn Wool and Mohair (USDA/ASCS)

Skill Needs Inventory Program (R-6) (USDA/FS)

Solicitation of Bids or Proposals for Procurement Contracts (USDA/ARS)

Special Use Permits, Easements, and Licenses (USDA/FS)

Special Uses — Forest Service (USDA/OGC)

State Cooperative Extension Service Employees (USDA/ES)

State Farm Census (USDA/SRS)

Subsidiary Personnel, Pay, and Travel Records (USDA/ASCS)

Telephone, Electric, and L.P. Gas Services Survey (USDA/SRS)

Temporary Employee Performance and Training Record (USDA/FS)

Tobacco (Flue-cured, Burley) Farm History Master File (USDA/ASCS)

Training File (USDA/ARS)

Training Files (USDA/FmHA)

Travel Records (USDA/FmHA)

Veterinary Services Programs — Animal Quarantine Regulatory Actions (USDA/APHIS)

Veterinary Services Programs — Animal Welfare and Horse Protection Regulatory Actions (USDA/APHIS)

Veterinary Services Programs — Candidates for Animal Disease Control Positions in Foreign Countries (USDA/APHIS)

Veterinary Services Programs — Records of Accredited Veterinarians (USDA/APHIS)

Warehouse Business Agents (USDA/ASCS)

Youth Conservation Corps (YCC) Enrollee Medical Records (USDA/FS)

Youth Conservation Corps (YCC) Enrollee Payroll Records (USDA/FS)

Youth Conservation Corps (YCC) Enrollee Records (USDA/FS)

Youth Conservation Corps (YCC) Recruitment System (USDA/FS)

Youth Conservation Corps (YCC) Research Files (USDA/FS)

U.S. Department of Commerce

Following is a list of the agencies and subagencies of the Department of Commerce, with their abbreviations:

Census	Census Bureau
DIBA	Domestic and International Business Administration
EDA	Economic Development Administration
MA	Maritime Administration
NBS	National Bureau of Standards
NOAA	National Oceanic and Atmospheric Administration
NTIS	National Technical Information Service
MBE	Minority Business Enterprise Office
Pat/TM	Patent and Trademark Office
SESA	Social and Economic Statistics Administration
USTS	United States Travel Service

The following pages list the files held by the Department of Commerce.

ACCOUNTS RECEIVABLE (COMMERCE/DEPT-2-DIBA)

Debtors owing money to organizational components, including employees, former employees, business firms, general public, and institutions.

Director, Office of Management and Systems, Dept. of Commerce/DIBA, 14th & Constitution Ave., NW, Washington, DC 20230, (202) 377-5436.

Request for information should contain: Individual's name, address, and invoice number, as appropriate.

ACCOUNTS RECEIVABLE (COMMERCE/DEPT-2-EDA)

Debtors owing money to organization components, including employees, former employees, business firms, general public, and institutions.

Director, Office of Public Affairs, Dept. of Commerce/EDA, 14th & Constitution Ave., NW, Washington, DC 20230, (202) 377-4901.

Request for information should contain: Individual's name, address, and invoice number, as appropriate.

ACCOUNTS RECEIVABLE (COMMERCE/DEPT-2-NFPCA)

Debtors owing money to organizational components, including employees, former employees, business firms, general public, and institutions.

Administration Officer, Dept. of Commerce/NFPCA, Washington, DC 20230, (202) 634-7663.

Request for information should contain: Individual's name, address, and invoice number, as appropriate.

ACCOUNTS RECEIVABLE (COMMERCE/DEPT-2-USTS)

Debtors owing money to organizational components, including employees, former employees, business firms, general public and institutions.

Executive Director, Dept. of Commerce/USTS, 14th & Constitution Ave., NW, Washington, DC 20230, (202) 377-4987.

Request for information should contain: Individual's name, address, and invoice number, as appropriate.

ACCOUNTS RECEIVABLE (COMMERCE/DEPT-2-OMBE)

Debtors owing money to organizational components, including employees, former employees, business firms, general public, and institutions.

Assistant Director, Field Operations and Administration, Dept. of Commerce/OMBE, 14th & Constitution Ave., NW, Washington, DC 20230, (202) 377-3024.

Request for information should contain: Individual's name, address, and invoice number, as appropriate.

ACCOUNTS RECEIVABLE (COMMERCE/DEPT-2-RAPC)

Debtors owing money to organizational components, including employees, former employees, business firms, general public, and institutions.

Director, Office of Organizations and Management Systems, 14th & Constitution Ave., NW, Washington, DC 20230, (202) 377-5113.

Request for information should contain: Individual's name, address, and invoice number, as appropriate.

ACCOUNTS RECEIVABLE (COMMERCE/DEPT-2-ARC)

Debtors owing money to organizational components, including employees, former employees, business firms, general public, and institutions.

Director, Office of Organization and Management Systems, 14th & Constitution Ave., NW, Washington, DC 20230, (202) 377-5113.

Request for information should contain: Individual's name, address, and invoice number, as appropriate.

ACCOUNTS RECEIVABLE (COMMERCE/DEPT-2-OFFICE OF FEDERAL COCHAIRMAN)

Debtors owing money to organizational components, including employees, former employees, business firms, general public, and institutions.

Director, Office of Organization and Management Systems, 14th & Constitution Ave., NW, Washington, DC 20230, (202) 377-5113.

Request for information should contain: Individual's name, address, and invoice number, as appropriate.

ACCOUNTS RECEIVABLE (COMMERCE/DEPT-2-NBS)

Debtors owing money to organizational components, including employees, former employees, business firms, general public, and institutions.

Associate Director for Administration, Dept. of Commerce/NBS, Administration Bldg., Washington, DC 20234, (202) 921-2477.

Request for information should contain: Individual's name, address, and invoice number, as appropriate.

ACCOUNTS RECEIVABLE (COMMERCE/DEPT-2-OTEL)

Debtors owing money to organizational components, including employees, former employees, business firms, general public, and institutions.

Administrative Officer, OTEL, 1325 G St., NW, Washington, DC 20005, (202) 377-1832.

Request for information should contain: Individual's name, address, and invoice number, as appropriate.

ACCOUNTS RECEIVABLE (COMMERCE/DEPT-2-NOAA)

Debtors owing money to organizational components, including employees, former employees, business firms, general public, and institutions.

Assistant Administrator for Administration, Dept. of Commerce/NOAA, 6010 Executive Blvd., Rockville, MD 20853, (301) 443-8134.

Request for information should contain: Individual's name, address, and invoice number, as appropriate.

ACCOUNTS RECEIVABLE (COMMERCE/DEPT-2-PAT-TM)

Debtors owing money to organizational components, including employees, former employees, business firms, general public, and institutions.

Assistant Commissioner for Administration, U.S. Patent and Trademark Office, Washington, DC 20231, (703) 557-3055.

Request for information should include: Individual's name, address, and invoice number, as appropriate.

APPLICANTS FOR FEDERAL PERMITS TO TAKE, BUY, OR TRANSPORT ENDANGERED SPECIES FOR SPECIFIC PURPOSES (COMMERCE/NOAA-1)

Applicants for permits to take, import, export, transport, or sell in interstate or foreign commerce, endangered species for scientific purposes, enhancement of propagation, enhancement of survival, or to minimize undue economic hardship.

Assistant Administrator for Administration, National Oceanic and Atmospheric Administration, 6010 Executive Blvd., Rockville, MD 20852, (301) 443-8134.

Request for information should include: Individual's name and address.

COMPLAINTS, INVESTIGATIONS AND DISCIPLINARY PROCEEDINGS RELATING TO REGISTERED PATENT ATTORNEYS AND AGENTS (COMMERCE/PAT-TM-2)

Attorneys and agents registered to practice before the Patent and Trademark Office in patent cases, disbarred or suspended attorneys and agents.

Assistant Commissioner for Administration, U.S. Patent and Trademark Office, Washington, DC 20231, (703) 557-3055.

Request for information should include: Individual's name and identification data.

EMPLOYEES EXTERNAL RADIATION EXPOSURE RECORDS (COMMERCE/NBS-7)

Individuals working with radioactive materials and machines who may be exposed to ionizing radiation.

Association Director for Administration, Room 1105, Administration Building, National Bureau of Standards, Washington, DC 20234, (301) 921-2477.

Request for information should include: Individual's name, Social Security number, and date of employment.

FISHERIES LAW ENFORCEMENT CASE FILES (COMMERCE/NOAA-11)

Violators and alleged violators of the criminal and/or civil provisions of certain laws and the regulations issued thereunder, within the responsibility of the Secretary of Commerce.

Assistant Administrator for Administration, NOAA, 6010 Executive Blvd., Rockville, MD 20852, (301) 443-8134.

Request for information should contain: Individual's name, address, and case number.

GENERAL AGENT'S PROTECTION AND IDEMNITY AND SECOND SEAMAN'S INSURANCE: WSA AND NSA (COMMERCE/MA-4)

Individuals (e.g., seamen, passengers, stevedores) filing claims against general agents for death, disability, loss of personal effects, detention, repatriation and property damage.

Secretary, Maritime Administration, Room 3099, 14th & Constitution Ave., NW, Washington, DC 20230, (202) 377-2746.

Request for information should contain: Seaman's name, vessel name, and date of incident.

INDIVIDUALS IDENTIFIED IN EXPORT ADMINISTRATION COMPLIANCE PROCEEDINGS OR INVESTIGATIONS (COMMERCE/DIBA-1)

Individuals identified in an export administration compliance proceeding or investigation; individuals alleged to have violated the Export Administration regulations; established violators of the regulations; certain other individuals identified by the FBI or other investigating agency or individual in the investigative process such as those involved in organized crime; and individuals who have received warning letters.

Director, Office of Management and Systems, Dept. of Commerce/DIBA, 14th & Constitution Ave., NW, Washington, DC 20230, (202) 377-5113.

Request for information should contain: Individual's name, address, and case or subject, if known.

INDIVIDUALS INVOLVED IN INTERNATIONAL BUSINESS TRADE COMPLAINTS (COMMERCE/DIBA-3)

Individuals filing trade complaints against foreign firms, or against whom foreign firms file complaints through United States embassies.

Director, Office of Management and Systems, Dept. of Commerce/DIBA, 14th & Constitution Ave., NW, Washington, DC 20230, (202) 377-5436.

Request for information should include: Individual's name and name of American party to the dispute.

INVESTIGATIVE RECORDS – CONTRACT AND GRANT FRAUDS AND EMPLOYEE CRIMINAL MISCONDUCT (COMMERCE/DEPT-12)

Past and present employees, when under or having been under investigation for suspected violation of criminal laws; employees and principal officers of contractors used by the department; and principal officers and employees of organizations, firms or institutions which are recipients or beneficiaries of grants, loans or loan guarantee programs of the department.

Director, Office of Organization and Management Systems, Department of Commerce, 14th & Constitution Ave., NW, Washington, DC 20230, (202) 377-5436.

Request for information should contain: Individual's name and association with the department.

NON-ATTORNEY PRACTITIONER APPLICATIONS AND "SECTION 807 REPORTS" (COMMERCE/MA-8)

Those representing others in agency proceedings.

Secretary, Maritime Administration, Room 3099, 14th & Constitution Ave., NW, Washington, DC 20230, (202) 377-2746.

Request for information should contain: Name of practitioner.

LITIGATION, CLAIMS, AND ADMINISTRATIVE PROCEEDINGS RECORDS (COMMERCE/DEPT-14)

Individuals making claims or bringing action against the department, and individuals who are the subject of the department's claims and actions, including tort and property claims and civil contract issues (but excluding Federal Employee Compensation Act claimants); individuals suspected of violations of criminal and civil statutes in connection with departmental programs and activities; individuals who are the subject of administrative proceedings where the department is involved; and individuals cited for violation of traffic and grounds regulations.

Office of the General Counsel, U.S. Department of Commerce, 14th and Constitution Ave., NW, Washington, DC 20230, (202) 377-4772.

Request for information should contain: Individual's name, address, Social Security number, case number, date of claim, and organization unit in which employed.

LITIGATION, CLAIMS, AND ADMINISTRATIVE PROCEEDINGS RECORDS (COMMERCE/DEPT-14-EDA)

Individuals making claims or bringing action against the department, and individuals who are the subject of the department's claims and actions, including tort and property claims and civil contract issues (but excluding Federal

Employee Compensation Act claimants); individuals suspected of violations of criminal and civil statutes in connection with departmental programs and activities; individuals who are the subject of administrative proceedings where the department is involved; and individuals cited for violation of traffic and grounds regulations.

Director, Office of Public Affairs, Dept. of Commerce/EDA, 14th & Constitution Ave., SW, Washington, DC 20230, (202) 377-4901.

Request for information should contain: Individual's name, address, Social Security number, case number, date of claim, and organization unit in which employed.

LITIGATION, CLAIMS, AND ADMINISTRATIVE PROCEEDINGS RECORDS (COMMERCE/DEPT-14-MARAD)

Individuals making claims or bringing action against the department, and individuals who are the subject of the department's claims and actions, including tort and property claims and civil contract issues (but excluding Federal Employee Compensation Act claimants); individuals suspected of violations of criminal and civil statutes in connection with departmental programs and activities; individuals who are the subject of administrative proceedings where the department is involved; and individuals cited for violation of traffic and grounds regulations.

Office of the General Counsel, U.S. Department of Commerce, 14th & Constitution Ave., NW, Washington, DC 20230, (202) 377-4772.

Request for information should contain: Individual's name, address, Social Security number, case number, date of claim, and organization unit in which employed.

LITIGATION, CLAIMS, AND ADMINISTRATIVE PROCEEDINGS RECORDS (COMMERCE/DEPT-14-NBS)

Individuals making claims or bringing action against the department, and individuals who are the subjects of the department's claims and actions, including tort and property claims and civil contract issues (but excluding Federal Employee Compensation Act claimants); individuals suspected of violations of criminal and civil statutes in connection with departmental programs and activities; individuals who are the subject of administrative proceedings where the department is involved; and individuals cited for violation of traffic and grounds regulations.

Associate Director for Administration, Dept. of Commerce/NBS, Administration Bldg., Washington, DC 20234, (301) 921-2477.

Request for information should contain: Individual's name, address, Social Security number, case number, date of claim, and organization unit in which employed.

LITIGATION, CLAIMS, AND ADMINISTRATIVE PROCEEDINGS RECORDS (COMMERCE/DEPT-14-NOAA)

Individuals making claims or bringing action against the department, and individuals who are the subject of the department's claims and actions, including tort and property claims and civil contract issues (but excluding Federal Employee Compensation Act claimants); individuals suspected of violations of criminal and civil statutes in connection with departmental programs and activities; individuals who are the subjects of administrative proceedings where the department is involved; and individuals cited for violation of traffic and grounds regulations.

Assistant Administrator for Administration, Dept. of Commerce/NOAA, 6010 Executive Blvd., Rockville, MD 20852, (301) 443-8134.

Request for information should contain: Individual's name, address, Social Security number, case number, date of claim, and organization unit in which employed.

LITIGATION, CLAIMS, AND ADMINISTRATIVE PROCEEDINGS RECORDS (COMMERCE/DEPT-14-PAT-TM)

Individuals making claims or bringing action against the department, and individuals who are the subjects of the department's claims and actions, including tort and property claims and civil contract issues (but excluding Federal Employee Compensation Act claimants); individuals suspected of violations of criminal and civil statutes in connection with departmental programs and activities; individuals who are the subject of administrative proceedings where the department is involved; and individuals cited for violation of traffic and grounds regulations.

Assistant Commissioner for Administration, Patent and Trademark Office, Washington, DC 20231, (703) 557-3055.

Request for information should contain: Individual's name, address, Social Security number, case number, date of claim, and organization unit in which employed.

LITIGATION, CLAIMS, AND ADMINISTRATIVE PROCEEDINGS RECORDS (COMMERCE/DEPT-14-CENSUS)

Individuals making claims or bringing action against the department, and individuals who are the subject of the department's claims and actions, including tort and property claims and civil contract issues (but excluding Federal Employee Compensation Act claimants); individuals suspected of violations of criminal and civil statutes in connection with departmental programs and activities; individuals who are the subject of administrative proceedings where the department is involved; and individuals cited for violation of traffic and grounds regulations.

Associate Director for Administration, Bureau of the Census, Federal Building 3, Washington, DC 20233, (202) 568-1200.

Request for information should contain: Individual's name, address, Social Security number, case number, date of claim, and organization unit in which employed.

PARTICIPANTS IN HUMAN FACTORS STUDIES (COMMERCE/NBS-5)

Individuals who have served as subjects in Human Factors Laboratory experiments and studies.

Associate Director for Administration, Room 1105, Administration Building, National Bureau of Standards, Washington, DC 20234, (301) 921-2477.

Request for information should contain: Individual's name and the title of experiment.

PARTICIPANTS IN PSYCHOACOUSTIC EXPERIMENTS (COMMERCE/NBS-6)

Applicants and participants in psychoacoustic experiments.

Associate Director for Administration, Room 1105, Administration Building, National Bureau of Standards, Washington, DC 20234, (301) 921-2477.

Request for information should contain: Individual's name and approximate date of experiment.

PARTIES INVOLVED IN PATENT INTERFERENCE PROCEEDINGS (COMMERCE/PAT-TM-6)

Applicants for patents and patentees who become involved in a conflict involving the question of priority of invention.

Assistant Commissioner for Administration, U.S. Patent and Trademark Office, Washington, DC 20231, (301) 921-2477.

Request for information should contain: Individual's name, address, and interference number, if known.

PRIVATE LEGISLATION CLAIMANTS – CENTRAL LEGISLATIVE FILES (COMMERCE/DEPT 15)

Individual claimants against the government seeking remedy through private relief bills in patent, contract, employee compensation and other similar areas which involve the department.

Director, Office of Organization and Management Systems, OS, Dept. of Commerce, 14th & Constitution Ave., NW, Washington, DC 20230, (202) 377-5113.

Request for information should contain: Individual's name, Social Security number, date of claim, and name of bill, if any.

UNFAIR LABOR PRACTICE CHARGES/COMPLAINTS (COMMERCE/DEPT-11-BEA)

Commerce employees filing unfair labor practice charges/ complaints.

Special Assistant to the Director, BEA, Tower Bldg., 1401 K St., NW, Washington, DC 20005, (202) 523-0893.

Request for information should contain: Individual's name, Social Security number, date of complaint, and organizational unit in which employed at the time of the complaint.

UNFAIR LABOR PRACTICE CHARGES/COMPLAINTS (COMMERCE/DEPT-11-EDA)

Commerce employees filing unfair labor practices charges/ complaints.

Director, Office of Public Affairs, Dept. of Commerce/EDA. 14th & Constitution Ave., NW, Washington, DC 20230, (202) 377-4901.

Request for information should include: Individual's name, Social Security number, date of complaint, and organizational unit in which employed at the time of the complaint.

UNFAIR LABOR PRACTICE CHARGES/COMPLAINTS (COMMERCE/DEPT-11-OEP)

Commerce employees filing unfair labor practice charges/ complaints.

Deputy Director, Dept. of Commerce/OEP, 14th & Constitution Ave., NW, Washington, DC 20230, (202) 961-6061.

Request for information should include: Individual's name, Social Security number, date of complaint, and organizational unit in which employed at the time of the complaint.

UNFAIR LABOR PRACTICE CHARGES/COMPLAINTS (COMMERCE/DEPT-11-NFPCA)

Commerce employees filing unfair labor practice charges/ complaints.

Administration Officer, Dept. of Commerce/NFPCA, Washington, DC 20230, (202) 634-7663.

Request for information should contain: Individual's name, Social Security number, date of complaint, and organizational unit in which employed at the time of the complaint.

UNFAIR LABOR PRACTICE CHARGES/COMPLAINTS (COMMERCE/DEPT-11-OMBE)

Commerce employees filing unfair labor practice charges/ complaints.

Assistant Director, Field Operations and Administration, Dept. of Commerce/OMBE, 14th & Constitution Ave., NW, Washington, DC 20230, (202) 377-3024.

Request for information should contain: Individual's name, Social Security number, date of complaint, and organizational unit in which employed at the time of the complaint.

UNFAIR LABOR PRACTICE CHARGES/COMPLAINTS (COMMERCE/DEPT-11-OFFICE OF FEDERAL COCHAIRMEN)

Commerce employees filing unfair labor practice charges/complaints.

Director, Office of Organization and Management Systems, 14th & Constitution Ave., NW, Washington, DC 20230, (202) 377-5113.

Request for information should contain: Individual's name, Social Security number, date of complaint, and organizational unit in which employed at the time of the complaint.

UNFAIR LABOR PRACTICE CHARGES/COMPLAINTS (COMMERCE/DEPT-11-DIBA)

Commerce employees filing unfair labor practice charges/complaints.

Director, Office of Management and Systems, Dept. of Commerce/DIBA, 14th & Constitution Ave., NW, Washington, DC 20230, (202) 377-5436.

Request for information should contain: Individual's name, Social Security number, date of complaint, and organizational unit in which employed at the time of the complaint.

UNFAIR LABOR PRACTICE CHARGES/COMPLAINTS (COMMERCE/DEPT-11-NBS)

Commerce employees filing unfair labor practice charges/complaints.

Associate Director for Administration, Dept. of Commerce/NBS, Administration Bldg., Washington, DC 20234, (301) 921-2477.

Request for information should contain: Individual's name, Social Security number, date of complaint, and organizational unit in which employed at the time of the complaint.

UNFAIR LABOR PRACTICE CHARGES/COMPLAINTS (COMMERCE/DEPT-11-NOAA)

Commerce employees filing unfair labor practice charges/complaints.

Assistant Administrator for Administration, Dept. of Commerce/NOAA, 6010 Executive Blvd., Rockville, MD 20852, (301) 443-8134.

Request for information should contain: Individual's name, Social Security number, date of complaint, and organizational unit in which employed at the time of the complaint.

UNFAIR LABOR PRACTICE CHARGES/COMPLAINTS (COMMERCE/DEPT-11-PAT-TM)

Commerce employees filing unfair labor practice charges/complaints.

Assistant Commissioner for Administration, U.S Patent & Trademark Office, Washington, DC 20231, (703) 557-3055.

Request for information should contain: Individual's name, Social Security number, date of complaint, and organizational unit in which employed at the time of the complaint.

UNFAIR LABOR PRACTICE CHARGES/COMPLAINTS (COMMERCE/DEPT-11-CENSUS)

Commerce employees filing unfair labor practice charges/complaints.

Associate Director for Administration, Bureau of the Census, Federal Building 3, Washington, DC 20233, (202) 568-1200.

Request for information should contain: Individual's name, Social Security number, date of complaint, and organizational unit in which employed at the time of the complaint.

Additional Files

Following is a list of the remaining files maintained by the Department of Commerce. Anyone interested in obtaining information from any of these files should contact the privacy officer for the Office of the Secretary or departmental staff offices.

Agriculture Census Records for 1964 (partial), 1969 and 1974 (COMMERCE/CENSUS-1)

Applicants for Hardship Exemptions under Marine Mammal Protection Act of 1972 (COMMERCE/NOAA-2)

Applicants for Marine Mammal Scientific Research and Display Permits (COMMERCE/NOAA-3)

Applicants for the NOAA Corps (COMMERCE/NOAA-4)

Applicants' Resumes for EDA–Funded Planning Grantee Positions (COMMERCE/EDA-1)

Applicants for Threatened Species Permits (COMMERCE/NOAA-5)

Applications to United States Merchant Marine Academy (USMMA) (COMMERCE/MA-1)

Atlantic Tropical Experiment (COMMERCE/NOAA-16)

Attendance, Leave, and Payroll Records of Employees and Certain Other Persons (COMMERCE/DEPT-1)

Attorneys and Agents Registered to Practice Before the Office (COMMERCE/PAT-TM-1)

Auditor Trainee Registrants (COMMERCE/IATC-1)

Cadet Files, State Merchant Marine Academies (COMMERCE/MA-2)

Citizenship Statements and Affidavits (COMMERCE/MA-3)

Commissioned Officer Official Personnel Folders (COMMERCE/NOAA-7)

Commissioned Officers Official Travel Orders Folders (COMMERCE/NOAA-6)

Commissioned Officers Retired Payroll (COMMERCE/NOAA-8)

Commissioners of International Fishery Commissions (COMMERCE/NOAA-9)

Conflict of Interest Records, Appointed Officials (COMMERCE/DEPT-3)

Congressional Files (COMMERCE/DEPT-4)

Customer Account Records (COMMERCE/NTIS-1)

Donors of Gifts and Bequests (COMMERCE/DEPT-5)

Employee Accident Reports (COMMERCE/DEPT-7)

Employee Applications for Motor Vehicle Operator's Card (COMMERCE/DEPT-8)

Employee Personnel Files Not Covered by U.S. Civil Service Commission (COMMERCE/DEPT-18)

Employee Production Records (COMMERCE/NOAA-10)

Employee Production Records (COMMERCE/PAT-TM-3)

Employee Productivity Measurement Records (COMMERCE/CENSUS-2)

Foreign Residence Requirements Waiver Applicants (COMMERCE/DEPT-10)

Government Employee Invention Rights (COMMERCE/PAT-TM-4)

Guest Workers at National Geophysical and Solar-Terrestrial Data Center (COMMERCE/NOAA-13)

ISMMA Midshipman Grade Transcripts (COMMERCE/MA-16)

Indian Industrial Development Intern Records (COMMERCE/EDA-2)

Indian Reservation Economic Development Planners and Applicants' Records (COMMERCE/EDA-3)

Individual and Household Statistical Surveys and Special Studies Records (COMMERCE/CENSUS-3)

Individuals Engaged in Weather Modification Activities (COMMERCE/NOAA-14)

Individuals Interested in NTIS Publications, Shipped Order Addresses, and Subscribers Files (COMMERCE/NTIS-2)

Individuals Involved in Export Transactions (COMMERCE/DIBA-2)

Inventors of Energy-Related Processes and Devices (COMMERCE/NBS-2)

Investigative Records — Persons Within the Investigative Jurisdiction of the Department (COMMERCE/DEPT-13)

Marine Recreational Fishermen's Catch Statistics (COMMERCE/NOAA-12)

Marine Training School Registrants (COMMERCE/MA-5)

Medical Records of Seamen Treated in Overseas Military Hospitals (COMMERCE/MA-6)

Members of United States Trade Missions (COMMERCE/DIBA–4)

Membership Information: District and Regional Export Councils (COMMERCE/DIBA-5)

Minority-Owned Business Enterprises Survey Records (COMMERCE/CENSUS-4)

NBS Guest Workers (COMMERCE/NBS-1)

National Defense Executive Reserve (COMMERCE/MA-7)

National Defense Executive Reserve Personnel Folders (COMMERCE/DIBA-6)

Nonregistered Persons Rendering Assistance to Patent Applicants (COMMERCE/PAT-TM-5)

Overseas Assignments for DIBA's Office of Field Operations (COMMERCE/DIBA-7)

Participants in Clinical Dental Projects (COMMERCE/NBS-4)

Participants in Human Factors Studies (COMMERCE/NBS-5)

Participants in Psychoacoustic Experiments (COMMERCE/NBS-6)

Patent Application Files (COMMERCE/PAT-TM-7) NOTE: This notice is broken down, where indicated, into three subsystems relating to the status of the files: Pending, Abandoned and Patented.

Patent Application Secrecy Order Files (COMMERCE/PAT-TM-8)

Patent Assignment Records (COMMERCE/PAT-TM-9)

Patent Deposit Accounts System (COMMERCE/PAT-TM-10)

Patent Examiner Testimony Files (COMMERCE/PAT-TM-11)

Patent Subscription Service System (COMMERCE/PAT-TM-12)

Petitioners for License to File for Foreign Patents (COMMERCE/PAT-TM-13)

Population Census Personal Service Records for 1900 and All Subsequent Decennial Censuses (COMMERCE/CENSUS-6)

Population and Housing Census Records for 1960 and 1970 (COMMERCE/CENSUS-5)

Property Accountability Files (COMMERCE/DEPT-16)

Records of Cash Receipts (COMMERCE/DEPT-17)

Research Associates (COMMERCE/NBS-3)

Sales Agents Authorized to Retail NOAA Aeronautical and Nautical Charts (COMMERCE/NOAA-15)

Scientist-Researchers in GATE (Global Atmospheric Research Program Atlantic Tropical Experiment) (COMMERCE/NOAA-16)

Seaman Awards and Nominations, for Service, Valor, etc. (COMMERCE/MA-9)

Seamen's Employment Analysis Records (COMMERCE/MA-10)

Seamen's Unclaimed Wages (Vietnam Conflict) (COMMERCE/MA-11)

Shipyard Labor Supply and Demand Program (COMMERCE/MA-12)

Special Censuses of Population Conducted for State and Local Government (COMMERCE/CENSUS-7)

Travel Records (Domestic and Foreign) of Employees and Certain Other Persons (COMMERCE/DEPT-9)

Trustees for Ship Sales (COMMERCE/MA-13)

USMMA Graduates (COMMERCE/MA-14)

USMMA Midshipman Account Records (COMMERCE/MA-15)

USMMA Midshipman Medical Files (COMMERCE/MA-17)

USMMA Midshipman Personnel Records (COMMERCE/MA-18)

USMMA Non-Appropriated Fund Employees (COMMERCE/MA-19)

USMMA Ship's Service Employees (COMMERCE/MA-20)

Visitor Logs and Permits for Facilities Under Department Control (COMMERCE/DEPT-6)

Waivers of Liability to Board Reserve Fleet Vessels (COMMERCE/MA-21)

U.S. Department of Defense

Following is a list of the agencies and subagencies of the Department of Defense, with their abbreviations:

DOD	Department of Defense
DARPA-E	Defense Advanced Research Projects Agency
CSS-Q	Central Security Service
DCPA-C	Defense Civil Preparedness Agency
DCA-K	Defense Communications Agency
DCAA-R	Defense Contract Audit Agency
DIA-V	Defense Intelligence Agency
DMA-B	Defense Mapping Agency
DNA-H	Defense Nuclear Agency
DSAA-T	Defense Security Assistance Agency
DSA-S	Defense Supply Agency
AF-F	Department of the Air Force
DA-A	Department of the Army
DON-N	Department of the Navy
NSA-G	National Security Agency
OSD-D	Office of the Secretary of Defense
JCS-J	Organization of the Joint Chiefs of Staff
USCG-P	United States Coast Guard
USMC-M	United States Marine Corps
USUHS-W	Uniformed Services University of the Health Sciences

The following pages list the files held by the Department of Defense.

EMPLOYEE RELATIONS: DISCIPLINE, GRIEVANCES, COMPLAINTS, AND APPEALS

Civilian employees paid from appropriated funds serving under career, career-conditional, temporary and excepted service appointments on whom discipline, grievances, and complaint records exist. Applicants for employment and former employees in appropriated and nonappropriated positions.

Director of Civilian Personnel, comparable official of the civilian personnel office servicing the Department of Defense activity/installation in question, or Department of Defense Privacy Board, The Pentagon, Washington, DC 20301, (202) 697-4122.

LABOR MANAGEMENT RELATIONS RECORDS SYSTEMS

Civilian employees paid from appropriated and nonappropriated funds who are involved in a grievance which has been referred to an arbitrator for resolution; civil employees involved in the filing of an unfair labor practice complaint which has been referred to the Assistant Secretary of Labor-Management Relations; union officials, union stewards, and representatives.

Director of Civilian Personnel, comparable official of the Civilian Personnel Office servicing the Department of Defense activity/installation in question, or Department of Defense Privacy Board, The Pentagon, Washington, DC 20301, (202) 697-4122.

Office of the Secretary of Defense

COMBAT AREA CASUALTIES

- Names of all military personnel who were killed, missing, captured, or interned in Southeast Asia.

Director for Information Operations and Control, Room 4B938, The Pentagon, Washington, DC 20301, (202) 697-7396.

• Any individual who has filed, or had filed on his or her behalf, a discrimination complaint.

Deputy for Plans and Policy, Office of the Deputy Assistant Secretary of Defense (Equal Opportunity), Room 3E319, The Pentagon, Washington, DC 20301, (202) 695-0107.

MILITARY ABSENTEES IN FOREIGN COUNTRIES (DESERTER)

Any military deserter known or believed to have gone to, or attempted to go to, a foreign country from July 1966 to the present (approximately 5000 individuals).

Assistant Director, Selected Policies, Office of the Deputy Assistant Secretary of Defense (Military Personnel Policy), Room 3C980, The Pentagon, Washington, DC 20301, (202) 697-4166.

PROTECTIVE SERVICES FILES

Any individual who initiates contact with the Secretary or Deputy Secretary of Defense in person, by United States mail or by telephone, who may possibly pose a threat to the personal safety of the Secretary or Deputy Secretary of Defense or other United States government officials.

Director, Physical Security, Washington Headquarters Services, the Pentagon, Washington, DC 20301, (202) 697-7396.

Additional Files

Following is a list of the remaining files maintained by the Office of the Secretary of Defense. Anyone interested in obtaining information from any of these files should contact the Office of the Secretary of Defense, Department of Defense, Pentagon Building, Washington, DC 20301, (202) 697-4122.

Administrative Files on Active Psychiatric Consultants to DOD
Administrative Files for Office of the Assistant Secretary of Defense for PA&E
Application for Pentagon Parking Permit
Assignment Folders
Biographic Data File
Biographical Record System
Biography File
Blood Donor Files
Cable Branch Personnel Administration Files
Case Files
Central Automated Inventory and Referral System (CAIRS)
Civilian Pay Time and Attendance Report
Classified Container Custodian Data SD 411
Computer Data Base
Contact Files
Contract Files
DOD Civilian Personnel Data File Extract

Department of Defense Distinguished Service Medal Files
Department of Defense Overseas Employment Program
Department of Defense Priority Placement Program (STOPPER LIST)
DOD Program for Stability of Civilian Employment
DOD-Wide Civilian Career Program for Comptroller/Financial Management Personnel
DRRI Student File
DSMS Academic Analysis System
DSMS Mailing List
DSMS Personnel Information Files
DSMS Student Files
DSMS Track Record System
Duty Status Cards
Employer Support File (PLEDGE)
Executive Development Programs File
Federal Employment Service Record Card
Files of Periodic Management Assessments of Certain Key Management Personnel and in DOD
Files of Personnel Evaluated for Employment in the Office of the ASD (H&E)
Files of Personnel Evaluated for Non-Career Employment in DOD
Files of Personnel Evaluated for Presidential Support Duties
Financial Interest Statement File
Flag and General Office File (FLAGS)
Freedom of Information Program Case Files
General Administrative File
General/Flag Officer Files
General/Flag Officer Roster
Health Benefits File
Health Benefits Preapproval Files
Health Facilities File
I&L Administrative Files
ISA Locator File
ISA Telephone Directory
Incentive Awards Records
Individual Personnel Files, 03-1b Consultants Files
Industrial Personnel Security Clearance Case Files
Job Opportunity Announcements
Joint Civilian Orientation Conference Files
Joint Service Commendation Medal Recommendations File
Key Personnel List
Legal Opinion Files
List of Female Employees of OSD/OJCS
List of Personnel and Security Clearances
Long Term Training Programs File
MARDAC Data Base
Management Intern File
Medical Care Inquiry Files
Medical Claim History Files
Navy Officer Personnel Service Records
Office of the Assistant Secretary of Defense (Intelligence) Personnel Roster
Office Director of Research and Development (ODDR&E), Inventor's File
Office Director of Research and Development (ODDR&E), Personnel Administration Files

Office of the DASD (Security Police) Personnel Files (ODASD (SP))

The Office of the Secretary of Defense Clearance File

OSD General Correspondence Files

The Office of the Secretary of Defense Identification Badge Suspense Card System

Office Social Roster and Locator Card

Organizational Personnel Files and 201 Files

Overseas Education Correspondence Files

Overseas Staffing Files

Pentagon Building Pass Application Files

Pentagon Computeride

Personnel File/Biography

Personnel Files

Personnel Leave Schedule

Personnel Records

Personnel Roster (Directorate for Procurement)

Personnel Roster (Directorate for Program and Financial Control)

Personnel Roster (Directorate for Research and Development)

Personnel Security Clearance Files

Policy and Precedent Files

Portrait-Photograph File

Private Relief Legislation File

Public Correspondence Files

Reduction-In-Force Case Files

Reenlistment Eligible File (RECRUIT)

Report of Personnel Assigned Outside of Department of Defense

Reports of Defense Related Employment

Request for Overtime Authorization

Requests for Two-Year Foreign Residence Waiver Files

Reserve Components Common Personnel Data System (RCCPDS)

Retired Personnel Master File

Roster of Military Personnel

Roster of When Actually Employed Employees

Security Clearance File

Security Inspector Duty Roster

Security Review Index File

Short Term Training Files

Staff Telephone Listing

Supergrade Correspondence, Reports, and Case Files

Survey Data Base

Teacher Application Files

Time and Attendance Report

Training Records

Travel Files

Variable Incentive Pay for Medical Officers—Data Management System

Worker's Compensation On-The-Job Injuries Report File

Defense Civil Preparedness Agency

CIVIL RIGHTS COMPLAINT AND COMPLIANCE FILES

Persons who file or could file a complaint with DCPA alleging discrimination by a state or local government in violation of Title VI of the Civil Rights Act of 1964.

Headquarters, DCPA, Pentagon Building, Washington, DC 20301, (202) 695-6498.

ENFORCEMENT (COMPLIANCE) – INDIVIDUALS OTHER THAN DCPA EMPLOYEES

Any individual who is not a DCPA employee (including state or local government employees, or volunteers), charged with, or who may be charged with, nonconformity to, noncompliance with, or violation of a law, rule, regulation, circular, or similar regulatory or program material which DCPA administers in whole or in part by participation in administration.

Headquarters, DCPA, Pentagon Building, Washington, DC 20301, (202) 695-6498.

EQUAL EMPLOYMENT OPPORTUNITY DISCRIMINATION COMPLAINT FILES

Any DCPA employee or applicant for employment, headquarters and field, including full-time permanent, part-time, temporary, consultants, military and civilian, who makes a discrimination-in-employment charge against DCPA.

Headquarters, DCPA, Pentagon Building, Washington, DC, 20301, (202) 695-6498.

Additional Files

Following is a list of the remaining files maintained by the DCPA. Anyone interested in obtaining information from any of these files should contact the Defense Civil Preparedness Agency, Department of Defense, Pentagon Building, Washington, DC 20301, (202) 695-6498.

ACC Payroll and Leave Accounting

ACC Travel and Transportation Accounting

COM Radio Amateur Civil Emergency Service (RACES) Plans

EMO Emergency Operating Planning

IND Liaison Services Industrial Coordinator, Guest Speaker, and National Organization List

INF Biographies

INF Civil Defense Awards

LEG Claims—Employees

LEG Claims—Other than Employees

LEG Enforcement, Compliance, and Supervision of DCPA Employees

LEG Interest Conflict Review

MGT Committee Management Files

MGT Defense Civil Preparedness Agency (DCPA) Central Files

MGT Delegations and Designations Files

MGT Program Management Information System

OSV Office Services File System

PER Bond, Charitable, and Blood Donor Drives Files

PER Classified Clearances

PER Emergency Notifications Lists

PER Executive Reserves
PER General Personnel
PER Handicapped Employees and Handicapped Veterans
PER Military Reserve Program
PER Publications Distribution Lists Computer Center
PUB Standard Publications Distribution Lists
PUB State Civil Defense Directors
RAD Maintenance and Calibration
RAD Radiation Exposure and Radioactive Materials; Radiation Committee Records
SEC Classified Documents Control Files
SHL Summer Hire
TES F.W. Dodge Company Reports
TNG, DCPA FORM 1353, Appl. for Enrollment in Architects and Engineers Professional Development Program
TNG Home Study Courses, DCPA Staff College
TNG Qualified Instructor File
TNG State and Local Civil Preparedness Instructional Program (SLCPIP)
TNG Student Academic and Course Records, DCPA Staff College
WNG Decision Info Distribution System (DIDS) Volunteers
WNG List of Custodians of Decision Info System (DIDS) Radio Receivers

Defense Communications Agency

The Director of the Defense Communications Agency (DCA) is also the Manager of the National Communications Systems (NCS), the Chairman of the Military Communications—Electronics Board (MCEB), and Director of the Worldwide Military Command and Communications System (WWMCCS) Systems Engineering. To the extent that the director performs these other functions, the records system described herein pertains to and is available to employees of these organizations, and may be corrected by means of the same process described for DCA files systems, unless specified otherwise herein.

With the exception of personnel records for navy officers assigned to DCA activities in the Washington metropolitan area, the official records of military personnel assigned to DCA are maintained by the parent department. That department has the only complete official copies of the military members' personnel records files. Responsibility for the completeness and accuracy of these files is vested in the military department. While the DCA commander or office chief may assist the military member in obtaining access or making corrections, DCA does not have the authority either to grant access or make corrections. The documents maintained by DCA on military personnel are copies of records provided by the military departments during the nomination process, copies of personnel correspondence generated during the members' tenure in DCA, promotion rosters furnished by the military departments, and copies of orders published by the departments. A few documents are maintained as a result of requirements

imposed by the departments (leave forms for army and air force personnel and SIDPERS for army personnel).

In the case of navy officers in the Washington area, DCA maintains the navy officers' service records and can grant access and make corrections within the purview of NAVPERS 15791, *Bureau of Naval Personnel Manual.*

CLASSIFIED CONTAINER INFORMATION ON FORM (DA FORM 727)

Civilian and military personnel assigned to DCA headquarters, and collocated field activities who have been designated responsible officials of a classified container, or who are to be notified if the container is found open and unattended.

Chief, Security Division, [name of staff element], Code 240, Headquarters, DCA, Washington, DC 20305, (202) 694-3245.

INCIDENT REPORT FILE

Any personnel (military or civilian) assigned to DCA Europe involved in a traffic, financial, criminal, or other incident that is reported to the DCA Europe commander for information or necessary action.

Commander, DCA Europe, APO New York 09131.

INVESTIGATION OF COMPLAINT OF DISCRIMINATION

Employees of, or applicants for employment with, DCA who have filed formal, written complaints alleging that they have been discriminated against.

Director, Equal Employment Opportunity, DCA (Code 107), Washington, DC 20305, (202) 694-3081.

SECURITY VIOLATION CASE FILE

- Civilian and military personnel assigned to DCA headquarters, and collocated field activities, who committed or contributed to a security violation involving classified defense information.

- Civilian and military personnel assigned to DCA headquarters and collocated field activities, who discovered the violation, were witnesses in connection with the violation, or were interviewed to determine whether they were involved.

- Civilian contractors under contractual obligation to the DCA and who were witnesses in connection with the violation, or were interviewed to determine whether they were involved.

- Any individual in the civilian community or government employ (military or civilian), who reported a security violation, or who could furnish information relative to the violation, or who may have been involved in the violation.

Chief, Security Division, Code 240, Headquarters, DCA, Washington, DC 20305, (202) 694-3245.

Additional Files

Following is a list of the remaining files maintained by the DCA. Anyone interested in obtaining information from any of these files should contact the Defense Communications Agency, Department of Defense, Washington, DC 20305, (202) 694-3245.

Access Listing to Classified Material (NATO)
Active Application Files (Applicant Supply Files)
Agency Access/Pass File System
Agency Training File System
Annual Classification Maintenance Review File
Armed Forces Courier Service Authorization Record
Authority to Review/Sign for Classified Messages at 1918 Communications Center
Authorization Lists
Authorization to Sign for Classified Material Lists
Awards Case History File
Card File for Forwarding Mail of Departed Personnel
Chronological Journal Files
Circulation File Charge Slip
Civil Service Certificate Files
Civilian Awards Program File
Claims Files, Requests for Waiver of Pay and Allowances
Classification Appeals File
Classification Container Information Form DA 727
Classified Material Receipt Authorization List
Clearance Card File for Defense Communications Agency (DCA) Personnel
Confidential Statement of Employment and Financial Interest
Courier Badge List
DA Form 727 Classified Container Information File
DCA Europe Form 62, Personnel Data Sheet
DCA Europe Form 132, Security Clearance Data
Duty Rosters
Education, Training, and Career Development Data System
Employee-Management Relations and Services Files
Employee Record File
Executive Level Position Files
Freedom of Information Act File (FOIA)
Identification Badge System
Injury Records
Military Financial File System
Military Personnel Files System
Military Personnel Management/Assignment Files
Minority Identification File List
NATO Subregistry Personnel Signature List
National Communications Systems Continuity of Operations Plan (NCS COOP)
National Communications System Emergency Action Group (NEAG)
National Communications System (NCS) Plan for Emergencies and Major Disasters

Navy Officers Service Record
Nominations/Enrollment for Training Courses
Official Personnel Folder Files (Standard Form 66)
Overseas Rotation Program Files
Parking Permit Control Files
Permanent Change of Station and Temporary Duty Travel Order File
Personnel Information System
Personnel Locator File System
Personnel Management Information System (PERMIS)
Personnel Security Files
Personnel Security Investigative Dossier File (PSIDF)
Postal Directory File
Priority Reassignment Eligibles File
Priority Repromotion Eligibles File
Promotion Register and Record Files
Records Relating to DCA Transactions under the Privacy Act of 1974
Report of Defense Related Employment
Request and Authorization for Temporary Duty Travel
Retention Register Files (Reduction-in-Force)
Security Clearance File
Sensitive Compartmented Info (SCI) Posn/Pers Accountability System
Service Record Card Files
Temporary Issue Receipt File
Time and Attendance Cards and Labor Distribution Cards
Travel Order and Voucher File
Travel Orders Records System
USAF Career Motivation Program
Vehicle Parking Registration Card
Vehicle Registration File
Visit Notification/Clearance Verification Records
Visitor Clearance File

Defense Contract Audit Agency

EEO BACKGROUND DOCUMENTS NOT INCLUDED IN CASE FILES

Any civilian employee of DCAA who has brought an EEO complaint against any organizational level of DCAA.

EEO Officer, HQ, DCAA, Room 4C346, Cameron Station, Alexandria, VA 22314, (202) 274-7319.

EEO CASES RESOLVED BY CSC

Any civilian employee of DCAA who has brought an EEO complaint against any organization level of DCAA.

EEO Officer, HQ, DCAA, Room 4C346, Cameron Station, Alexandria, VA 22314, (202) 274-7319.

EEO COMPLAINTS RESOLVED BY DCAA

Any civilian employee of DCAA who has brought an EEO complaint against any organizational level of DCAA.

EEO Officer, HQ, DCAA, Room 4C346, Cameron Station, Alexandria, VA, 22314, (202) 274-7319.

FREEDOM OF INFORMATION ADMINISTRATIVE APPEALS

Any individual who appeals an initial denial of information by the agency.

Records Administrator, Defense Contract Audit Agency, Cameron Station, Building 4, Room 4A320, Alexandria, VA 22314, (202) 274-7285.

GENERAL EEO FILES

Any civilian employee of DCAA who has contacted an EEO Counselor regarding any form of discrimination against them by any organizational level of DCAA.

EEO Officer, HQ, DCAA, Room 4C346, Cameron Station, Alexandria, VA 22314, (202) 274-7319.

GRIEVANCE & APPEAL FILES

Employees who have filed formal grievances pursuant to Chapter 58, DCAAM 1400.1.

Personnel office of the region in which the grievance originated, or HQ, DCAA.

Request for information should contain: Individual's name, current address, telephone number, and office of assignment.

Personal visits may be made to the personnel office of the region in which the grievance was filed.

LEGAL OPINIONS

Any DCAA employee who files a complaint with regard to personnel problems that require a legal opinion for resolution.

Records Administrator, Defense Contract Audit Agency, Cameron Station, Building 4, Room 4A320, Alexandria, VA 22314, (202) 274-7285.

NAME FILES

Civilian employees of DCAA on whom copies of communications, favorable or unfavorable, have been received.

Director of Personnel, HQ, DCAA, Cameron Station, Alexandria, VA 22314, (202) 274-6025.

Request for information should contain: Individual's name, current address, telephone number, and office of assignment.

OTHER COPIES OF EEO COMPLAINT CASE FILES

Any civilian employee of DCAA who has brought an EEO complaint against any organizational level of DCAA.

EEO Officer, HQ, DCAA, Room 4C346, Cameron Station, Alexandria, VA 22314, (202) 274-7319.

PRIVACY ACT ADMINISTRATIVE APPEALS

Any individual who appeals an initial denial of information by DCAA under the Privacy Act of 1974.

Records Administrator, Defense Contract Audit Agency, Cameron Station, Building 4, Room 4A320, Alexandria, VA 22314, (202) 274-7285.

STANDARDS OF CONDUCT, CONFLICT OF INTEREST

Any DCAA employee who has accepted gratuities from contractors or who has business, professional, or financial interests that would indicate a conflict between their private interests and those related to their duties and responsibilities as DCAA personnel.

Any DCAA employee who is a member or officer of an organization that is incompatible with his or her official government position, using public office for private gain, or affecting adversely the confidence of the public in the integrity of the government.

Records Administrator, Defense Contract Audit Agency, Cameron Station, Building 4, Room 4A320, Alexandria, VA 22314, (202) 274-7285.

Additional Files

Following is a list of the remaining files maintained by the DCA. Anyone interested in obtaining information from any of these files should contact the Defense Contract Audit Agency, Department of Defense, Washington, DC 20305, (202) 694-3245.

Applicant Correspondence
Applicant Supply File Index
Career Files
Clearance Certification
Congressional Committee Correspondence
Congressional Correspondence
Cross Reference Index to Legal Opinions
DCAA Automated Personnel Inventory System (APIS)
DCAA Management Information System (MIS)
Delegations of Authority
Disbursement Vouchers
Executive Development Program
General (Permanent Change of Station)
Inactive Service Records
Key Control Records
Letters of Commendation and Appreciation
Locator Records
Notification of Security Clearance Status
Notification of Security Determinations
Notification of Visits
Official Personnel Folders
Parking Permits and Vehicle Registration
Personnel Security Adjudication File
Personnel Security Data Files
Property Pass Files
Regional Security Clearance Request Files
Reports of Personnel Security Investigations
Security Status Master List
Security Training and Orientation

Service Record File
Statements of Employment and Financial Interest
Students and Instructors
Supervisor Personnel Records
Temporary Passes and Permits for Visitors and Vehicles
Time and Attendance Reports
White House Correspondence

Defense Intelligence Agency

For information about any Defense Intelligence Agency (DIA) system of records, individuals should contact the following office, stating in which system of records they are interested:

Records Management Office, Defense Intelligence Agency, attention: SCIPA 1974, Washington, DC 20301, (202) 695-1222. Personal visits: The Secretariat, Room 3E268, The Pentagon, Washington, DC 20301, (202) 695-6669.

Requests for information should contain: Individual's name, Social Security number, date and place of birth, and military status.

COMPLAINTS

Civilian and military personnel employed by the DIA who have made a complaint to the inspector general or who have been interviewed during the inquiry into a complaint.

COMPLAINTS/INVESTIGATIONS

Any civilian employee or applicant who has filed a formal written EEO complaint.

DEFENSE ATTACHE INVESTIGATION FILE

Individuals who were subjects of security or criminal investigations while assigned to the Defense Attache System.

DEFENSE INTELLIGENCE AGENCY, DIRECTORATE FOR INFORMATION SYSTEMS SECURITY FILES

Military and civilian clearance levels, security violation files, security records, access controls to areas and computers and computer programs, and visitor requests.

EMPLOYEE GRIEVANCES AND APPEALS

Civilian employees who have filed formal written grievances.

INVESTIGATIONS

Civilian and military personnel employed by the DIA, who are interviewed by the inspector general during a formal investigation.

LEGAL OPINIONS AND RELATED DOCUMENTATION

Individuals who have been involved in legal matters.

SECURITY

Any individual assigned to DS-4A who has been involved in security violations, investigations, destruction of classified material, whose name appears on access rosters for areas with the branch and/or authorizations to access specific types of intelligence; any individual whose name and clearance has been passed through DIA security in order to gain access to the DIA library or any of its annexes; any individual assigned to DS-4A whose name and clearance have been forwarded to another agency or department; individuals within the branch with DIAOLS authorization.

SECURITY VIOLATIONS FILES

Any individual who, while assigned or employed by the DIA, has been found, upon inquiry or investigation, to be responsible for a violation of established security directives or procedures resulting in the compromise or possible compromise of classified information.

Additional Files

Following is a list of remaining files maintained by the DIA. Anyone interested in obtaining information from any of these files should contact the Defense Intelligence Agency, Department of Defense, Washington, DC 20301, (202) 695-1222.

ASDIA All Source Document Index
Administrative Publications
Agency Checkout File
Applicants for Employment
Application, Change, Cancellation for U.S. Savings Bond
    Class A Pay Reservation
Attaches and Human Resources Personnel Information
    Files
Automated Bibliographic Data Files, ASDIA, IRISA,
    IRFLA
Biographical Sketch (Military and Civilian)
Board of Visitors File (BOV)
Cancellation of Allotment of Pay for Credit to Financial
    Institution
Civilian Employee Compensation Records
Civilian Payroll/Earnings and Leave Statements
Civilian Personnel Administrative Records
Claim for Reimbursement for Expenditures on Official
    Business
Classified Letters of Appreciation File
Clearance Certification File
Collection of Indebtedness Due U.S. Government
Contract Correspondence
Cost of Annual Leave Balance Report
DIA Awards Files
DIA Employee Bond Issuances Schedule DD 1084C
DIS Employee Civilian Payroll Checks Listing
DIA Employee Payroll Authorization for Disposition of
    Salary Check, Bond DIA 945
DIA Employee Personal Services DA 2449
DIA 53 Payclerk/Supervisor Name Card
DIA Form 209
DIA Prisoner of War Intelligence Analysis and Debriefing
    Files

DIA Travel Record DIA 766
DOD Priority Placement and Overseas Employment
  Programs
Defense Attache Roster
Defense Intelligence Agency Personnel Roster
Defense Intelligence Special Career Automated System
  (DISCAS)
Defense Special Career Automated System
Director's Correspondence File
Emergency Alert and Recall Rosters
Employee Performance Appraisals
Field Personnel Folder
Freedom of Information Act (FOIA) Files
Graphic Arts Management System (GAMS)
Guest Lecturer File
Health, Welfare, and Charities
Health, Welfare, and Recreation
Incentive Awards
Individual Identification Records
Intelligence Collection Records
Intelligence Report Indexing System (IRISA)
Job Opportunities (Selection of High Potential Employees)
Joint Table of Distribution
Library Circulation File
Local Transportation Records
Locator Cards/Rosters
Locator Service/Postal Directory
Management Analysis
Military Personnel Procurement, DIA Form 83
Military Service Administrative Records
Movement of Personnel/Travel
Off Duty Employment Report
Office Administration—Dining Room Passes
Organization Planning and Manpower
Passports and Visas
Payroll Service Request Form
Personnel Actions (Civilian)
Personnel File Index
Personnel Management Information System (PMIS)
Personnel Security Case Records Retirement Retrieval
  Index
Personnel Security Investigation Files
Personnel Security and Security Clearance Status
  Index
Position Descriptions
Production Control System
Project Files
Qualifications, Placements, and Promotions
Reduction in Force (RIF) Case Files
Reemployment Rights File
Reports of Survey
Request for Clearance
Request for DOD Management Education and Training
Program Courses
Request by Employee for Allotment of Pay for Credit to
  Savings Account
Request for Irregular Overtime
Request for Training
Requests for Reassignment

Requests for Waiver of Indebtedness Resulting from
  Erroneous Payments
Reserve Personnel Status (DIA Form 2-6) File
Reserve Training Records
Retirement Records SF2806
Rotary Card File
Security Management Information System (SMIS)
Sensitive Compartmented Information (SCI) Access Files
Service Record Card File
Signature Card DD 577, Individual Signature Card
Student Information Files
Supervisor's Records of Employees
Supply, Space and Facilities, Policy and Planning
System Access Log and Directory
Telephone Records
Timekeeper Station Listing
Training Facilities Records
Training Locator Cards
Transportation Officers Lists
Travel Voucher or Subvoucher
Vehicle Parking
Visitor Accreditation File

Defense Investigative Service

ADVERSE ACTIONS, GRIEVANCE FILES, AND
ADMINISTRATIVE APPEALS

Affected civilian employees of the DIS.

Chief, Civilian Personnel Office (D0151), DIS HQ, Room 2H086, Forrestal Building, Washington, DC 20314, (202) 693-7521.

DEFENSE CASE CONTROL SYSTEM (DCCS)

Any person or activity which is the subject of an ongoing or recently completed DIS investigation.

Assistant for Information, Defense Investigative Service (D0020), Washington, DC 20314, (202) 693-1740.

Request for information should contain: Individual's name and all maiden or alias names under which files may be maintained, personal identifiers which include data and place of birth, Social Security number, and last four digits of military service number.

Personal visits may be made to the Assistant for Information, DIS, 1000 Independence Avenue, Washington, DC 20314. Personal visitors will be subject to routine check of personal documents.

DEFENSE CENTRAL INDEX OF INVESTIGATIONS (DCII)

Any person described as a subject, a victim, or a cross-reference in an investigation completed by or for a DOD investigative organization when that investigation is retained by the organization and the name is submitted for central indexing.

Assistant for Information, Defense Investigative Service (D0020), Washington, DC 20314, (202) 693-1740.

Request for information should contain: Individual's name and all maiden and alias names under while files may be maintained, and personal identifiers. Note: Social Security account numbers may be necessary for positive identification of certain records.

EEO COMPLAINTS

Persons involved in complaints and DIS civilian employees who have been officially counselled.

Chief, Civilian Personnel Officer (DO151), DISH HQ, Room 2H086, Forrestal Building, Washington, DC 20314, (202) 694-7521.

INSPECTOR GENERAL COMPLAINTS

Past and present civilian employees of the DIS and military personnel currently or formerly assigned to DIS for duty who have made a complaint, or requested assistance from the inspector general, or whose complaint or request has been referred to the inspector general for action, assistance, or information.

Assistant for Information (D0020), Room 2H043, Forrestal Building, Washington, DC 20314, (202) 693-1740.

INVESTIGATIVE FILES SYSTEMS

Military personnel who are on active duty, applicants for enlistment or appointment, and reservists and national guardsmen; DOD civilian personnel who are paid from appropriated funds; industrial or contractor personnel who are working in private industry in firms that have contracts involving access to classified DOD information or installations; Red Cross personnel and personnel paid from non-appropriated funds who have DOD affiliation; ROTC cadets; former military personnel; individuals residing on, having authorized official access to, or conducting or operating any business or other functions at any DOD installation or facility. Individuals not affiliated with DOD when, during the previous year, their activities have directly threatened the functions, property or personnel of the DOD or they have engaged in, or conspired to engage in, criminal acts on DOD installations or directed at the DOD.

Assistant for Information, Defense Investigative Service (D0020), Washington, DC 20314, (202) 693-1740.

Request for information should contain: Individual's name, date and place of birth, and Social Security number. More information or a notarized statement verifying the identity of requesters may be required.

Personal visits may be made to the Information Office, Room 2H043, 1000 Independence Avenue, Washington, DC. Visitors will be subject to routine check of personal documents.

NATIONAL AGENCY CHECK (NAC) CASE CONTROL SYSTEM (NCCS)

Any person the subject of an active or recently completed national agency check conducted by DIS.

Assistant for Information, Defense Investigative Service (D0020), Washington, DC 20314, (202) 693-1740.

Request for information should contain: Individual's name and all maiden or alias names under which files may be maintained, personal identifiers such as date and place of birth, Social Security number, and last four digits of military service number.

Personal visits may be made to Assistant for Information, DIS, Room 2H043, 1000 Independence Avenue, Washington, DC 20314. Visitors will be subject to routine check of personal documents.

Additional Files

Following is a list of remaining files maintained by the DIS. Anyone interested in obtaining information from any of these files should contact the Defense Investigative Service, Department of Defense, Washington, DC 20314, (202) 693-1740.

Civilian Applicant Records
Civilian Employee Personnel Records
Civilian Personnel Management Information System
Incentive Awards
Manpower Personnel Assignment Document (MPAD)
Merit Promotion Plan Records
Military Personnel Management Information System
Optional Personnel Management Records (OPMR)
Personnel Security Files
Privacy and Freedom of Information Request Records
Special Compartmented Intelligence (SCI) Access File

Defense Mapping Agency

ADVERSE ACTION FILES

Civilian employees who have had adverse action taken against them.

Personnel Office, Building 56, Defense Mapping Agency, U.S. Naval Observatory, Washington, DC 20305, (202) 254-4066.

AGENCY CLAIM FILES

Individuals against whom the agency has legal claims.

Counsel, Building 56, Defense Mapping Agency, U.S. Naval Observatory, Washington, DC 20305, (202) 254-4431.

BASIC LABOR RELATIONS FILES

Civilian employees who file grievances under negotiated grievance procedure.

Personnel Office, Building 56, Defense Mapping Agency, U.S. Naval Observatory, Washington, DC 20305, (202) 254-4066.

CHRONOLOGICAL JOURNAL FILES

Civilian employees of the agency who have personnel actions pertaining to them.

Personnel Office, Building 56, Defense Mapping Agency, U.S. Naval Observatory, Washington, DC 20305, (202) 254-4066.

EQUAL EMPLOYMENT OPPORTUNITY COMPLAINT CASE FILES

Employees who file complaints of discrimination.

Personnel Office, Building 56, Defense Mapping Agency, U.S. Naval Observatory, Washington, DC 20305, (202) 254-4066.

GRIEVANCE FILES

Civilian employees who have filed a grievance.

Personnel Office, Building 56, Defense Mapping Agency, U.S. Naval Observatory, Washington, DC 20305, (202) 254-4066.

OFFICIAL PERSONNEL FOLDER FILES

Civilian employees.

Indebtedness—Allegations of indebtedness made by creditors requesting help from personnel office.

Personnel Office, Building 56, Defense Mapping Agency, U.S. Naval Observatory, Washington, DC 20305, (202) 254-4066.

PERSONAL PROPERTY CLAIM FILES

Employees having claims against the government for loss, damage, or destruction of personal property.

Counsel, Building 56, Defense Mapping Agency, U.S. Naval Observatory, Washington, DC 20305, (202) 254-4431.

REPORT OF SURVEY FILES

Employees that have lost, damaged, or destroyed accountable government property.

Administrative and Communications Office, Building 56, Defense Mapping Agency, U.S. Naval Observatory, Washington, DC 20305, (202) 254-4401.

SECURITY COMPROMISE CASE FILES

Employees with security violations.

Security Office, Building 56, Defense Mapping Agency, U.S. Naval Observatory, Washington, DC 20305, (202) 254-4411.

SECURITY VIOLATION CARD FILE

Any employee of DMA Aerospace Center who has a security violation.

Director, DMA Aerospace Center, Security Office (SO), St. Louis Air Force Station, MO 63118, (314) 268-4941.

TORT CLAIM FILES

Any individual filing a tort claim against DMA for damage, loss, or destruction of property and for personal injury or death resulting from negligence, wrongful act, or omission of acts by DMA personnel.

Counsel, Building 56, Defense Mapping Agency, U.S. Naval Observatory, Washington, DC 20305, (202) 254-4431.

VEHICLE REGISTRATION AND DRIVER RECORD FILE

Any person privileged to operate a motor vehicle on a military installation and who has been involved in a chargeable traffic accident or whose commission of a moving traffic violation has been verified.

Security Office, Building 56, Defense Mapping Agency, U.S. Naval Observatory, Washington, DC 20305, (202) 254-4411.

Additional Files

Following is a list of the remaining files maintained by the DMA. Anyone interested in obtaining information from any of these files should contact the appropriate agency head or the Secretary of Defense, The Pentagon, Washington, DC 20301.

Accidental Injury/Death Reporting Records Files
Active Application Files (Applicant Supply Files)
Alcoholism and Drug Abuse Files
Appeals Files
Billet Access Record
Biography Files
Blood Donors Files
Civilian Employee Health Clinic Records
Civilian Personnel Program Reporting Files (Employee Retirement Record)
Civilian Personnel Program Reporting Files (Master File Printout)
Civilian Training Program Files
Civilian Training Reporting Files
Classified Material Access Files
Collateral Individual Training Record Files
Communications Center Release Authorization
Compensation Data Request Files
Comptroller/Financial Management Civilian Career Referral System
Congressional Correspondence Files (Civilian Personnel—Congressional Inquiries)

Contract Training Files
Contracting Officer Designation Files
DMA Central Clearance Group Pre-Employment Files
DMA HQ Military Personnel Reference Paper Files
Decedent Claim Files
Differential and Allowance Files
Duty Roster Files
Employee Record Card Files
Employee Service Record File
Equal Employment Opportunity Reporting Files
Expert and Consultant Data Files
Faculty Development Program Files
Federal, State, and Professional Safety Councils and Committees Files
Firearms Authorization Files
Historical Photographic Files
Hours of Work Files
Incentive Awards
Individual Academic Record Files
Individual Government Transportation Files
Individual Overseas Employment Referral Files
Individual Pay Record Files
Individual Retirement Record Control Files
Inspector General Complaint Files
Inspector General Investigative Files
Installation Historical Files
Key Accountability Files
Leave Record Files
Legal Assistance Case Files
Military Personnel Reference Paper Files
Military Services Administrative Record Files
Motor Vehicle Operator's Permits and Qualifications Files
Occupational Inventory Files
Occupational Qualification List Files
Office General Personnel Files
Office Personnel Information Files
Office Personnel Locator Files
Official Records (Military) Files and Extracts
Organization File
Parking Permit Control Files
Passport Files
Pending Application Files
Personnel Assistance Files
Personnel Locator Files (Alpha Listing)
Personnel Security Clearance Information Files
Personnel Security Files
Personnel Security Investigative Files
Property Officer Designation Files
Record of Training Files
Record of Travel Payments
Records Access Files
Reduction-in-Force Card Files
Referral and Selection Files
Retention Register Files
Safety Awards Files
School Faculty Board Review Files
School Reporting Files
Security Awareness Files

Security Briefing and Debriefing Files
Security Identification Accountability Files
Security Identification Issue Files
Self Service Store Authorization Card Files
Special Security Briefing and Debriefing Files
Standard of Conduct
Statements of Employment and Financial Interest Files
Temporary Duty Travel Files
Traffic Law Enforcement Files
Training Files
Transportation Officer Appointment Files

Defense Nuclear Agency

EMPLOYEE RELATIONS

Civilian employees paid from appropriated funds serving under career, career-conditional, temporary, and excepted service appointments on whom discipline, grievances, and complaints records exist; discrimination complaints of civilian employees, paid from appropriated and nonappropriated funds, applicants for employment and former employees in appropriated and nonappropriated positions.

Civilian Personnel Officer, Defense Nuclear Agency, Washington, DC 20305, (202) 325-7592.

LABOR MANAGEMENT RELATIONS RECORDS SYSTEM

Civilian employees paid from appropriated and nonappropriated funds, who are involved in a grievance that has been referred to an arbitrator for resolution, and union officials, union stewards, and representatives.

Civilian Personnel Officer, Defense Nuclear Agency, Washington, DC 20305, (202) 325-7592.

Additional Files

Following is a list of the remaining files maintained by the DNA. Anyone interested in obtaining information from any of these files should contact the appropriate agency head or the Secretary of Defense, The Pentagon, Washington, DC 20301.

AFRRI Personnel Roster
Biography Files
DNA 001 Employee Assistance Program Case Record Systems
FCDNA Personnel Data Systems
Headquarters Personnel Roster
Personnel Radiation Exposure Records
Personnel Security Files
Training and Employee Development Record Systems
Visitor Access Control System

Defense Supply Agency

CLAIMS & LITIGATION, OTHER THAN CONTRACTUAL

Employees, groups of employees, members of the general public, and public-interest organizations.

Counsel, Headquarters DSA, Cameron Station, Alexandria, VA 22314, (202) 274-6156; counsel, DSA field activities.

Request for information should contain: Name of litigant, year of incident, and court case number in order to insure proper retrieval in those situations where a single litigant has more than one case with the agency.

COMPLAINTS

Individuals who have submitted written or oral complaints to the inspector general.

Inspector General, Headquarters, DSA, Cameron Station, Alexandria, VA 22314, (202) 274-6057

COMPLAINTS

DSA civilian and military personnel, and former personnel, contractor employees, union representatives, other individuals, and organizations who have presented complaints— to the president, members of congress, secretary of defense, director of Defense Supply Agency, or other official—which have been referred to staff director of civilian personnel, DSA headquarters, for response, action, or information.

Staff Director, Civilian Personnel, Headquarters, DSA, Cameron Station, Alexandria, VA 22314, (202) 274-6025.

Request for information should contain: Individual's name, the name of any DSA activity involved, and general nature of complaint individual believes to be filed in this system.

CRIMINAL INCIDENTS/INVESTIGATIONS FILE

Civilian and military personnel of DSA, contractor employees, and other persons who have committed or are suspected of having committed a felony or misdemeanor on DSA-controlled activities or facilities; or outside of those areas in cases where DSA is or may be a party of interest.

Command Security Officer, Headquarters DSA, Cameron Station, Alexandria, VA 22314.

DEBT RECORDS FOR INDIVIDUALS

Current and former civilian and military personnel who are indebted to the United States government.

Chief, Finance Systems Branch, Accounting and Finance Division, Office of Comptroller, Headquarters DSA, Cameron Station, Alexandria, VA 22314, (202) 274-6213.

FRAUD & IRREGULARITIES

Any individual or group of individuals or other entity, involved in or suspected of being involved in any fraud, criminal conduct, or antitrust violation relating to DSA procurement, property disposal, or contract administration.

Counsel, Headquarters DSA, Cameron Station, Alexandria, VA 22314, (202) 274-6156; DSA field activity counsels.

Requests for information should contain name of subject and sufficient identification of the incident in order to insure correct retrieval.

GRIEVANCE EXAMINERS AND EQUAL EMPLOYMENT OPPORTUNITY INVESTIGATORS PROGRAM

Military and civilian employees of the DSA, or former employees, who have been nominated by commanders of primary level field activities (PLFAs) to serve as DSA grievance examiners and EEO investigators and have been approved by DSA headquarters, are listed by name on regional rosters as available for serving in those areas. Also, retired federal civilian employees and others approved by DSA headquarters as grievance examiners and EEO investigators for the Agency and as available to serve under a nonpersonnel services contract are listed by name on regional rosters.

Staff Director, Civilian Personnel, Headquarters DSA, Cameron Station, Alexandria, VA 22314, (202) 274-6025.

Request for information should contain: Individual's name, and, if a current DSA employee, name of DSA activity at which employed.

INDIVIDUAL ACCIDENT CASE FILES

Civilian and military personnel, contractor employees, and other personnel who are injured on the premises of DSA or performing assignment incidental to DSA operations. Also relates to accidental damage to vehicles, equipment, and property.

Staff Director, Civilian Personnel, Headquarters DSA, Cameron Station, Alexandria, VA 22314, (202) 274-6025; safety officers, DSA primary level field activities.

Request for information should contain: Individual's name and name of DSA activity at which incident occurred; or if individual is or was a DSA employee, name of employing activity is also required.

LEGAL ASSISTANCE

Authorized military personnel and dependents who have requested legal assistance.

Counsel, Headquarters DSA, Cameron Station, Alexandria, VA 22314, (202) 274-6156; Office of Counsel, PLFAs.

Request for information should contain: Individual's name and, if appropriate, date assistance was requested.

PATENT INFRINGEMENT

Individuals and firms involved in potential or actual claims or litigation against government for infringement of patents.

Counsel, DSAH-G, Commission of Patents and Trademarks, Patent and Trademark Office, Washington, DC 20231, (703) 557-3158; and Clerk, United States Court of Customs and Patent Appeals, 717 Madison Place, NW, Washington, DC 20439, (202) 347-1552.

PERSONNEL SECURITY FILES

All civilian employees and military personnel who have been the subject of a background investigation (BI) or special background investigation (SBI) pertaining to their qualifications for access to classified information.

Command Security Officer, Headquarters DSA, Cameron Station, Alexandria, VA 22314, (202) 274-6066; Security Officers, PLFA.

SECURITY VIOLATIONS FILES

Civilian and military personnel currently or formerly employed by or assigned to DSA, employees of DOD contractor facilities, and other persons who may be involved in security violations.

Command Security Officer, Headquarters DSA, Cameron Station, Alexandria, VA 22314, (202) 274-6066; Security Officers, PLFA.

Request for information should contain: Individual's name and the identity of DSA activity at which the violation occurred, as well as the date of its occurrence.

SEIZURE AND DISPOSITION OF PROPERTY RECORDS

- Any person identified on DSA-controlled property as being in possession of contraband or physical evidence connected with criminal offense.
- Heads of PLFAs who are responsible for investigating suspected criminal acts.

STANDARDS OF CONDUCT

Includes DSA employees, General Schedule 13s and above, and lieutenant colonel, commander, and above, involved in approving awards for contracts or contractor audits (DSA Regulation 5500.1, Standards of Conduct Regulations) or any employee of DSA involved in potential violation of standards of conduct.

Office of Counsel, Headquarters DSA, DSAH-G; Counsel, PLFA.

Request for information should contain: Individual's name, subject matter of information requested, and date of form of (alleged) violation.

Additional Files

Following is a list of the remaining files maintained by the DSA. Anyone interested in obtaining information from any of these files should contact the appropriate agency head or the Secretary of Defense, The Pentagon, Washington, DC 20301.

Atlanta Personnel Data Bank System
Attorney Personal Information and Applicant Files
Auditor Profile
Authorization File
Automated Payroll, Cost, and Personnel System (APCAPS)
Automated Payroll, Cost, and Personnel System (APCAPS) Personnel Subsystem
Biography File
Bye-Bye Retirement System
Central Inventory, Comptroller/Financial Management
Civilian Medical Case Files
Civilian Personnel Administration Career Program
Civilian Personnel and Manpower Control System
Contracting Officer Files
Dallas Internal Personnel Management Information System (DIPMIS)
Data Processing Project Control Assignment and Machine Utilization
Defense Contract Administration Services Region (DCASR) Dallas Personnel
Defense Personnel Support Center (DPSC) Civilian Personnel File
Dependents Travel
Emergency Assignment and Training Records
Emergency Transportation of Essential Personnel
Employment Inquiries
Enrollment, Registration, and Course Completion Record
Firearms Registration Records
Guest Instructor Introduction Card
Headquarters Defense Supply Agency (DSA) Automated Civilian Personnel Data
Individual Access Files
Individual Development Plan (IDP)
Individual Vehicle Operators File
Industrial Personnel Security Clearance File
Information Military Personnel Records
Invention Disclosures
Local Civilian Personnel Data Bank
Manufacturing Payroll System; Weekly Piece Work
Mechanization of Contract Administration Services—1B Payroll (MOCAS 1B)
Military Personnel Data Bank System
Monthly Quality Assurance Activity Report by Person
Motor Vehicle Registration Files
Nomination for Awards
Nonappropriated Fund (NAF) Membership Records
Officer/Enlisted Evaluation Report File and File Summary
Official Personnel Folders for Non-Appropriated Fund Employees
Official Records for Host Enrollee Programs
Patent Licenses and Assignments
Personnel Cost Forecast System
Personnel Security Clearance Status – CAPSTONE
Police Force Records
Position Classification Appeals
Position Surveys
Quality Assurance Activity Certification Report
Quality Assurance Staff Development Program
Request for Assistance and Information
Reserve Affairs

Rotation of Employees from Foreign Areas and the Canal
    Zone
Royalties
Schedule and Record of Overtime Assignment and Request
Supervisors' Personnel Records
Supervisors' Records and Reports of Employee Attendance
    and Leave
Traffic Violations File
Travel Record
Vehicle Accident Investigation Files
Visitors and Vehicle Temporary Passes and Permits File
Work Assignment, Performance, and Productivity Records
    and Reporting Systems

Department of the Air Force

AAC QUALITY FORCE RECORDS SYSTEM

Maintained on military personnel assigned to Alaskan Air
Command who have three or more incidents recorded on
Air Force Form 1137, Unfavorable Information File
Summary, Alaskan Air Command, Elmendorf Air Force
Base, Alaska 99506.

ABSENTEE AND DESERTER INFORMATION FILES

All active-duty personnel who are or have been in absentee
status more than 10 days or in deserter status.

Assistant Deputy Chief of Staff Personnel for Military Personnel, Randolph Air Force Base, TX 78148.

ACCOUNTS PAYABLE RECORDS

Individuals who have monies owed to them by the air force
or who have performed an official function resulting in a
valid debt payment by the air force to a third party. Such
individuals include, but are not limited to, contractors, military and civilian personnel and their dependents, assignees,
trustees, guardians, survivors, claimants having tort or compensation claims against the air force for personal injuries
or property damage.

AFAFC/RMAD, 3800 York Street, Denver, CO 80205,
(303) 825-1161, ext. 6341.

ADMINISTRATIVE DISENROLLMENT AND
INVESTIGATIONS

Air Force Academy cadets.

Director, Cadet Personnel and Administration, USAF
Academy, Colorado Springs, CO 80840.

ADVANCED PERSONNEL DATA SYSTEM, CONSOLI-
DATED BASE PERSONNEL OFFICE OPTIONAL DIN Y07

Computer records coded with identity of marijuana experi-

menters on personnel assigned at Chanute.

Chief, Consolidated Base Personnel Office, 3345 Air Base
Group, Chanute AFB, IL 61868.

AIR FORCE DISCHARGE REVIEW BOARD
ORIGINAL CASE FILES

Former air force personnel who submit applications for
review of discharge/separation/dismissal.

Director, Secretary of the Air Force Personnel Council,
Washington, DC 20030, (202) 694-4016.

Requests for information should contain: Individual's
name, service number and Social Security account number
of the requestor. Personal visits may be made to room 920,
Commonwealth Building, 1300 Wilson Blvd., Arlington,
VA.

Personal visitors must supply full name, service number,
Social Security account number and some form of identification such as driver's license, credit cards, etc.

AIR FORCE RESERVE AIRMAN DEMOTIONS

Air force reserve personnel.

Command Documentation Officer ARPC/DAES, 3800
York Street, Denver, CO 80205, (303) 370-7553. Records
may be reviewed in Records Review Room ARPC, 3800
York Street, Denver, CO 80205, in building 2, unit G,
between 8 A.M. and 3 P.M. on normal workdays.

AIR FORCE RESERVE OFFICER TRAINING
CORPS (AFROTC) CONTRACT VIOLATORS

Air force reserve personnel.

Command Documentation Officer ARPC/DAES, 3800
York Street, Denver, CO 80205, (303) 370-7553.

Request for information should contain: Individual's
name, Social Security account number, current address,
and the case control number shown on correspondence
received from the center.

Records may be reviewed in Records Review Room ARPC,
3800 York Street, Denver, CO 80205, building 2, unit G,
between 8 A.M. and 3 P.M. on normal workdays.

AIRCRAFT ACCIDENTS AND INCIDENTS
COMPUTER FILE

Any person in control of aircraft at time of United States
Air Force accident or incident.

Chief, Reports and Analysis Division, Air Force Inspection
and Safety Center, Norton AFB, CA 92409, (714) 382-2325.

AIRMEN UTILIZATION RECORDS SYSTEM

Enlisted personnel on active duty who: write or visit the Air Force Military Personnel Center, Airmen Management Division (AFMPC/DPMRA) regarding assignment information; or request reassignment or deferment from assignment under the Children Have A Potential (CHAP) humanitarian programs; or are released from a hospital and made available for reassignment; or are nominated or volunteer for special assignment; or request information or action through high-level channels; or volunteer for PALACE GUN or PALACE DRAGON; or are restricted, along with their dependents, from assignment to certain oversea areas; or are subject to special assignment procedures, such as reassignment of personnel with known deficiencies; reassignment of threatened personnel; disposition of personnel involved in disciplinary/legal problems enroute to permanent change of station (PCS) assignment; or reassignment for trial; curtailment of oversea tour for cause or are permanently disqualified from the Human or Personnel Reliability Programs; and master, senior master, and chief master sergeants on active duty in the air force who are considered/selected for an assignment. Enlisted club stewards on active duty in the air force.

Assistant Deputy Chief of Staff Personnel for Military Personnel, Randolph Air Force Base, TX 78148, (512) 652-2115.

ALASKAN AIR COMMAND (AAC) QUALITY FORCE RECORD SYSTEM

Pertains to all active-duty air force personnel who write dishonored checks.

Director of Personnel, Consolidated Base Personnel Office, Elmendorf Air Force Base, Alaska, APO Seattle 98742 and Eielson Air Force Base, Alaska, APO Seattle 98737, (907) 752-4478.

ALCOHOL ABUSE CONTROL CASE FILES

All active-duty military personnel, civilian employees, and dependents of military personnel who are enrolled in an alcohol rehabilitation program.

Director of Administration, Headquarters United States Air Force, Washington, DC 20030, (202) 695-9492.

APPEAL AND GRIEVANCE LOG

Civilian employees.

Civilian Personnel Officer, Lackland Air Force Base, TX 78236, (512) 671-4117.

ARTICLE 15 RECORDS

All persons subject to the Uniform Code of Military Justice (UCMJ) (10 USC 802) upon whom Article 15 punishment is imposed.

The Judge Advocate General, Headquarters United States Air Force, Washington, DC 20030, (202) 694-5732.

Staff Judge Advocate at all levels of command and the Military Personnel Records Division, Directorate of Personnel Data Systems, Air Force Military Personnel Center (AFMPC/DPMDR), (202) 693-0205.

AUTOMATED MILITARY JUSTICE ANALYSIS AND MANAGEMENT SYSTEM (AMJAMS)

All persons subject to the Uniform Code of Military Justice (10 USC 802) who receive Article 15 punishment or against whom court-martial charges are preferred.

The Judge Advocate General, Headquarters United States Air Force, Washington, DC 20030, (202) 694-5732; or Major Command Staff Judge Advocates; or requester may visit the office of the Judge Advocate General, Forrestal Bldg., Washington, DC.

BEHAVIORAL AUTOMATED RESEARCH SYSTEM (BARS) (B-3500)

Air force prisoners who serve sentences to confinement at 3320 Retraining Group and 3415 special training squadron students.

Commander, 3320 Retraining Group/RGP, Lowry AFB, CO 80230, (303) 370-3002.

CADET DISCIPLINARY SYSTEM

Air Force Academy cadets.

Commandant of Cadets, USAF Academy, Colorado Springs, CO 80840, (303) 472-4290.

CHAIN OF CUSTODY RECEIPT

Blood alcohol testing is accomplished on military personnel at the direction of proper military authority.

Commander, USAF Hospital, Elmendorf Air Force Base, Alaska, APO Seattle 98742, (907) 752-3500.

CHILD ADVOCACY CASE FILES

All personnel assigned at air force installations whose drug use or neglect was brought to the attention of appropriate medical authorities.

The Surgeon General, Headquarters United States Air Force, Washington, DC 20030, (202) 767-4343.

Clinics, major command surgeons, commanders of medical centers and hospitals.

Request for information should contain: Individual's name, Social Security account number of sponsor, and place of incident.

CIVIL LITIGATION RECORDS

All those individuals who have brought suit against, or have been involved in litigation with, in a United States jurisdiction, the United States or its officers or employees concerning matters related to the Department of the Air

Force, excepting those cases involving claims arising under the provisions of the Federal Tort Claims Act, 28 USC 2671–80.

The Judge Advocate General, Headquarters United States Air Force, Washington, DC 20030, (202) 694–5732.

CLAIMS ADMINISTRATIVE MANAGEMENT PROGRAM (CAMP) E064

All military personnel and civilians filing administrative claims against the air force or against whom the air force has filed an administrative claim.

HQ USAF/JACC, James Forrestal Bldg., Washington, DC 20314, (202) 693–0353.

CLAIMS CASE FILE — MISSING IN ACTION DATA

Missing-in-action air force members; dependents of missing air force members; next of kin of missing air force members; and spouses of missing air force members.

AFAFC/RMAD, 3800 York Street, Denver, CO 80205, (303) 825–1161, ext. 6341.

CLAIMS RECORDS

All military personnel and civilians filing administrative claims against the air force or against whom the air force has filed an administrative claim.

HQ USAF/JACC, 1900 Half Street, SW, Washington, DC 20324, (202) 693–0353.

Request for information should contain: Individual's full name, date of incident, date of claim, type of claim, claim number, location of incident. Driver's license, military identification, birth certificate, or equivalent must be presented for personal visit.

COMMANDER'S OPERATIONAL REPORTING SYSTEM INCIDENT REPORTS

Any air force member involved in a racial incident.

Deputy Chief of Staff/Personnel, Headquarters United States Air Force, Washington, DC 20030, (202) 697–6088.

COMMUNICABLE DISEASE REPORT SYSTEM

Any patient diagnosed as, or suspected of, having a reportable communicable disease.

The Surgeon General, Headquarters United States Air Force, Washington, DC 20030, (202) 767–4343.

COMPLAINTS AND INCIDENTS (DELIVERY AGREEMENT)

Military personnel arrested by civilian police.

Chief, Security Police Sq., Holloman AFB, NM 88330, (505) 479–4034.

COMPLAINTS AND INQUIRIES

Civilian and military personnel who have submitted complaints or congressional inquiries.

General, Alaskan Air Command, Elmendorf Air Force Base, Alaska 99506.

CORRECTION RECORDS

Records are maintained on any individual who was placed in confinement at an installation, assigned to the 3320th Retraining Group and the U.S. Disciplinary Barracks for purposes of retraining or confinement, placed in a federal prison system as the result of criminal conviction, or spent time in the correctional custody program at any air force installation.

Chief of Security Police, Headquarters United States Air Force, Washington, DC 20030, (202) 697–6366; The Judge Advocate General, Headquarters United States Air Force, Washington, DC 20030, (202) 694–5732; Unit commander at the individual's last assignment; the commander of the 3320th Retraining Group, Lowry AFB, Colorado; installation chief of security police; commandant, U.S. Disciplinary Barracks; chairman of the Air Force Clemency and Parole Board.

COURT-MARTIAL RECORDS

All persons subject to the Uniform Code of Military Justice (10 USC 802) who are tried by court-martial.

The Judge Advocate General, Headquarters United States Air Force, Washington, DC 20030, (202) 694–5732; staff judge advocates at all levels of command.

CRIMINAL RECORDS

All active-duty military personnel; civilian employees; former civilian employees; Air Force Reserve personnel; Air National Guard; retired air force military personnel; contracting officers and representatives; Air Force Academy cadets; dependents of military personnel; foreign nationals residing in the United States; American Red Cross personnel; Peace Corps and State Department personnel; exchange officers.

The Judge Advocate General, Headquarters United States Air Force, Washington, DC 20030, (202) 694–5732.

DISASTER TEAMS AND TRAINING

All air force active-duty military personnel, air force civilian employees.

Disaster preparedness officer at all installations.

DISCIPLINARY AND ADVERSE ACTION LOG

Air force civilian employees.

Civilian Personnel Officer, Lackland Air Force Base, TX 78236, (512) 671–4117.

DISHONORED CHECK CONTROL RECORD

All personnel, military and civilian, whose personal checks are returned to NAFIs by the banking system and are dishonored for such reasons as insufficient funds, closed accounts, invalid signatures, bank errors, etc.

Individuals may inquire of the appropriate Nonappropriated Fund custodian/manager in order to exercise their rights under the Privacy Act.

Air Force Accounting and Finance Center, Denver, CO 80279.

DRUG ABUSE CONTROL CASE FILE

All air force active-duty military personnel; air force civilian employees, dependents of military personnel who are enrolled in a drug rehabilitation program.

Chief, social actions servicing air force installation.

Requests to determine existence of a file should contain: Individual's name, grade, and unit of assignment. Personal visit proof of identity requires full name and possession of DOD form 2 AF, Armed Forces Identification Card; DOD Form 1173, Uniformed Services Identification and Privilege Card; or driver's license and personal recognition of counselor.

Commander, Air Force Medical Service Center, Brooks Air Force Base, TX 78235.

DRUG ABUSE LEDGER

All rated or flying training students who have drug abuse files.

DCS/P Randolph Air Force Base, TX 78148, (512) 652-3109.

DRUG ABUSE REHABILITATION REPORT SYSTEM

Any active-duty military personnel who are confirmed as drug abusers as a result of drug abuse urinalysis testing.

The Surgeon General, Headquarters United States Air Force, Washington, DC 20330, (202) 767-4343.

DRUG/ALCOHOL INTAKE INTERVIEW AND CHECKLIST

All air force active-duty military personnel assigned to March Air Force Base, California.

Social Actions Officer, March Air Force Base, CA 92508, (714) 655-4646.

DUTY AND TRAVEL RESTRICTION NOTIFICATION LETTERS

Military members, civilian employees and defense contractors whose travel and duty assignments have been restricted because of current knowledge of certain sensitive classified information.

Chief of Security Police, Headquarters United States Air Force, Washington, DC 20030, (202) 697-6366; installation chief of consolidated personnel office (military or civilian, as applicable); installation chief of security police; commander of unit issuing the restriction letter.

Write or visit the installation where currently assigned/employed or, if applicable, where separated from the air force. Written requests for information must be notarized; personal visits require positive identification. Provide full name, Social Security account number, and current military/civilian status. Former members also provide approximate date (month and year) when active military duty or civilian employment terminated.

EQUAL OPPORTUNITY IN OFF-BASE HOUSING

Military member, Department of Defense (DOD) civilian employee, and adult dependent for military member submitting a housing discrimination complaint.

Deputy Chief of Staff/Personnel, Headquarters United States Air Force, Washington, DC 20030, (202) 697-6088, or individuals may contact agency officials at the respective base level housing referral office in order to exercise their rights under the Act.

FILE DESIGNATION, DRUG ABUSE, WAIVER REQUESTS

Applicants for enlistment or commissioning who have a history of preservice drug abuse and who have requested a waiver of their disqualification.

Deputy Chief of Staff/Personnel, Headquarters United States Air Force, Washington, DC 20030, (202) 697-6088.

FOREIGN CIVIL LITIGATION RECORDS

All individuals who initiate litigation against the United States in a foreign court in respect to a matter pertaining to the air force.

The Judge Advocate General, Headquarters United States Air Force, Washington, DC 20030, (202) 694-5732.

HUMAN FACTORS IN AIRCRAFT ACCIDENT/INCIDENT COMPUTER FILE

Any individual aboard aircraft during a United States Air Force accident or who suffered injury/fatality as a result of accident/incident.

Chief, Reports and Analysis Division, Air Force Inspection and Safety Center, Norton AFB, CA 92409, (714) 382-2325.

INCIDENT INVESTIGATION FILES

Persons who become involved in criminal acts or incidents on an air force installation.

Chief of Security Police, Headquarters United States Air Force, Washington, DC 20030, (202) 697-6366.

INDEBTEDNESS AND CLAIMS

All active-duty military personnel; civilian employees; former civilian employees; Air Force Reserve personnel; Air National Guard personnel; retired air force military personnel; Air Force Academy cadets; dependents of military personnel; exchange officers; former spouses of military personnel, survivors of deceased military and civilian personnel, foreign nationals.

AFAFC/RMAD, 3800 York Street, Denver, CO 80205, (303) 825-1161, ext. 6341.

INDEBTEDNESS, NONSUPPORT, PATERNITY

Active-duty and retired personnel.

Assistant Deputy Chief of Staff Personnel for Military Personnel, Randolph AFB, TX 78148, (512) 652-2115.

INDIVIDUAL ACCIDENT/VIOLATION AND SAFETY TRAINING RECORD

Active-duty military personnel assigned within Air Force Communications Command (AFCC).

Chief of Ground/Explosives Safety Division, Office of the Inspector General, Headquarters AFCC, Explosives Division (714) 382-3137; Ground Division (714) 382-3614; general information (714) 382-3012; and commanders at all AFCC units.

INFORMATIONAL PERSONNEL RECORDS

All special agents trained in fraud, criminal, polygraph, and technical services and counterintelligence assigned to the Air Force Office of Special Investigations (AFOSI) and USAF Defense Investigative Service (DIS).

Commander, Air Force Office of Special Investigations, Washington, DC 20314, (202) 693-6680.

INSPECTOR GENERAL RECORDS

All those who have registered a complaint or query with the inspector general or base inspector on matters related to the Department of the Air Force.

INVESTIGATIONS/COMPLAINTS FILES

Any individual specified in a formal complaint action.

Chief, Equal Opportunity Branch, Directorate of Personnel Plans, Deputy Chief of Staff/Personnel, Washington, DC 20330, (202) 697-8200.

Request for information should contain: Individual's name, military status, dates of service, unit of last or present assignment, Social Security account number, and type of record involved. For personal visits, the requester may present proof of identity to include full name from driver's license or military identification card.

LABORATORY RECORDS SOBRIETY DETERMINATION REPORT

All active duty military personnel; civilian employees; Air Force Reserve personnel; Air National Guard personnel; retired air force military personnel; dependents of military personnel, as requested by security police.

The Surgeon General, Headquarters United States Air Force, Washington, DC 20030, (202) 767-4343; commanders of air force hospitals, medical centers and clinics; air force base where medical record was last maintained.

LINE OF DUTY DETERMINATIONS AND INVESTIGATIONS

All air force military personnel on extended active duty; members of the Air Force Reserve and Air National Guard on active duty for training or inactive duty training; Air Force Reserve Officers' Training Corps (AFROTC) cadets on training duty for 14 days or more; cadets of the Air Force Academy; persons who are either provisionally accepted for duty or are initially selected under the Military Selective Service Act of 1967 and are traveling to or from, or are present at, a place for final acceptance or entry on active duty with the air force. *Note*: Records are accomplished on the above categories of individuals only if they have an injury or disease that is treated by a doctor — whether or not they are hospitalized — and which results in inability to perform their duties for more than one day as determined by competent authority, or likelihood of a permanent disability or future claim against the government.

Assistant Deputy Chief of Staff/Personnel for Military Personnel, Randolph Air Force Base, TX 78148, (512) 652-2115.

LITIGATION RECORDS; TORT CLAIMS, ADMIRALTY, COLLECTION, AND HOSPITAL RECOVERY ACTS

All military personnel and civilians filing litigation against the air force or against whom litigation has been filed under 28 USC 1346b, 46 USC 741-52, 781-90, 31 USC 71, 951-3, 42 USC 2651-3.

The Judge Advocate, Headquarters, United States Air Force, Washington, DC 20030, (202) 694-5732.

LOCATOR OR PERSONNEL DATA (LISTS OF KNOWN CIVILIAN CRIMINALS)

Lists of known civilian criminals.

Judge Advocate, 317th Combat Support Group, Pope Air Force Base, NC, (919) 394-2341.

MILITARY AIRLIFT COMMAND (MAC) DISHONORED CHECK PROGRAM

All active-duty military personnel; civilian employees; Air Force Reserve personnel; Air National Guard personnel;

retired air force military personnel; dependents of military personnel; all DOD civilian employees; all retired military personnel.

Chief, Consolidated Base Personnel Office, Quality Force Section, National Personnel Records Center, Military Airlift Command Records, United States Air Force, 9700 Paige Blvd., St. Louis, MO 63132.

MILITARY JUSTICE ADMINISTRATION

Air-force-duty enlisted personnel nominated to serve on general court-martial.

Headquarters, 15 Air Force Staff Judge Advocate, March Air Force Base, CA 92508, (714) 655-4247.

NOTIFICATION LETTERS TO PERSONS BARRED FROM ENTRY TO AIR FORCE INSTALLATIONS

Persons prohibited from entering United States military installations for cause.

Chief of Security Police, Headquarters United States Air Force, Washington, DC 20030, (202) 697-6366; installation chief of security police.

PATENT INFRINGEMENT AND LITIGATION RECORDS

All claimants or petitioners who have alleged unlicensed use of their patents by the air force or who have brought suit against the United States concerning patent, trademark, or copyright matters related to the Department of the Air Force.

The Judge Advocate General, Headquarters United States Air Force, Washington, DC 20030, (202) 694-5732.

PERSONAL APPEARANCE COMMENDATION/ VIOLATION CITATION

Air force active-duty officer personnel or air force active-duty enlisted personnel assigned to 15 Air Force units.

Squadron commander.

PERSONNEL QUALITY CONTROL REPORT

All assigned military personnel whose conduct and performance were substandard.

Commander, Pease Air Force Base, NH 03801, (603) 436-3303.

PICKUP OR RESTRICTION ORDER

The record applied to any air force member whose actions require the unit commander to issue the order.

Chief of Security Police, Headquarters United States Air Force, Washington, DC 20030, (202) 697-6366; installation chief of security police.

PREPARATORY SCHOOL REPORT OF OFFENSE

Preparatory school students.

Commander, Preparatory School, USAF Academy, CO 80840, (303) 472-2580.

RECORD OF INDIVIDUAL COUNSELING

All military personnel assigned to Air Training Command counseled for offenses or incidents.

Immediate commander.

Request for information should contain: Individual's name and Social Security account number. Requester may visit commander for information.

REPORTING CRIMES AND SERIOUS INCIDENTS

Armed forces personnel, their dependents, DOD civilian employees and their dependents stationed or going through Alaskan Air Command installations.

Chief, security police of units.

REPORTS, CONTROLLED AND UNCONTROLLED (BAD CHECK REPORT)

All active-duty military personnel, dependents of military personnel, all air force active duty military personnel, retired military and their dependents, selected DOD civilian employees, survivors of deceased active duty military personnel, disabled veterans and their dependents.

Judge Advocate General, Headquarters, United States Air Force, Washington, DC 20030, (202) 694-5732.

SERIOUS INCIDENT REPORTS

Persons who become involved in crimes or serious incidents on air force installations, or air force personnel and dependents who become involved in these incidents regardless of the location.

Major command chief of security police and installation chief of security police.

SOURCE SUPPORT OR CONTROL DATA (DISCIPLINARY OVERWEIGHT CHART)

Individuals who have been punished, are pending administrative discharge, or are not meeting air force weight standards.

Squadron commander.

STATUS OF INEFFECTIVE RECRUITER

Active-duty Air Training Command enlisted recruited personnel relieved from duty.

DCS/P Randolph Air Force Base, TX 78148, (512) 652-3109.

TEMPORARY PRIVATE VEHICLE IMPOUNDMENT RECORD

Any individual who abandons or leaves a disabled or derelict privately owned motor vehicle in a public parking area over five consecutive days.

Chief, Security Police, 21 Security Police Squadron, Elmendorf Air Force Base, APO Seattle 98742, (907) 752-2167.

TRAFFIC ACCIDENT AND VIOLATION REPORTS

Persons who become involved in traffic violations or accidents on an air force installation.

Chief of Security Police, Headquarters United States Air Force, Washington, DC 20030, (202) 697-6366.

Installation chief of security police.

UNFAVORABLE INFORMATION FILES (UIF) ON OFFICERS AND AIRMEN

Air Force Reserve personnel.

Commander, Air Reserve Personnel Center (ARPC), 3800 York Street, Denver, CO 80205, (303) 370-4634. Records may be reviewed in Records Review Room, ARPC, 3800 York Street, Denver, CO 80205, building 2, unit G, between 8 A.M. and 3 P.M. on normal workdays.

USAF FOREIGN CRIMINAL JURISDICTION CASES

All those air force personnel, United States nationals employed by the air force, and dependents of the foregoing who become involved with foreign law enforcement authorities or who are subject to trial in foreign courts for serious criminal offenses.

Chief, International Law Division, Office of The Judge Advocate General, Forrestal Building, Washington, DC 20314, (202) 695-9631; or staff judge advocate of the concerned subordinate command or installation. Personal visits may be made to AF/JACI, Forrestal Building, Washington, DC 20314.

UNITED STATES AIR FORCE (USAF) GROUND ACCIDENT FATALITY FILE

All air force active-duty military and civilian employee fatalities.

Director of Aerospace Safety, Air Force Inspection and Safety Center, Norton AFB, CA 92409, (714) 382-2302.

VENEREAL DISEASE EPIDEMIOLOGIC REPORT SYSTEM

Any patient, military or civilian, upon whom the diagnosis of venereal disease is confirmed.

Information may be obtained from the environmental health officer of the medical facility where the individual received treatment for venereal disease.

For any Department of the Air Force files not previously listed, individuals should contact:

- Military: National Personnel Records Center, Military Personnel Records – Air Force, 9700 Paige Blvd., St. Louis, MO 63132.

- Civilian: Civilian Personnel Records, 111 Winnebago St., St. Louis, MO 63118.

Request should cite the Privacy Act of 1974 and should include individual's full name, date and place of birth, and reasonable verification of identity.

Additional Files

Following is a list of the remaining files maintained by the air force. Anyone interested in obtaining information from any of these files should contact the appropriate agency head or the Secretary of Defense, The Pentagon, Washington, DC 20301.

ANG Rated Report
Academic Completion Report
Academic Counseling Record
Academic Grades
Academic Requirements
Academic Scheduling
Access Records
Accession Listing
Account Receivable Records Maintained by Accounting and Finance
Accounting and Finance Officer Accounts and Substantiating Documents
Accounts Receivable
Accrued Military Pay System, Discontinued (AMPS 360/390)
Accreditation References
Active Cadet Counseling File
Activities Therapy Referral
Additional Airmen Performance and Officer Evaluation Report Information
Administrative Discharge for Cause on Reserve Personnel
Administrative Discharge File
Administrative Discharge Information Summary
Admission and Disposition System
Advanced Data Personnel System Optional DIN Y06
Advanced Degree File
Advanced Personnel Data System (APDS)—ADS: E300
Advanced Personnel Data System (APDS) CBPO Optional DINS Y01-Y05
Aero Club Membership/Training Records
Aerobics Status
Aeromedical Research Data
Aerospace Medicine Program Medical Recommendation Missile Duty
Aerospace Physiology Personnel Career Information System
Air Force Academy Administrative Record
Air Force Academy Appointment and Separation Records
Air Force Academy Candidate System
Air Force Academy Liaison Officers Listing
Air Force Academy Pre-Candidate
Air Force Advisory Personnel in Latin America
Air Force Aerospace Physiology Training Programs
Air Force Air Society (AFAS) Financial Assistance Record System

Air Force Attache Record System

Air Force Audit Agency (AFAA) Management Information System—Plan File

Air Force Audit Agency Management Information System—Report File

Air Force Audit Agency Office File

Air Force Audit Agency Office Personnel File

Air Force Audit Agency Office Training File

Air Force Audit Agency (AFAA) Personnel Electronic Evaluation, Reporting System (PEERS)

Air Force Blood Program

Air Force Clinical Laboratory Automation Systems (AFCLAS)

Air Force Discharge Review Board Case Control/Locator Cards

Air Force Discharge Review Board Retain Files

Air Force Discharge Review Board Voting Cards

Air Force Educational Assistance Loans

Air Force Enlistment/Commissioning Records System

Air Force Institute of Technology Education (AFIT) Historical File

Air Force Junior ROTC (AFJROTC) Instructor Applicant System

AFJROTC Instructor Records System

Air Force Junior ROTC (AFJROTC) Unit Files

Air Force Logistics Command (AFLC) Supergrade Information Files

Air Force Officer Confirmed Nomination Lists

Air Force Office of Information/OI Personnel Background Record

Air Force Open Mess Program

Air Force Personnel Test 851, Test Answer Cards

Air Force Postal Directory File

Air Force Reserve Applications

Air Force Reserve Applications for Extended Active Duty

Air Force Reserve Medical School Tour Allocations

Air Force ROTC Cadet Pay System

Air Force Reserve Officer Training Corps Evaluation Information Record Files

Air Force ROTC Field Training Administration System

AFROTC Field Training Assignment System

Air Force Reserve Officer Training Corps (AFROTC) Guest Lecture Files

Air Force Reserve Officer Training Corps (AFROTC) Membership System

Air Force Reserve Officer Training Corps Qualifying Test Scoring System

Air Force Security Program Cases

Air Force Service Data of Employees and Relatives

Air Force Service Number/Social Security Account Number Cross Reference Rosters

Air Force System Command Personnel Data Retrieval System

Air Force Systems Command (AFSC) Personnel Resource Management System

Air Intelligence Manpower Management System (AIMMS)

Air National Guard Information Personnel Background File

Air Reserve Information Squadron Biographical Files

Air Reserve Pay and Allowance System (ARPAS)

Air Reserve Technician (ART) Officer Selection Folders

Air Traffic Control (ATC) Certification Documentation

Air Traffic Control Rating and Training Program Documentation

Air Training Command Aircraft Accident Board Resources List

Air Training Command Management Analysis Awards Program

Air Training Command (ATC) Officer Add-On Data

Air Training Command (ATC) Officers Effectiveness Analysis File

Air Training Command (ATC) Personnel VIP Roster

AU OER-TR Reviewing Sheet

Air University Academic Records

Air University (AU) Advanced Degree Application

Air University Outstanding Junior Officer of the Year

AU Potential Faculty List

Aircrew Data

Aircrew Instruction Records (Flying Training Records)

Aircrew Intelligence Training Report

Aircrew Positive Control Study Record

Aircrew Qualification

Aircrew Resource Management System (SACARMS)/Aircrew Qualification Report

Aircrew Standards Case File

Aircrew Training Records, Aerospace Defense Command (ADC)

Aircrew Training Records F4 Aircraft

Aircrew Training Records F102 Aircraft

Aircrew Training Records F106 Aircraft

Aircrew Training Records T33 Aircraft

Airman Assignment Action Number Listing

Airman NCO Recognition Program

Airman Projected Status Listing

Airman Promotion Master Select/Non-Select Listings/Promotion Sequence Number Listing

Airman Promotion Status File

Airmen Name Roster

Alaskan Air Command Civilian Identification Cards

Allergy Worksheet

Alphabetical Listing of Approved Retirements

Annual Outstanding Air Force Administration and Executive Support Awards

Applicant Supply Files

Application for Advanced Aeronautical Rating File (Senior and Chief Flight Surgeon)

Application for Appointment and Extended Active Duty Files

Application for Separation from the Regular AF to AF Reserve/Air National Guard

Applications for Appointment Medical Corps

Applications for Identification (ID) Cards

Arbitrations

Armed Services Vocational Aptitude Battery (ASVAB) Test Cards

Assessments Screening Records

Assignment Action File

Assignment Preference Application Data

Assignment Record Files for Personnel Selected for Presidential Support Duties

Athletic Squad List

Automated Inpatient Data Systems

Bachelor Airmen's Quarters (BAQ) Temporary Issue Receipt

Background Information Questionnaire

Background Material

Bad Address Card Files

Badge and Credentials

Base Automated Mobility System (BAMS) Personnel Extract Tape

Base Housing Management

Base, Unit and Organizational Military and Civilian Personnel Locator Files

Bicycle Registration File

Bioenvironmental Engineer Personnel Career Information System

Biographical File

Biographical and Personal Data on Very Important Personnel

Biographies

Biographies of Officers and Key Civilians Assigned to SAF/OI

Bomber Mobilization Recovery Roster

Brigadier General Screening Board Results

Cadet Accounting and Finance, System Code RZ, Data System Designator E 516

Cadet Appointment System

Cadet Awards Case Files

Cadet Counseling Interview Files

Cadet Evaluation

Cadet Information Card

Cadet Injury/Illness Report

Cadet Personality File

Cadet Promotion List

Cadet Records

Cadet Records System (Research and Evaluation Files)

Cadet Religious Information Card

Cadet Summer Training

Cadet Wing Movements

Cadet Wing Strength Accounting System

Career Development Course Enrollees

Career Development Folder

Career Development Graduates Historical Roster

Career Development Graduates Monthly Report

Casualties in Southeast Asia

Casualty Files

Central Medical Registry Files

Chaplain Applicant Processing Folder

Chaplain Biographical Files

Chaplain Fund Service Contract File

Chaplain Information Sheet

Chaplain Personnel Action Folder

Chaplain Personnel Management Files

Chaplain Personnel Record

Chaplain Personnel Roster

Chaplain Privileged Communication Files

Child Care Attendance Records

Children Have a Potential (CHAP) Files

Civil Air Patrol (CAP) Membership

Civil Engineer Personnel Data Cards

Civilian Attorney Qualifying Committee Records

Civilian Health/Medical Program of Uniformed Services (CHAMPUS) Case Claim Files

Civilian Pay—Control Data

Civilian Pay Records

Civilian Personnel/Allowance Appeals

Civilian Personnel/Classification Appeal Records

Civilian Personnel/Classification Survey Sheets

Civilian Personnel/Compensation Case Files

Civilian Personnel Files

Civilian Personnel Management Information System (CPMIS)

Civilian Personnel Occupational and Suitability Employment Examinations

Civilian Personnel Statistical Accounting System

Civilian Personnel Test Score Record

Claims Case File—Corrected Military Pay and Allowances

Claims Case File—Death Gratuity Records

Claims Case File—Missing in Action Data

Class Biographies

Classification Screening Records

Clearance Certificate Records

Clinical Records and Related Documents

Clipping Files

Collateral Training Records

Columnist Files

Combat Intelligence Crew Training Record

Command Airman Promotion Eligibility Rosters

Command Officers Eligibility Rosters

Command Secondary Zone Board Proceedings

Commander Identification

Commander Selection File

Commander's Patient Status Report (Cadet)

Committee Management Records

Community College of the Air Force Student Record System

Compartmented Intelligence Access Roster

Completion of Courses/Degrees Under Operation Bootstrap

Computation of Promotion Select/Non-Select Status

Confidential Statement of Employment and Financial Interest

Congressional Correspondence

Congressional/High Level/Correction Military Records Inquiries and Replies

Congressional Inquiries

Congressional Inquiries/Legislative Liaison

Congressional Inquiry File

Consolidated Base Personnel Office Academic Rank

Consolidated Base Personnel Office Academic Rank, Appointment, Date

Consolidated Base Personnel Office, Name, Spouse

Contingency Planning Support Capability (CPSC)—Data Systems Designator (DSD) A349

Control Card for Vouchers for Medical Services

Control Log for Civilian Medical Care

Control Logs

Cooperative Degree Accounting System

Correction of Military Record Card

Correction of Military Records of Officers and Airmen

Correspondence, Message and Project Files (Civil Reserve Air Fleet Personnel)

Counterintelligence Operations and Collection Records

Current Official Active Duty Chaplains Mailing List

Curriculum Vitae

Daily Report of First Aid, Dental Assistance, and Outpatient Workload Data

Daily Strength Report

Data Change/Suspense Notifications

Date, Last Name, Officer Career Objective Statement

Deceased Investigation Dependent Military Burial

Deceased Service Member's Dependent File

Defense Language Institute Student History

Dental Health Records

Dental Personnel Actions

Dental Professional Activities

Department of Defense Medical Examination Review Board Medical Examination Files

DIA Source Administration Program for Foreign Intelligence Collection Activities

Diagnostic X-Ray Film

Directory of Active Duty and Retired Chaplains

Disability Retirement Correspondence Files

Disability Retirement Retain Folders

Discharge and Separation Records

Distinguished Visitors Program Documentation

Documentation for Identification and Entry Authority

E201S/RG Advanced Logistic System Mission Training Scheduling and Measurement Subsystem

E246 Civilian Skills Locator System

Education Levels of Air Force Military Personnel

Education and Research Data Base

Education Services Program Records (Individual)

Education Services Test Control Officers

Education and Training Fact Sheets

Educational Delay Board Findings

Effectiveness/Performance Reporting Systems

Effectiveness Report Review

Electronic Warfare Officer Examination Answer Sheet

Employee Group Life and Health Insurance Plan

Employee Orientation Checklist

Employee's Quarterly Federal Tax Return

Enlistee Quality Control Monitoring System E818

Entry Control Roster

Events and Installation File

Exception Time Accounting (ETA) System (G001A)

Executive Development Council File

Faculty Biographical Sketch

Faculty Board Ledger

Faculty, Staff, Graduate Writing File

Family Services Volunteer of Year

Fee Case File

Field Grade Officer Promotion Analysis Worksheet

Field Training Student Attendance and Rating Records

Files on AF Reserve General Officers; Colonels Assigned to General Officer Positions

Files on General Officers and Colonels Assigned to General Officer Positions

Files of Nominations for Award

Files of Waiver from Flying Duty (WAVR File)

Firearm Authorization for Civilian Employees

Flight Instruction Program (FIP)

Flight Management Data Systems (FMDS) Data System Designator A020

Flying Evaluation Board (FEB) File

Flying Status Actions

Flying Status Branch File

Flying Training Records (Air Force active duty officer personnel, Air Force Reserve personnel, Air National Guard personnel, attending flying training courses)

Flying Training Records (All rated personnel being trained in C118, T39 UH1)

Flying Training Records (All students entered in T41 training at Lackland Air Force Base)

Flying Training Records (Flight crew members and flying supervisors)

Flying Training Records (Minority students in flying training)

Flying Training Records (Personnel undergoing upgrade or instructor training)

Flying Training Records (Undergraduate pilot and navigator training students)

For Cause Separations of Personnel With Duty and Travel Restrictions (FCS/DTR)

Four Year Reserve Officer Training Corps (AFROTC) Scholarship Program Files

Freedom of Information Act Appeals

Funded Legal Education and Excess Leave Program Records

General/Colonel Personnel Data Action Report

General/Colonel Status Board

General Officer Personnel Data System

Geographically Separated Unit Copy Officer Effectiveness and Airman Performance Report

Graduate Evaluation Master File

Graduate Programs

Graduate Record System

Graduates of Air Force Short Course in Communication (Oklahoma University)

Ground Safety Accident Briefing

Group Scheduling Listing

Guest Lecturer Biographical Sketch File

Harold Brown Award

Health Education Records

Health and Outpatient Records

High Level Inquiry File

Historical Airman Promotion Interim Eligibility File (IEF)

Historical Airman Promotion Master Test File (MTF)

Historical Files

Household Goods Nontemporary Storage Account System (NOTEMPS)

Human Reliability for Special Missions

Humanitarian/Permissive Reassignment Files

Inactive Duty Training, Extension Course Institute (ECI) Training

Incoming Clearance Record

Individual Academic Records (Flying training instructors and students)

Individual Academic Records – Survival Training
  Students
Individual Academic Training Record
Individual Class Record Form
Individual Decorations Approved or Disapproved
Individual Earning Data
Individual Flight and Aircrew Evaluation Records
Individual Flight Records
Individual Progress Record – Synthetic Trainers
Individual Retirement Record
Individual Weight Control File
Individual Weight Loss Record
Informal Airmen/Reserve Information Record
Information Officer Background Record
Information Officer Short Course Eligibility File
Information Program Reference and Guidance Material
Information Requests – Freedom of Information Act
Informational Personnel Files (Management Folders)
Informational Personnel Records
Informational Personnel Records (Air Force Reserve
  personnel)
Informational Personnel Records (All active duty military
  personnel)
Informational Personnel Records (Mobilization Augmentee
  File)
Informational Personnel Records (NORAD/ADC Subordin-
  ate Public Affairs/Information Personnel Chief, NORAD/
  ADC OIII)
Informational Personnel Records (OI Personnel Background)
Informational Personnel Training Records
Inpatient Data System
Input Transaction Registers
Inquiries (Presidential, Congressional)
Inquiries on the Reserve Program
Inspector General Records Freedom of Information Act
Instructor of the Month Records
Integrated Aircrew Resource Management System
Integrated Management Information and Control System
  (IMICS)
Internal Accounts Receivable System
Internal Audit and Control Records
Internal Personnel Data System
Interservice Photography Contest Entry Records
Interview Evaluation Files
Intramural Absentee and Injury Report
Intramural/Intercollegiate Participation Roster
Intramural Season Participation Record
Intramural Team Roster
Invention, Patent Application, and Patent Files
Investigative Applicant Processing Records
Investigative Support Records
Involuntary Recall
Job Element Questionnaires for Civilian Trades and Labor
  Occupations
Joint Uniform Military Pay System (JUMPS)
Judge Advocate Command Roster
Judge Advocate Officer Personnel Records
Key Personnel Status Report
Laboratory Course Phase II

Laboratory Records
Lackland Entry Airmen Pay System (LEAPS)
Legal Administration Records of the Staff Judge Advocate
Legal Assistance Administration
Listing of Potential Humanitarian/Permissive Reassignment
  Cases
Locator Personnel Data
LOG-DP A 7303 Apprentice Training Report
Long-Term Full-Time Training File
Loss of Funds Case Files
MAMS-R (Medical Administration Management System –
  Revision)
Maintenance Management Information and Control System
  (MMICS)
Major Command (MAJCOM) Secondary Zone Promotion
  Nomination Board Results
Management Control System (MCS)
Management Oriented Personnel System (MOP)
Manhour Accounting System (MAS)
Manning Specialist Evaluation
Manpower Standards Study Reports
Master Alpha Resource List (MARLA)
Master Cadet Personnel Record (RR)/Active, Directorate
  of Cadet Records
Master Cadet Personnel Record (RR)/Historical
Medical Actions Card File
Medical Mobilization Augmenter Personnel Management
  Files
Medical Officer Personnel Utilization Records
Medical Opinions on Board for Correction of Air Force
  Military Records Cases (BCMR)
Medical Recommendation for Flying Duty
Medical Service Account – Authorization for Supplemental
  Care
Medical Service Accounts
Medical Service Corps Personnel Files
Medical Service Liaison Officer Program Card File
Merit Promotion File
Microfilm of Military Pay Records
Microfilm Records Congressional/Executive Inquiries
Military Affiliate Radio System (MARS) Personnel
  Action
Military Affiliate Radio System (MARS) Station Question-
  naire
Military Airlift Command Aircrew Resource Management
  System
Military Airlift Command (MAC) Special Executive Devel-
  opment Program
Military Decorations
Military Justice Administration
Military and Leadership Order of Merit System
Military Pay Records
Military Personnel Expense Distribution Listing
Military Personnel Folders
Military Personnel Management System
Military Personnel Microform Records System
Military Personnel Records System
Military Records Processed by the Air Force Correction
  Board

Minnesota Multiphase Personality Inventory Research Program

Minutes of 354 TFW Quality Review Committee

Missile Procedures Training (MPT) Accomplishment

Mobilization Augmentee Training Forces

Motor Vehicle Operator's Records

Name Index of Board and Committee Members

National Agency Check—Status

National Civilian Consultant Files

Navigation Course Number 470, Flight Mission Report

Navigator Background Information

Nelson Denny Reading Test Answer Sheets

Next of Kin Inquiries Civilian MIA/PW's

Night Manager's Log

Nomination Files of Personnel Evaluated for Presidential Support Duties

Nonappropriated Fund (NAF) Civilian Personnel Records

Nonappropriated Funds Standard Payroll System

Non-Chaplain Ecclesiastical Endorsement Files

Nursery Attendance Sheet

Nursing Service Records

Nursing Skill Inventory

OASIS (Outpatient Appointment Scheduling Information System)

Off-Base Housing Referral Service

Off Duty Education File

Office File

Office Personnel Data Informational Files

Office Projects/Studies (Behavioral Service Program)

Office, Secretary of Air Force Travel Files

Officer Assignment Files

Officer Assignment Logs

Officer Duty Air Force Specialty Code Roster

Officer Effectiveness Report (OER)/Airman Performance Report (APR) Appeal Case Files

Officer Effectiveness Report Data Card

Officer Projected Status Listing

Officer Promotion Eligibility Report

Officer Promotions

Officer Promotions and Appointments, Branch Administrative File

Officer Selection Brief File

Officer Status File

Officer Utilization Records System

Officers Electronic Warfare Officer (EWO) Training Record

Official Biographies, Office of the Secretary of the Air Force

Official Personnel Folders (Temporary Records)

On/Off Base Housing Records

Operational Reference File

Operations Security File for Foreign Intelligence Collection Activities

Operations Training Records

Orientation Checklist and Placement Followup

Outgoing Clearance Record

Outstanding Airman of Year

PCS Funds Control Log

Palace Chase Assignment Applications

Patient Evacuation Manifest

Patient Index and Locator System

Pay and Allotment Records

Performance Awards and Outstanding Performance Ratings

Periodic Occupation Vision Record

Periodic Reconciliation File

Personal Clothing and Equipment Record

Personal Property Movement Records

Personnel Action File (Digest File)

Personnel Appraisal Pacific Air Command (PACAF) Executive Development Program

Personnel Cost Accounting System (PCAS)

Personnel Data System

Personnel Data Used for Management Engineering (ME) Program Manning Purposes

Personnel Files on Statutory Tour Officers

Personnel Information File

Personnel Interview Record

Personnel Management Files

Personnel Locator Cards

Personnel Locator Roster

Personnel Management Information System

Personnel Movement Program

Personnel Research Laboratory Historical Data Base File

Personal Security Access Records

Personnel Security Clearance Investigation Records

Personnel Security Record Files

Personnel Selected for Relocation

Physical Education Record

Physical Examination Reports Suspense File

Physician Assistant Evaluation

Physician Personnel Files

Picture and Roster Index

Planning and Resource Management Information System

Potential Faculty Rating System

Potential Program Managers Tracking System (PPMTS)

Predischarge Education Program Certifying Officers

Preparatory School Automated Grade Retrieval System

Preparatory School Instructor's Comments

Preparatory School Instructor's Grade Sheet

Preparatory School Military Training Evaluation

Preparatory School Physical Fitness Program

Preparatory School Record of Disenrollment

Preparatory School Standard Answer Sheet

Preparatory School Student Record Card

Preparatory School Theme Cover Sheet

Presentation Aids and Office Projects and Studies

Privacy Act Request File

Processed Transactions

Processing and Classification of Enlistees (PACE)

Professional Inquiry Records System

Professional Military Educational (PME) Rosters

Professional Military Education (PME)

Professional Officer Course (POC) and Financial Assistance Program Cadets

Program Administration Records (Flying training students)

Program Administration Records (Synthetic training instructors)

Progress Report, Undergraduate Pilot Training

Promotion and Regular Appointment Propriety Monitor File

Prospective Cadet Athlete Records/Cadet Athlete Recrods

Prospective Instructor Files

Provisional Pass

Psychiatric Treatment Records

Pupil Registration and Cumulative Records Cards

Radiology Records X-Ray Photo Identification and File

Randolph Air Force Base Women Officers Listing

Record of Air Force Personnel Assigned Outside the Department of Defense

Recorder's Roster

Records on Baptisms, Marriages and Funerals by Air Force Chaplains

Recreation Volunteer and Application Records

Recruiter Manning Personnel Listing

Recruiting Advertising Evaluation (RAE) System E806

Redline Control Report

Registration Records (Excluding private vehicle reports)

Regular Air Force Appointment Management File

Regular Air Force Appointment Program

Regular Air Force Officer Promotion List (Lineal List)

Regular Air Force Officer Selection Board Support File

Regular Officer History Card File

Religious Education Registration and Attendance Records

Relocation Preparation Project Folders

Removal of Government Operators HCCNSC

Report of Personnel Deployed in Support of Specific Contingency Plan

Report of Personnel on Temporary Duty (TDY)

Report of Processing Time for Administrative Discharge Actions

Reports of Survey

Request for and Authorization of Academic Absence

Request for Clinical Privilege at USAF Hospital Beale

Request for Enrollment, Part-Time Professional Education Program

Request for and Report of Pulmonary Function Study

Request for Variable Reenlistment Bonus (VRB) and/or Advance Payment of VRB

Request for Discharge from the Air Force Reserve

Request for Access to Classified Information by Historical Researchers

Research and Development (R&D) Projects Records

Reserve Judge Advocate Training Report

Reserve Management and Mobilization System (RMAMS)

Reserve Manning Report

Reserve Medical Service Corps Officer Appointments

Reserve Mobilization Augmentee Records

Reserve Officer/Airman Personnel Data Card Index

Reserve Promotion Administrative File

Reserve Supplement Officer (RSO) Case File

Responses to Congressional Inquiries

Results of Intramural Competition

Retirements/Separation Records System

Review of Application for Correction of Military Personnel Records

Rome Air Development Center (RADC) Manpower Resources Expenditure System

Safety Education File

Secretary of the Air Force Historical Records

Secretary of the Air Force Military Personnel Administration

Security Assistance Training Management Information System

Security Case Files

Security Records on Patent Applications

Security and Related Investigative Records

Security Squadron Office Alpha Roster and Squadron Roster

Selection Record System (Historical Files)

Selective Reenlistment Consideration

Senior Officer Information File

Senior Officer Management Office Files

Senior Officers Roster

Sensitive Compartmented Information (SCI), Personnel Security Records (PSR)

Separation Case Files (Officer and Airman)

Separation Relocation Project Folders

Seriously Ill Reporting System

Service Retirement Case File—Airmen

Service Retirement Case File—Officers

Servicemen's Group Life Insurance (SGLI) Entitlement Case Files

Sound Recordings

Source Support—Control Data

Source Support and Control Data Basic Trainee Records

Source Support and Control Data Special Training Records

Special Awards File

Special Events Planning—Protocol Roster

Special General Chemistry and Hematology Worksheets

Special Interest Assignment Files

Special Security Files

Speech Files

Squad List Alpha

Squadron Officer School (SOS) Eligibility Roster

Staff Background Information

Standardization Evaluation Program

Statutory Tour Program

Storage and Special Permits for Recreational and Utility Trailers

Student Collateral Training Records

Student Information Cards

Student Questionnaire

Student Record

Student Record of Training

Supervisor's Management Training Profile

Supervisor's Record of Employees

Supplement Military Payroll System

Survival Training Elimination Messages

Technical Training Course Management Information System

Temporary Disability Retired List

Temporary Duty History File—List of Updated Transactions

Temporary Promotion Sequence File

Temporary Quarters Subsistence Expense

Third Party Liability Notification

Thomas D. White National Defense Award Nomination Records

Tool Kit Control Card

Trailer Lot Registration

Training Aids Usage (Simulator Student Training Records)

Training Instructors (Academic Instructor Improvement/
Evaluation
Training Progress
Training Progress (Permanent Student Record)
Training Progress Reading Proficiency Case Files
Training Progress Student Data Records
Training Status Code
Training Summaries Alphabetical Roster
Training Summaries Class Roster
Training Summaries Entering Class Rosters
Training Summaries Graduation Roster
Training Work Sheet (GRF Form 36)
Training Systems Research and Development Materials
Travel Records
Uncommon Tours of Duty
Undergraduate Pilot and Navigator Records
Undergraduate Pilot and Navigator Training
Unfavorable Information Files (UIFs)
Uniformed Services Savings Deposit Program (USSDP)
Unit Assigned Personnel Information File
Unit Training Program
USAF Academy Cadet Honor Committee Case Files
U.S. Air Force Academy Honor Guard Membership Record
United States Air Force (USAF) Airman Retraining Program
USAF Aerospace Medicine Personnel Career Information
System
USAF Compression Chamber Operation
USAF Hearing Conservation Record System
United States Air Force (USAF) Inspection Scheduling
System
USAF Master Radiation Exposure Registry
USAF Prisoner of War (POW) Debriefing Files
USAF Reconstitution Requirements for Office of JCS and
HQ USAF
USAF Research and Development Award
U.S. Air Force Reserve/Air National Guard of U.S. (USAFR/
ANGUS) Appointment Management File
United States Air Force Retired Pay System
United States Air Force Special Investigations School
Individual Academic Records
Upgrade Training Missile Procedures Training (MPT)
Critique Form
Unusual and Incoherent Translation Material
Vehicle Administration Records
Vehicle Integrated Management System (VIMS)
Veterinary Personnel Files
Veterinary Records
Visiting Officer Quarters—Transient Airman Quarters
Reservation
Visual Air
Workers' Compensation Claims File
X-Ray Film Identification Card
X-Ray Nominal Index File

Department of the Army
ABSENTEE CASE FILES

Any active army member absent without proper authority
and administratively designated as a deserter in accordance
with AR 630-10 on absenteeism and desertion.

Commander, USACICD, Attention: CIJA-RI, 5611 Columbia
Pike, Falls Church, VA 22041.

ALCOHOL AND DRUG REFERENCE PAPER FILES

Military, retired military, military dependents, and civilian
employees with drug or alcohol problems.

Headquarters and Installation Support Activity (ECOM),
Alcohol and Drug Control Office, Fort Monmouth, NJ
07703, (201) 532-2415.

ARMY COUNCIL OF REVIEW BOARDS FILES

Members of active army and former members of active
army and prospective enlistees/inductees eliminated or
denied enlistment who have cases pending or under consideration by the Army Council of Review Boards or any
of its component boards.

Office, Secretary of the Army, Army Council of Review
Boards, Room 1E474, The Pentagon, Washington, DC
20310, (202) 697-3071.

ARMY PROPERTY CLAIM FILES

Individuals who, having damaged government property,
were not subject to the collection activities of other agencies
or organizations and therefore require litigation on behalf
of the Department of the Army.

Chief, Litigation Division, Office of the Judge Advocate
General, Department of the Army, The Pentagon, Washington, DC 20310, (202) 695-1721.

Request for information should contain: Individual's name,
current address, telephone number, the case number that
appears with the office symbol on all correspondence received from this office and any other personal identifying
data (such as driver's license number, if any) which would
assist in determining the identity of the requester. For
personal visits, the individual should be able to provide
some positive identification (driver's license, identification
card) and give some information that could be verified
within his or her "case" folder. Visits may be made to any
staff judge advocate office.

BANKRUPTCY PROCESSING FILES

Any army military member or Department of the Army
civilian (DAC) or former military member DAC for whom
bankruptcy notice has been received.

Chief, Field Services Office, USAFAC, Indianapolis, IN
46249, (317) 542-3127.

CENTRAL FILES, OFFICE OF THE CHIEF
OF STAFF (DACS-DAS)

Any military or civilian employee or correspondent of the
army who may have been the subject of, or initiated

correspondence referred to, the office of the chief of staff of the army.

HQDA (DACS-DSA), Room 3D-671, The Pentagon, Washington, DC 20310, (202) 695-3503 or 695-2765.

CHECK-CASHING PRIVILEGE FILES

Persons whose checks, written at these facilities, have been dishonored and/or whose check-cashing privileges have been suspended or revoked.

Installation commander.

CIVIL PROCESS CASE FILES AND REFERENCE FILES

USAREUR personnel against whom German civil court documents have been forwarded to the United States armed forces for service.

Office of the Judge Advocate HQ USAREUR and 7th Army, Heidelberg, Federal Republic of Germany.

CLAIMS BACK-UP FILE

Individuals who file claims, through RCPAC, against United States government.

Staff Judge Advocate, RCPAC, 9700 Paige Blvd., St. Louis, MO 63132, Attention: AGUZ-RPC-JA, (314) 268-7533.

COMPLAINT FILE

Any employee who has filed an equal opportunity complaint which requires Department of the Army headquarters review.

OSA (SAMR), Room 2E-600, The Pentagon, Washington, DC 20310, (202) 695-3721.

COUNTERINTELLIGENCE OPERATIONS FILES

Active and retired military personnel, DOD-affiliated civilians including contractor personnel employed by civilian firms having defense contracts, and individuals not affiliated with the DOD only if there is a reasonable basis to believe that one or more of the following situations exist:

- Theft, destruction or sabotage of weapons, ammunition, equipment, facilities, or records belonging to DOD units or installations.

- Possible compromise of classified defense information by unauthorized disclosure or by espionage.

- Subversion of loyalty, discipline, or morale of Department of the Army military or civilian personnel by actively encouraging violation of laws, disobedience of lawful orders and regulations, or disruption of military activities.

- Demonstrations on active or reserve army installations or demonstrations immediately adjacent to them which are of such a size or character that they are likely to

interfere with the conduct of military activities. Armed forces induction centers, army recruiting stations located off-post, and facilities of federalized national guard units are considered to be active DOD installations. For the purpose of the subparagraph, Reserve Officer Training Corps (ROTC) installations on campuses are not considered to be active or reserve army installations and coverage of demonstrations at or adjacent to such installations is not authorized.

- Direct threats to DOD military or civilian personnel regarding their official duties or to other persons authorized protection by DOD resources.

- Activities or demonstrations endangering classified defense contract facilities or key defense facilities, including the Panama Canal, approved by Department of the Army headquarters as crucial to the defense and operation of the Panama Canal.

Commanding General, United States Army Intelligence and Security Command, The Pentagon, Washington, DC 20310, (202) 545-6700.

COUNTERINTELLIGENCE RESEARCH FILE SYSTEM (CIRFS)

Individuals who have come to the attention of the United States Army counterintelligence community during the course of intelligence operations or normal mission requirements.

Commanding General, United States Army Intelligence and Security Command, The Pentagon, Washington, DC 20310, (202) 545-6700.

CRIMINAL INVESTIGATION CASE FILES, CRIME LABORATORY REPORTING FILES

Any individual, civilian or military, involved or suspected of being involved in or reporting possible criminal activity affecting the army's interests, property, and/or personnel.

Commander, USACIDC, Attention: CIJA-RI, 5611 Columbia Pike, Falls Church, VA 22041, (202) 756-2263.

DIRECTORY OF KNOWN OR SUSPECT HOSTILE INTELLIGENCE PERSONALITIES – DOKSHIP

DOKSHIP contains a master listing by name, country, and address of intelligence (known or suspect) personalities employed by each agency that is of interest to the Counterintelligence Analysis Detachment and the army counterintelligence community.

Concerning the Freedom of Information Act: United States Army, Office of the Secretary of the Army, The Pentagon, Washington, DC 20310, (202) 545-6700; concerning the Privacy Act: Department of the Army, Office for Privacy Act Matters, Forrestal Bldg., 1000 Independence Ave., SW, Washington, DC (202) 693-0973.

EQUAL OPPORTUNITY INVESTIGATIVE FILES

All national guard technicians and military members who have filed complaints of discrimination and those national guard technicians and military members who are involved in these complaints.

NGB-EO, Room 301, Nassif Building, 5611 Columbia Pike, Falls Church, VA 22041, (202) 756-1563.

EXPELLED OR BARRED PERSON FILES

Any citizen who is expelled or barred from an army installation.

Personnel, Office of the Secretary of the Army, The Pentagon, Washington, DC 20310, (202) 545-6700.

FBI CRIMINAL-TYPE REPORTING FILES

Any member or civilian employee of the active army or reserve components involved in criminal activity.

HQDA, Forrestal Building, 1000 Independence Avenue, SW, Washington, DC 20314, (202) 693-0973.

FOREIGN JURISDICTION CASE FILES

All members of the United States Army, civilians in the employ of, serving with, or accompanying the United States Army abroad, and the dependents of individuals in such categories, who have been subject to the exercises of civil or criminal jurisdiction of foreign courts or foreign administrative agencies.

Chief, International Affairs Division, Office of the Judge Advocate General, HQDA (DAJA-IA), Washington, DC 20319, (202) 697-1567, and the staff judge advocate office where the case originates.

Request for information should contain: Individual's name, current address, telephone number, the case number that appears with the office symbol on all correspondence received from this office, and any other personal identifying data (such as driver's license number, if any) which would assist in determining the identity of the requester. Personal visits may be made to any staff judge advocate office. For personal visits, the individual should be able to provide some positive identification (driver's license, identification card) and give some information that could be verified with his or her "case" folder.

FOREIGN JURISDICTION REPORTING FILES

All members of the United States Army, civilians in the employ of, serving with, or accompanying the army abroad, and the dependents of individuals in such categories, who have been subject to the exercise of criminal jurisdiction by foreign courts and sentenced to unsuspended confinement.

Chief, International Affairs Division, Office of The Judge Advocate General, HQDA, Washington, DC 20319, (202) 697-1567, and the staff judge advocate office where the case originates.

Request for information should contain: Individual's name, current address, telephone number, the case number that appears with the office symbol on all correspondence received from this office, and any other personal identifying data (such as driver's license number) which would assist in determining the identity of the requester. Personal visits may be made to any staff judge advocate office. For personal visits, the individual should be able to provide some positive identification (driver's license, identification card) and give some information that could be verified within his or her "case" folder.

GENERAL PERMIT FILES

Any person or persons applying for permits, permittees, and persons having done unauthorized work in navigable waters.

HQDA, Office of the Chief of Engineers, Attention: DAEN-CWO-N, Washington, DC 20314, (202) 272-0001.

Information may also be obtained by writing or visiting the nearest corps of engineers district office.

INDIVIDUAL CORRECTIONAL TREATMENT FILES

Any military member confined at an army confinement facility as a result of, or pending, trial by court-martial.

The Deputy Chief of Staff for Personnel, Headquarters, Department of the Army, The Pentagon, Washington, DC 20310, (202) 695-6003; installation commanders having installation and area confinement facilities.

INDIVIDUAL FLIGHT RECORD FILE

Army personnel on flying status; army personnel on flying status who are prohibited from participating in aerial flights; army personnel on flying status who are prohibited by statute from participating in aerial flight; foreign students; flight crews, observers, technicians, flight medical personnel, photographers, gunners, and mechanics; national guard aviators; army reserve aviators.

U.S. Army Agency for Aviation Safety, Ft. Rucker, AL 36360, (205) 255-3410, for all active army, national guard, and army reserve flying status personnel; U.S. Army Reserve Components Personnel and Administration Center, 9700 Paige Blvd., St. Louis, MO 63112, (314) 268-7600, for all separated, retired, or deceased flying status personnel.

INDIVIDUAL PRISONER PERSONNEL FILES

Any military member confined at the United States Disciplinary Barracks who have been considered for clemency, restoration, or parole by the Deputy Chief of Staff for Personnel Restoration Board or the Army Clemency and Parole Board; any military member transferred from the United States Disciplinary Barracks to a federal penal institution.

The Deputy Chief of Staff for Personnel, HQDA, The Pentagon, Washington, DC 20310, (202) 695-6003.

INDIVIDUAL RADIATION PROTECTION FILES

All army personnel, military and civilian, occupationally exposed to hazards of ionizing radiation.

HQDA (DASG-AOM), Room 2D453, The Pentagon, Washington, DC 20310, (202) 695-2090.

INSPECTOR GENERAL COMPLAINT FILES

Any person, civilian or military, who presents to an inspector general in writing or in person a complaint/request for assistance.

HQDA (DAIG-AC), Room 1D736, The Pentagon, Washington, DC 20310, (202) 695-1578.

Request for information must include full name, grade, Social Security number, unit of assignment, nature of complaint, proof of personal identification, and the identity of the command inspector general to whom complaint was submitted.

INSPECTOR GENERAL INVESTIGATIVE FILES

Any person who has been the subject of, witness for, or referenced in an inspector general investigation.

Because reports are seldom filed by surname or Social Security number, requests to determine if the system contains a record about requester should include full name, rank (if applicable), Social Security account number (if applicable, address or army post office (APO), if applicable, approximate date of investigation, subject of investigation, location of inspector general office conducting the investigation, and the requester's role in the investigation.

HQDA (DAIG-IN), Room 1D731, The Pentagon, Washington, DC 20319, (202) 695-7385.

INSURANCE CLAIMS FILES — WORKMEN'S COMPENSATION

All employees who suffer on-the-job accidents, illness, or death.

Headquarters, AAFES, Comptroller, Insurance Branch, Dallas, TX 75222, (214) 330-2271.

INTERCEPTION OF WIRE AND ORAL COMMUNICATIONS QUARTERLY REPORTS AND MOTIONS FOR DISCOVERY

DOD-affiliated and nonaffiliated United States citizens who are or were subject to, or party to, a United States Army wiretap; names of individuals who have filed a motion for discovery with the army to determine whether or not they were the subject of an army wiretap.

HQDA (DAMI-DOS), Room 2E463, The Pentagon, Washington, DC 20310, (202) 697-8874.

JUDICIAL INFORMATION RELEASE FILE

Individuals connected in any manner with army aircraft accidents, to include crew members, passengers of the aircraft, witnesses to the accident, technical experts who testified at the investigation into the accident, and members of the investigating boards; individuals and legal entities who have requested information from army files for which the Litigation Division, Office of The Judge Advocate General of the Army, is the releasing authority.

Chief, Litigation Division, Office of the Judge Advocate General, Department of the Army, Washington, DC 20310, (202) 695-1721.

Request for information should contain: Individual's name, current address, telephone number, the case number that appears with the office symbol on all correspondence received from this office, and any other personal identifying data (such as driver's license number, if any) which would assist in determining the identity of the requester. Personal visits may be made to any staff judge advocate office. For personal visits, the individual should be able to provide some positive identification (driver's license, identification card) and give some information that could be verified within his or her "case" folder.

LEGAL ASSISTANCE CASE FILES

Persons having sought legal assistance in their personal and private affairs.

Chief, Legal Assistance Office, HQDA (DAJA-LA), The Pentagon, Washington, DC 20310, (202) 695-1750, and the staff judge advocates of organizations listed in the DOD directory.

Request for information should contain: Individual's name, current address, telephone number, the case number that appears with the office symbol on all correspondence received from this office, and any other personal identifying data (such as driver's license number, if any) which would assist in determining the identity of the requester. Personal visits may be made to any staff judge advocate office. For personal visits, the individual should be able to provide some positive identification (driver's license, identification card) and give some information that could be verified within his or her "case" folder.

LEGAL ASSISTANCE INTERVIEW RECORD FILES

Persons having sought legal assistance in their personal and private affairs.

Decentralized System Chief, Legal Assistance Office, Office of the Judge Advocate General, Department of the Army, The Pentagon, Washington, DC 20310, (202) 695-4321; staff judge advocate offices at organizations listed in the DOD organizational directory.

Request for information should contain: Individual's name, current address, telephone number, the case number that appears with the office symbol on all correspondence received from this office, and any other personal identifying data (such as driver's license number, if any) which would assist in determining the identity of the requester. Personal visits may be made to any staff judge advocate office. For personal visits, the individual should be able to provide some positive identification (driver's license, identification card) and give some information that could be verified within his or her "case" folder.

LEGAL OPINION PRECEDENT FILES

Individuals who have been subjected to disciplinary action under the Uniform Code of Military Justice.

Chief, Criminal Law Division, Office of the Judge Advocate General, HQDA (DAJA-CL), The Pentagon, Washington, DC 20310, (202) 695-6433.

Request for information should contain: Individual's name, current address, telephone number, the case number that appears with the office symbol on all correspondence received from this office, and any other personal identifying data (such as driver's license number, if any), which would assist in determining the identity of the requester. Personal visits may be made to any staff judge advocate office. For personal visits, the individual should be able to provide some positive identification (driver's license, identification card) and give some information that could be verified within his or her "case" folder.

LIST OF HOSTILE INTELLIGENCE COLLECTORS OF UNCLASSIFIED MIL INFO

Contains names of suspected hostile collectors of unclassified military information.

Intelligence and Threat Analysis Center, Arlington Hall Station, Arlington, VA 22212, (202) 692-5223.

LITIGATION CASE FILES

Active duty and former military personnel, civilian employees of the army, dependents and heirs of military or civilian personnel of the army, and nonaffiliated agencies and personnel who have filed a complaint against the United States Army or its personnel in the federal civil court system; military and civilian personnel of the army who are named individually as defendants in civil litigation initiated against or by the army.

Chief, Litigation Division, Office of The Judge Advocate General, Department of the Army, The Pentagon, Washington, DC 20310, (202) 695-1721.

Request for information should contain: Individual's name, current address, telephone number, the case number that appears with the office symbol on all correspondence received

from this office, and any other personal identifying data (such as driver's license number, if any), which would assist in determining the identity of the requester. Personal visits may be made to any staff judge advocate office. For personal visits, the individual should be able to provide some positive identification (driver's license, identification card) and give some information that could be verified within his or her "case" folder.

LOCAL CRIMINAL INFORMATION FILES

Any citizen or group of citizens suspected of or involved in criminal activity directed against or involving the army.

Commander, USACIDC, Attention: CIIO, 5611 Columbia Pike, Falls Church, VA 22041, (202) 756-2263.

MEDICAL EVALUATION FILES

Army members whose medical fitness for continued service has been questioned either by the member or by his or her commander.

HQDA (DASG-AOM), Room 2D453, The Pentagon, Washington, DC 20310, (202) 695-2090.

MEDICAL EXPENSE CLAIMS FILES

Individuals who have received medical treatment at the expense of the United States Army as a result of a tortious or negligent act of a third party; third parties causing medical care to be furnished to individuals entitled to medical care at government expense.

Chief, Litigation Division, Office of The Judge Advocate General, Department of the Army, The Pentagon, Washington, DC 20310, (202) 695-1721.

Request for information should contain: Individual's name, current address, telephone number, the case number that appears with the office symbol on all correspondence received from this office, and any other personal identifying data (such as driver's license number, if any), which would assist in determining the identity of the requester. Personal visits may be made to any staff judge advocate office. For personal visits, the individual should be able to provide some positive identification (driver's license, identification card) and give some information that could be verified within his or her "case" folder.

MISCONDUCT/UNFITNESS/UNSUITABILITY DISCHARGE BOARD PROCEEDINGS FILE

Any army member whose unfitness, unsuitability, or misconduct is of such a nature to warrant an appearance before a properly constituted board for a determination of continuance in the service or discharge therefrom.

Commander, U.S. Army Military Personnel Center, 200 Stovall Street, Alexandria, VA 22332, (202) 325-9060.

MP REPORTING FILES

Any citizen who is the subject, victim, complainant, or witness in connection with a complaint.

Commander, USACIDC, Attention: CIJA-RI, 5611 Columbia Pike, Falls Church, VA 22041, (202) 756-2263.

NAF COMPLAINT, APPEAL & GRIEVANCE CASE FILES

Any individual who has applied for employment with, is employed by, or was employed by a nonappropriated fund (NAF) instrumentality within the Department of the Army and who has filed (individually or collectively) a complaint, grievance, or appeal.

HQDA (PECA), The Pentagon, Washington, DC 20310, (202) 693-1596.

PATENT, COPYRIGHT, AND DATA LICENSE PROFFERS, INFRINGEMENT CLAIMS, AND LITIGATION FILES

Claimants or defendants in administrative proceedings or litigation with the government for improper use, infringement, enforcement of agreements, or comparable claims concerning patents or copyrights; individuals having copyrights in material Department of the Army is interested in; individuals who own patents which they offer to license to Department of the Army; individuals seeking private relief before Congress because of right in inventions, patents, copyrights, or data.

Chief, Intellectual Property, HQDA (DAJA-PA), The Pentagon, Washington, DC 20310, (202) 695-6822, and the senior patent attorney at each location listed.

Request for information should contain: Individual's name, current address, telephone number, the case number that appears with the office symbol on all correspondence received from this office, and any other personal identifying data (such as driver's license number, if any), which would assist in determining the identity of the requester. Personal visits may be made to any Department of the Army patent location. For personal visits, the individual should be able to provide some positive identification (driver's license, identification card) and give some information that could be verified within his or her "case" folder.

PECUNIARY CHARGE APPEAL FILES

Any army military member or civilian employee held pecuniarily liable for charges for which an appeal is filed.

Chief, Field Services Offices, USAFAC, Indianapolis, IN 46249, (317) 542-3217.

PERSECTORIAL FILES

Any individual who is pending trial by court-martial.

United States Court of Military Appeals, 450 E Street, NW, Washington, DC 20442, (202) 693-7100.

PRESS INTEREST REFERENCE FILES

Army members and civilians, active and retired and discharged, who are, have been, or are likely to again become, the subject of press interest.

HQDA (DAIO-IO), Room 2D 641, The Pentagon, Washington, DC 20310, (202) 695-5136.

PRIVACY ACT REQUEST FILE

All individuals who request information on records concerning them which are in the custody of Department of the Army, or individuals who request access or amendment to such records under the provisions of Title 5, United States Code, section 552a (The Privacy Act of 1974).

HQDA (DAAG-AMR), Forrestal Building, 1000 Independence Ave., SW, Washington, DC 20314, (202) 693-0631.

PROCUREMENT MISCONDUCT FILES (FRAUD CASES)

Individuals or legal entities investigated for alleged procurement misconduct, such as fraudulent activities in securing or performing a government contract.

Chief, Litigation Division, Office of The Judge Advocate General, Department of the Army, The Pentagon, Washington, DC 20310, (202) 695-1721.

PUBLIC INFORMATION, ADMINISTRATIVE, AND REFERENCE PAPER FILES

Any individual, civilian or military, involved or suspected of being involved in any criminal activity affecting the army's interest or property; and/or personnel involved in one or more public affairs actions of U.S. Army Criminal Investigation Command (USACIC).

Commander, USACIC, Attention: CIIO, 5611 Columbia Pike, Falls Church, VA 22041, (202) 756-2263.

RACE RELATIONS/EQUAL OPPORTUNITY & EQUAL EMPLOYMENT OPPORTUNITY COMPLAINT FILES

Any member of the army (active and reserve components) who submits a complaint to this office, orally, telephonically, or in writing, or whose complaint is forwarded by a major command to this office for appropriate action.

HQDA (DAPE-HRR), Room 2D745, The Pentagon, Washington, DC 20310, (202) 695-4200 or 697-1860.

RECRUITER ASSIGNMENT REPORT

Individuals who have been relieved from or not accepted for recruiting duty.

Director, Recruiting Force Management, USARCRFM-MP-A, U.S. Army Recruiting Command, Ft. Sheridan, IL 60037, (312) 926-3910.

RECRUITER MALPRACTICE FILES

Individuals who have alleged recruiter malpractice or processing irregularities against members of the recruiting command; members of the recruiting command who have been investigated for alleged recruiter malpractice or processing irregularities.

Director, Recruiting Force Management, USARCRFM-SS, Army Recruiting Command, Fort Sheridan, IL 60037, (312) 926-3147.

RESERVOIR PERMIT FILES

Any person or persons applying for permits, permittees, and persons having done unauthorized work at water resource development projects of the Army Corps of Engineers.

Write project resource manager at project concerned.

SERIOUS INCIDENT REPORTING FILES

Any citizen identified as the subject or victim of a serious incident reportable to Department of the Army in accordance with Army Regulation 190-40, military police serious incident report. This includes in general any criminal act or other incident which — because of its sensitivity or nature, publicity, or other considerations — should be brought to the attention of Headquarters, Department of the Army.

Office of the Secretary, The Pentagon, Washington, DC 20310, (202) 545-6700.

SHORT/LONG TERM DISABILITY FILES

- Short Term: All insured headquarters employees who file claims for disabilities extending beyond 17 days.

- Long Term: All insured employees who file claims for disabilities extending beyond 6 months.

Headquarters AAFES, Comptroller, Insurance Branch, Dallas, TX 75222, (214) 330-2271.

SOLICITATION BAN LIST FILES

Any individual whose on-base solicitation privileges have been withdrawn by the Department of the Army or the Department of the Navy.

HQDA (DAAG-AMP), Room GA 172, Forrestal Building, Washington, DC 20314, (202) 693-0718.

SUBVERSION AND ESPIONAGE DIRECTED AGAINST THE ARMY (SAEDA)

Selected reports of individuals who have reported incidents which indicate subversion and/or espionage directed against the army. Only army personnel are referenced in this file.

Intelligence & Threat Analysis Center, Arlington Hall Station, Arlington, VA 22212.

TORT CLAIM FILES

Personnel, military affiliated, or civilians with no military connection, who have filed a complaint against the United States Army in the United States District Court under the Federal Tort Claims Act.

Chief, Litigation Division, Office of The Judge Advocate General, Department of the Army, The Pentagon, Washington, DC 20310, (202) 695-1721. Personal visits may be made to any staff judge advocate office.

TRAFFIC LAW ENFORCEMENT FILES

Any citizen who, at a military installation, registers a privately owned motor vehicle; is the subject of a traffic violation/summons; is a subject, victim, complainant, or witness to a traffic accident; or has a parking permit.

Office of the Secretary of the Army, Personnel, The Pentagon, Washington, DC 20310, (202) 545-6700.

UNFAVORABLE INFORMATION FILES

Army personnel on whom unfavorable information has been discovered, considered, referred to individual, and disposition determination reached.

HQDA (DAPE-MPO-C), Room 2B 724, The Pentagon, Washington, DC 20310, (202) 697-5100.

UNSOLICITED CORRESPONDENCE FILE

Individuals who voluntarily communicate with army officials to express concern or complaints about army operations or personnel.

Intelligence and Threat Analysis Center, Arlington Hall Station, Arlington, VA 22212.

USAINTA INVESTIGATIVE FILES SYSTEM

Military personnel of the army, to include active duty, national guard members, reservists, and retirees; civilian employees of the Department of the Army, to include contract temporary, part-time, advisory, and volunteer including citizen and alien employees located both in the United States and in overseas areas; industrial or contractor personnel who are civilians working in private industry for firms which have contracts involving access to classified DOD information; aliens granted limited access authorization to defense information; DOD alien personnel investigated for visa purposes; individuals about whom there is a reasonable basis to believe that they are engaged in, or plan to engage in, activities such as (1) theft, destruction, or sabotage of ammunition, equipment, facilities, or records belonging to DOD units or installations; (2) possible compromise of classified defense information by unauthorized disclosure or by espionage; (3) subversion of loyalty, discipline, or morale of Department of the Army military or civilian personnel by actively encouraging violation of lawful orders and regulations or disruption of military activities; (4) demonstrations on active or reserve army installations or immediately adjacent thereto which are of such character that they are likely to interfere with the conduct of military operations; (5) direct threats to DOD military or civilian employees regarding their official duties or to other persons authorized protection by DOD resources; (6) activities or demonstrations endangering classified defense contract facilities or key defense facilities of the Panama Canal approved by Headquarters, Department of the Army (HQDA); certain non-DOD-affiliated persons whose activities involve them with the DOD; namely, activities involving requests for admission to DOD facilities or requests for certain information regarding DOD personnel, activities, or facilities; persons formerly affiliated with DOD; persons who applied for or are/were being considered for employment with or access to DOD such as applicants for military service, pre-inductees and prospective contractors; visa applicants, individuals residing on, having authorized official access to, or conducting or operating any business or other function at any DOD installation or facility; and USAINTA sources.

Commander, U.S. Army Intelligence Agency, Fort Meade, MD 20755, (301) 677-4743 or 4011.

U.S. ARMY CLAIMS SERVICE MANAGEMENT INFORMATION SYSTEM (USARCS MISO)

All individuals, corporations, associations, countries, states, territories, political subdivisions presenting a claim against the United States cognizable under the following statutes and army regulation 27-30: (1) The Military Claims Act (10 U.S.C. 2733); (2) The Federal Tort Claims Act (28 U.S.C. 2671-2680); (3) The Act of 9 October 1962 (10 U.S.C. 2737); (4) The National Guard Claims Act (32 U.S.C. 715); (5) Title 10, U.S.C. section 2734a and 2734b (NATO claims); (6) The Maritime Claims Settlement Act (10 U.S.C. 4801-4808); (7) Article 139, Uniform Code of Military Justice (10 U.S.C. 939); (8) The Foreign Claims Act (10 U.S.C. 2734); and (9) The Military Personnel and Civilian Employees' Claims Act (31 U.S.C. 240-243).

Chief, United States Army Claims Service, Fort Meade, MD 20755, (301) 677-7034.

Request for information should contain: Individual's name, current address, and telephone number, the claim number if known, the date and place of the incident giving rise to the claim, and any other personal identifying data (such as driver's license number, if any) which could assist in determining the identity of the requester. Personal visits may be made to any staff judge advocate office. For personal visits, the individual should be able to provide some positive identification (driver's license, identification card) and give some information that could be verified within his or her "case" folder.

USMA LEGAL FILES ON MILITARY AND CIVILIAN PERSONNEL

Military personnel (officers, enlisted personnel, and cadets) who have been the subject of official board proceedings, court-martial, criminal investigations, investigations regarding offenses against civil authorities, or matters involving potential litigation (estates, personal and property injury); civilian personnel who have been the subject of military or civil authority board proceedings, civil or criminal investigations, or matters involving potential litigation (estates, personal and property injury), or misconduct or adverse actions.

Professor and Head of the Department of Law, United States Military Academy, West Point, NY 10996, (914) 938-2310.

VALIDATION FILES

Any army member or Department of the Army civilian (DAC) or former military member or DAC suspected of fraud or improper payment.

Chief, Field Services Office, USAFAC, Indianapolis, IN 46249, (317) 542-3127.

VIOLATION WARNING FILES

Any individual who, on lands administered by the Army Corps of Engineers, violates the provisions of Chapter III, Parts 313 or 327, of Title 36, Code of Federal Regulations which governs public use of water resource development projects.

HQDA (DAEN-PM), Forrestal Building, Washington, DC 20314, (202) 693-6608.

WITNESS APPEARANCE FILES

Witnesses requested by United States Attorneys for federal court proceedings.

Chief, Litigation Division, Office of The Judge Advocate General, Department of the Army, The Pentagon, Washington, DC 20310, (202) 695-1721.

Request for information should contain: Individual's name, current address, telephone number, the case number that appears with the office symbol on all correspondence received from this office, and any other personal identifying data (such as driver's license number, if any), which would assist in determining the identity of the requester. Personal visits may be made to any staff judge advocate office. For personal visits, the individual should be able to provide some positive identification (driver's license, identification card) and give some information that could be verified within his or her "case" folder.

For any files not previously listed, individuals should contact:

- Out-of-service, rehired, reserved: National Personnel Center – Army, 9700 Paige Blvd., St. Louis, MO 63132, (314) 268-7600.

- Officers, active: Military Personnel Center, 200 Stovall St., Alexandria, VA 22332, (202) 325-9060.

- Enlisted, active: Command U.S. Army, Enlisted Record Center, Fort Benjamin Harrison, IN 46429, (317) 442-3111.

Following is a list of the remaining files maintained by the Department of the Army. Anyone interested in obtaining information from any of these files should contact the appropriate agency head or the Secretary of Defense, The Pentagon, Washington, DC 20301.

AAFES Time Sheets
AAFMPS Active and Inactive Theater Employees Payroll Register
AAFMPS Individual Earnings Record
ADP Master and Operating Files
AYA Registration File
Accident and Incident Case Files; Army Safety Management Information System
Accident and Incident Files
Accidental Death and Dismemberment Administrative Files
Alphabetical Listing of Scientists
Alumni Affairs and Gifts Program Division Donor Data System
American Red Cross Consultation Service Case Files
American Red Cross Dental Files
Annuity Eligibility Files
Application for Employment Files
Appointment of Unit Postal Officers and Unit Mail Clerks
Appraisal of Past Performance AGUZ Form 651
Army Athletic Association Membership File
Army Community Service (ACS) Volunteer Record
Army Emergency Relief Transaction Files
Army Medical Department Personnel Management and Manpower Control System
Army Medical X-Ray Film Files
Army National Guard Automated Personnel Reporting System
Army School Files
Army School Student Files
Army Service School/Senior Service College Selections — US Army Reserve
Authorized Supply Representative Card Files
Authorized Supply Representatives Card Register Files
Badge and Credential Files
Baptism, Marriage, and Funeral Files
Blackmarket Monitoring Files
Blood Donor Files
Burial Register Files
Cadet Academic Management Information System
Cadet Counseling File
Career Management Files of Dual Component Personnel
Career Management Individual Files
Casualty Case Files
Casualty Information System (CIS)
Check-Cashing Privilege Files
Check-Cashing Privilege Suspense Files

Civilian Attorney/Patent Adviser Career Files
Civilian Consultation Service Case Files
Civilian Dental Files
Civilian Employee Pay System
Civilian Personnel Information System
Civilian School Files
Claims Inventory of Active Claims for Medical Care Under CHAMPUS
Classified Material Access Files
Classified Matter Inventory Reporting Files
Clemency Project
Clinical Psychology Individual Case Files
Congressional Correspondence Files
Congressional Inquiry File
Contract Surgeon Personnel Files
Contract Training File
Contractor Personnel Files
Contractor Qualification Files
Control Card Files
Controller Training and Proficiency Record Files
Conversion Files
Correction Case Folders
Correspondence (Civilian Aides to the Secretary of the Army)
Correspondence Course Files
Cross Reference List Report of Claims for CHAMPUS
DD Form 1300 Files
Debriefing Acknowledgment Files
Dental Health Record Files
Department of the Army Operational Support Activities Files
Departure Clearance Files
Dependent Children School Program Files
Disbursing Office Establishment and Appointment Files
Emergency Data Files
Employee Examination Records
Employee Service Record Card Files
Employee Travel Files
Employer's Copy of Income Tax Withheld
Employer's Quarterly Federal Tax Return Files
Enlisted Master File (EMF)
Enlisted Year Group Management File
Entertainment Case Files
Entrance Medical Examination Files
Equipment Operator Permit Files
Evaluation Files on Cadets and Potential Instructors
Extra Oral Dental X-ray Files
Family Index Files
Federal Housing Administration (FHA) Mortgage Payment Insurance Files
Fidelity Bond Files
Field Military Personnel Information System
File Search Microfilm Storage and Retrieval System
Financial Counseling Reference Paper Files
Flight Examination Files
Flight Regulation Violation Files
Food Taste Test Reference Files
General Educational Development (GED) Individual Record
Group Insurance Card Files

Group Insurance Printout Files
Hand Receipt Files
Health Nursing Case Files
Historian's Background Material
Historical Inquiry Files
Historical Photographic Files
Homeowners Assistance Case Files
Household Goods Shipment Excess Cost Collection File
Household Shipment Contract Files
Identification Card Accountability Files
Incentive Awards Case Files
Individual Deceased Personnel Files
Individual Gravesite Reservation Files
Individual Interment Report Files
Individual Leave Record — Annual and Sick
Individual Patient Diet Files (Department Army Form 2924)
Individual Retirement Files
Individual Travel Files
Indoctrination/Debriefing/Travel Restriction Data Files
Informant Register
Inspector General Management Information System
Installation X-ray Index Files
Intelligence Collection Files
Joint Uniform Military Pay System — Active Army (JUMPS-AA)
Joint Uniform Military Pay System — Army — Retired Pay
Joint Uniform Military Pay System — Reserve Components Army
Levy and Garnishment Files
MARS Member Files
MBA USAR Reserve Field System
MCP Civilian Personnel Information System
MCT USAR Civilian Technician System
MPA Civilian Pay and Leave System
Master Index (NMI)
Mechanized Reporting System (MRS) 130
Medal of Honor Recipient Files (Vietnam Era)
Media Contact Files
Medical Classification Files
Medical and Dental Registrant Case Files
Medical Facility Individual Reporting Files
Medical Prescription Files
Medical Review Files
Medical Services Account Files
Medical Treatment Indices
Medical Treatment Record Files
Memorialization Board Files
Mental Competency Review Files
Military Award Case File
Military and Civilian Waiver Files
Military Consultation Service Case Files
Military Dental Files
Military Identification Application Files
Military Personnel Action File
Military Personnel Assignment Files
Military Personnel Records Jacket Files (MPRJ)
Military Police Investigator Certification Files
Miscellaneous Employee Claim Files
NAF Personnel Records

Nonappropriated Fund Employee Insurance Files
Nursing Service Schedule Files
OCS Waiver Requests
Occupational Inventory Files
Office Personnel Register Files
Office Master File (OMF)
Officer Personnel Information Files
Officer Availability and Civil School Mgt. System
Official Military Personnel File
Official Personnel Folders (OPF)
Operator's Examination and Qualification Record Files
Oversea Processing Records
Paid Death Claim Files
Paid Disbursement Files
Passenger Reservation Reference Paper Files
Passport Files
Patent, Copyright, Trademark, and Proprietary Data Files
Patent, Copyright, and Trademark Soliciting Files
Patient Accountability Files
Patient Condition Reporting File
Patient Treatment X-ray Films
Patient Trust Fund and Baggage Files
Payroll Adjustment Files
Payroll Allotment Files
Payroll Register Files
Payroll Report Files
Personal Affairs Case File
Personal Clothing Record Files
Personal Property Accounting Files
Personal Property Claim Files
Personnel Clearance Records
Personnel Data Card and Locator Card Files
Personnel Management/Action Working Files
Personnel Records Maintained at Supervisory Level
Personnel Security Case Files
Personnel Security Status Files
Personnel Utilization Reporting System
Philippine Army Files
Photographer Identification Files
Photographic Caption Files
Physical Profile
Postal Directory Files
POV and Firearm Registration Files
Privilege Care Application Files
Program Management and Review System (PROMARS)
Property Officer Designation Files
Prosthetic Case Files
Rapid Electric Ad Coupon Transmission (REACT)
Referral Program for NAF Employees
Registration and Permit Files
Release of Information Action Files
Relief Legislative Files
Report of Casualty Department of Defense (DD) Form 1300
Request for Information Files
Resettlement Files
Retired Personnel Data File
Retirement Assistance Files
Retirement Card Files
Retirement Extension Files

Retirement Services Control Reference Paper Files
ROTC Member File
Safety Award Files
School Employee File
School Health Files
Security Access Information Files
Security Clearance Case Files (SCCF)
Security Clearance Information Files
Small Arms Sales Record Files
Social Work Individual Case Files
Special Review Board (SRB) Appeal Case Summary
  File
Spectacle Issue and Receipt Files
Standing Delivery Order Files
Statistical Tabulation Files — Household Goods and Baggage
  System
Still Picture Files (Personalities)
Systems Magnetic Tape Files
Technician Personnel Management Information System
  (TPMIS)
Temperature, Pulse, and Respiration Files
Training Summary
Transfer of POW Files
Travel Advance Accounting System (TAAS)
Travel Advance Register Files
Travel Advance Trial Balance Files
Trophy Firearm Registration
Tuberculosis Registry
Tuition Assistance Case Files
US Army Criminal Investigation Fund Vouchers
USA Individual Ready, Standby, and Retired Reserve
  Personnel Information System
USA Reserve Officer Training Corps (ROTC) Medical
  Examination Files
United States Corps of Cadets Personnel Records
United States Military Academy Cadet Files
USMA Cadet Pay and Accounts System
United States Military Academy Candidate Files
United States Military Academy Entrance Examination
  Result Files
USMA Institutional Research Survey File
United States Military Academy (USMA) Medical Qualifi-
  cation Files
United States Savings Bond Register Files
Vehicle Registration System (VRS) and Correctional Re-
  porting System (CRS)
Visiting Scientist Research Associates Reference Files
Wage and Separation Information Report Files
Waiver of Premium Files
World War I Awards and Decorations Card File

Department of the Navy

ADMIRALTY CLAIMS FILES

All individuals who have asserted claims under the Public
Vessels Act and Suits in Admiralty Act against the Department of the Navy.

Assistant Judge Advocate General (Civil Law), Office of
the Judge Advocate General, Navy Department, Washington,
DC 20370, (202) 694-5436.

AFFIRMATIVE CLAIMS FILES

All individuals against whom the navy has claims sounding
in tort, and all individuals who are in the military or are dependents of military members and have been provided
medical care by a naval medical facility for injuries resulting
from such tortious conduct.

Assistant Judge Advocate General (Civil Law), Office of the
Judge Advocate General, Navy Department, Washington,
DC 20370, (202) 694-5436.

AIRCRAFT MISHAP

Designated naval aviators, naval flight officers, crew members,
and maintenance personnel involved in or contributing to a
navy or marine aircraft accident, incident, or ground accident.

Director of Aviation Safety, Naval Safety Center, NAS,
Norfolk, VA 23511, (804) 444-4200.

Request for information should contain: Individual's name,
current address, military status, and Social Security account
number. Visitors will be required to provide military or
comparable civilian identification cards.

ARTICLE 69 PETITIONS

Navy and Marine Corps personnel who were tried by courts-
martial which were not reviewed by the Navy Court of Military Review, when such service members have petitioned
the judge advocate general pursuant to Article 69, Uniform
Code of Military Justice, for review.

Deputy Assistant Judge Advocate General (Military Justice),
Office of the Judge Advocate General, Navy Department,
Washington, DC 20370, (202) 694-5436.

Request for information should contain: Individual's name,
address, military status, and Social Security account number.
Personal visits may be made to the Military Justice Division,
Office of the Judge Advocate General, Room 2518, Navy
Annex, Arlington, VA. Visitors will be required to provide
military or comparable civilian identification, e.g., armed
forces identification card, driver's license, etc.

ARTICLE 73 PETITIONS FOR NEW TRIAL

Navy and marine corps personnel who submitted petitions
for new trial to the judge advocate general within two years
after approval of their court-martial sentence by the con-
vening authority but after their case had been reviewed by
the Navy Court of Military Review or Court of Military
Appeals, if appropriate.

Deputy Assistant Judge Advocate General (Military Justice),
Office of the Judge Advocate General, Navy Department,

Washington, DC 20370, (202) 694-5436. Written requests for information must be signed by the requesting individual. Personal visits may be made to the Military Justice Division, Office of the Judge Advocate General, Room 2518, Navy Annex, Arlington, VA. Visitors will be required to provide military or comparable civilian identification cards.

ARTICLE 138 COMPLAINT OF WRONGS

Active duty navy and marine corps personnel who have submitted complaints of wrong pursuant to Article 138, UCMJ, which have been forwarded to the Secretary of the Navy for final review of the complaint and the proceedings had thereon.

Deputy Assistant Judge Advocate General (Military Justice), Office of the Judge Advocate General, Navy Department, Washington, DC 20370, (202) 694-5436. Personal visits may be made to the Military Justice Division, Office of the Judge Advocate General, Room 2815, Navy Annex, Arlington, VA. Visitors will be required to provide military or comparable civilian identification cards, e.g., armed forces identification card, driver's license, etc.

BAD CHECK LIST

Individuals who have passed bad checks.

Consolidated Package Store Manager, Naval Support Activity, 136 Flushing Avenue, Brooklyn, NY, (212) 522-1928.

Requests for information should contain: military identification or civilian identification containing description of individual.

BAD CHECKS AND INDEBTEDNESS LISTS

Patrons of navy exchanges and commissary stores who have passed bad checks; recruits who have open accounts with navy exchanges; patrons who have made COD mail order transactions; those patrons who make authorized charge or credit purchases where their accounts are maintained on the basis of an identifying particular such as name, Social Security account number or service number.

Director, Controller Division (FM), Navy Resale System Office, 3rd Avenue and 29th Street, Brooklyn, NY 11232, (212) 965-5000.

Request for information should contain: Individual's name, Social Security account number, and activity where he had his dealings. A list of other offices the requester may visit will be provided after initial contact is made at the office listed above. Visitors must provide the following proof of identity: Name, date of birth, place of birth, father's first name, and mother's maiden name.

BASE SECURITY INCIDENT SYSTEM

Individuals involved in or witnessing incidents requiring the attention of base security personnel.

Commanding officer of the activity in question.

CIVIL LITIGATION FILES

Applicants or navy civilian employees paid from appropriated or nonappropriated funds who have filed civil suit or are anticipated to file suit in connection with pre- or post-employment actions.

Director of Civilian Manpower Management (Code 1A), Department of the Navy, Washington, DC 20390, (202) 694-4547.

Request for information should contain: Individual's name and the requester's signature. Personal visits may be made to the Office of Legal Counsel, OCMM, Room 106, Pomponio Plaza, 1735 N. Lynn Street, Arlington, VA.

COMMERCIAL FIDELITY BOND
INSURANCE RECORDS

Civilian and military personnel assigned to navy exchanges, whom the duly constituted authority (usually a board of investigation appointed by the base commanding officer) has established to be guilty of a dishonest act which has resulted in a loss of money, securities, or other property, real or personal, for which the exchange is legally liable.

Director, Controller Division (FM), Navy Resale System Office, 3rd Avenue and 29th Street, Brooklyn, NY 11232, (212) 965-5000.

Request for information should contain: Individual's name, payroll or military service number, and activity where individual had dealings. A list of other offices the requester may visit will be provided after initial contact is made at the office listed above. At the time of a personal visit, requesters must provide the following proof of identity: Name, date of birth, place of birth, father's first name, and mother's maiden name.

CONFLICTS OF INTEREST AND
EMPLOYMENT ACTIVITIES

Active-duty, reserve, or retired military personnel and present and former civilian employees of the navy or marine corps who, by reason of their own inquiries or inquiries or complaints of Department of the Navy or other federal officials or other appropriate persons, have been the subject of correspondence with the judge advocate general concerning the legality of outside federal, state, or private employment or financial interests; dual federal employment; postretirement employment; defense-related employment; foreign employment; acceptance of gifts, gratuities, or benefits from government contractors, foreign governments, or other sources; or other possible violations of federal conflicts of interest or standards of conduct laws or regulations.

Assistant Judge Advocate General (Civil Law), Office of the Judge Advocate General, Navy Department, Washington, DC 20370, (202) 694-5436. Personal visits may be made to: Administrative Law Division (Code 13), Office of the Judge Advocate General, Room 2511, Navy Annex, Arlington, VA. Visitors will be required to provide military or comparable civilian identification cards.

COUNTRY FILES AND TRIAL OBSERVER FILES

Any members of the navy or marine corps, their dependents, or civilian employees of the Department of the Navy who were tried before a foreign criminal tribunal.

Office of the Judge Advocate General of the Navy, International Law Division (Code 10), Navy Department, Washington, DC 20360, (202) 697-9161.

COURT-MARTIAL CASE REPORT

All individuals having appeared before a special or general court-martial within the preceding two fiscal years.

Circuit Military Judge, ATLANTIC Judicial Circuit, Navy-Marine Corps Trial Judiciary, Washington Navy Yard, Washington, DC 20374, (202) 433-4160.

Request for information should contain: Individual's name, branch of service, military status, where stationed when tried, and when tried.

COURT-MARTIAL INDEX AND SUMMARY

All accused individuals tried by court-martial convened by a subordinate command.

Staff Judge Advocate, Commander Light Attack Wing, U.S. Pacific Fleet, Naval Air Station, Lemoore, CA 93245, (209) 998-3679 (Chief of Staff).

Request for information should contain: Individual's name, Social Security account number, and year of court-martial. Visitors will be required to provide military or comparable civilian identification cards.

COURT-MARTIAL STATISTICS

Navy and marine corps personnel tried by general courts-martial and by special courts-martial when the special court-martial sentence as finally approved includes a punitive discharge.

Deputy Assistant Judge Advocate General (Military Justice), Office of the Judge Advocate General, Navy Department, Washington, DC 20370, (202) 694-5436. Personal visits may be made to: The Military Justice Division, Office of the Judge Advocate General, Room 2518, Navy Annex, Arlington, VA. Visitors will be required to provide military or comparable civilian identification cards.

DEFENSE CENTRAL INDEX OF INVESTIGATIONS (DCII)

Any person described as a subject, a victim, or a cross-reference in an investigation completed by or for a DOD investigative element when that investigation is retained by the element and the name is submitted for central indexing.

Assistant for Information, Defense Investigative Service (D0020), Washington, DC 20314, (202) 325-9257.

Request for information should contain: Individual's name, and all maiden and alias names under which files may be maintained and personal identifiers listed. Note: Social Security account numbers may be necessary for positive identification of certain records. Personal visits may be made to DIS Information Office, 1000 Independence Avenue, Washington, DC 20314. Visitors will be required to provide military or comparable civilian identification cards.

EMPLOYEE GRIEVANCES, COMPLAINTS, AND ADVERSE ACTION APPEALS

Former and present civilian employees of the Department of the Navy, and applicants for employment with the Department of the Navy.

Department of the Navy Employee Appeals Review Board, Washington, DC 20360, (202) 696-4621.

Request for information should contain: Individual's name, employing office, and appropriate identification card.

EMPLOYEE RELATIONS INCLUDING DISCIPLINE, EMPLOYEE GRIEVANCES, COMPLAINTS, ETC.

Navy civilian employees, applicants, and former employees paid from appropriated funds who are serving under career, career-conditional, temporary, and excepted service appointments on whom discipline, grievances, or complaints records exist and who have made discrimination complaints; civilian employees paid from appropriated funds; Filipino employees who have appealed cases or had cases reviewed by CINCPAC under Filipino employment policy instructions.

Director of Civilian Manpower Management, Department of the Navy, Washington, DC 20390, (202) 694-4547; Commanding officers or heads of navy staff headquarters and field activities.

Request for information should contain: Individual's name, Social Security account number, and signature of the requester. Personal visits may be made to the Director of Civilian Manpower Management, Department of the Navy, Washington, DC, or the navy activity at which the requesting individual is employed.

EQUAL OPPORTUNITY INFORMATION AND SUPPORT SYSTEM

Navy personnel who are involved in formal or informal investigations involving aspects of equal opportunity and/or who have initiated, or were the subject of, correspondence concerning aspects of equal opportunity.

Privacy Act Coordinator, Washington, DC 20370, (202) 694-3390.

Request for information should contain: Individual's name, Social Security account number, rank/rate, military status, and signature of the requester. Personal visits may be made to the Chief of Naval Personnel, Arlington Annex (FB 2), Room 1066, Washington, DC for assistance with records located in that building; or the individual may visit the local activity to which attached, for access to locally maintained records. Visitors will be required to provide military or comparable civilian identification cards.

ETHICS FILE

Civilian and military lawyers authorized to practice before a court-martial or Navy Court of Military Review and who by their personal or professional conduct have demonstrated that they are so lacking in competency, integrity, or ethical or moral character as to be unacceptable as counsel before a court-martial or Navy Court of Military Review.

Deputy Assistant Judge Advocate General (Military Justice), Office of the Judge Advocate General, Navy Department, Washington, DC 20370, (202) 694-5436. Written requests must be signed by the requesting individual. Personal visits may be made to the Military Justice Division, Office of the Judge Advocate General, Room 2518, Navy Annex, Arlington, VA. Visitors will be required to provide military or comparable civilian identification cards.

FEDERAL TORT CLAIMS FILES

Any individuals who have filed claims against the navy under the Federal Tort Claims Act.

Assistant Judge Advocate General (Civil Law), Office of the Judge Advocate General, Navy Department, Washington, DC 20370, (202) 694-5436.

FIDUCIARY AFFAIRS RECORDS

All active duty, fleet reserve, and retired members of the navy and marine corps who have been medically determined to be mentally incapable of managing their financial affairs, their appointed or prospective trustees, and members' next of kin.

Assistant Judge Advocate General (Civil Law), Office of the Judge Advocate General, Navy Department, Washington, DC 20370, (202) 694-5436.

FOREIGN CLAIM FILES

All individuals who have filed claims against the Department of the Navy under the Foreign Claims Act.

Assistant Judge Advocate General (Civil Law), Office of the Judge Advocate General, Navy Department, Washington, DC 20370, (202) 694-5436.

GENERAL COURT-MARTIAL RECORDS OF TRIAL

Active-duty navy and marine corps personnel tried by general court-martial.

Deputy Assistant Judge Advocate General (Military Justice), Office of the Judge Advocate General, Navy Department, Washington, DC 20370, (202) 694-5436.

Request for information should contain: Individual's name, date of trial, and signature of the requesting individual. Personal visits may be made to the Military Justice Division, Office of the Judge Advocate General, Room 2518, Navy Annex, Arlington, VA. Visitors will be required to provide military or comparable civilian identification cards.

INDEBTEDNESS CORRESPONDENCE FILE

Enlisted personnel who have been the subjects of letters of indebtedness.

Legal office, USS KITTY HAWK (CV063), FPO San Francisco, CA 96601.

INTERNATIONAL LEGAL HOLD FILES

Military personnel, members of the civilian component, and their dependents who have had criminal charges lodged against them in the Philippine judicial system.

Staff Judge Advocate, Commander, U.S. Naval Base, Subic Bay, FPO San Francisco, CA 96651.

Request for information should contain: Individual's name, rate, and service number. Personal visits may be made to Room 202, Building 156, U.S. Naval Base, Subic Bay. Visitors will be required to provide military or comparable civilian identification cards.

INVESTIGATORY (FRAUD SYSTEM)

Individuals suspected or convicted of fraud in navy procurement; individuals suspected of being involved in theft of government property or conflict of interest in matters relative to navy procurement.

Deputy IG (Investigations), Naval Material MAT 01G1, CP 5, Room 422, Washington, DC 20360, (202) 325-0198.

Request for information should contain: Individual's name, address, Social Security account number, and business affiliation. Personal visits, after written visit notification, may be made to Chief of Naval Material, Deputy IG (Investigations), MAT 09G1, GP 5, Room 422, Washington, DC 20360, between 9:00 A.M. and 3:00 P.M. Visitors will be required to provide military or comparable civilian identification cards.

JAG MANUAL INVESTIGATIVE RECORDS

Any individual who participated in, who was involved in, who incurred an injury, disease, or death in, who was intoxicated (drugs or alcohol) during, before, or after, or who had an interest in any accident, incident, transaction, or situation involving or affecting the Department of the Navy, naval personnel, or any procedure, operation, material, or design involving the Department of the Navy.

Assistant Judge Advocate General (Civil Law), Office of the Judge Advocate General, Navy Department, Washington, DC 20370, (202) 694-5436.

LABOR MANAGEMENT RELATIONS RECORDS SYSTEM

Navy civilian employees paid from appropriated and nonappropriated funds, who are involved in a grievance which has been referred to an arbitrator for resolution; navy civilian employees involved in the filing of an unfair labor practice complaint which has been referred to the Assistant Secretary of Labor-Management Relations; union officials; union stewards; and representatives.

Director of Civilian Manpower Management (Attention: Code 04), Department of the Navy, Washington, DC 20390, (202) 694-5911.

LEGAL ASSISTANCE CARD FILES

Authorized military and civilian personnel and dependents who have sought legal assistance from a legal assistance office established within the Department of the Navy.

Assistant Judge Advocate General (Civil Law), Office of the Judge Advocate General, Navy Department, Washington, DC 20370, (202) 694-5436.

LEGAL DIARY

Individuals, both staff and student, who have caused other than routine actions to be taken by the Legal Division of the Administrative Department, Naval Air Technical Training Center, Lakehurst, NJ.

Legal Assistance Referral Officer, NATTCL, (201) 323-2571.

LEGAL OFFICE LITIGATION/CORRESPONDENCE FILES

Criminal and civil plaintiffs/defendants involved in litigation against or involving Puget Sound Naval Shipyard.

Commander, Puget Sound Naval Shipyard, Bremerton, WA, 98314, (206) 478-3161; legal officer (Code 107), Puget Sound Naval Shipyard.

Request for information should contain: Individual's name, rank/rate, shop or badge number, and Social Security account number.

LIST OF CUBAN EXILE FAMILIES AT U.S. NAVAL BASE GUANTANAMO BAY, CUBA

Navy civilian employees at Unites States Naval Base Guantanamo Bay, Cuba, who are Cuban exiles.

Financial Management Officer, Shore Activities Readiness Division, CINCLANTFLT, Norfolk, VA 23511, (804) 444-6873.

Request for information should contain: Employment dates of head of household while employed at GITMO, activity employed by, ARC number and names, and location of dependents. Personal contacts with Cuban exiles are not normally envisioned. However, any personal contacts will be at CINCLANTFLT Compound, Building 3 North, Room 206. Visitors will be required to produce military or comparable civilian identification cards and to answer same questions required by letter inquiry.

MILITARY CLAIMS FILES

All individuals who have filed claims under the Military Claims Act against the Department of the Navy.

Assistant Judge Advocate General, Civil Law, Office of the Judge Advocate General, Navy Department, Washington, DC 20370, (202) 694-5436.

MILITARY JUSTICE CASE FILE

All personnel who, while attached to command, have had charges referred to either non-judicial punishment under Article 15, UCMJ, or summary, special, or general courts-martial; or who are under investigation pursuant to Article 32, UCMJ; or who have been returned to command in custody of shore patrol or civil authorities with civil or military charges pending.

Legal Office, USS KITTY HAWK (CV-63), FPO San Francisco, CA 96601.

MILITARY JUSTICE CORRESPONDENCE FILE

Active duty, retired, and discharged navy and marine corps personnel who were the subject of military justice proceedings.

Deputy Assistant Judge Advocate General (Military Justice), Office of the Judge Advocate General, Navy Department, Washington, DC 20370, (202) 694-5436. Personal visits may be made to the Military Justice Division, Office of the Judge Advocate General, Room 2518, Navy Annex, Arlington, VA.

MILITARY JUSTICE DOCKET CARD FILE, ACTIVE/CLOSED

Military personnel who are faced with the possibility of disciplinary or administrative action and who have been assigned counsel.

Officer in Charge, Naval Legal Service Office, Pensacola, FL 32508, (904) 452-2551.

Request for information should contain: Individual's name, Social Security account number and military rank.

MILITARY PERSONNEL AND CIVILIAN EMPLOYEES' CLAIMS

All individuals who have filed claims against the Department of the Navy under the Military Personnel and Civilian Employees' Claims Act and all common carriers against whom recovery has been sought by the Department of the Navy.

Assistant Judge Advocate General (Civil Law), Office of the Judge Advocate General, Navy Department, Washington, DC 20370, (202) 694-5436.

MISSING PERSONS AND DEATH CASES

Dependents of employees of the navy missing or deceased as a result of their employment.

Director of Civilian Manpower Management, Department of the Navy, Washington, DC 20390, (202) 694-4547.

Request for information should contain: Requester's name, job or position title, series and grade, organizational assignment, employing activity name and address, and official signature or witnesses mark. Personal visits may be made to the Office of Civilian Manpower Management, 1735 North Lynn Street, Arlington, VA. Proof of identification will consist of a Department of Defense (DOD) or navy building pass or identification badge, driver's license, or other type of identification bearing a photograph or signature or both, or by providing verbal information that can be verified by reference to the file information requested.

MOTOR VEHICLE ACCIDENTS AND INJURIES

Navy military personnel, regardless of duty status, who are injured as a result of a motor vehicle accident or are the operator of one of the vehicles involved in such an accident; navy military and civilian personnel who are involved in a government motor vehicle accident or a private motor vehicle accident on navy property; navy civilian employees who are injured in a motor vehicle accident during the course of their official duties.

Director of Occupational Safety, Health, and Support Programs, Naval Safety Center, NAS, Norfolk, VA 23511, (804) 444-3345.

Request for information should contain: Individual's name, address, military status, and Social Security account number. Visitors will be required to provide military or comparable civilian identification cards.

NAD HAWTHORNE POLICE RECORDS SYSTEM (NADHPRS)

Persons who have committed crimes and offenses; persons suspected of crimes or offenses; victims of crimes and offenses; witnesses to crimes and offenses; persons contacted during field interviews because of proximity to a crime or offense, resemblance to suspects, or possession of property or instruments similar to those involved in crime or offense; juveniles involved in offenses peculiar to nonadults; persons involved in proposed and actual adverse personnel actions that require police services for accomplishment; persons who have requested police services.

Security Office, Building 15, NAD Hawthorne, Hawthorne, NV 89415. For information by phone, Office of the Secretary of the Army, (202) 545-6700.

Request for information should contain: Individual's name, Social Security account number, military status, sex, date and place of birth, and current address. Visitors will be required to provide military or comparable civilian identification cards.

NAVAL EDUCATIONAL DEVELOPMENT

Individuals on whom there have been formal/informal investigations or inquiries conducted as directed by CNET and higher authority.

Staff inspector general and his immediate staff.

Information is available to individuals but is restricted to the extent that the source of the information is not revealed.

NAVY PERSONNEL REHABILITATION SUPPORT SYSTEM

Navy personnel (officers and enlisted) who have been identified as drug or alcohol abusers, or who have undergone counseling and rehabilitation for drug or alcohol abuse in navy drug or alcohol rehabilitation facilities; recovered alcoholic and nonalcoholic professional personnel who work part-time helping alcoholics; active duty navy recovered alcoholics who voluntarily help their commands develop alcoholism prevention programs; navy personnel convicted by court-martial and sentenced to confinement; or who were in pretrial confinement.

Privacy Act Coordinator, Navy Department, Washington, DC 20370, (202) 694-3390; or the local activity to which the individual is assigned.

Request for information should contain: Individual's name, Social Security account number, military status, address and signature of requester. Those inquiring about records at confinement centers must have their signature notarized, if not confined at time of request. Personal visits may be made to the Chief of Naval Personnel, Arlington Annex

(FOB 2), Room 1066, for assistance with records located in the Bureau of Naval Personnel; individual may also visit the local activity concerned. Visitors will be required to provide military or comparable civilian identification cards.

NAVSEA RADIATION INJURY CLAIM RECORDS

Individuals employed by the navy and navy contractors who have alleged radiation injury from radiation exposure associated with naval nuclear propulsion plants.

Naval Sea Systems (Code 08), Washington, DC 20362, (202) 692-3381.

Request for information should contain: Individual's name, organization where employed at time of alleged injury, and supporting evidence.

NIS INVESTIGATIVE FILES SYSTEM

Persons in the following categories who require access to classified defense information prior to August 1972: Active and inactive members of the naval service, civilian personnel employed by the Department of the Navy (DON); industrial and contractor personnel, civilian personnel being considered for sensitive positions, boards, conferences, etc.; civilian personnel who worked or resided overseas; Red Cross personnel; civilian and military personnel accused, suspected, or victims of felonious type offenses, or lesser offenses impacting on the good order, discipline, morale, or security of the DON; civilian personnel seeking access to or seeking to conduct or operate any business or other function aboard a DON installation, facility, or ship; civilian or military personnel involved in the loss, compromise, or unauthorized disclosure of classified material/information; civilian and military personnel who were of counter-intelligence interest to the DON.

Director, Naval Investigative Service, 2461 Eisenhower Avenue, Alexandria, VA 22331, (202) 325-0198.

Request for information should contain: Individual's name and at least one additional personal identifier such as date and place of birth; Social Security number, or military service number. Persons submitting written requests must properly establish their identity to the satisfaction of the NIS. Where a question exists a signed, notarized statement or other certified form of identification will be required. Personal visits by requesters should be confined to the Naval Investigative Service headquarters at the above address. Visitors will be required to provide military or comparable civilian identification cards. Attorneys or other persons acting on behalf of a subject of a record must provide a notarized authorization from the subject of the record.

"NONSCOPE" CLAIMS FILES

All individuals who have filed claims under the "Nonscope" Claims Act against the Department of the Navy.

Assistant Judge Advocate General (Civil Law), Office of the Judge Advocate General, Navy Department, Washington, DC 20370, (202) 694-5436.

OTSU PRISON HEALTH AND COMFORT ITEMS

Individuals who have been imprisoned under Japanese law and jurisdiction for various offenses.

Commander, Fleet Activities, FPO Seattle 98762.

Request for information should contain: Individual's rank/rate, name, branch of service, and Social Security account number. Files are maintained in logistics within command; requesters may visit this office for review of their files during normal working hours. Proof of identification is limited to armed forces identification cards or passports.

RECORDS OF LITIGATION

Individuals who have filed suit in federal or state court within southern California seeking relief other than monetary damages.

Commandant, Eleventh Naval District, San Diego, CA 92132, (714) 235-3022.

Request for information should contain: Individual's name, case caption, and year court action filed. Personal visits may be made to the District Legal Office, Headquarters Eleventh Naval District, San Diego, CA 92132. Visitors will be required to provide military or comparable civilian identification cards.

RELIEF OF ACCOUNTABLE PERSONNEL FROM LIABILITY FOR LOSSES OF PUBLIC FUNDS

Accountable navy and marine corps military and civilian disbursing personnel and collection agents who request relief from liability for losses of public funds in their custody.

Assistant Judge Advocate General (Civil Law), Office of the Judge Advocate General, Navy Department, Washington, DC 20370, (202) 694-5436. Personal visits may be made to the Administrative Law Division, Office of the Judge Advocate General, Room 2511, Navy Annex, Arlington, VA. Visitors will be required to provide military or comparable civilian identification cards.

SAVINGS DEPOSIT

Navy members still declared missing in action in the Vietnam conflict.

Command Officer, Navy Finance Center, Celebrezze Federal Building, Cleveland, OH 44199, (216) 522-5511.

Only the member or executor or beneficiary of estate will be provided information. Request for information should contain: Individual's name and Social Security account number. Personal visits may be made to the Navy Family Allowance Activity, Room 967, Celebrezze Federal Building, 1240 E. 9th St., Cleveland, OH 44199.

SECURITY INSPECTION AND VIOLATION SYSTEM

Individuals involved in security violations.

Commanding officer of the activity in question.

SHOPLIFTING

Individuals having previously been picked up for shoplifting.

Navy Exchange Officer, Naval Support Activity, 136 Flushing Avenue, Brooklyn, NY 11251, (212) 522-1028.

Request for information should contain: Individual's name and Social Security account number. Visitors will be required to provide military or comparable civilian identification cards.

SPECIAL COURTS-MARTIAL RESULTING IN BAD CONDUCT DISCHARGES OR CONCERNING COMMISSIONED OFFICERS

Navy and marine corps personnel tried by special court-martial and awarded a bad conduct discharge, and all navy and marine corps commissioned officers tried by special court-martial.

Deputy Assistant Judge Advocate General (Military Justice), Office of the Judge Advocate General, Navy Department, Washington, DC 20370, (202) 694-5436.

Request for information should contain: Individual's name and date of trial of the individual concerned. Personal visits may be made to the Military Justice Division, Office of the Judge Advocate General, Room 2518, Navy Annex, Arlington, VA. Visitors will be required to provide military or comparable civilian identification cards.

STAFF JUDGE ADVOCATE'S MEMORANDUM FILE

Any navy or marine corps personnel facing disciplinary or administrative action requiring the personal attention of the commandant, Fourth Naval District.

Staff Judge Advocate, Fourth Naval District, Naval Base, Philadelphia, PA 19112, (215) 755-4526.

Request for information should contain: Name and address of requester, military status of requester, Social Security account number of requester, and subject matter of request. Personal visits may be made to Room 103, Building 6, Naval Base, Philadelphia, PA. Visitors will be required to provide military or comparable civilian identification cards.

STUDENTS AWAITING LEGAL, MEDICAL ACTION ACCOUNT

All student personnel assigned to NATTCL, whether or not they successfully completed training; all students on board that are not enrolled in class.

Personnel Office Supervisor, Office of the Secretary of the Army, The Pentagon, Washington, DC 20310, (202) 545-6700.

SUMMARY COURTS-MARTIAL AND NON–BAD CONDUCT DISCHARGE COURTS-MARTIAL NAVY AND MARINE CORPS

Navy and marine corps enlisted personnel tried by summary court-martial or by special court-martial which did not result in a bad conduct discharge.

Deputy Assistant Judge Advocate General (Military Justice), Department of the Navy, Washington, DC 20370, (202) 694-5436.

Request for information should contain: Individual's name, the type of court-martial (summary or special), the name of the command which held the court-martial, and the date of the court-martial proceedings. Personal visits may be made to the Military Justice Division, Office of the Judge Advocate General, Room 2518, Navy Annex, Arlington, VA. Visitors will be required to provide military or comparable civilian identification cards.

TENANT COMMAND DISCIPLINARY ACTION FILE

Members of tenant commands at Naval Air Station, Lemoore, CA, who are suspected of having violated the Uniform Code of Military Justice and who are the subject of investigative reports.

Station Judge Advocate, Naval Air Station, Lemoore, CA 93245, (209) 998-3254. Personal visits may be made to the Office of the Station Judge Advocate, Naval Air Station, Lemoore, CA. Visitors will be required to provide military or comparable civilian identification cards.

UNCOLLECTIBLE ACCOUNTS

Any individual incurring indebtedness to the United States by receiving health care treatment or examination services funded by the Navy Medical Department.

Chief, Bureau of Medicine and Surgery, 23rd and E Streets, NW, Washington, DC 20070, (202) 254-4153.

Request for information should contain: The full name of the debtor, the military or dependency status of the debtor, and the location and approximate dates of treatment or examination. Personal visits may be made to the Comptroller, Bureau of Medicine and Surgery, 23rd and E Streets, NW, Washington, DC 20070. Visitors will be required to provide military or comparable civilian identification cards.

U.S. POSTAL SERVICE INDEMNITY CLAIMS FILES

All persons who have filed claims with the U.S. Postal Service for loss of or damage to mailed matter, and which claims have been paid by the U.S. Postal Service and thereafter forwarded for reimbursement by the Department of the Navy pursuant to 39 U.S.C. 712.

Assistant Judge Advocate General (Civil Law), Office of the Judge Advocate General, Navy Department, Washington, DC 20370, (202) 694-5436.

For any Department of the Navy file not previously listed, individuals should contact:

- Active and civilian: Chief of Naval Personnel, The Pentagon, Washington, DC 20370.
- Reserve: Naval Reserve Personnel Center, 4400 Dauphine Street, New Orleans, LA 70146.
- Retired: National Personnel Records Center, Military Personnel Records — Navy, 9700 Paige Blvd., St. Louis, MO 63132.

Following is a list of the remaining files maintained by the Department of the Navy. Anyone interested in obtaining information from any of these files should contact the individual agency or the Secretary of Defense, The Pentagon, Washington, DC 20301.

ADP Budget
Academic Potential Coding
Academic Registration System
Access Control System
Active Duty Navy and Marine Corps Death System (Civilian/ Overseas Death Certificate)
Administrative Civilian Personnel Management System
Administrative Files System
Administrative Personnel Management System
Application for U.S. Navy Ration Permit
Appraisals of Performance Record System
Area Coordinator Information and Operation Files
Armed Forces Health Professional Scholarship System
Author Publication Index
Automated Student Information System
Aviation Medical Officer's Report
Aviation Training Jacket
Bibliography
Bingo Winners
Blood Donor Program Files
Bond Accounting
Bureau of Medicine and Surgery Headquarters Personnel System
Bureau of Medicine and Surgery Personnel Management Information System
Career Development Program for Communicators
Casualty Information Support System
Civilian Pay System
Civilian Personnel Administrative Services Record System
Civilian Personnel Security Files
Civilian Volunteer Form Disaster Preparedness Unit 2.1.1
Claims File, Navy Exchange, Guam
Combined Federal Campaign
Commercial Invoice Payments History System
Commissary Control Program
Commissary Store Monetary Allowance Records
Commonwealth Pass Application Form

Communications Security Report (Personnel Section)
Computer Assisted Manpower Analyses System (CAMAS)
Congressional Biographical Data Index
Continuing Education Tutor File
Contract Field Service File
Correspondence Files
Curricular Office Student Grade Summary
Curricular Officer Student Training and Information Files
DODCI Course Evaluation System
DODCI Student Biography System
DODCI Student Record System
Decedent Affairs Records System
Design of Training Systems Data Base — Instructor File
Determinations on Origins of Disabilities for Which Military Members Have Retired
Directory of Retired Regular and Reserve Judge Advocates
Diving Accidents and Injuries
Diving Log
Duty Free Vehicle Log
Employee Assistance Program Case Record System
Employee Explosives Certification Program
Employee Salary and Overtime Report/Budget Book
Enlisted Development and Distribution Support System
Enlisted Master File Automated System
Faculty Activity Record — Report of Teaching and Professional Activities
Family Housing Assignment Application System
Family Housing Requirements Survey Record Systems
Federal Housing Administration Mortgage Insurance System
Field Training Assistance Representatives (FTAR) File
File of Records of Acquisition, Transfer and Disposal of Privately Owned Vehicles
Fleet Ballistic Missile Submarine Demo and Shakedown Operation Crew Evaluation
Flight Instruction Standardization and Training (FIST) Jacket
Gasoline Ration System
Health Programs, Insurance and Annuities
Housing Referral Services Records System
Individual Faculty/Support Personnel Files
Individual Flight Activity Report
Individual Merchandise Control Record
Industrial Relations Personnel Records
Intelligence Reserve Personnel Management File
JAG Corps Officer Personnel Information
Job Evaluation, Position Classification, Job Grading, Position Management, Etc.
Joint Uniform Military Pay System (JUMPS)
Kidney Transplant Histocompatibility Study
Laboratory Information System (LABIS)
Large Dollar Volume Purchasers
Large Purchases in Navy Exchange
Large Sales Slips; Navy Exchange, Guam
Layaway Sales Records
Legal Records System
Listing of Personnel — Sensitive Compartmented Information
Living Quarters Allowance
Local Automated Personnel Information System (LAPIS) — Prototype
Low Quality Recruiting Report (CNET Report 1130-1)

Mail Order Customer Listing
Mail Orderly
Maintenance of Housing Unit
Manhour Accounting System
Medical Department Training Records System
Medical Treatment Record System
Midshipman Pay System
Military and Civilian Employee Dependents Hurricane
  Shelter Assignment List
Military Pay System
Minority Group Identification File
Models for Organizational Design and Staffing (MODS)
NAME/LEAD Processing System
NPS Graduates Historical File
NROTC Educational Development Records
Naval Attache Files
Naval Audit Personnel Development System
Naval Educational Development Records
Naval Health Research Center Data File
Naval Home Resident Information System
Naval Material Command Contingency/Emergency Plan-
  ning Cadre
Naval Officer Development and Distribution Support System
Naval Research Reserve Program Personnel Accounting System
Naval Reserve Law Program Officer Personnel Information
Naval Reserve Officer Training Corps Pay System
Naval Reserve Security Group Personnel Records
Naval Security Group Personnel Security/Access Files
Naval Training Information System
Navy Automated Civilian Manpower Information System
  (NACMIS)
Navy Central Clearance Group (NCCG) Records
Navy Civilian Career Management Inventory and Referral
  System
Navy Clemency and Parole Board Files
Navy Discharge Review Board Proceedings
Navy Exchange, Guam — Major Appliance Contracts
Navy Exchange Security Investigation
Navy Lodge Records
Navy Medical Department, Inpatient Data System
  MED-6300-2
Navy Medical Department, Medical Board Data System
Navy Personnel Evaluation System
Navy Personnel Records System
Navy Recruiting Command Attrition Tracking System
Navy Recruiting Support System
Navy Research and Development Planning Summary
  (DD-1634) System
Navy Strategic Weapons System Personnel and Training
  Evaluation Program
Navy Technical Reports System
Navy Work United Information System
Next of Kin Information for Sea Trial Riders
Nonappropriated Fund Activity Information Support
  System
Nuclear Program Interview and Screening
Occupational Injury and Illness
Office of the Judge Advocate General, Reporting
  Questionnaire

Officer Master File Automated System
Officer Promotion System
Officer Selection and Appointment System
Organization Locator and Social Roster
POW/MIA Captivity Studies
Payroll and Employee Benefits Records
People Files
Personal Commercial Affairs Solicitation Privilege File
  System
Personal Injury and Illness Reports on Civilian and
  Government-Service Seamen Employed on MSC Ships
Personal Services and Dependents Services Support System
Personnel Automated Data System (PADS)
Personnel Data Base Application/Student Instructor Per-
  formance Module
Personnel Information System
Personnel Management and Training Research Statistical
  Data System
Personnel Resources Information System for Management
  (PRISM)
Personnel Security Eligibility Information System
Personnel Transportation System
Pet Registration
Physical Disability Evaluation Proceedings
Pre-registration System
Principal Investigator Record of Active Contracts
Private Relief Legislation
Privately-owned Tax-free Vehicle Records Cards, Tax-free
  Gasoline Record Cards
Professional Qualifications Records (PQR's)
Project Analysis and Control System (PAC)
Property Accountability Records
Puget Sound Naval Shipyard, Navy Exchange Tobacco Sales
Ration Card, Luxury Permit Record Cards
Record of Import and Export of Foreign Made Auto Vehicles
  Into and Out of Australia
Record of Issue, Prescription Safety Glasses
Record System for Civilian Employees of Nonappropriated
  Fund (NAF) Activities
Recruiting Enlisted Selection System
Recruitment, Employment, and Internal Placement
Resale System Military Management Information System
Reserve Pay System
Reserve Personnel History File
Reservists Reporting for Active Duty for Training, Back-
  ground Questionnaires
Retired Pay System
Roster, Naval Reserve Law Companies
Salary Report for Budget for PARS, IMMS, and Non-ADP
Seismic Survey List of Companies Involved in Outer
  Continental Shelf
Sight Conservation Program
Slot Machine Winnings
Special Intelligence Personnel Access File
Special Membership Listing of the Organizational
  Recreation Association
Special Order Record; NEX Guam
Statements of Employment (Regular Retired Officers)
Statements of Employment and Financial Interest

Status of Downed Naval Aviation Personnel, Southeast Asia
    Operations
Students at Civilian Universities
Suggestions and Awards Record System
Summary Debriefs of Former Prisoners of War
Supervisor's Authorization for Issuance of Prescription
    Ground Safety Glasses
Supervisor's Report of Potential to Perform and Reference
    Check Records System
Support Personnel – Faculty Personnel Billet
    Count/Billet Cost System
Technical Paper/Author Cross Index System
Temporary Lodging Allowance
Tests and Examinations Record System
Training and Employee Development Record System
Travel Allowance Claims Record System
Travel Pay System
USAREU/USAFE Ration Card
VGA Personnel and Manpower Information System
    (PERMIS)
Vehicle Control System
Volunteer Tutorial Program
Weapons Registration
Welfare and Recreation Ticket Selection Program
Youth Activities Association Membership Record

National Security Agency/Central Security Service

Persons calling or corresponding with the National Security
Agency/Central Security Service (NSA/CSS) concerning
Congressional inquiries; job opportunities; Freedom of
Information and Privacy Act requests; suggestions, comments, or other requests for information; registering complaints; requesting appropriate security clearance and permission to visit; requesting or requiring information relating
to litigation or anticipated litigation; and employees or
assignees registering complaints or requesting information
with respect to equal employment opportunities; requesting inquiry or investigation by the inspector general; requesting advice, opinions, or assistance from the general
counsel or provided the general counsel, with respect to con-
flict-of-interest issues.

Information Officer, National Security Agency/Central
Security Service, Ft. George G. Meade, MD 20755, (301)
688-6311.

Following is a list of the files maintained by the NSA
agency. Anyone interested in obtaining information from
any of these files should contact the appropriate agency
head or the Secretary of Defense, The Pentagon, Washington,
DC 20301.

NSA/CSS Access, Authority and Release of Information File
NSA/CSS Applicants
NSA/CSS Cryptologic Reserve Mobilization Designee List
NSA/CSS Equal Employment Opportunity Data

NSA/CSS Health, Medical and Safety Files
NSA/CSS Motor Vehicles and Carpools
NSA/CSS Payroll and Claims
NSA/CSS Personnel File
NSA/CSS Personnel Security File
NSA/CSS Time, Attendance and Absence
NSA/CSS Training

United States Marine Corps

ABSENTEE PROCESSING FILE

Marine corps absentees and deserters; marines in the custody
of civil authorities, foreign and domestic; marines who fail
to comply with orders to new duty stations; suspected and
convicted absentees and deserters who have returned to
military control within the last two years.

Commandant of the Marine Corps (Code MP), Headquarters,
U.S. Marine Corps (Code MP), Washington, DC 20380,
(202) 694-2500; or the commanding officer of the activity
in question.

ACCIDENT AND INJURY REPORTING SYSTEM

Military or civilian employees who are involved in accidents
which result in lost time, government or private property
damage, or destruction and personal injury or death.

Commanding officer of the activity in question.

BASE SECURITY INCIDENT REPORTING SYSTEM

Individuals involved in witnessing or reporting incidents requiring the attention of base security or law enforcement
personnel.

Commanding officer of the activity in question.

BUSINESS COMPLAINT FILE

Businesses which have generated complaints by clients at
the Marine Corps Legal Assistance Office.

Commanding General (Attention: Tri-Command Legal), Marine Corps Base, Camp Lejeune, NC 28542, (919) 451-
3218.

CIGARETTES SALES ABUSE FILE

PX patrons who have bought large quantities of cigarettes
over a period of time.

Exchange Officer, Marine Corps Exchange 2 21, Marine
Corps Supply Activity, Philadelphia, PA 19146. (Closed
down in 1976, but information available by mail.)

CORRESPONDENCE BRANCH, JA DIVISION, HQMC CORRESPONDENCE CONTROL FILES

Marines or former marines who have been the subject of
correspondence from a member of Congress, a high level

official in the federal executive branch, parents of such an individual, individual marines, or members of the general public which correspondence concerns legal matters.

Director, Judge Advocate Division, Headquarters, U.S. Marine Corps (Code JA), Washington, DC 20380, (202) 694-2737.

DELINQUENT MAIL ORDER ACCOUNT SYSTEM

Any woman marine who purchases clothing until payment has been completed or payment is delinquent in excess of 90 days.

Women Marine's Clothing Outlet, Depot Service and Supply Department, Marine Corps Recruit Depot, Parris Island, SC 29905, (803) 525-3391.

DELIVERY AGREEMENT

Marines arrested under criminal warrant by civilian authorities.

Staff judge advocate/legal officer, local marine corps activity.

If local activity concerned is not known, contact the Director, Judge Advocate Division, Headquarters, U.S. Marine Corps (Code JAC), Washington, DC 20380, (202) 694-2737.

DESERTER INQUIRY FILE

Marine corps absentees and deserters; marines in the hands of civil authorities, foreign and domestic; marines who fail to comply with orders to new duty stations; suspected and convicted absentees and deserters who have returned to military control within the last 90 days.

The Commandant of the Marine Corps (Code MP), Headquarters, U.S. Marine Corps, Washington, DC 20380, (202) 694-2927.

DISHONORED PERSONAL CHECK RECORDS AND WITHDRAWAL OF CHECK CASHING PRIVILEGES LISTS

All military personnel, active and retired; their authorized dependents and dependents of deceased military retirees; marine corps exchange employees.

Commanding officer of activity concerned.

DRUG/ALCOHOL ABUSE REPORTING PROGRAM

All military personnel who have been tested for, identified, evaluated, apprehended, or rehabilitated for drug or alcohol abuse; all military personnel who have been granted drug abuse exemption; all military personnel who are seeking assistance in drug or alcohol abuse programs.

Commanding officer of the activity in question.

IN HANDS OF CIVIL AUTHORITIES CASE FILE

All military personnel who are in the hands of civil authorities or have charges pending against them by civil authorities.

Commanding General (Attention: Adf), Marine Corps Base, Camp Lejeune, NC 28542, (919) 451-2414.

INDEBTEDNESS CORRESPONDENCE RECORD

All marines with respect to whom indebtedness correspondence has been received at Headquarters, U.S. Marine Corps.

Director, Judge Advocate Division, Headquarters, U.S. Marine Corps (Code JA), Washington, DC 20380, (202) 694-2737.

MAGISTRATE COURT CASE FILES

Civilians pending or tried by the assigned federal magistrate for crimes committed on military reservation at Camp Lejeune, NC.

Commanding General (Attention: SJA), Marine Corps Base, Camp Lejeune, NC 28542, (919) 451-5177.

MARINE CORPS COMMAND LEGAL FILES

Civilian employees of the DOD or guests who have visited marine corps installations, who have allegedly committed criminal offenses at a military installation, or whose conduct has been subject to investigation; any marine or navy service member who is the subject of disciplinary action under the provisions of the Uniform Code of Military Justice (Title 10, U.S. Code 801, et seq.); who has been the subject of administrative discharge action pursuant to the current edition of Marine Corps Order P1900.16); or who has been the subject of an investigation (JAG Manual investigations) convened pursuant to the provisions of the Uniform Code of Military Justice or the Manual of the Judge Advocate General (the current edition of JAG Instruction 5800.7) or any other type of investigation or inquiry.

Commanding officer of the unit concerned. If unit is not known, information may be obtained from Director, Judge Advocate Division, Headquarters (Code JA), U.S. Marine Corps, Washington, DC 20380, (202) 694-2737.

Request for information should contain: Individual's name, Social Security account number, and military status. Proof of identity may be established by military identification card or DD-214 and driver's license.

MILITARY POLICE INFORMATION SYSTEM (MILPINS)

Military personnel and civilians who have come in contact with the military police as victims, suspects, or witnesses to incidents or complaints reported to the provost marshal.

Installation provost marshal of activity concerned.

PERFORMANCE FILE

All members of the marine corps on active duty or in a reserve status who are under investigation, indictment, or in the process of a criminal proceeding by military or civilian authorities.

Director, Judge Advocate Division, Headquarters, U.S. Marine Corps (Code JA), Washington, DC 20380, (202) 694-2737.

PET REGISTRATION

Owners of pets residing on naval reservations; owners of pets in quarantine as the result of biting complaints; owners of pets who are subject of nuisance complaints.

Commanding officer of the activity in question.

PRISONER RECORDS

All military personnel who are confined in a detailed, adjudged, or sentenced status.

Commanding officer of the activity in question.

2ND MARINE AIRCRAFT WING GENERAL CORRESPONDENCE FILES FOR LEGAL ADMINISTRATION

Individuals who have appealed nonjudicial punishment; individuals who have been recommended for administrative discharge whose cases have been reviewed by a staff judge advocate; individuals who have been served with civil process; individuals on whom correspondence has been received from civilian and military agencies or persons requesting assistance in the completion of legal-related problems.

Staff Judge Advocate, Staff Code 17, Marine Corps Air Station, Cherry Point, NC 28533, (919) 466-2444.

STAFF JUDGE ADVOCATE WORKING PAPERS

Persons appealing Article 15 punishment and traffic court rulings; persons referred to a court-martial; persons awaiting special and general court-martial; persons confined at a correctional facility in excess of 30 days; lawyers assigned to be on call for a given period; officers punished under Article 15, Uniform Code of Military Justice; and persons selected to sit as members of a court-martial.

Commanding General, Marine Corps Development and Education Command (Code b 052), Marine Corps Base, Quantico, VA 22134, (703) 640-2776.

UNIT PUNISHMENT BOOK

Any enlisted marine who is charged with a violation of the Uniform Code of Military Justice.

Unit commanders of USMC or Marine Reserve units authorized to administer nonjudicial punishment. If unit imposing punishment cannot be determined, information may be sought from Director, Judge Advocate Division, Headquarters, U.S. Marine Corps (Code JA), Washington, DC 20380, (202) 694-2737.

Request for information should contain: Individual's name, Social Security account number, and military status. Proof of identity may be established by military identification card or DD 214 and driver's license.

Following is a list of the remaining files maintained by the USMC. Anyone interested in obtaining information from any of these files should contact the appropriate agency head or the Secretary of Defense, The Pentagon, Washington, DC 20301.

Activity Check In/Check Out File
Adjutant Services Selection Discharge Working Files
Alphabetical Roster of Officers Attached to HQMC in the Washington D.C. Area
Amateur/Citizen Band Radio Operation Request and Authorization File
Amateur Radio Operator's File
Armory Access and Individual Weapons Assignments
Assignment and Occupancy of Family Housing Records
Automated Leave and Pay System (ALPS)
Bachelor Housing Registration Records System
Biographical Files
Bond and Allotment (B&A) Systems
Car Pool Locator List
Centralized Automated Reserve Pay System (CAREPAY)
Civilian Labor Projection, Operations and Maintenance, MC Budget Report (Job Procedure 5576)
Customer Service Records/Special Accounts
Dealer's Record of Sale of Rifle or Pistol, State of California
Depot Maintenance Management Subsystem (DMMS)
Directory and Locator Mail Service
Employment Referral Questionnaire for Members of Reserve Units
Equipment and Weapons Receipt or Custody Files
Examination Division Records System
Exchange Privilege Authorization Log
Federal Building Number 2 (FB 2), Car Pool Locator File
File of Confidential Statements of Employment and Financial Interests
Financial Assistance/Indebtedness Files
Firearms Transaction Record
First Marine Division Personnel Assigned to Operation New Arrivals
Flight Qualification Record
Flight Readiness Evaluation Data System (FREDS)
Headquarters Marine Corps Locator Files
Headquarters, U.S. Marine Corps Emergency Recall Listing Essential Personnel
Housing Referral Services Records System
Identification Card Control

Individual Accounts of Mail Order Clothing (Bill File)

Individual Drill Attendance and Retirement Transaction Card (IDART) File

Individual Training Records/Files for Training Related Matters

Individual Uniform Clothing Records

Inspection of Government Property Assigned to Individual

Insurance Files

Joint Military Pay System/Manpower Management System (JUMPS/MMS)

Judge Advocate Division "D" Files

Laundry Charge Accounts Records

Library Patron File

Listing of Retired Marine Corps Personnel

MDSVEN Vendor Directory

Manpower Management System (MMS)

Marine Corps Aircrew Performance/Qualification Information

Marine Corps Club and Mess Membership

Marine Corps Education Program Applicant/Participant Information File

Marine Corps Enlisted Aircrewman Qualification Jacket

Marine Corps Exchange Service Station Work Orders

Marine Corps Locator Files

Marine Corps Military Personnel Records (OQR/SRB)

Marine Corps Military Personnel Records Access Files

Marine Corps Motion Picture/Instructional Television (ITV) Archives

Marine Corps Naval Aviator/Naval Flight Officer Qualification Jacket

Marine Corps Recreation Facilities

Marine Corps Still Photographic Archives

Message Release/Pickup Authorization File

Narrative Biographical Data With Photos (NAVMC Form 10573)

Naval Aviator/Naval Flight Officer Reporting Management System (NANFORMS)

Non-Appropriated Fund (NAF) Employee and Applicant Personnel Records

Organization Clothing Control File

Passenger Transportation Program

Pay Vouchers for Marine Corps Junior Reserve Officer Training Course Instructors

Per Diem and Travel Payment System

Permanent Record of Enlisted Flight Time

Personal History Card File

Personal Property Program

Personnel Management Subsystem, Resource Control System (RCS)

Personnel Management Working Files

Personnel Procurement Working Files

Personnel Security Eligibility and Access Information System

Personnel Services Working Files

Primary Management Efforts (PRIME)/Operations Subsystem

Recreation Fund Property Records

Register/Lineal Lists

Reserve Personnel Management Information System (REPMIS)

Retired Pay/Personnel System (RPPS)

Source Data Automated Fitness Report System (SDAFRS)

Standard Licensing Procedures for Operators of Military Motor Vehicles

Temporary Record of Enlisted Flight Time

Transportation Data Financial Management System (TDFMS)

Truth Teller/Static Listings

Vehicle Control System

Weapons Registration

Work Measurement Labor Distribution Cards

Working Files, Division Supply Sections and Wing Supply Sections

Working Files, Inspection Division, Headquarters, U.S. Marine Corps

For any USMC files not previously listed, individuals should contact:

- Active and reserve: Commandant of the Marine Corps (Code MSRB), The Pentagon, Washington, DC 20380, (202) 694-2578.

- Retired, terminated, or deceased: National Personnel Records Center, Military Personnel Records — Marine Corps, 9700 Paige Blvd., St. Louis, MO 63132.

- Civilian: Civilian Personnel Records, 111 Winnebago St., St. Louis, MO 63118.

Uniformed Services University of the Health Sciences

For information concerning any files maintained by the Uniformed Services University of the Health Sciences, contact the Registrar Office, 6917 Arlington Road, Bethesda, MD 20014, (301) 295-2120.

Applicant Record System

Employee Assistance Program Case Record System

Payroll System

Personnel Files

Student Record System

Training and Employee Development Record System

Office of the Joint Chiefs of Staff

For information concerning any files maintained by the Office of the Joint Chiefs of Staff, contact the Director of Administrative Services, Office of the Joint Chiefs of Staff, The Pentagon, Washington, DC 20301, (202) 695-0866.

Directorate Administrative Services Message Information System (DASMIS)

Military Personnel Files

OJCS Medals and Awards Files and Reports System: Microfilmed Historical Awards
Personnel Security File, Security Division, DAS

Defense Advanced Research Projects Agency

For information concerning any files maintained by the
Defense Advanced Research Projects Agency, contact the
Administrative Officer, ARPA, 1400 Wilson Blvd., Arlington,
VA 22209, (202) 694-1440.

ARPA Basic File
ARPA Personnel
Biographical Sketch
Travel File

U.S. Department of Health and Human Services

Following is a list of the agencies and subagencies of the U.S. Department of Health and Human Services, with their abbreviations.

HHS	U.S. Department of Health and Human Services
OS	Office of the Secretary
ASAM	Assistant Secretary for Administration and Management
ASC	Assistant Secretary, Comptroller
ASL	Assistant Secretary for Legislation
ASPA	Assistant Secretary for Public Affairs
ASPE	Assistant Secretary for Planning and Evaluation
ES	Executive Secretary
IATF	Interagency Task Force
OCA	Office of Consumer Affairs
OCR	Office for Civil Rights
OGC	Office of the General Counsel
SP	Office of Special Projects
R	Regions
RD	Regional Director
RO	Regional Office
OHD	Office of Human Development
AOA	Administration on Aging
OCD	Office of Child Development
ONAP	Office of Native American Programs
ORS	Office of Rehabilitation Services
OYD	Office of Youth Development
RSA	Rehabilitation Services Administration
FDA	Food and Drug Administration
PHS	Public Health Service
ADAMHA	Alcohol, Drug Abuse, and Mental Health Administration
CDC	Center for Disease Control
HRA	Health Resources Administration
HSA	Health Services Administration
NIH	National Institutes of Health
OASH	Office of Assistant Secretary for Health
SRS	Social and Rehabilitation Service
OCSE	Office of Child Support Enforcement
SSA	Social Security Administration
C	Commissioner
EA	External Affairs
HA	Hearings and Appeals
HI	Health Insurance
MA	Management and Administration
PO	Program Operations
PP	Programs Policy and Planning

Office of the Secretary

ADMINISTRATIVE CLAIMS, HHS/OS/OGC

Individuals who are involved in litigation with HHS (regarding matters within the jurisdiction of the department) either as plaintiffs or as defendants in both civil and criminal matters; individuals who file administrative complaints with HHS alleging discrimination in health and social services, or discrimination under government financial contracts, and also individuals subject to personnel actions which they consider adverse.

The General Counsel, Office of the General Counsel, HHS, North Building, Room 5228, 200 Independence Ave., SW, Washington, DC 20201, (202) 245-7741.

CASE FOLLOWING SYSTEM, HHS/OS

Persons filing complaints or involved in litigation concerning discrimination in employment, education, benefits, or services on the basis of race, color, sex, national origin, or handicap in programs and institutions using funds controlled by HHS.

Assistant Director (Administration and Management, Office for Civil Rights, 200 Independence Ave., SW, Room 3557, North Building, Washington, DC 20201, (202) 245-6585.

CLAIMS FOR DAMAGE, INJURY, OR DEATH, HHS/RO

Federal employees and nonfederally employed individuals submitting claims for financial remuneration due to damage, injury, or death which is government-related.

Director, Administrative Services Division, DHHS/Regional III, Room 3300, 3535 Market St., Philadelphia, PA 19104, (215) 596-6460.

Request for information should contain: Individual's name, relationship to claim/claimant, work address, and phone.

COMPLAINT FILES, CONTRACT COMPLIANCE DIVISION, HHS/OS

Individuals who file complaints with HHS alleging race, color, religion, sex, or national origin discrimination in employment by employers who receive federal contracts and for whom HHS has been assigned compliance-agency responsibility.

Assistant Director (Administration and Management), Office for Civil Rights, 200 Independence Ave., SW, Room 3557, North Building, Washington, DC 20201, (202) 245-6585.

Request for information should contain: Individual's name and address as well as a copy or summary of allegations contained in the original complaint.

COMPLAINT FILES, HEALTH & SOCIAL SERVICES DIVISION, HHS/OS

Individuals who file complaints with HHS concerning race/ethnic/sex discrimination in the delivery of health and social services or in admission to certain federally funded training programs.

Assistant Director (Administration and Management), Office for Civil Rights, 200 Independence Ave., SW, Room 3557, North Building, Washington, DC 20201, (202) 245-6585.

Request for information should contain: Individual's name and address as well as a copy or summary of allegations contained in the original complaint.

COMPLAINT FILE, HIGHER EDUCATION DIVISION, HHS/OS

Individuals who file complaints with HHS concerning discrimination under Executive Order 11246, Title VI, Title IX, and PHSA.

Assistant Director (Administration and Management), Office for Civil Rights, 200 Independence Ave., SW, Room 3557, North Building, Washington, DC 20201, (202) 245-6585.

Request for information should contain: Individual's name and address, and contractor/institution and address.

COMPLAINT FILES ON NURSING HOMES, HHS/R RD OLTCSE

Persons who make complaints on nursing homes certified under Title XVIII (Medicare) and XIX (Medicaid) of the Social Security Act.

Assistant Director (Administration and Management), Office for Civil Rights, 200 Independence Ave., SW, Room 3557, North Building, Washington, DC 20201, (202) 245-6585.

Request for information should contain: Individual's name and address, as well as a copy or summary of allegations contained in the original complaint.

COMPLAINT LOG, ELEMENTARY-SECONDARY DIVISION, HHS/OS

Persons filing complaints with HHS alleging discrimination on the basis of race, color, sex, or national origin in elementary and secondary education programs receiving federal funds through HHS.

Assistant Director (Administration and Management), Office for Civil Rights, 200 Independence Ave., SW, Room 3557, North Building, Washington, DC 20201, (202) 245-6585.

Request for information should contain: Individual's name and address, as well as a copy or summary of allegations contained in the complaint.

COMPLAINTS AND INQUIRIES RECORDS— MISCELLANEOUS HHS

Current federal employees of HHS.

Employee's supervisor of personnel office.

Request for information should contain: Individual's name, organization in which employed, and date of birth.

CONFLICT OF INTEREST RECORDS SYSTEM, HHS

Incumbents of HHS positions, the duties of which are such that an incumbent's financial interests, debts, ownership of real property, or outside employment may come in conflict with the incumbent's official duties.

For incumbents who are in position under the executive schedule, office of the secretary staff office heads, or regional directors: Deputy Assistant Secretary for Personnel and Training, Office of Personnel and Training, HHS, 200 Independence Ave., SW, Washington, DC 20201, (202) 245-6746. For incumbents of other positions included in this record system, the employee's personnel officer.

Request for information should contain: Individual's name, position title, grade and series, and organization in which located.

CONFLICT OF INTEREST – STANDARDS OF CONDUCT RECORDS, HHS/OS/OGC

Current and past HHS employees who are or have been the subject of conflict of interest or standards of conduct inquiries or determinations.

The General Counsel, Office of the General Counsel, HHS, North Building, Room 5228, 200 Independence Ave., SW, Washington, DC 20201, (202) 245-7741.

CONSUMER COMPLAINT CORRESPONDENCE SYSTEM HHS/OS/OCA

Individual consumers.

Director, Administrative Management & Finance, Room 3332, North Building, 200 Independence Avenue, SW, Washington, DC 20201, (202) 245-6396.

DISCRIMINATION COMPLAINTS RECORDS SYSTEM, HHS

Individuals or organizations which have consulted an EEO counselor or have filed a complaint alleging discrimination on the basis of race, color, religion, sex, national origin or age, because of a determination or decision made by an HHS official.

Assistant Director (Administration and Management), Office for Civil Rights, 200 Independence Ave., SW, Washington, DC 20201, (202) 245-6585.

Request for information should contain: Individual's name, date of birth, agency in which employed or agency in which the complaint arose if different from employing agency, the approximate date, and the kind of action taken.

EMPLOYEE ALCOHOLISM, DRUG ABUSE, AND EMOTIONAL PROBLEM COUNSELLING AND REFERRAL RECORDS, HHS

Department employees who have been counselled for work adjustment, or personal or emotional health problems which may be related to the misuse of alcohol or drugs.

Employee's personnel officer.

Request for information should contain: Individual's name, grade, organization in which employed, and date of birth.

FAMILY EDUCATIONAL RIGHTS AND PRIVACY ACT–SCHOOL RECORDKEEPING PRACTICES CORRESPONDENCE AND COMPLAINT SYSTEM, HHS/OS/FERPA

Individuals who have made inquiries regarding complaints or have filed complaints alleging violations of the provisions of the Family Educational Rights and Privacy Act of 1974; and those who have commented to HHS on its proposed rules and practices.

Head, FERPA Office, Room 5643, North Building, 200 Independence Ave., SW, Washington, DC 20201, (202) 245-7488.

Request for information should contain: Individual's name and date of previous correspondence, if known; for complaint/investigative material, name, and any identification number assigned.

GRIEVANCE RECORDS FILED UNDER PROCEDURES ESTABLISHED BY LABOR-MANAGEMENT NEGOTIATIONS, HHS

Current federal employees of HHS covered by a collective bargaining agreement.

Employees' personnel officers.

Request for information should include: Individual's name, grade, title, and organizational unit when contacting the system manager.

GRIEVANCES FILED UNDER THE INFORMAL GRIEVANCE PROCEDURES, HHS

HHS employees individually or as a group who have requested personal relief in a matter of concern or dissatisfaction which is subject to the control of HHS management.

Employee's personnel officer. Individuals who have filed grievances are aware of that fact and have been provided information in writing concerning the disposition of the grievance.

Request for information should contain: Individual's name, organization in which employed, date of birth, and approximate date of the filing of the informal grievance.

INDOCHINA REFUGEE AND SPONSOR SYSTEM, HHS/OS/IATF

Individuals who are refugees from Indochina as defined in the authorizing legislation and individuals who offer to sponsor or assist refugees.

Interagency Task Force, Department of State, Washington, DC 20520, (202) 632-5184.

Additional Files

Following is a list of the remaining files maintained by this agency. Anyone interested in obtaining information from any of these files should contact the appropriate agency head or the Secretary of Health and Human Services, 200 Independence Ave., SW, Washington, DC 20201.

Accounting Records of Payments to Individuals from Agency and Regional Financial Management and Disbursing Offices, HHS/OS/ASC 1
Applicants for Employment Records, HHS
Biographies and Photographs of HHS Officials, HHS/OS/ASPA
Central Registry of Individuals Doing Business with HHS, HHS/OS/ASC 2
Congressional Biographies, HHS/OS/ASL

Congressional Correspondence Unit, HHS/OS/ASL
Congressional Grants Notification Unit, HHS/OS/ASL
Consumer Liaison Contacts, HHS/OS/OCA
Consumer Mailing Lists, HHS/OS/OCA
Departmental Parking Control Policy, HHS/OS/ASAM/FE
DHHS Motor Vehicle Operator Records, HHS
Directory, Federal, State, County, and City Government
  Consumer, HHS/OS/OCA Offices
Employee Appraisal Program Records, HHS
Employee Housing Service, HHS/OS/OSPO
Employee Suggestion System, HHS/OS/DMPD
Executive Development Records System, HHS
Federal Advisory Committee Membership Files, HHS/OS
Federal Employees Occupational Health Program Records,
  HHS
Freedom of Information Case File and Correspondence
  Control Index, HHS/PA/FOIA
Garn Income Maintenance Experiment, HHS/OS/ASPE
Health Insurance Study, HHS/OS/ASPE
Interviews with Selected Women in the Health Professions
  Schools, HHS/OS/ASPE
Invention Reports Submitted to the Department of Health
  and Human Services by Its Employees, Grantees,
  Fellowship Recipients, and Contractors
Investigatory Material Compiled for Law Enforcement
  Purposes System, HHS/OS/ASAM/IS
Investigatory Material Compiled for Security and Suit-
  ability Purposes System, HHS/OS/ASAM/IS
Massachusetts Sample Survey of Developmentally Disabled
  Persons, HHS/OS/ASPE
New Orleans Louisiana Review, HHS/OS
Office of External Liaison— Consumer Correspondence
  Files, HHS/OS/OCA
OGC — Attorney Applicant Files in the Executive Office
OGC Directory
OS Federal Women's Program and Privacy Act — Talent Bank,
  HHS/OS/FWP
OS Spanish Speaking Program and Privacy Act — Talent Bank,
  HHS/OS
Panel Study of Income Dynamics (Annual National Sample
  of Heads of Households); Also Known as the Michigan
  Longitudinal Study, HHS/OS/ASPE
Pay, Leave, and Attendance Records, HHS
Personnel Records in Operating Offices, HHS
Photo Identification Cards System, HHS/OS/ASAM/IS
Rural and Urban Income Maintenance Experiments, HHS/
  OS/ASPE
Safety Management Information System (DHHS Accident,
  Injury, and Illness Reporting System), HHS/OS/ASAM/
  SM
Seattle/Denver Income Maintenance Experiments, HHS/
  OS/ASPE
Secretary's Correspondence Control System, HHS/OS/ES
Secretary's Official Files, HHS/OS/ES
Suitability for Employment Records, HHS
Telephone Directory/Locator System, HHS/OS/ASAM/
  OMPT
Volunteer EEO Support Personnel Records, HHS

Office of the Assistant Secretary of Health

ALASKA PIPELINE COLD STRESS STUDY–HHS/CDC/
NIOSH

Persons exposed to cold weather while working directly
on the Trans-Alaska Pipeline.

Office of the Assistant Secretary of Health, HHS, 200 Independence Avenue, SW, Washington, DC 20201, (202)
245-1824.

BYSSINOSIS STUDY–HHS/CDC/NIOSH

Employees at cotton textile mills and a sample of people
from the general population.

Office of the Assistant Secretary of Health, HHS, 200 Independence Avenue, SW, Washington, DC 20201, (202)
245-1824.

COMPLAINTS AND INQUIRIES RECORDS–
MISCELLANEOUS, HHS/OS

Current federal employees of the department.

Employee's personnel officer.

CONFLICT OF INTEREST RECORDS SYSTEM,
HHS/OS

Incumbents of HHS positions, the duties of which are of
such a nature that incumbent's financial interests, debts,
ownership of real property, or outside employment may
come in conflict with the incumbent's official duties.

For incumbents who are in position under the executive
schedule: office of the secretary staff office heads; or
regional directors: Deputy Assistant Secretary for Personnel and Training, Office of Personnel and Training,
HHS, 200 Independence Avenue, SW, Washington, DC
20201, (202) 245-6746. For incumbents of other positions
included in this records system, the employee's personnel
officer.

CONTROL SYSTEM FOR DELAYED, CRITICAL, OR
SENSITIVE CASE INQUIRIES, HHS/SSA

Social Security beneficiaries or persons inquiring on their
behalf who are reporting failure to receive a check or
checks which they believe are due, or are inquiring about
other matters which have been determined to be of a
critical or sensitive nature.

Nearest Social Security Administration office.

COURT CASE RECORD FILE, HHS/SSA

Plaintiffs who have filed court actions against the Secretary of HHS.

Director, Bureau of Retirement and Survivors Insurance,
6401 Security Boulevard, Baltimore, MD 21235, (301)
594-1900.

DISCRIMINATION COMPLAINTS RECORDS SYSTEM, HHS/OS

Individuals or organizations which have consulted an EEO counselor or have filed a complaint alleging discrimination on the basis of race, color, religion, sex, national origin, or age, because of a determination or decision made by an HHS official.

Employee's personnel officer.

EMPLOYEE CONDUCT INVESTIGATIVE RECORDS, HHS/FDA

Employees or former employees, or special government employees of FDA, who are alleged to have violated FDA or departmental regulations and/or federal statutes.

Privacy Coordinator (HF-50), Food and Drug Administration, 5600 Fishers Lane, Rockville, MD 20852, (301) 443-1814.

GENERAL CRIMINAL INVESTIGATION FILES, HHS/SSA

Reported violators of federal and state criminal laws on Social Security Administration property.

Chief, Protective Security Section, Office of Management, Budget and Personnel, 6401 Security Blvd., Baltimore, MD 21235, (301) 594-6970.

GRIEVANCE RECORDS FILED UNDER PROCEDURES ESTABLISHED BY LABOR-MANAGEMENT NEGOTIATIONS, HHS/OS

Current federal employees of the department covered by a collective bargaining agreement.

Employee's personnel officer.

GRIEVANCES FILED UNDER THE INFORMAL GRIEVANCE PROCEDURES, HHS/OS

Department employees, individually or as a group, who have requested personal relief in a matter of concern or dissatisfaction which is subject to the control of department management.

Employee's office head.

HEALTH EFFECTS STUDY OF DUST AND DIESEL EXHAUST ON NON-COAL UNDERGROUND MINERS, HHS/CDC/NIOSH

Metal and non-metal underground miners (excluding coal miners).

Privacy Act Coordinator, Center for Disease Control, Management Analysis Office, Atlanta, GA 30333, (404) 329-3061.

LITIGATION ACTIVITY FILE, HHS/SSA

Plaintiffs who have filed court actions against the Secretary of HHS.

Director, Bureau of Retirement and Survivors Insurance, 6401 Security Boulevard, Baltimore, MD 21235, (301) 594-1900.

MEDICAL AND TEST RECORD RESULTS OF INDIVIDUALS INVOLVED IN NIOSH LABORATORY STUDIES, HHS/CDC/NIOSH

Volunteer subjects from the general population.

Privacy Act Coordination Center for Disease Control, Management Analysis Office, Atlanta, GA 30333, (404) 329-3061.

MORTALITY STUDY OF TENNESSEE VALLEY AUTHORITY (TVA) WORKERS EXPOSED TO COAL HANDLING PROCESSES, HHS/CDC/NIOSH

TVA workers exposed to coal handling processes from 1955 to 1965.

Privacy Act Coordinator, Center for Disease Control, Management Analysis Office, Atlanta, GA 30333, (404) 329-3061.

MORTALITY AND MORBIDITY STUDY AMONG OIL SHALE WORKERS, HHS/CDC/NIOSH

United States Bureau of Mines employees from 1948 to 1956 in Rifle, CO; employees at five oil companies in Rifle, CO from 1966 through 1969; employees in retort process at Bureau of Mines in Laramie, WY.

Privacy Act Coordinator, Center for Disease Control, Management Analysis Office, Atlanta, GA 30333, (404) 329-3061.

PROGRAM INTEGRITY CASE FILES, HHS/SSA

Persons suspected of having violated the criminal provisions of the Social Security Act where substantial basis for criminal prosecution exists, and defendants in criminal prosecution cases.

Branch Chief, Investigations Branch, Office of Management, Budget and Personnel, 6401 Security Boulevard, Baltimore, MD 21235, (301) 934-3235.

Request for information should contain: Individual's name and Social Security account number, any Social Security account number on which he has filed for or received benefits, the type of such claim, and current claim status.

RECORDS OF RESEARCH ON ALCOHOL ABUSERS AND ADDICTS, HHS/ADAMHA/NIAAA

Alcohol abusers and addicts.

Chief, Intramural Research Branch, National Institute on Alcohol Abuse and Alcoholism, Room 493, Wm. A. White Building, Saint Elizabeth's Hospital, Washington, DC 20032, (202) 443-4375.

SOCIAL SECURITY CODE CARDS, HHS/OS/OGC

Individuals who are Social Security claimants or wage-earners who have been the subject of Social Security precedent opinions.

Regional Attorney, HHS, 19th and Stout Streets, Denver, CO 80202.

For information on the following files, contact: Privacy Act Coordinator, Center for Disease Control, Management Analysis Office, Atlanta, GA 30333, (404) 329-3061.

- STUDY OF HEALTH HAZARDS IN ANIMAL CONFINEMENT HOUSING, HHS/CDC/NIOSH

  Persons working in settings where many animals are confined.

- STUDY OF NOISE AND HEARING IN PAPER WORKING INDUSTRY, HHS/CDC/NIOSH

  Paper workers in Ohio.

- STUDY AT WORK-SITES WHERE AGENTS SUSPECTED OF BEING OCCUPATIONAL HAZARDS EXIST, HHS/CDC/NIOSH

  Volunteer subjects employed at specific sites under study.

- STUDY OF WORKERS EXPOSED TO AIRBORNE CARCINOGENS IN WOODWORKING SHOPS, HHS/CDC/NIOSH

  Woodworkers exposed to sawdust and other wood-shop environments.

- STUDY OF WORKERS EXPOSED TO HEAVY METALS (LEAD, CADMIUM, ETC.), HHS/CDC/NIOSH

  Employees exposed to heavy metals at various industrial plants.

- STUDY OF WORKERS EXPOSED TO INORGANIC CHEMICALS, HHS/CDC/NIOSH

  Employees exposed to inorganic chemicals at various industrial plants.

- STUDY OF WORKERS EXPOSED TO MINERAL FIBERS, HHS/CDC/NIOSH

  Employees exposed to mineral fibers at various industrial plants.

- STUDY OF WORKERS EXPOSED TO ORGANIC CHEMICALS, HHS/CDC/NIOSH

  Employees exposed to organic chemicals at various industrial plants.

- STUDY OF WORKERS EXPOSED TO TOLUENE DIISOCYANATE (TDI), HHS/CDC/NIOSH

  Male volunteers at the Olin Chemical Company at Lake Charles, Louisiana.

Additional Files

Following is a list of the remaining files maintained by the Office of the Assistant Secretary of HHS. Anyone interested in obtaining information from any of these files should contact the appropriate agency head or the Secretary of Health and Human Services, 200 Independence Ave., SW, Washington, DC 20201.

Accounts Payable, HHS/HSA/BMS
Accounts Receivable, HHS/HSA/BMS
Administration: Employee Health Records, HHS/NIO/OD
Administration: General Files, HHS/NIH/NEI
Administration: Journal of the National Cancer Institute, HHS/NIH/NCI
Administration: Reader Registration, HHS/NIH/NLM
Adminstrative Disallowance Records for Technical Denials, HHS/SSA
Administrative Services Record System, HHS/HSA/IHS
Advisory Groups: Consultant File, HHS/NIH/NHLI
Alcohol and Drug Education Program—List of National Action Committee for Drug Abuse Education Consultants, HHS/E
American College Testing Service National Sample of 1972-73 High School Juniors, HHS/E
Applicants for Employment Records, HHS/OS
Assistant Secretary for Health Correspondence Control System, HHS/OASH/OPI
Automated Controlled Correspondence Extraction System, HHS/SSA
Biographies: Curricula Vitae, HHS/NIH/NIAMDD
Biographies: Employees and Consultants, HHS/NIH/NIAID
Biographies: Who's Who in the National Cancer Institute, HHS/NIH/NCI
Carrier Medicare Claims Records, HHS/SSA
Claims Folders and Post-Adjudicative Records of Applicants and Beneficiaries for Social Security Administration Benefits, HHS/SSA
Clinical Research: Burkitt's Lymphoma Registry, HHS/NIH/NCI
Clinical Research: Disseminated Breast Cancer, HHS/NIH/NCI
Clinical Research: Urinary Steroid Levels in Breast Cancer Patients, HHS/NIH/NCI
Collaborative Perinatal Project, HHS/NIH/NINCDS
Compensatory Education Study, HHS/E
Concept 71, The National Logitudinal Study of the High School Class of 1972, HHS/E
Congressional Inquiry File, HHS/SSA
Consultant and Site Visitor List, Network of Innovative Schools, HHS/E
Consultants Used in Production of Film on New Opportunities in Education for Women, HHS/E
Contracts: Administration, HHS/NIH/FIC
Contracts: Administration, HHS/NIH/NEI
Contracts: Administration, HHS/NIH/NHLI
Contracts: Administration, HHS/NIH/NIAMDD
Contracts: Administration, HHS/NIH/NICHD
Contracts: Administration, HHS/NIH/NIDR

Contracts: Administration, HHS/NIH/NIGMS

Contracts: Administration, HHS/NIH/NINCDS

Contracts: Carcinogenesis Contracts and Intramural Projects, HHS/NIH/NCI

Contracts: Contract Management System, HHS/NIH/NCI

Contracts: Division of Cancer Control and Rehabilitation, HHS/NIH/NCI

Contracts: NIH Management Records, HHS/NIH/DCG

Contracts: Viral Oncology Contracts, HHS/NIH/NCI

Cooperative Mycoses Study, HHS/CDC/OCD

Correspondence: Executive Secretariat, NIH-HHS/NIH/OD

Correspondence Files, HHS/ADAMHA

Development of Biologic Standards by Breath Analysis, HHS/CDC/NIOSH

Disability Data Record, HHS/SSA

Division of Federal Employee Health, Employee Health Records, HHS/HSA/BMS

Early Warning Indicators of Pesticides Exposure, HHS/CDC/NIOSH

Earnings Recording and Self-Employment Income System, HHS/SSA

Employee Housing Requirements Files, HHS/SSA

Employee Identification Card Files (Building Passes), HHS/SSA

Employee Production and Accuracy Records, HHS/SSA

Environmental Education Program—Curriculum Vitae and Lists of Field Readers, HHS/E

Epidemiologic Study of Special Disease Problems, HHS/CDC/BE

Equipment Field Test Studies, HHS/CDC/NIOSH

ESEA, Title III — Supplementary Educational Centers and Services; Guidance, Counseling and Testing Validators, HHS/E

Federal Private Relief Legislation, HHS/OS/OGC

Fee Ledger System for Representatives, HHS/SSA

Field Reader Candidates in Vocational Education, HHS/E

Field Reader File System

Field Reader Retrieval System, Bureau of Education for the Handicapped, HHS/E

Field Readers Field for HEA, II-B (Library Research and Demonstration and Training Programs), HHS/E

Field Readers to the Office of the Gifted and Talented, HHS/E

Financial Management Systems, HHS/HSA/IHS

Grants: Research, Research Training, Fellowship, and Construction Applications and Awards, HHS/NIH/OD

Group Health Plan System, HHS/SSA

Handicapped Children's Early Education Development Data, HHS/E

Health Insurance Master Record, HHS/SSA

Health Insurance Overpayment Ledger Cards, HHS/SSA

Interpreters of the Deaf, National Advisory Committee on the Handicapped, HHS/E

Investigation of Vascular Access Site Infections, HHS/CDC/BE

Learning Disabilities Mailing List of Potential Applicants for Funding, Bureau of Education for the Handicapped, HHS/E

Mailing List: NIH Guide to Grants and Contracts, HHS/NIH/DRG

Mailing List: NIH Publications and Information, HHS/NIH/DAS

Mailing List: Reprints, HHS/NIH/NIAID

Maryland Psychiatric Case Register, HHS/ADAMHA/NIMH

Master Beneficiary Record, HHS/SSA

Master Files of Social Security Number Holders, HHS/SSA

Medical Fellowships and Educational Loans, HHS/HSA/OA

Medicare Beneficiary Correspondence Files, HHS/SSA

Mortality of Dairymen, HHS/CDC/NIOSH

Motor Vehicle Accident Reports, HHS/OS/OGC

National Council on Educational Research Attendance Lists, HHS/E

National Council on Educational Research Current and Past Information on Members of the Council and Consultants, HHS/E

National Council on Educational Research Mailing Lists, HHS/E

National Health Service Corps (NHSC) Applicant Recruitment and Provider File, HHS/HSA/BCHS

Occupational and Educational Attainments of 1974-1975 College Graduates

Office of Federal Property Assistance, Concerned with Administration of the DHHS Office of Surplus Property Utilization, HHS/RO9

Operation Follow-Up, the National Longitudinal Study of the High School Class of 1972, HHS/E

Panelists for ETV and Special Projects of ESAA for Technical Review of Applications, HHS/E

Panelists for General Assistance Centers — Type B (Lau) for Technical Review of Applications Under CRA, Title IV, HHS/E

Participants in ESEA Title VII Bilingual Education Program National Impact Evaluation of Elementary Programs, HHS/E

Patients Medical Record System PHS Hospitals/Clinics, HHS/HSA/BMS

Pay, Leave and Attendance Records, HHS/OS

Personnel: Guest Workers Visiting Fellows, Student Scientists, HHS/NIH/DPM

Personnel Records in Operating Offices, HHS/OS

PHS Commissioned Corps General Personnel Files and Records, HHS/OASH/OAM

PHS Commissioned Corps Medical Records, HHS/OASH/OAM

PHS Commissioned Corps Officer Board Proceedings, HHS/OASH/OSM

PHS Commissioned Corps Training Files and Materials, HHS/OASH/OAM

PHS Commissioned Corps Unofficial Personnel Files, Leave, Identification, and Privilege Cost Records in Operating Program Offices and Field Stations

PHS Commissioned Officer Grievance, Equal Employment Opportunity, and Disciplinary Files, HHS/OASH/OAM

PHS Commissioned Officer Personnel Data System, HHS/OASH/OAM

Pilot Agricultural Noise Study, HHS/CDC/NIOSH

Presidential Scholars Files of Selected Participants, HHS/E

Quality Assurance Case File

Readers from Community and Junior Colleges

Readers for Cooperative Education Program
Readers for the Developing Institutions Program
Readers for Domestic Mining and Mineral and Mineral Fuel
Conservation Fellowship Program
Readers for the Ethnic Heritage Studies Program
Readers for Higher Education Personnel Training Programs
Readers for International Studies Programs
Readers for Planning Demonstration Centers for Extension
and Continuing Education Programs
Readers for the Public Service Education Program
Readers for Special Community Service and Continuing
Education Projects
Record of Earnings Information Furnished for Non-Program
Purposes, HHS/SSA
Research Resources: H-2 Soluble Antigen and H-2 An-
tiserum, HHS/NIH/NIAID
Research Resources: HL-A Antiserum and Tray Users,
HHS/NIH/NIAID
Resources: Viral Oncology Human Specimen Program,
HHS/NIH/NCI
Requests for Review of Proposed Contracts with Experts
and Consultants, HHS/SSA
St. Elizabeth's Hospital Biometrics System, HHS/ADAMHA/
NIMH
St. Elizabeth's Hospital Social Services Record System,
HHS/ADAMHA/NIMH
Social Security Administration Claims Control System,
HHS/SSA
Social Security Administration Contract Files, HHS/SSA
Suitability for Employment Records, HHS/OS
Supervisory Effects on Worker Safety in the Roofing
Industry, HHS/CDC/NIOSH
Training Manpower Information System, HHS/OS
Unfair Labor Practice Records, HHS/OS
Volunteer EEO Support Personnel Records, HHS/OS

Alcohol, Drug Abuse, and Mental Health Administration

ADMINISTRATIVE RECORDS ON CIVILLY
COMMITTED DRUG ABUSERS UNDER THE
NARCOTIC ADDICT REHABILITATION ACT–
HHS/ADAMHA/NIDA

Civilly committed narcotic addicts.

Medical Records Administrator, Division of Community
Assistance, National Institute on Drug Abuse, Room 712,
Rockwall Building, 11400 Rockville Pike, Rockville, MD
20852, (301) 443-6780.

NATIONAL INSTITUTE ON DRUG ABUSE ADDICTION
RESEARCH CENTER FEDERAL PRISONER AND
NON-PRISONER PATIENT FILES–HHS/ADAMHA/
NIDA

Federal prisoners and nonprisoner volunteers in drug
addiction research program.

Program Assistant, NIDA Addiction Research Center, P.O.
Box 12390, Leestown Road, Lexington, KY 40511,
(606) 255-6812.

PATIENT MEDICAL RECORDS ON PHS BENEFICIARIES
AND CIVILLY COMMITTED NARCOTIC ADDICTS
TREATED AT THE PHS HOSPITALS AT LEXINGTON,
KENTUCKY AND FORT WORTH, TEXAS–HHS/
ADAMHA/NIDA

PHS beneficiaries treated prior to 1967 and civilly committed narcotic addicts treated after 1966.

Medical Record Administrator, Division of Community
Assistance, National Institute on Drug Abuse, Room 7601,
Rockwall Building, 11400 Rockville Pike, Rockville, MD
20852, (301) 443-6780.

SAINT ELIZABETH'S HOSPITAL COURT-ORDERED
FORENSIC INVESTIGATORY MATERIALS FILE–
HHS/ADAMHA/NIMH

Past and present patients committed to Saint Elizabeth's
Hospital pursuant to the District of Columbia and United
States Criminal Codes; alleged criminal offenders sent for
pretrial examination; persons committed after having been
found not guilty by reason of insanity; and mentally ill,
sentenced prisoners transferred from penal institutions.

Chief, Pre-trial Section or, Chief, Post-trial Section, Division
of Forensic Programs, Saint Elizabeth's Hospital, Washington, DC 20032, (202) 562-4000.

STATISTICAL RESEARCH DATA ON ADOLESCENT
RUNAWAYS IN PRINCE GEORGES COUNTY,
MARYLAND, 1962-1965–HHS/ADAMHA/NIMH

Adolescent runaways in Prince Georges County, MD,
1962-1965.

Chief, Mental Health Study Center, 2340 University Boulevard East, Adelphi, MD 20783, (301) 436-6343.

Additional Files

Following is a list of the remaining files maintained by the
Alcohol, Drug Abuse, and Mental Health Administration.
Anyone interested in obtaining information from any of
these files should contact the appropriate agency head or
the Secretary of Health and Human Services, 200 Independence Ave., SW, Washington, DC 20201.

Grant Files Containing Information on Individual Grantees
and Personnel at Grantee Institution, HHS/ADAMHA
Intramural Research Program Records of Research Per-
formed on In- and Out-Patients with Various Types of
Mental Illness, HHS/ADAMHA/NIMH
Maryland Psychiatric Case Register, HHS/ADAMHA/
NIMH

Medical Record Files of Patients Seen in Therapy at the Mental Health Study Center, HHS/ADAMHA/NIMH

Official Contract Files Containing Personal Information on Individual Contractors and Contractors' Employees Used by HHS/ADAMHA

Record of Follow-Up Study of NIMH-Supported Trainees and Fellows, HHS/ADAMHA/NIMH

Record of Guest Workers, HHS/ADAMHA/OA

Record of Staff Fellows, HHS/ADAMHA/OA

Saint Elizabeth's Hospital Area D Community Mental Health Center Citizens Advisory Groups Records, HHS/ADAMHA/NIMH

Saint Elizabeth's Hospital Central Admission Service Non-Admission File System, HHS/ADAMHA/NIMH

Saint Elizabeth's Hospital Clinical Support Services Record Systems, HHS/ADAMHA/NIMH

Saint Elizabeth's Hospital Financial Systems, HHS/ADAMHA/NIMH

Saint Elizabeth's Hospital General Administrative Record System, HHS/ADAMHA/NIMH

Saint Elizabeth's Hospital General Medical/Clinical Records System and Related Indexes, HHS/ADAMHA/NIMH

Saint Elizabeth's Hospital General Security System, HHS/ASAMHA/NIMH

Saint Elizabeth's Hospital Juvenile Education Monitoring System, HHS/ADAMHA/NIMH

The Saint Elizabeth's Medical-Surgical Support Program File System, HHS/ADAMHA/NIMH

Saint Elizabeth's Hospital Multidisciplinary Raw Data Consultation Files, HHS/ADAMHA/NIMH

Saint Elizabeth's Hospital Patients Personal Property Record System, HHS/ADAMHA/NIMH

Saint Elizabeth's Hospital Pre-Service Education Records, HHS/ADAMHA/NIMH

Saint Elizabeth's Hospital Research Project Record, HHS/ADAMHA/NIMH

Saint Elizabeth's Hospital Research Subjects Data Record, HHS/ADAMHA/NIMH

Saint Elizabeth's Hospital Social Services Record System, HHS/ADAMHA/NIMH

Saint Elizabeth's Hospital Training Videotape Records, HHS/ADAMHA/NIMH

Saint Elizabeth's Legal Office Record System, HHS/ADAMHA/NIMH

Center for Disease Control

For information about any CDC system of records, write to the following address, stating which system of records are of interest:

Privacy Act Coordinator, Management Analysis Office, Center for Disease Control, Atlanta, GA 30333.

- BERYLLIOSIS/SARCOIDOSIS STUDY OF BERYLLIUM PLANT WORKERS – HHS/CDC/NIOSH

  Beryllium plant workers, sarcoid registry, sample of general population.

- BETA-NAPTHYLAMINE WORKERS STUDY–HHS/CDC/NIOSH

  Workers using beta-napthylamine.

- COSMETOLOGY WORKERS STUDY (THESAUROSIS)–HHS/CDC/NIOSH

  Workers exposed to cosmetic aerosols.

- DIAGNOSIS OF OCCUPATIONAL DISEASE BY ANALYSIS OF BODY FLUIDS OR TISSUES THROUGH BIOCHEMICAL OR CLINICAL CHEMICAL ANALYSIS–HHS/CDC/NIOSH

  Industrial workers.

- EPIDEMIC INVESTIGATION CASE RECORDS–HHS/CDC/BE

  Patients with disease, their contacts, others with possible exposure, and appropriate controls.

- MACHINISTS EXPOSED TO CUTTING OIL MIST 1938-1967–HHS/CDC/NIOSH

  Male machinists employed between 1938 and 1967 in an industrial plant in Michigan.

- MEDICAL RECORDS OF PATIENTS EXAMINED AT NIOSH IN MORGANTOWN, WEST VIRGINIA–HHS/CDC/NIOSH

  Individuals at excess risk to occupational respiratory diseases, plus a sample of the general population.

- RESPIRABLE INSULATION FIBERS STUDY–HHS/CDC/NIOSH

  Workers exposed to respirable fibers.

- SILICOSIS (BRICK LAYERS) STUDY, NORTH CAROLINA–HHS/CDC/NIOSH

  Brick layers exposed to dust.

- STUDY OF NEW JERSEY MOTOR VEHICLE EXAMINERS EXPOSED TO CARBON MONOXIDE–HHS/CDC/NIOSH

  New Jersey motor vehicle examiners.

- STUDY OF WORKERS EXPOSED TO BENZENE–HHS/CDC/NIOSH

  Workers in the chemical industry exposed to benzene.

- STUDY OF WORKERS EXPOSED TO BLADDER CARCINOGENS–HHS/CDC/NIOSH

  Dichlorobenzidine-exposed workers.

- STUDY OF WORKERS EXPOSED TO CHLORINATED HYDROCARBONS–HHS/CDC/NIOSH

  Tri-chloroethylene, polychlorinated biphenols, ethyline biodiomine, and chloropreme exposed workers in selected plants.

- STUDY OF WORKERS EXPOSED TO FIBROUS GLASS–HHS/CDC/NIOSH

  Employees exposed to fibrous glass from several plants.

- STUDY OF WORKERS EXPOSED TO METHYL BUTYL KETONE–HHS/CDC/NIOSH

  Workers exposed to methyl butyl ketone from selected plants.

- STUDY OF WORKERS EXPOSED TO POLYVINYL CHLORIDE IN THE PLASTICS INDUSTRY AT ASHTABULA, OHIO, AVON LAKE, OHIO, AND LOUISVILLE, KENTUCKY–HHS/CDC/NIOSH

  Workers in the plastic industry at selected plants.

- STUDY OF WORKERS EXPOSED TO TALC–HHS/CDC/NIOSH

  Talc-exposed workers from several locations.

- STUDY OF WORKERS IN TYLER, TEXAS, ASBESTOS PLANT–HHS/CDC/NIOSH

  Employees of Tyler, Texas, asbestos plant.

- SURVEILLANCE OF ACCIDENTAL RUBELLA VACCINATION OF PREGNANT WOMEN–HHS/CDC/BSS

  Women who were vaccinated against rubella immediately preceding pregnancy or accidentally vaccinated during pregnancy.

- SURVEY OF ARIZONA ASBESTOS MINERS AND MILL WORKERS (1969)–HHS/CDC/NIOSH

  Persons working in Arizona asbestos operations in 1969.

- UNION PACIFIC RAILROAD WORKERS, CARBON MONOXIDE STUDY–HHS/CDC/NIOSH

  Selected Union Pacific Railroad workers exposed to carbon monoxide.

- WORKERS EXPOSED TO BIS (CHLOROMETHYL) ETHER AND CHLOROMETHYL METHYL ETHER–HHS/CDC/NIOSH

  Workers exposed to bis (chloromethyl) ether and chloromethyl methyl ether.

- WORKERS EXPOSED TO COTTON-DUST BYSSI-NOSIS, HHS/CDC/NIOSH

  Workers from selected plants in the cotton industry.

Additional Files

Following is a list of the remaining files maintained by the Center for Disease Control. Anyone interested in obtaining information from any of these files should contact the appropriate agency head or the Secretary of Health and Human Services, 200 Independence Ave., SW, Washington, DC 20201.

Alien Mental Waiver Program, HHS/CDC/BE
Alien Tuberculosis Follow-up Program, HHS/CDC/BE
Appalachian Coal Miner Study (1963–1966), HHS/CDC NIOSH
Aspirin Myocardial Infarction Study Files, HHS/CDC/BL
BCG Vaccination Studies for Tuberculosis–Puerto Rico, HHS/CDC/BSS
Bakers (White Lung) Study, HHS/CDC/NIOSH
Biochemical Data System, HHS/CDC/NIOSH
Biodynamics of Lifting in the Sagittal Plane, HHS/CDC/ NIOSH
Bureau of Mines Study in Morgantown, West Virginia, HHS/CDC/NIOSH
Byssinosis Research at Burlington Industries in Ashville, North Carolina, HHS/CDC/NIOSH
Byssinosis Study at Cordova, North Carolina, Klopman Steel Plant, HHS/CDC/NIOSH
Children's Pulmonary Function Study, HHS/CDC/NIOSH
Clinical Associates Roster, HHS/CDC/BSS
Coal Mine Hearing Study, HHS/CDC/NIOSH
Coal Miner Medical Information Processing System, HHS/CDC/NIOSH
Coal Miner Study in Charleston-Beckley, West Virginia, HHS/CDC/NIOSH
Coal Miner Workers Study, HHS/CDC/NIOSH
Control Study Group from the University of Utah for the Cosmetology Study, HHS/CDC/NIOSH
Coronary Drug Project Files, HHS/CDC/BL
Dengue and Schistosomiasis Research Studies, HHS/CDC/ BL
Determination of Normal Baseline Pulmonary Values, HHS/CDC/NIOSH
Diagnosis Program for Detection of Chromosomal Abnormalities in High Risk Patients, HHS/CDC/BL
Diagnostic Methods for Identification of Occupational Diseases Through Biopsy and/or Autopsy Specimens, HHS/CDC/NIOSH
Division of Training Mailing Lists, HHS/CDC/NIOSH
Drug Resistance Study for Tuberculosis, HHS/CDC/BSS
Effects of Carbon Monoxide on Vigilance Performance of College Students, HHS/CDC/NIOSH
Epidemic Intelligence Service Officers Files, HHS/CDC/BE
Epidemiological Study of United States Surface Coal Miners
Fireman Hearing Study, HHS/CDC/NIOSH
Gold Mine (Home Stake) Silicosis Study, HHS/CDC/NIOSH
Hard Rock Miner Mortality Study, HHS/CDC/NIOSH
Hearing and Noise Study of Industrial Workers, HHS/CDC/ NIOSH
Histocompatibility Association of Pneumoconiosis (Black Lung) in Coal Workers, HHS/CDC/NIOSH
Indicators of Physiological and Psychological Strain, HHS/CDC/NIOSH
Individuals Listed in the 1960 American Dental Association Directory, HHS/CDC/NIOSH
Kaiser Aluminum Employees at Ravenswood, West Virginia Study, HHS/CDC/NIOSH
Kennecott Sulfur Dioxide Study, HHS/CDC/NIOSH
Leukemia-Lymphoma Case Surveillance, HHS/CDC/BE

Malaria Surveillance, HHS/CDC/BE

Metabolic Costs and Physiological Responses to Heat in Laboratory Studies, HHS/CDC/NIOSH

Metal Mining Mortality Survey System, HHS/CDC/NIOSH

Metropolitan Atlanta Congenital Malformations Surveillance Program, HHS/CDC/BE

Microbiology Specimen Handling for Testing and Related Data, HHS/CDC/BL

Mine Enforcement Safety Administration (MESA) Dust Measurement, HHS/CDC/NIOSH

Miner/Neighbor Study in Pineville, West Virginia, HHS/CDC/NIOSH

National Coal Miner Study, HHS/CDC/NIOSH

New Mexico Potash Miner Study, HHS/CDC/NIOSH

Noise-Induced Temporary Threshold Shift Data, HHS/CDC/NIOSH

Occupational Vibration Field Studies (Experimental Group), HHS/CDC/NIOSH

Passport File, HHS/CDC/FMO

Pennsylvania Coal Miners Study, HHS/CDC/NIOSH

Potential Grant Applicant File, HHS/CDC/NIOSH

Pre-Test Cosmetology Convention Study, HHS/CDC/NIOSH

Purseglove Mine (West Virginia) Shift Study, HHS/CDC/NIOSH

Rabies Serum Antibody Study ('Blue Sheet' CDD4.332), HHS/CDC/BE

Radiation Exposure Records for NIOSH Employees in Morgantown, HHS/CDC/NIOSH

Research/Demonstration and Training Grants Application File, HHS/CDC/NIOSH

Respiratory Infections Study in Guyan Valley, West Virginia, HHS/CDC/NIOSH

Rifampin in Initial Treatment of Pulmonary Tuberculosis, HHS/CDC/BSS

Rifampin-Isoniazid in Initial Treatment of Pulmonary Tuberculosis, HHS/CDC/BSS

Silicosis Study in 30 Metal Mines, 1958–1962, HHS/CDC/NIOSH

Study of Bakers and Confection Workers, and Other Associated Industries, HHS/CDC/NIOSH

Study of Behavioral Performance of Kentucky Toll Booth Operators Exposed to Auto Exhaust, HHS/CDC/NIOSH

Study of Chemotherapy of Pulmonary Tuberculosis, HHS/CDC/BSS

Study of Cincinnati Fireworkers, HHS/CDC/NIOSH

Study of Colloids, Inc. Workers, HHS/CDC/NIOSH

Study of Columbus Coated Fabrics Study, HHS/CDC/NIOSH

Study of Metal Mine Workers, HHS/CDC/NIOSH

Study of Metals Industry Workers, HHS/CDC/NIOSH

Study of Mineral Wool Workers, HHS/CDC/NIOSH

Study of Phosphate Fertilizer Industry, HHS/CDC/NIOSH

Study of Pottstown, Pennsylvania Chemical Plant Workers, HHS/CDC/NIOSH

Study of Selected Environmental Protection Agency Employees in Cincinnati for Respiratory Disease, HHS/CDC/NIOSH

Study of Union Carbide, Charleston, WV, Plant, HHS/CDC/NIOSH

Subacute Sclerosing Panencephalitis Surveillance, HHS/CDC/BSS

Surveillance of Persons on Isoniazid Preventive Treatment for Tuberculosis, HHS/CDC/BSS

Textile Workers Audiogram Results, HHS/CDC/NIOSH

Tuberculin Testing Study, HHS/CDC/BSS

Tuberculosis Prophylaxis Studies—Alaska and Puerto Rico, HHS/CDC/BSS

Tuskegee Study of Untreated Syphilis Medical Care Program, HHS/CDC/BSS

Uranium Mill Worker Study in Colorado, HHS/CDC/NIOSH

Uranium Miner Study in Far West, HHS/CDC/NIOSH

Vibration Laboratory Studies (Experimental Group), HHS/CDC/NIOSH

West Virginia Pulp and Paper Company Study, HHS/CDC/NIOSH

Workers Exposed to Benzidine (Bladder Cancer), HHS/CDC/NIOSH

Zoster Immune Globulin Records on High Risk Immunosuppressed Children Exposed to Chicken Pox, HHS/CDC/BSS

Food and Drug Administration

For information concerning any files maintained by the Food and Drug Administration (FDA), contact the Privacy Coordinator, FDA, 5600 Fishers Lane, Rockville, MD 20852, (301) 443-3170.

Association of Official Analytical Chemists (AOAC) Member File, HHS/FDA

Certified Retort Operators, HHS/FDA

Clinical Investigator Records, HHS/FDA

Communications (Oral and Written) with the Public

FDA Credential Holder File, HHS/FDA

Individual and Household Statistical Surveys and Special Studies on FDA-Regulated Products, HHS/FDA

Quality Assurance Program, HHS/FDA

Radiation Protection Program Personnel Monitoring System, HHS/FDA

Radiation Registry of Physicians, HHS/FDA

Regulated Industry Employee Enforcement Records, HHS/FDA

Science Advisor Research Associate Program (SARAP), HHS/FDA

State Food and Drug Official File, HHS/FDA

Health Resources Administration

For information concerning any files maintained by the Health Resources Administration, contact the Director, HRA, 3700 East-West Highway, Hyattsville, MD 20782, (301) 436-7200.

Affidavits of Nondisclosure, HHS/HRA/NCHS

American Dental Association Directory Tape HHS/HRA/RHM

American Occupational Therapy Association Membership Tape, HHS/HRA/BHM

America Osteopathic Association Tape, HHS/HRA/BHM

American Podiatry Association Membership Tape, HHS/HRA/BHM

American Veterinary Medical Association Membership Tape, HHS/HRA/BHM

Applied Statistics Training Institute Applicants and Students, HHS/HRA/NCHS

Biographical Sketches of Witnesses at Appropriations Hearings, HHS/HSA/OA

Biographical Sketches of Witnesses at Appropriations Hearings, HRA/OA

Central Cost Advisory Files, HHS/HRA/OA

Chattanooga Incremental Care Program, HHS/HRA/BHM

Clinical Laboratory Technologists Proficiency Exam Results (Medicare), HHS/HSA/BQA

Consultant Roster, HHS/HRA/OHRO

Contract Physicians and Consultants, HHS/HSA/BMS

Contracts, Division of Nursing (Unofficial), HHS/HRA/BHM

Cooperative Research Studies System: Pyelonephritis, HHS/HSA/BMS

Cooperative Research Studies System: Coronary Artery Disease, HHS/HSA/BMS

Cooperative Research Studies System: Essential Hypertension, HHS/HSA/BMS

Cuban Loan Program, HHS/HRA/BHM

Cycle II Dentist Survey, HHS/HRA/BHM

Cytotechnologists Proficiency Exam Results (Medicare), HHS/HSA/BQA

Death and Disability Claims in the Health Professions Student Loan Program, HHS/HRA/BHM

Death and Disability Claims of the Nursing Student Loan Program, HHS/HRA/BHM

Dental Patient Records, HHS/HRA/BHM

Dental Research-Evaluation of Restorative Materials, HHS/HRA/BMS

Dental Residency Program, HHS/HRA/BHM

Division of Federal Employee Health, Employee Health Records, HHS/HSA/BMS

Emergency Non-PHS Treatment Authorization File, HHS/HSA/BMS

End Stage Renal Disease (ESRD) Medical Information System (Registry), HHS/HSA/BQA

Federal Employee Occupational Health Data System, HHS/HSA/BMS

Health and Demographic Surveys Conducted in Random Samples of the U.S. Population, HHS/HRA/NCHS

Health Manpower Inventories and Surveys, HHS/HRA/NCHS

Health and Medical Records Systems, HHS/HSA/ISH

Health Professions Student Loan Cancellation, HHS/HRA/BHM

Health Professions Student Loan Repayment Program, HHS/HRA/BHM

Hospital Manpower Characteristics Survey, HHS/HRA/BHM

Independent Laboratory Directors Proficiency Exam Results (Medicare), HHS/HSA/BQA

Medicare Beneficiary Claims for Emergency Services, HHS/HSA/BQA

National Center for Health Services Research Contract Records System, HHS/HRA/NCHSR

National Center for Health Services Research Grants Records System, HHS/HRA/NCHSR

National Health Service Corps (NHSC) Applicant Recruitment and Provider File, HHS/HSA/BCHS

National Register of Licensed Dental Manpower, HHS/HRA/BHM

1972–73 Survey of Optometrists File, HHS/HRA/BHM

1972–73 Survey of Pharmacists, HHS/HRA/BHM

Nurse Long-Term Trainee File, HHS/HRSA/BHM

Operation MEDIHC (Military Experience Directed Into Health Careers) File, HHS/HRA/BHM

PHS Clinical Affiliation Trainee Records, HHS/HSA/BMS

Patient's Medical Record System PHS Hospitals/Clinics, HHS/HSA/BMS

Physical Therapists Proficiency Exam Results (Medicare), HHS/HSA/BQA

Physician Shortage Area Scholarship Program, HHS/HRA/BHM

Plaque Study in a School Setting, HHS/HRA/BHM

Professional Nurse Traineeships, HHS/HRA/BHM

Psychiatric Technician Proficiency Exam Results (Medicare), HHS/HSA/BQA

Public Health Service Scholarship Program, HHS/HRA/BHM

Records of Patients' Personal Valuables and Monies, HHS/HSA/BMS

Register of Dental Licensure, HHS/HRA/BHM

Sample Survey of Dentists for Non-Licensed Personnel, HHS/HRA/BHM

Special Nursing Research Fellowship Grants, HHS/HRA/BHM

Survey of Medical Technologists, HHS/HRA/BHM

Unofficial Vital Records System, HHS/HSA/IHS

Vietnamese Refugee Physicians and Medical Students, HHS/HRA/BHM

Vital Statistics for All Births, Deaths, Fetal Deaths, Marriages and Divorces Occurring in the United States During Each Year, HHS/HRA/NCHS

Waivered Licensed Practical Nurse Proficiency Exam Results (Medicare), HHS/HSA/BQA

Social and Rehabilitation Service

FEDERAL PARENT LOCATOR SYSTEM, HHS/SRS

Parents being sought for the purpose of enforcing support obligations.

Office of Child Support Enforcement, HHS, 330 C Street, SW, Washington, DC 20201, (202) 443-4442.

Request for information should contain: Individual's name and Social Security account number.

Following is a list of the remaining files maintained by the Social and Rehabilitation Service. Anyone interested in obtaining information from any of these files should contact the appropriate agency head or the Secretary of Health and Human Services, 200 Independence Ave., SW, Washington, DC 20201.

Cuban Refugee Registration Records, HHS/SRS
Repatriate Records System, HHS/SRS

Social Security Administration

ANALYSIS OF NARCOTICS ADDICTS IN BALTIMORE (STATISTICS), HHS/SSA

Narcotics addicts in Baltimore, selected from police reports; 1951-1971.

Assistant Commissioner for Research and Statistics, Social Security Administration, Room 112, 1875 Connecticut Avenue, NW, Washington, DC 20009, (202) 673-5602.

Request for information should contain: Individual's Social Security account number, and, for verification purposes, name (woman's maiden name, if applicable), address, date of birth, sex, and to ascertain whether the individual's record is in the system, indication of previous Baltimore, MD, residence.

APPEALS FILE, HHS/SSA

Social Security and black-lung claimants.

Bureau of Hearings and Appeals, Social Security Administration, 801 North Randolph Street, Arlington, VA 22203, (703) 724-0151.

CONTROL SYSTEM FOR DELAYED, CRITICAL, OR SENSITIVE CASE INQUIRIES, HHS/SSA

Social Security beneficiaries or persons inquiring on their behalf who are reporting failure to receive a check or checks that they believe are due or who are inquiring about other matters that have been determined to be of a critical or sensitive nature.

Contact the most convenient Social Security office and provide the system name, Social Security account number, and return address or phone number.

COURT CASE RECORD FILE, HHS/SSA

Plaintiffs who have filed court actions against the Secretary of HHS.

Director, Bureau of Retirement and Survivors Insurance, 6401 Security Boulevard, Baltimore, MD 21235, (301) 594-1900.

CRIMINAL INVESTIGATIONS FILE, HHS/SSA

Persons alleged to be in violation of either personnel regulations or criminal provisions of the Social Security Act.

Branch Chief, Investigations Branch, Office of Management and Administration, 6401 Security Boulevard, Baltimore, MD 21235, (301) 934-3235.

DEBIT VOUCHER FILE (SUPPLEMENTAL SECURITY INCOME), HHS/SSA

Aged, blind, or disabled individuals who have negotiated two checks for the same month incorrectly or who have refunded money to the Bureau of Supplemental Security Income by check only to have their checks bounce.

Director, Office of Assistance, Social Security Administration, 6401 Security Boulevard, Baltimore, MD 21235, (301) 594-1234.

DEBTORS, CREDIT COUNSELING, AND CONSUMER PROTECTION, HHS/SSA

Employees of Social Security Administration headquarters who request services or employees about whom the administration receives written inquiries because of employees' alleged delinquency in paying taxes and just debts.

Employee Relations Branch, Social Security Administration, 6401 Security Boulevard, Baltimore, MD 21235, (301) 594-6775.

GENERAL CRIMINAL INVESTIGATION FILES, HHS/SSA

Reported violators of federal and state criminal laws on Social Security Administration property.

Chief, Protective Security Section, Office of Management and Administration, 6401 Security Boulevard, Baltimore, MD 21235, (301) 594-6970.

HEALTH INSURANCE OVERPAYMENT LEDGER CARDS, HHS/SSA

All Social Security health and supplemental medical insurance enrollees who received incorrect medicare payments or services, who are determined liable, and against whom it is not possible to adjust subsequent Part A (hospital) or Part B (supplementary medical) benefits.

Retirement and Survivors Insurance Program Centers, Division of International Operations, Bureau of Disability Insurance, 6401 Security Boulevard, Baltimore, MD 21241, (301) 594-6580.

HEARING FILE, HHS/SSA

Social Security and black-lung claimants.

Bureau of Hearings and Appeals, Social Security Administration, 801 North Randolph Street, Arlington, VA 22203, (703) 724-0151.

HEARING OFFICE MASTER CALENDAR, HHS/SSA

Social Security and black-lung claimants.

Bureau of Hearings and Appeals, Social Security Administration, 801 North Randolph Street, Arlington, VA 22203, (703) 724-0151.

HEARINGS AND APPEALS CASE CONTROL CARD FILE, HHS/SSA

Social Security and black-lung claimants.

Bureau of Hearings and Appeals, Social Security Administration, 801 North Randolph Street, Arlington, VA 22203, (703) 724-0151.

HEARINGS AND APPEALS CASE LOCATOR SYSTEM, HHS/SSA

Social Security and black-lung claimants.

Bureau of Hearings and Appeals, Social Security Administration, 801 North Randolph Street, Arlington, VA 22203, (703) 724-0151.

LITIGATION ACTIVITY FILE, HHS/SSA

Plaintiffs who have filed court actions against the Secretary of HHS.

Director, Bureau of Retirement and Survivors Insurance, 6401 Security Boulevard, Baltimore, MD 21235, (301) 594-1900.

OVERPAYMENT FILE (SUPPLEMENTAL SECURITY INCOME), HHS/SSA

Any supplemental security income payment recipient having a potential supplemental security income overpayment.

Director, Bureau of Supplemental Security Income, 6401 Security Boulevard, Baltimore, MD 21235, (301) 594-3800.

PRESIDING OFFICER FILE, HHS/SSA

Social Security and black-lung claimants.

Bureau of Hearings and Appeals, Social Security Administration, 801 North Randolph Street, Arlington, VA 22203, (703) 724-0151.

PRESIDING OFFICER'S DOCKET, HHS/SSA

Social Security and black-lung claimants.

Bureau of Hearings and Appeals, Social Security Administration, 801 North Randolph Street, Arlington, VA 22203, (703) 724-0151.

PROGRAM INTEGRITY CASE FILES, HHS/SSA

Persons suspected of having violated the criminal provisions of the Social Security Act where substantial basis for criminal prosecution exists, and defendants in criminal prosecution cases.

Appropriate program center for retirement and survivor cases: the Bureau of Disability Insurance for disability, black lung, or supplemental security income for the disabled or blind; the appropriate health insurance regional offices for health insurance; the appropriate quality assurance field staff for supplemental security income.

Request for information should contain: Individual's name and Social Security account number, any Social Security account number on which he has filed for or received benefits, the type of such claim, and current claim status.

PROGRAM INTEGRITY MANAGEMENT INFORMATION AND CONTROL SYSTEM, HHS/SSA

All individuals suspected of criminal violations involving the supplemental security income (SSI) program.

Director, Division of Program Integrity, Office of Quality Assurance, Office of Management and Administration, 6401 Security Boulevard, Baltimore, MD 21235, (301) 594-3470.

RECONSIDERATION AND HEARING CASE FILES (PART A) HOSPITAL INSURANCE PROGRAM, HHS/SSA

Individuals dissatisfied with an initial determination as to the amount of benefits payable on the beneficiary's behalf under the hospital insurance program who have filed either an expressed or implied request for reconsideration.

Request for information should be addressed to the most convenient Social Security office or to the carrier that conducted the hearing. The individual should furnish his or her health insurance claim number and name as shown on Social Security records.

RECOVERY ACCOUNTING FOR OVERPAYMENTS, HHS/SSA

All Social Security beneficiaries who received an overpayment of benefits, all persons holding conserved (accumulated) funds received on behalf of a Social Security beneficiary, and persons who received Social Security payments on behalf of a beneficiary and were found to have misused those payments.

Request should be addressed to the most convenient Social Security office or program center.

REVIEW AND FAIR HEARING CASE FILES—SUPPLEMENTARY MEDICAL INSURANCE PROGRAM, HHS/SSA

Beneficiary, physician, provider, or other supplier of service who is dissatisfied with the carrier's denial of a request for payment, or with the amount of the payment, or with the length of time being taken to process the claim for payment.

Requests for information should be addressed to the most convenient Social Security office or to the Health Care Financing Administration, Bureau of Health Insurance, Reconsideration Branch, Baltimore, MD 21235, (301) 594-9008. Request for information should contain: Individual's insurance claim number and name as shown on Social Security records.

STORAGE OF HEARING RECORDS: TAPE CASSETTES AND AUDIOGRAPH DISCS, HHS/SSA

Social Security and black-lung claimants.

Social Security Administration, Bureau of Hearings and Appeals, 801 North Randolph Street, Arlington, VA 22203, (703) 724-0151.

Request for information should contain: Individual's Social Security account number for identification.

Additional Files

Following is a list of the remaining files maintained by the Social Security Administration. Anyone interested in obtaining information from any of these files should contact the appropriate agency head or the Secretary of Health and Human Services, 200 Independence Ave., SW, Washington, DC 20201.

Actuarial Sample Health Insurance and Supplementary Medical Insurance (Medicare), HHS/SSA

Actuarial Sample Hospital Stay Record Study, HHS/SSA

Actuarial Sample of Supplementary Medical Insurance Payments, HHS/SSA

Adjudication of Supplemental Security Income Claims Study, HHS/SSA

Administrative Award and Termination File (Statistics), HHS/SSA

Administrative Disallowance File (Statistics), HHS/SSA

Administrative Disallowance Records for Technical Denial, HHS/SSA

Advance Payment File (Supplemental Security Income), HHS/SSA

Age at Death and History of Covered Employment and Entitlement (Statistics), HHS/SSA

Agricultural Worker Data File (Statistics), HHS/SSA

Alphabetical Name File (Folder) of Health Insurance Program Consultants, HHS/SSA

Ambulatory Prescription Drug Study (Statistics), HHS/SSA

Analysis of Factors in Recurring Dependency among Welfare Cases Closed in New York City (Statistics) HHS/SSA

Annual 5 Percent Summary File of Services Reimbursed under the Medicare Program (Statistics), HHS/SSA

Automated Control System for Case Folders, HHS/SSA

Automated Controlled Correspondence Extraction System, HHS/SSA

Beneficiaries Residing Aboard File (Statistics), HHS/SSA

Billing and Collection Master Record System, HHS/SSA

Black Lung Payment System, HHS/SSA

Carrier Medicare Claims Records, HHS/SSA

Cases Currently in Process File (Supplemental Security Income), HHS/SSA

Changing Commitments to Work and Family Among Women in Chicago, Aged 25–54 (Statistics), HHS/SSA

Chronic Renal Disease Beneficiary History File, HHS/SSA

Claims Development Record, HHS/SSA

Claims Folders and Post-Adjudicative Records of Applicants and Beneficiaries for Social Security Administration Benefits, HHS/SSA

Claims Index File (Supplemental Security Income), HHS/SSA

Claims Leads, HHS/SSA

Coal Miners Covered by the Health and Safety Act (Statistics), HHS/SSA

Commissioner's Correspondence File, HHS/SSA

Completed Determination Record—Continuing Disability Determinations, HHS/SSA

Congressional Inquiry File, HHS/SSA

Consultative Physician File, HHS/SSA

Control File for Cases Before Presiding Officers, HHS/SSA

Continuous Disability History Sample (Statistics), HHS/SSA

Continuous Work History Sample (Statistics), HHS/SSA

Correspondence File of the Bureau of Data Processing, HHS/SSA

Critical Case Processing Time, HHS/SSA

Current Medicare Survey (Statistics), HHS/SSA

Curriculum Vitae and Professional Qualifications of Staff Physicians and Medical Advisors, HHS/SSA

Daily Record of Certified Benefits, HHS/SSA

Direct Input Source Documents, HHS/SSA

Disability Data Record, HHS/SSA

Disability Hearing Processing Time, HHS/SSA

Disabled Persons Operations File (Annual) (Statistics), HHS/SSA

Disposition of Vocational Rehabilitation Report to Social Security Administration, HHS/SSA

Earnings Recording and Self-Employment Income System, HHS/SSA

Effect of the Annual Earnings Test (Statistics), HHS/SSA

Employee Housing Request Files, HHS/SSA

Employee Identification Card Files (Building Passes), HHS/SSA

Employee Production and Accuracy Records, HHS/SSA

Evaluation of the Impact of Surgical Screening Based upon Union Member Utilization of the Pre-Surgical Consultant Benefit (Statistics), HHS/SSA

Explanation of Medicare Benefit Records, HHS/SSA

Family Benefits File (Annual) (Statistics), HHS/SSA

Fee Ledger System for Representatives, HHS/SSA

Forced Payment File (Supplemental Security Income), HHS/SSA

Group Health Plan System, HHS/SSA

Group Practice Prepayment Plan Line Item Sample of Medicare Utilization (Statistics), HHS/SSA

Health Insurance Benefit and Actuarial Sample Control System, HHS/SSA

Health Insurance Enrollment Statistics–General Enrollment Statistics–General Enrollment Period, HHS/SSA

Health Insurance Master Record, HHS/SSA

Health Insurance Utilization Microfilm, HHS/SSA

Hospital Insurance Open Admission Item File (Statistics), HHS/SSA

Initial Agency Disability Cases Time Study, HHS/SSA

Initial and Continuing Disability Determination File, HHS/SSA

Intermediary Medicare Claims Records, HHS/SSA

Issuance of Social Security Numbers (Statistics), HHS/SSA

Lag Period Between Initial Denial Notice and Reconsideration Study, HHS/SSA

List of Designated Presiding Officers, HHS/SSA

List of Physicians Utilized as Readers of Black Lung X-Ray Films, HHS/SSA

Local Birth Records, HHS/SSA

Local School Records, HHS/SSA

Longitudinal Retirement History Study (Statistics), HHS/SSA

Longitudinal Sample of Disability Insurance Applicants (Statistics), HHS/SSA

Longitudinal Supplemental Security Income File (Statistics), HHS/SSA

Master Beneficiary Record, HHS/SSA

Master Beneficiary Record Research Extract (Statistics), HHS/SSA

Master Files of Social Security Number Holders, HHS/SSA

Matches of Internal Revenue Service and Social Security Administration Data (Joint Social Security Administration/Treasury Department Statistics Development Project), HHS/SSA

Matches of Internal Revenue Service and Social Security Administration Data with Census Survey Data (Joint Social Security Administration/Census Statistics Development Project), HHS/SSA

Medical Services Microdata Project (Statistics), HHS/SSA

Medicare Beneficiary Correspondence Files, HHS/SSA

Medicare Benefit Check Records, HHS/SSA

Medicare Bill File (Statistics), HHS/SSA

Medicare Enrollment Records (Statistics), HHS/SSA

Monthly Benefit Disability Freeze Study (Statistics), HHS/SSA

Motor Vehicle Operator Files, HHS/SSA

Multiple Social Security Number Study (Statistics), HHS/SSA

Non-Contributory Military Service Reimbursement System, HHS/SSA

One-Time Payment File, HHS/SSA

Optional State Supplemental Payment Program Design (Statistics), HHS/SSA

Panel Listings for Vocational Experts and Medical Advisors, HHS/SSA

Parking Assignment and Recordkeeping Files, HHS/SSA

Payment Record File of Supplementary Medical (Medicare) Enrollees (Statistics), HHS/SSA

Pending Social Security Number Applications, HHS/SSA

Personnel Research and Test Validation Records, HHS/SSA

Problem Case File, HHS/SSA

Problem Case File (Supplemental Security Income), HHS/SSA

Public Inquiry Correspondence File, HHS/SSA

Quality Assurance Casefile

Quality Evaluation Data Records, HHS/SSA

Quality of Service Measurement Program Based upon Consumer Opinions, HHS/SSA

Record of Claims (Microfiche), HHS/SSA

Record of Earnings Information Furnished for Non-Program Purposes, HHS/SSA

Record of Employees Authorized to Review Bureau Records, HHS/SSA

Records of Usage of Medical Advisors, HHS/SSA

Redetermination File (Supplemental Security Income), HHS/SSA

Reimbursement from Trust Funds for Vocational Rehabilitation Services, HHS/SSA

Requests for Review of Proposed Contracts with Experts and Consultants, HHS/SSA

Retirement, Survivors, and Disability Insurance Claims Study, HHS/SSA

Retirement and Survivors Insurance Awards and Disallowances Appraisal System, HHS/SSA

Retirement and Survivors Insurance Postadjudicative Appraisal System, HHS/SSA

Sample of Newly Entitled Worker Beneficiaries, HHS/SSA

Social Security Administration–Rehabilitation Service Agency Data Link of Closed Cases (Statistics), HHS/SSA

Social Security Administration Claims Control System, HHS/SSA

Social Security Administration Contract Files, HHS/SSA

Social Security and the Changing Life Ethos, HHS/SSA

Special Age 72 Benefit Trust Fund Transfer Project, HHS/SSA

Special Sample of Earnings Records (Statistics), HHS/SSA

State Data Exchange System (Supplemental Security Income), HHS/SSA

Studebaker Plant Closure Data File (Statistics), HHS/SSA

Study to Determine Impact of State Supplementation of Domiciliary Care of Supplemental Security Income Recipients, HHS/SSA

Study of Medical Use Under the United Medical Clinic Plan or the Kaiser Health Plan (Statistics), HHS/SSA

Substantive Awards File (Statistics), HHS/SSA

Supplemental Security Income Audit Trail Microfiche

Supplemental Security Income Claims Data, HHS/SSA

Supplemental Security Income Congressional Inquiries File

Supplemental Security Income File of Refunds, HHS/SSA

Supplemental Security Income, Impact Research Project of Persons in Multnomah County, Oregon, HHS/SSA

Supplemental Security Income Quality Assurance System, HHS/SSA

Supplemental Security Income Monetary Alert Planning System, HHS/SSA

Supplemental Security Income Priority Correspondence Staff Files, HHS/SSA

Supplemental Security Income Record, HHS/SSA

Supplementary Medical Insurance Premiums (Buy-In) Master Records, HHS/SSA

Supplementary Medical Sample Bill Summary File of Medicare Utilization (Statistics), HHS/SSA

Survey of the Aged (Demographic and Economic Characteristics of the Aged) (1968), HHS/SSA

Survey of Disabled Adults (Statistics), HHS/SSA

Survey of Institutionalized Supplemental Security Income Recipients (Statistics) (1974), HHS/SSA

Survey of Low Income Aged and Disabled (Statistics), HHS/SSA

Survey of Student Beneficiaries (1973), HHS/SSA

Tax Assessment Records, HHS/SSA

Total Resources and Information Management (TRIM) System of Assistant Bureau Director Systems, HHS/SSA

Vocational Rehabilitation Savings Calculation, HHS/SSA

Wage Item File, HHS/SSA

Welfare Eligibility Lists for December 1973, HHS/SSA

National Institutes of Health

ADMINISTRATION: NIH CHEMICAL CARCINOGEN REGISTRY, HHS/NIH/DRS

Researchers, laboratory workers, and NIH employees potentially exposed to chemical carcinogens.

Chief, Engineering and Sanitation Section, ESB, Building 13, Room 3-K04, NIH, 9000 Rockville Pike, Bethesda, MD 20014, (301) 496-5601.

ADMINISTRATION: PRINCIPAL INVESTIGATORS PROTECTION FROM RESEARCH RISKS, HHS/NIH/OD

Persons submitting research proposals to the NIH involving hazards to subjects or ethical problems.

Director, OPRR, Westwood Building, Room 303, NIH, 5333 Westbard Avenue, Bethesda, MD 20014, (301) 496-7005.

ADMINISTRATION: RADIATION WORKERS MONITORING, HHS/NIH/DRS

NIH workers using radioactive materials or radiation producing equipment.

Radiation Safety Officer, Building 21, Room 108, NIH, 9000 Rockville Pike, Bethesda, MD 20014, (301) 496-5774.

CLINICAL RESEARCH: PREGNANT REGISTERED NURSES EXPOSED TO INFECTIOUS DISEASES – DELIVERY HISTORY, HHS/NIH/NINCDS

Registered nurses in the NIH study who were exposed to infectious diseases during their pregnancies.

Head, Administration Management Section, Building 31, Room 8A47, NIH, 9000 Rockville Pike, Bethesda, MD 20014, (301) 496-2511.

RESEARCH RESOURCES: REGISTRY OF MICROBIAL AGENTS, TISSUE CULTURES AND ANIMAL & USERS, HHS/NIH/DRS

Individuals potentially exposed to biohazardous microbial agents.

Chief, Biological Control Section, Building 13, Room 3K-04, NIH, 9000 Rockville Pike, Bethesda, MD 20014, (301) 496-4000.

Following is a list of the remaining files maintained by the NIH. Anyone interested in obtaining information from any of these files should contact the appropriate agency head or the Secretary of Health and Human Services, 200 Independence Ave., SW, Washington, DC 20201.

Administration: Authorized Radionuclide Users File, HHS/NIH/DRS

Administration: NIH Library Circulation and User I.D. File, HHS/NIH/DRS

Administration: NIH Safety Glasses Issuance Program, HHS/NIH/DRS

Administration: Visitor Locator, HHS/NIH/NLM

Clinical Research: Blood Donor Records, HHS/NIH/CC

Clinical Research: Baltimore Cancer Research Center Patients, HHS/NIH/NCI

Clinical Research: Breast Cancer Patients at Selected Hospitals, HSS/NIH/NCI

Clinical Research: Burkitt's Lymphoma Registry, HHS/NIH/NCI

Clinical Research: Cancer End Results File, HHS/NIH/NCI

Clinical Research: Cancer Incidence File–1973, HHS/NIH/NCI

Clinical Research: Candidate Normal Volunteer Records, HHS/NIH/CC

Clinical Research: Collaborative Clinical Epilepsy Research, HHS/NIH/NINCDS

Clinical Research: Collaborative Perinatal Project, HHS/NIH/NINCDS

Clinical Research: Comanche County Multiple Sclerosis Study, HHS/NIH/NINCDS

Clinical Research: Creutzfeldt-Jacob Disease Study, HHS/NIH/NINCDS

Clinical Research: DCT Clinical Investigations, HHS/NIH/NCI

Clinical Research: Diabetes Mellitus Research Study of Southwestern American Indians, HHS/NIH/NIAMDD

Clinical Research: Disseminated Breast Cancer, HHS/NIH/NCI

Clinical Research: Genetic Counseling, HHS/NIH/NINCDS

Clinical Research: Genetics of Neurological Disorders, HHS/NIH/NINCDS

Clinical Research: Gerontology Research Center Longitudinal Aging Study, HHS/NIH/NIA

Clinical Research: Guam Patient/Control Registry, HHS/NIH/NINCDS

Clinical Research: Guam Studies, HHS/NIH/NINCDS

Clinical Research: Head and Neck Cancer Patients — Memorial Hospital, New York City, HHS/NIH/NCI

Clinical Research: Hodgkin's Disease Pathology Studies, HHS/NIH/NCI

Clinical Research: Hodgkin's Disease Pathology Study — Connecticut, HHS/NIH/NCI

Clinical Research: Malignant Melanomas, HHS/NIH/NCI

Clinical Research: Maternal Smoking-Birth Weight, Washington City, Maryland, HHS/NIH/NCI

Clinical Research: Mayo Clinic Neurological Studies, HHS/NIH/NINCDS

Clinical Research: Medical Neurology Branch Medical Histories, HHS/NIH/NINCDS

Clinical Research: Multiple Sclerosis Twin Study, HHS/NIH/NINCDS

Clinical Research: National Cancer Incidence Survey, HHS/NIH/NCI

Clinical Research: National Cancer Institute/American Cancer Society National Breast Cancer Screening of Antihypertensives, HHS/NIH/NCI

Clinical Research: National Institute of Dental Research Patient Records, HHS/NIH/NIDR

Clinical Research: NIH Clinical Center Admissions, DCBD, HHS/NIH/NCI

Clinical Research: NIH Clinical Center Admissions, DCCP, HHS/NIH/NCI

Clinical Research: NIH Clinical Center Admissions and Other Selected Patient Files-DCT, HHS/NIH/NCI

Clinical Research: Nervous System Studies, HHS/NIH/NINCDS

Clinical Research: Neuropharmacology Studies, HHS/NIH/NINCDS

Clinical Research: Parkinson's Disease Studies, HHS/NIH/NINCDS

Clinical Research: Patient Data, HHS/NIH/NIAMDD

Clinical Research: Patient Medical Histories, HHS/NIH/NINCDS

Clinical Research: Patient Medical Records, HHS/NIH/CC

Clinical Research: Patient Records, HHS/NIH/NHLI

Clinical Research: Pharyngeal Development, HHS/NIH/NIDR

Clinical Research: Phonocardiogram, HHS/NIH/DCRT

Clinical Research: Polymyositis Study, HHS/NIH/NINCDS

Clinical Research: Preadmission Medical Records, HHS/NIH/CC

Clinical Research: Radiotherapy Patient File, HHS/NIH/DRS

Clinical Research: Sensory Testing Research Program, HHS/NIH/NIDR

Clinical Research: Serological and Virus Data in Studies Related to the Central Nervous System, HHS/NIH/NINCDS

Clinical Research: Soft Tissue Sarcoma Staging, HHS/NIH/NCI

Clinical Research: Southwestern American Indian Patient Data, HHS/NIH/NIAMDD

Clinical Research: Student Records, HHS/NIH/CC

Clinical Research: Survey of Prostatic and Bladder Cancer, HHS/NIH/NCI

Clinical Research: Urinary Steroid Levels in Breast Cancer Patients, HHS/NIH/NCI

Clinical Research: Veterans Administration Bladder and Prostate Cancer Clinical Trials, HHS/NIH/NCI

Clinical Research: Veterans Administration Ulcer Study, HHS/NIH/NINCDS

Grants: Application Control File, HHS/NIH/DRG

Grants: Associates Program, HHS/NIH/DRG

Grants: IMPAC (Grant/Contract Information), HHS/NIH/DRG

International Activities: Fellowships Awarded by Foreign Organizations, HHS/NIH/FIC

International Activities: Scholars Program, HHS/NIH/FIC

International Activities: U.S. Foreign Health Exchange Programs, HHS/NIH/FIC

Research Resources: Hormone Distribution, HHS/NIH/NIAMDD

Research Resources: Viral Oncology Human Specimen Program, HHS/NIH/NCI

Office of Human Development

DEVELOPMENTAL DISABILITIES COMPLAINTS AND CORRESPONDENCE FILES, HHS/OHD DDO RO7

Individuals who have made inquiries regarding complaints or requested information regarding services from the developmental disabilities program, and those who have commented to HSS on its proposed rules and practices.

Director, Developmental Disabilities Office, 601 East 12th Street, 5th Floor, Kansas City, MO 64106, (816) 374-5211.

Request for information should contain: Individual's name and date of previous correspondence, if known. For complaint or investigative material, include name and any identification number assigned.

NATIONAL CENTER ON CHILD ABUSE AND NEGLECT MAILING LIST

Persons interested in the national center's publications; persons interested in making grant applications; project directors; social workers; and others interested in information on child abuse and neglect.

Administrative Assistant, Room 5564, 400 6th Street, SW, Washington, DC 20201, (202) 245-2885.

RUNAWAY YOUTH ACT MAILING LISTS
HHS/OHD OYD

Individuals who make inquiries regarding publications, grant programs, and other matters related to the Runaway Youth Act.

Head, OYD Office, Room 1651, Donahoe Building, 400 6th Street, SW, Washington, DC 20201, (202) 755-7724.

Request for information should contain: Individual's name and date of previous correspondence, if known.

Additional Files

Following is a list of the remaining files maintained by the Office of Human Development. Anyone interested in obtaining information from any of these files should contact the appropriate agency head or the Secretary of Health and Human Services, 200 Independence Ave., SW, Washington, DC 20201.

Children's Bureau General Mailing List, HHS/OHD/OCD/ CB

Children Today Mailing List, HHS/OHD/OCD/CB

Consultants for Federal Technical Assistance Program, Vocational Rehabilitation Services, HHS/OHD/ORS/IX

Education for Parenthood Mailing List, HHS/OHD/OCD/ CB

Mailing List for ONAP Publications

National Center for Child Advocacy Mailing List, HHS/ OHD/OCD/CB

National Clearing House on Aging—Mailing Keys, HHS/AOA/ NCA

OCD Mailing List, HHS/OCD/RIO

OCD Project Staff Lists, HHS/OHD/CCD/IX

OCD Research and Development Program Mailing List, HHS/OHD/OCD R&F

Office of Rehabilitation Services Mailing Lists

Office of Research, Demonstrations, and Manpower Resources Project Reviewers, HHS/OHD/AOA/ORD

Parent Council Advisory Members, HHS/OHD/OCD/ IX-2

U.S. Department of Education

CLIENT LIST FOR DIRECT SERVICES FROM
REGIONAL RESOURCE CENTERS

Individuals who because of lack of financial means are requesting federal funds for diagnosis and educational programming for a handicapped condition.

Regional Resource Centers, Client List Program Manager, Regional Office Building, 400 Maryland Ave., SW, Washington, DC 20202, (202) 245-6996.

Request for information should contain: Individual's name, position, and purpose of request.

GUARANTEED STUDENT LOAN PROGRAM – CLAIMS
AND COLLECTIONS MASTER FILE

Students for whom the United States government reimbursed lending institutions for claims submitted due to defaults.

Director, Program Systems Division, Room 4051, Regional Office Building 03, 7th and D Streets, SW, Washington, DC 20202, (202) 245-2292.

GUARANTEED STUDENT LOAN PROGRAM
COLLECTION FILES

Defaulted borrowers under the guaranteed student loan program, by regional office.

Director, guaranteed student loan program in the region in which the inquirer resides.

GUARANTEED STUDENT LOAN PROGRAM—
COLLECTION LETTERS

Students for whom the United States government reimbursed lending institutions for claims submitted due to defaults.

Director, Program Systems Division, Room 4501, Regional Office Building 03, 7th and D Streets, SW, Washington, DC 20202, (202) 245-2292.

GUARANTEED STUDENT LOAN PROGRAM—
COMPLIANCE FILES

Student borrowers, lenders, or school personnel in the guaranteed student loan program against whom there are proved or alleged acts of misconduct.

Associate Commissioner, Office of Guaranteed Student Loans, Room 4051, Regional Office Building 03, 7th and D Streets, SW, Washington, DC 20202, (202) 245-9717.

GUARANTEED STUDENT LOAN PROGRAM—
DEFAULTED LOANS SUBMITTED TO GENERAL
ACCOUNTING OFFICE

Student borrowers for whom defaulted claims have been paid on federally insured student loans and subsequently submitted to General Accounting Office (GAO) for further action.

Guaranteed Student Loan Branch, Division of Program Operations, Student Financial Assistance, Claims and Collections Center, Room 4621, Regional Office Building 03, 7th and D Streets, SW, Washington, DC 20202, (202) 447-8960.

GUARANTEED STUDENT LOAN PROGRAM –
PRE-CLAIMS ASSISTANCE

Students reported by lending institutions who are delinquent on their educational loan.

Director, Program Systems Division, Room 4051, Regional Office Building 03, 7th and D Streets, SW, Washington, DC 20202, (202) 245-2292.

GUARANTEED STUDENT LOAN PROGRAM—STUDENT COMPLAINT FILES

Student borrowers and applicants for student loans in the guaranteed student loan program who have made complaints or allegations of irregularities by schools or lenders.

Associate Commissioner, Officer of Guaranteed Student Loans, Room 4051, Regional Office Building 03, 7th and D Streets, SW, Washington, DC 20202, (202) 245-9717.

INSURANCE CLAIM FILE GUARANTEED STUDENT LOAN PROGRAM

Guaranteed student loan program borrowers on whose accounts the federal government has been requested to pay a claim by lenders, because of default, bankruptcy, death, or disability.

Associate Commissioner, Office of Guaranteed Student Loans, Room 4051, Regional Office Building 03, 7th and D Streets, SW, Washington, DC 20202, (202) 245-9717; director, guaranteed loan program in the region in which the inquirer resides.

Additional Files

Following is a list of the remaining files maintained by the Department of Education. Anyone interested in obtaining information from any of these files should contact the appropriate agency head or the Secretary of the Department of Education, Federal Office Building, 400 Maryland Ave., SW, Washington, DC 20202.

ATS-6 Participant Panel
Alaska Education Satellite Project Teacher Participants
Alum Rock Education Voucher Project
Appalachian Educational Laboratory Experienced Based Career Education Record System
Appalachian Education Satellite Project Teacher Enrollment Record
Basic Educational Opportunity Grant Alternate Disbursement System
Basic Educational Opportunity Grant Student Validation File
Basic Grant Application File
Basic Grant Student Eligibility Report Sub-system
Berkeley Unified School District Experimental School Project
Captioned News Newsletter Mailing List—Captioned Films for the Deaf Program
Carbon County School District 02 Experimental Schools Project
Career Education Project Client Information Data Base
Career Education Rural Needs Assessment
Comprehensive Career Education Model Acceptability Survey
Computer Management Instruction (CMI)

Constantine Public Schools Experimental Schools Project
Craig City School District Experimental School Project
Debt Counseling Records
Deinstitutionalization Research Client File System
Deinstitutionalization Research Consent
Development Studies
Differential Cognitive Development in Infants and Toddlers Longitudinal Study
Edgewood Independent School District Experimental School Project
Education Resources Information Center Document File
Educational Testing Service, Beginning Teacher Evaluation Study
Educational Testing Service Experienced Based Career Education Record System
Effective Teacher Education Program, and Flexible Learning System
Employment Inquiries, Suggestions, and Resources for the Basic Skills Group
Evaluation Comment (Journal of the Center for the Study of Evaluation)
Evaluation of the Use and Interpretation of the Guidelines for Assessment of Sex Bias and Sex Fairness in Career Interest Inventories
Evaluation of a Workshop on Freeing Sex Roles
Far West Laboratory, Beginning Teacher Evaluation Study
Far West Laboratory Experienced Based Career Education Records Systems
Fellows Program Nominees
Field Test of Comprehensive Career Education Model (CCEM) Curriculum Units
Follow-up Study of Mountain-Plains Participant and Control Group Families
Franklin Pierce School District Experimental Schools for Project
Gibboney Multimodal Data Analysis and Retrieval System for the Career Intern Program
Guaranteed Student Loan Program — Inactive Loan Control Master File
Guaranteed Student Loan Program — Lender's Report
Guaranteed Student Loan Program — Loan Control Master File
Guaranteed Student Loan Program — Paid Claims File
Hancock County Public Schools Experimental Schools Project
Hyperkinesis and Food Additives Study
Index of Career Decision-Making Data Bank
Instructional Development and Evaluation
Kansas Reflection Impulsivity Scale for Preschoolers (KRISP)
Language Assessment Research Subject Records
Language Training Project Research Subject Records
Lead/Deadwood Independent School District 0106 Experimental Schools Project
Life Plans Study: The Impact of the Women's Movement on Educational and Occupational Behavior and Attitudes of Married Women
Longitudinal Studies — Learning and Development Work
Longitudinal Study — Toward a Theoretical Model of Infant Competency

Longitudinal Survey on the Nature and Antecedents of Psychosocial Maturity Among Students

MITT Team Teaching Research Data

Mailing Lists for the Office of Policy Communications: Public Affairs and External Affairs

Management Information System for Vocational Education (MISVE)

Manpower Economic Education and the Transition from School to Work

Migrant Student Record Transfer System (MSRTS)

Migration and Refugee Assistance Act of 1962—United States Loan Program for Cuban Students

Mountain-Plains Education and Economic Development Program

Mutual Educational and Cultural Exchange Act—Doctoral Dissertation Research Abroad and Faculty Research Abroad, Fellows and Alternates

Mutual Educational and Cultural Exchange Act Teacher Exchange Grantees and Applicants

NIE Child Study Center

NIE Controlled Correspondence

NIE Mailing Label System

NIE Outside Experts

NIE Project Management System

NIE 3002 Title I Evaluation Reports System

National Advisory Committee for NCES Manual of Terms and Definitions about Students

National Association of the Deaf Film Evaluator Records System—Captioned Films for the Deaf Program

National Defense Education Act Foreign Language Fellowship Program—Fellows and Alternates

National Defense Student Loan Program—Request for Cancellation of Loan on Ground of Permanent and Total Disability

National Direct (formerly Defense) Student Loan Program— NDSL Student Loan Files

National Institute of Education—Sources and Effects of Teacher Expectations

National Longitudinal Study Mailing List

Northwest Regional Educational Laboratory, Experienced Based Career Education Record System

Northwest Regional Educational Laboratory, Improving Teacher Competencies Program

Office of Education Financial Management Information System

Opportunities Industrialization Center of America, Urban Career Education Center (UCEC) Program Data Storage and Retrieval System

Oral History of the Office of Education as Dictated by Former Commissioners of Education

Parent Participants in Deaf-Blind Programs Provided by Regional Centers for Deaf-Blind Children

Participants of Projects Serving Severely Handicapped Children and Youth

Participant Waiting List for Projects Serving Severely Handicapped Children and Youth

Participants in Workshops Concerning Severely Handicapped Children and Youth

Perry County Schools Experimental Schools Project

Pilot Test of Occupational Exploration Program

Program on Teacher Effectiveness, Stanford Center for Research and Development in Teaching

Project MORE Research Subject Records

Purchasers of CSE Evaluation Products

Quilcene Public Schools Experimental Schools Project

The R&D Center for Teacher Education, Effective Teacher Programs

Rand Interactive CCTV Evaluation (Research Subjects)

Record of Advances of Funds for Employees Traveling for the Office of Education (SF-1038, Application and Account for Advance of Funds)

Referred Children Lists

Registry of Deaf-Blind Children—Regional-National

Research for Better Schools Experienced Based Career Education Record System

Research for Better Schools, Information on Teacher Attitudes and Student Learning Related to RBS-Developed Products

Research Data on Organizational Change Projects in Urban Schools and on Users of the Data

Research on Learning and Adaptive Education

Responsiveness Project: Case Study Data File

Responsiveness Project: Community Demands for School District Response File

Resource File for Teacher Center Network Feasibility Study

Safe School Study

School Participant's Evaluation Workshop Data

School Supervisory Union 058 Experimental Schools Project

Science Curriculum Evaluation Subject Records

Sociometric System—Development of Peer Group Formation in Children

South Umpqua Public Schools Experimental Schools Project

Southwest Regional Laboratory Curriculum Development Program

Student Participants in Deaf-Blind Programs Under Centers and Services for Deaf-Blind Children

Support for Improvement of Postsecondary Education; Field Readers to Review Proposals for FIPSE

Support for Improvement of Postsecondary Education Contract to Formative Evaluation Research Associates to Evaluate Women's Programs at Four Types of Postsecondary Institutions

Support for Improvement of Postsecondary Education Contract to Help Colleges or Develop a Model Prospectus for Potential Students

Support for Improvement of Postsecondary Education Contract to the National Radio Institute (NRI) to Develop a Prospectus for Correspondence Study

Support for Improvement of Postsecondary Education Mailing List for Program Information

Survey of Career Education Implementation in Six School Districts

Teacher Corps Application File

Teacher Corps Corpsmember Profile

Travel-Official Travel of NIE Personnel

Upward Bound Information System

Wilcox Public Schools Experimental Schools Project

U.S. Department of Housing and Urban Development

Following is a list of the agencies and subagencies of the U.S. Department of Housing and Urban Development, with their abbreviations:

HUD   Housing and Urban Development Department
FDAA   Federal Disaster Assistance Administration
FIA   Federal Insurance Administration
GNMA   Government National Mortgage Association
ILSRO   Interstate Land Sales Registration Office

Requests for the following files should be made to the Privacy Office, 451 7th Street, SW, Washington, DC 20410, (202) 755-6420.

ACCIDENTS, EMPLOYEES, AND/OR GOVERNMENT VEHICLES

HUD employees in on-the-job accidents, including accidents involving government-owned vehicles; other individuals who have sustained injury or illness as a result of such accidents.

CONSTRUCTION COMPLAINTS FILES

Mortgagors, builders, developers, and contractors under HUD programs.

CONTRACTORS – ADVERSE ACTIONS

Individuals or firms debarred or suspended from participation in HUD programs; corporations, companies, or individuals determined to be unsatisfactory risks; suspended, debarred, or ineligible grantees; builders of single-family homes whom HUD will not insure; individuals and firms disqualified from doing business with HUD; individuals and firms on the no-business list; mortgagors writing to HUD concerning complaints; builders who fail to adjust valid construction complaints; individuals and firms debarred by

executive agencies; dealers and contractors in home improvements and repairs; individuals and firms subject to precautionary measures for practices not consistent with the standards and objectives of the FHA Property Improvement Program; defaulted contractors; developers and contractors who have allegedly not paid prevailing wage rates; individual workers underpaid by a contractor on a HUD project.

EQUAL OPPORTUNITY HOUSING COMPLAINTS

Individuals filing housing discrimination complaints; individuals, officials, and organizations complained about; managers; grant, or project applicants; builders; developers; contractors; appraisers; attorneys; individuals in disaster and EO files; Title VI, VIII, and IX complainants.

FEDERAL CRIME INSURANCE

Federal crime insurance policyholders.

GRANT AND LOAN CONTRACTS

Grant and loan applicants; grantees and loan debtors; grantee personnel under research and categorical grant programs.

INTERSTATE LAND SALES REGISTRATION INVESTIGATIONS

Litigants; attorneys; developers; realtors; lot purchasers; lenders; contractors; appraisers; government officials; others involved in relation to investigations under the Interstate Land Sales Full Disclosure Act.

INVESTIGATION FILES

HUD program participants and HUD employees under investigation including mortgagors, mortgagees, grant and project applicants, builders, developers, real estate firms, contractors, and appraisers.

LEGAL ACTIONS FILES

Litigants; potential and past claimants against the government.

MORTGAGES – DELINQUENT/DEFAULT

Mortgagors under single- and multi-family housing programs seeking assistance in preventing foreclosures; mortgagors whose mortgages are held by the Secretary and whose payments are delinquent; mortgagors complaining about loan servicing; mortgagees under single- and multi-family housing programs; mortgagees servicing defaulted loans; banks lending money; builders, developers, and other firms under multi-family housing programs; contractors, developers, or lien holders under multi-family programs; builders, developers, real estate firms, contractors, appraisers, other corporations, and firms making repair bids; defaulted borrowers; project owners; project managing agents; former owners; tenants; area managers; HUD personnel in area and regional offices.

WAGE COMPLAINTS AND COMPLIANCE

Construction and maintenance employees of builders and contractors working on HUD-assisted projects.

Additional Files

Following is a list of the remaining files maintained by HUD. Anyone interested in obtaining information from any of these files should contact the Department of Housing and Urban Development, Privacy Office, 451 7th St., SW, Washington, DC 20401.

Accounting Records
Appraisal Review Files
Appraisals/Appraisers Files
Architects and Engineers
Audits and Financial Reports Files
Board of Contract Appeals Files

Builder, Contractor, and Developer Evaluations – Workmanship Adjustment Records
Casualty/Hazard Insurance
Contractors', Brokers', and Management Agents, Qualifications and Bidders' Lists
Cost Analyses of Projects
Credit Processing
Equal Opportunity Programs – Construction
Experimental Housing Allowance Program – Participant Files
Federal Disaster Assistance Administration Files
Fellowship Files, Urban Studies
Flood Insurance Files
Freedom of Information Act Files
Homeownership Assistance and Recertification Application (HARAS)
Housing Assistance Applicants
Housing Counselling
Housing Management Section 8 Management Information
Housing Production and Mortgage Credit Monitoring System
Insured and Terminated Single-Family Cases
Interstate Land Sales Registration Investigations
Loan Management Files
Local Housing Mortgage Insurance
Mobile Home Improvement and Rehabilitation Loans– Delinquent/Default
Mobile Home Park Inspection
Mortgage Servicing Files on HUD-Held Properties
Multifamily Projects Case Files
Pay and Leave Records of Employees
Personnel Medical Records
Personnel Timekeeping System
Personnel Travel System
Pre-Construction Plans, Bids, and Contracts
Project Files
Property Inspection Reports System
Public Housing Rent Subsidy Programs
Real Estate Files
Relocation Assistance
Repair and Maintenance Contractors
Single Family Case Files
Spanish-Speaking Program
Standards of Conduct Files
Subdivision Files

U.S. Department of the Interior

Following is a list of the agencies and subagencies of the U.S. Department of the Interior, with their abbreviations:

Interior	U.S. Department of the Interior
BPA	Bonneville Power Administration
BIA	Bureau of Indian Affairs
BLM	Bureau of Land Management
FWS	Fish and Wildlife Service
GS	Geological Survey
MESA	Mining Enforcement and Safety Administration
Mines	Mines Bureau
NPS	National Park Service
OHA	Office of Hearings and Appeals
Oil and Gas	Office of Oil and Gas
—	Bureau of Reclamation

Note: All inquiries regarding Department of Interior systems of records must be in writing and signed by the requester.

ACCOUNTS RECEIVABLE–INTERIOR/GS

Debtors owing money to the U.S. Geological Survey, including employees, former employees, business firms, institutions, and private individuals. (The records contained in this system that pertain to individuals contain principally proprietary information concerning sole proprietorships. However, some of the records in the system that pertain to individuals may reflect personal information. Only the records reflecting personal information are subject to the Privacy Act. The system also contains records concerning corporations and other business entities. These records are not subject to the Privacy Act.)

Chief, Branch of Financial Management, Geological Survey, National Center, Reston, VA 22092, (703) 860-6181.

ACCOUNTS RECEIVABLE–INTERIOR/OFFICE OF THE SECRETARY

All debtors, including employees, former employees, business firms, private citizens, and institutions. (The records contained in this system which pertain to individuals contain principally proprietary information concerning sole proprietorships. Some of the records in the system which pertain to the individuals may reflect personal information, however. Only the records reflecting personal information are subject to the Privacy Act. The system also contains records concerning corporations, other business entities, and organizations. These records are not subject to the Privacy Act.)

Chief, Office of Secretarial Operations–Fiscal, Department of the Interior, 18th and C Streets, NW, Washington, DC 20240, (202) 343-5027.

AUDIT FILES AND WORKPAPERS–INTERIOR/OFFICE OF THE SECRETARY

Individuals who are or have been the subject of an audit.

Director, Office of Audit and Investigation, 18th and C Streets, NW, Washington, DC 20240, (202) 343-6777.

CIVIL TRESPASS CARE INVESTIGATIONS–INTERIOR/BLM

Individuals suspected of trespass or confirmed as trespassers on national resource lands.

Assistant Director–Technical Services, Bureau of Land Management, Department of the Interior, 18th and C Streets, NW, Washington, DC 20240, (202) 343-4201.

CLAIMS FILES INTERIOR/OFFICE OF THE SOLICITOR

Individuals who have filed tort, federal employee, admiralty, or irrigation claims.

System manager or, with respect to records maintained in the office or implementing the statute, rule, regulation, order, or license violated for which he is responsible, a regional or field solicitor; Administrative Officer, Office of the Solicitor, Department of the Interior, Washington, DC 20240, (202) 343-6115.

CLAIMS INTERIOR/RECLAMATION

Individuals who have filed tort, federal employee, or irrigation claims.

Chief, Division of General Services, Bureau of Reclamation, Department of the Interior, Washington, DC 20240 (202) 343-8937.

COAL MINE HEALTH AND SAFETY SPECIAL INVESTIGATIONS INTERIOR/MESA

Any individual alleged to have committed or have information concerning willful or knowing violations of the Coal Mine Health and Safety Act and related sections of the United States Code.

Assistant Administrator—Coal Mine Health and Safety, Room 814, Ballston Tower 03, 4015 Wilson Blvd., Arlington, VA 22203, (703) 235-1140.

CRIMINAL CASE INVESTIGATION INTERIOR/BLM

Individuals suspected of violation of federal law concerning national resource lands, resources, or facilities.

Assistant Director—Technical Services, Bureau of Land Management, Department of the Interior, 18th and C Streets, NW, Washington, DC 20240, (202) 343-4201.

DISCRIMINATION COMPLAINTS INTERIOR/OFFICE OF THE SECRETARY

Individuals who claim to have been discriminated against on the basis of race, color, sex, religion, or national origin in violation of Title VI of the Civil Rights Act of 1964 (42 U.S.C. 2000d), in violation of Section 403 of the Trans-Alaska Pipeline Authorization Act (87 Stat. 576), or in violation of Executive Order 11246, as amended (3 CFR 169 [1974 ed.]).

For complaints arising under Executive Order 11246, as amended (3 CFR 169 [1974 ed.]), and under Title VI of the Civil Rights Act of 1964 (42 U.S.C. 2000d)—Director, Office for Equal Opportunity, Office of the Secretary, Department of the Interior, 18th and C Streets, NW, Washington, DC 20240, (202) 343-5693. For complaints arising under Section 403 of the Trans-Alaska Pipeline

Authorization Act (87 Stat. 576)—Authorized Officer, Alaska Pipeline Office, Department of the Interior, 808 E Street, Anchorage, AL 99501, (907) 276-7422.

EMPLOYEE CONDUCT INVESTIGATIONS INTERIOR/BLM

Bureau of Land Management employees.

Associate Director, Bureau of Land Management, Department of the Interior, 18th and C Streets, NW, Washington, DC 20240, (202) 343-3897.

EMPLOYEE CONDUCT INVESTIGATIONS INTERIOR/MESA

Any Mesa employee against whom any allegation of misconduct, illegal acts, conflict of interest, etc., has been made.

Chief, Office of Internal Affairs, MESA, 4015 Wilson Blvd., Arlington, VA 22203, (703) 235-1580.

HEARINGS AND APPEALS FILES INTERIOR/OHA

Individual persons involved in hearings and appeals proceedings before the hearings division, appeals boards, and the director of OHA.

Field Interior, 4015 Wilson Boulevard, Arlington, VA 22203; or Director, Office of Hearings and Appeals, Department of the Interior, 18th and C Streets, NW, Washington, DC 20240, (202) 557-1500.

INDUSTRIAL ACCIDENT FILES AND EMPLOYEE CLAIMS INTERIOR/BPA

Employees, contractors, or private parties involved in serious accidents with BPA facilities or employees filing claims for lost or damaged personal property.

Safety Manager, Bonneville Power Administration, 1002 NE, Holladay Street, P.O. Box 3621, Portland, OR 97208, (503) 234-3361, ext. 4751.

INVESTIGATIVE CASE FILE SYSTEM INTERIOR/FWS

Subjects of investigation relative to violation of fish and wildlife laws.

Chief, Division of Law Enforcement, U.S. Fish and Wildlife Service, P.O. Box 19183, Washington, DC 20240, (202) 343-9242.

LAW ENFORCEMENT SERVICES INTERIOR/BIA

Individuals violating laws on Indian reservations and those who appear in court for violations of 25 CFR regulations, and individuals primarily interested in Indian affairs who advocate violence as a means of obtaining their goals.

Director, Office of Indian Services, Bureau of Indian Affairs, 18th and C Streets, NW, Washington, DC 20245, (202) 343-2111.

LAW ENFORCEMENT STATISTICAL REPORTING SYSTEM, INCIDENT CARD REFERENCE, AND RELATED FILES INTERIOR/NPS

Individual complainants in criminal cases, individuals investigated or arrested for criminal or traffic offenses, or involved in motor vehicle accidents or certain types of noncriminal incidents.

Associate Director, Park Systems Management, National Park Service, Department of the Interior, Washington, DC 20240, (202) 343-2015.

LITIGATION, APPEAL, AND CASE FILES INTERIOR/ OFFICE OF THE SOLICITOR

Individuals involved in litigation with the United States, or the Department of the Interior, officials or constituent units thereof; individuals involved in administrative proceedings before the department, to which the department is a party or in which it has an interest; individuals suspected of violations of criminal and civil statutes or regulations or orders, the violation of which carries criminal penalties; individuals who have applied to the department for permits, grants, or loans; individuals who have appealed to the office of the solicitor from the decisions of other constituent units of the department; individuals involved in negotiations, claims, or disputes with the department; individuals for whom the department has performed legal services.

Office of the Solicitor, Department of the Interior, 18th and C Streets, NW, Washington, DC 20240, (202) 343-4423.

LITIGATION INTERIOR/RECLAMATION

Individuals against whom the Bureau of Reclamation has brought suit or who have brought suit against the Bureau of Reclamation.

Chief, Division of General Services, Bureau of Reclamation, Department of the Interior, Washington, DC 20240, (202) 343-8937.

NEGOTIATED GRIEVANCE PROCEDURE FILES INTERIOR/OFFICE OF THE SECRETARY

Interior employees filing grievances/complaints.

Applicable chief of personnel.

PERSONNEL INVESTIGATIONS RECORDS INTERIOR/GS

Current USGS employees who have been granted access to classified information; are selected applicants considered for access to classified information; are selected applicants found unsuitable for access to classified information because unfavorable information was developed during the conduct of their security investigations; are selected employees fulfilling sensitive or critical-sensitive positions not requiring access to classified information; and are selected employees fulfilling nonsensitive positions whose employment suitability investigation disclosed unfavorable or questionable information. Former USGS employees who were granted access to classified information, and about whom unfavorable or questionable information was disclosed as a result of a security or employment suitability investigation.

Security Officer/Alternate Security Officer, USGS, 12201 Sunrise Valley Drive, Reston, VA 22092, (703) 860-6089.

PRIVATE RELIEF CLAIMANTS, BUREAU INTERIOR/ OFFICE OF THE SECRETARY

Individual claimants against the United States seeking remedy through private relief bills for claims involving the programs and activities of the Department of the Interior.

Director, Congressional and Legislative Staff, Room 4639, Bureau of Indian Affairs, 1951 Constitution Avenue, NW, Washington, DC 20245, (202) 343-8877; or Legislative Specialist, Geological Survey, National Center, Reston, VA. 22092; or Chief, Division of Legislation and Regulatory Management, Bureau of Land Management, 18th & C Streets, NW, Washington, DC 20240.

SAFETY FILES INTERIOR/MINES

Persons who have had an accident, injury, illness, or fatality or are associated with a health hazard, radioactive materials, or radiation-producing media in performance of job-related duties or while a visitor.

Bureau Safety Manager, Division of Management Services, Bureau of Mines, Department of the Interior, 2401 E Street, NW, Washington, DC 20241, (202) 634-4764; or, with respect to records maintained at field facilities, the safety officer of the facility.

SAFETY MANAGEMENT INFORMATION INTERIOR/BIA

Employee operators and incidental operators of government-owned vehicles and equipment; federal employees who have had an accident or incident; injured employees who submit claims for medical attention or loss of earning capability due to on-the-job injury; individuals filing tort claims against the United States government.

Director, Office of Administration, Bureau of Indian Affairs, Department of the Interior, 1951 Constitution Avenue, NW, Washington, DC 20245, (202) 343-2111; or, with respect to records maintained in the office responsible, the agency or the school superintendent within the area of a field office director.

THEFTS LISTING INTERIOR/RECLAMATION

Individuals reporting loss or theft.

Chief, Division of General Services, Department of the Interior, Bureau of Reclamation, Washington, DC 20240, (202) 343-8937.

TIMBER CUTTING AND FIRE TRESPASS CLAIMS FILES INTERIOR/BIA

Indian landowners who have filed trespass claims for fire or cutting damage to Indian forest lands under Bureau of Indian Affairs supervision.

Director, Office of Trust Responsibilities, Bureau of Indian Affairs, 1951 Constitution Avenue, NW, Washington, DC 20242, (202) 343-4513; or the agency, or the area office director.

TORT CLAIM RECORDS INTERIOR/FWS

Claimants for damages to personal property or personal injury.

Chief, Division of Contracting and General Services, U.S. Fish and Wildlife Service, Department of the Interior, Washington, DC 20240, (202) 634-1853; or the appropriate regional office.

TRESPASS CASES INTERIOR/RECLAMATION

Individuals who trespass on government-owned property.

Chief, Division of General Services, Bureau of Reclamation, Department of the Interior, Washington, DC 20240, (202) 343-8937.

UNFAIR LABOR PRACTICE CHARGES/COMPLAINTS INTERIOR/OFFICE OF THE SECRETARY

Interior employees filing unfair labor practice charges/complaints.

Applicable chief of personnel.

Additional Files

Following is a list of the remaining files maintained by the Department of the Interior. Anyone interested in obtaining information from any of these files should contact the Department of the Interior, 18th and C Streets, NW, Washington, DC 20240, (202) 343-4201.

Accident Reports and Investigations, Interior/GS
Accident and Injury Records, Interior/MESA
Accident, Interior/BOR
Accidents, Interior/Southwestern Power Administration
Accounts Receivable, Interior/BOR
Administrative Management and Fiscal Records, Interior/ Alaska Power Administration
Advisory Council on Historic Preservation Membership, Interior/NPS
Aircraft Crew/Mechanic Information File, Interior/OS
Aircraft Crew/Mechanic Information File (Commercial Operations), Interior/OS

Aircraft Instructor Qualification File, Interior/OS
Aircraft Passenger Manifest ecords—Fire Control, Interior/ BLM
Aircraft Services Administrative Management and Fiscal Records, Interior/OS
Alaska Native Claims, Interior/BLM
American Attitudes Toward Animals, Interior/FWS
Animal Damage Control Authorization Records, Interior/ FWS
Applicant Files, Interior/OS
Attendance at Meetings, Interior BOR
Audiograms (Hearing Test Record), Interior/OS
Audiometric Testing Forms, Interior/BPA
Audiovisual Performance Selection Files, Interior/NPS
Authorized Cashier, Alternate Cashier, Certifying Officer and Cashier, Collection Officers, Interior/GS
Automated Data Files, Interior/OS
Automotive Accident Files, Interior/BPA
Biography File, Interior/OS
Biographical Reference File, Interior/BOM
Budget Forecast System, Interior/Southwestern Power Administration
Cartographic Information Customer Records, Interior/GS
Cash Receipts, Interior/OS
Central Employee Locator Index, Interior/OS
Central Files, Interior/NPS
Classified Documents, Interior/OS
Coal Lease Data System, Interior/BLM
Coal Mine Noise Level Program, Interior/MESA
Collection, Certifying and Disbursing Officers, and Imprest Fund Cashiers, Interior/NPS
Collection Contracts, Interior/BOR
Committee Management Files, Interior/OS
Computer Services Users, Interior/GS
Concessioner Financial Statement and Audit Report Files, Interior/NPS
Concessioners, Interior/NPS
Concessions, Interior/BOR
Concessions Management Files, Interior/NPS
Congressional Correspondence, Advisory Council on Historic Preservation, Interior/NPS
Congressional Correspondence File, Interior/BOR
Contract Files, Interior/BLM
Contract Files, Interior/GS
Contract and Procurement Records, Interior/FWS
Contracts System, Interior/Southwestern Power Administration
Correspondence, Interior/GS
Correspondence Control, Interior/BIA
Correspondence Control, Interior/BLM
Correspondence Control System, Interior/FWS
Correspondence Files System, Interior/BIA
Diagnostic-Extension Service Records, Interior/FWS
Distribution Center and Film Borrower Record Cards, Interior/BOM
Driver's License, Interior/BOR
Emergency Defense Mobilization Files, Interior/OS
Emergency Loan Fund Committee Loan Records, Interior/OS

Employee Experience, Skills, Performance and Career Development Records, Interior/OS

Employee Financial Irregularities, Interior/NPS

Employee Identification Card Files, Interior/OS

Employee Locator System, Interior/MESA

Employee Trip Reports, Interior/BOR

Employee Work Report Edit and Individual Employee Production Rates, Interior/GS

Employee Workloand and Production Reports, Interior/GS

Employees' Compensation Records, Interior/BOR

Employment Assistance Case Files, Interior/BIA

Endangered Species License System, Interior/FWS

Equipment, Supply, and Service Contracts, Interior/BOR

Farm Pond Stocking Program, Interior/FWS

Financial Interest Statements and Ethics Counselor Decisions, Interior/OS

Financial Management, Interior/BLM

Financial Management System, Interior/BOR

Fish Disease Inspection Report, Interior/FWS

Fish Tag Returns, Interior/FWS

Foreign Visitors and Observers, Interior/BOR

Freedom of Information Files, Interior/OS

Government of American Samoa Administrative Management and Fiscal Records, Interior/OS

Great Lakes Commercial Fisheries Catch Records, Interior/FWS

Health and Safety Training Records Including Qualifications and Certification Data, Interior/MESA

Health Unit Medical Records, Interior/OS

Hunting and Fishing Survey Records, Interior/FWS

Identification Cards, Interior/BOR

Identification Cards, Interior/MESA

Identification Cards and Passes, Interior/BLM

Imprest Fund Cashiers, Interior/Southwestern Power Administration

Incentive and Honor Awards, Interior/BLM

Indian Association Stock Purchase Records, Interior/BIA

Indian Business Development Program (Grants), Interior/BIA

Indian Housing Improvement Program, Interior/BIA

Indian Land Leases, Interior/BIA

Indian Land Records, Interior/BIA

Indian Loan Files, Interior/BIA

Indian Social Services Case Files, Interior/BIA

Indian Student Records, Interior/BIA

Indian Trust Land Mortgages, Interior/BIA

Individual Indian Monies, Interior/BIA

Individual Records of Issues, Interior/BOR

Inventions and Patents, Interior/Reclamation

Investigative Records, Interior/OS

Irrigation Management Service, Interior/BOR

Labor Cost Information Records, Interior/FWS

Land Acquisition and Relocation Files, Interior/NPS

Land Case File, Interior/BLM

Land Exchange, Interior/BOR

Land Records, Interior/BPA

Land Settlement Entries, Interior/BOR

Lands-Leases, Sales, Rentals, and Transfers, Interior/BOR

Lease of Housing, Interior/BOR

Library Borrowers' Records, Interior/BOM

Library Circulation Control System, Interior/OS

Lunar Sample, Interior/GS

Management Information System, Interior/NPS

Management Information System, Publication Division, Interior/GS

Management by Objectives, Interior/BOR

Manpower Management, Interior/BLM

Manuscript Processing System, Interior/GS

Metal and Nonmetal Mine Health and Safety Management Control, Interior/MESA

Migratory Bird Populations and Harvest Systems, Interior/FWS

Mineral Lease Management, Interior/BLM

Mineral Lease and Royalty Accounting Files, Interior/GS

Mineral Location Entries, Interior/Reclamation

Mineral Surveyor Appointment File, Interior/BLM

Mineral and Vegetable Material Sales, Interior/BLM

Mining Claim Title Clearance, Interior/BLM

Motor Vehicle Operations Program, Interior/BOR

Motor Vehicle Operator Identification Records, Interior/BPA

Motor Vehicle Operator's Identification Card Applications, Interior/OS

Motor Vehicle Permit Log, Interior/FWS

Movable Property ADP Records, Interior/BOR

Movable Property Individual Responsibility, Interior/BOR

National Fish Hatchery Special Use Permits, Interior/FWS

National Mine Health and Safety Academy Records, Interior/MESA

National Park Service Historical Library, Interior/NPS

National Research Council Grants Program, Interior/GS

National Wildlife Refuge Special Use Permits, Interior/FWS

Navajo-Hopi Joint Use Project, Interior/BIA

North American Breeding Bird Survey, Interior/BWS

Office of Minerals Exploration (OME), Interior/GS

Office Operations Records on Employees, Bureau System, Interior/OS

Office Operations Records on Employees, Department System, Interior/OS

Oil and Gas Applications, Interior/BOR

Outer Continental Shelf Lease Sale, Interior/BLM

Parking, Interior/BOR

Parking Assignment Records, Interior/OS

Patent Files, Interior/Office of the Solicitor

Payroll, Interior/BIA

Payroll, Interior/BLM

Payroll, Interior/BOM

Payroll, Interior/FWS

Payroll, Interior/NPS

Payroll, Attendance, and Leave Records (PAYPERS), Interior/BOR

Payroll, Attendance, and Leave Records, Interior/GS

Payroll, Attendance, and Leave, Interior/OS

Payroll Files, Interior/BPA

Payroll Records, Interior/MESA

Payroll System, Interior/BOR

Payroll System, Interior/Southwestern Power Administration

Permits, Interior/BOR

Permits System, Interior/FWS
Personal Author Reports, Interior/BOR
Personal Property Accountability Records, Interior/GS
Personnel Identification, Interior/Mines
Photo File System, Interior/GS
Photographic Files, Interior/BOR
Plant Services History Files, Interior/BPA
Plant Services Personal Accountability Property System, Interior/BPA
Position and Manpower Reporting System (PMRS), Interior/NPS
Privacy Act Files, Interior/OS
Project Descriptions and Work Plans and Accomplishments, Interior/GS
Property Accountability, Interior/OS
Property Control, Interior/MESA
Property Control, Interior/Mines
Property Hand Receipt File, Interior/BOR
Property Loan Agreement Files, Interior/BIA
Property Management System, Interior/Southwestern Power Administration
Property and Supplies Accountability, Interior/BLM
Property and Supplies Accountability, Interior/NPS
Publication Sales, Interior/BOR
Publications Division Management Information System, Interior/GS
Range Management System, Interior/BLM
Real Property Records, Interior/FWS
Real Property and Right-Of-Way Acquisitions, Interior/BOR
Recordable Contracts, Interior/BOR
RELOS Records, Interior/GS
Retirement Record, Interior/NPS
Right-Of-Way Applications, Interior/BOR
Safe Driving Records, Interior/BOR
Safety Career Opportunity Plan for Employees, Interior/OS
Safety Management Information, Interior/GLM
Safety Management Information System, Interior/OS
Safety Training Files, Interior/BPA
Sale of Power to Individuals, Interior/BOR
Secretarial Correspondence Card File, Interior/OS
Secretarial Subject Files, Interior/OS
Security, Interior/GS
Security Clearance Files, Interior/BLM
Security Clearance Files, Interior/FWS
Security Clearance Files, Interior/OS
Security Clearance Records, Interior/MESA
Security Files, Interior/Mines
Special Use Applications, Licenses, and Permits, Interior/ BOR
Special Use Permits, Interior/NPS
Speeches, Interior/BOR
Supervisors' Records of Employees, Interior/OS
Traders License Files, Interior/BIA
Travel, Interior/BLM
Travel, Interior/MESA
Travel, Interior/OS
Travel Accounting System, Interior/BIA
Travel Advance File, Interior/BOM
Travel Advance File, Interior/MESA

Travel Approval Authorizations and Reports, Interior/BOR
Travel Files, Interior/BIA
Travel Files, Interior/GS
Travel Record System, Interior/Southwestern Power Administration
Travel Records, Interior/BPA
Travel Records, Interior/FWS
Travel Records, Interior/NPS
Travel Records, Interior/OS
Travel and Transportation Automated Accounting System, Interior/BOR
Travel Vouchers and Authorizations, Interior/Mines
Tribal Rolls, Interior/BIA
Trip Reports, Interior/BIA
Trust Territory Administrative Management and Fiscal Records, Interior/OS
U.S. Deputy Game Warden System, Interior/FWS
U.S. Park Police Personnel Photograph File, Interior/NPS
Vehicle Use Authorization, Interior/BLM
Vendor Payment Records, Interior/BOR
Visitor Statistical Survey Forms, Interior/NPS
Water Development Project and/or Effluent Discharge Permit Application Reviews, Interior/FWS
Water Rights Applications, Interior/BOR
Water Rights Acquisition, Interior/BOR
Water Sales and Delivery Contracts, Interior/BOR
Waterfowl Hunter Attitude Study, Interior/FWS
Workload Analysis, Interior/Office of the Solicitor
Youth Conservation Corps (YCC) Enrollee Medical Records, Interior/OS
Youth Conservation Corps (YCC) Enrollee Payroll Records File, Interior/OS
Youth Conservation Corps (YCC) Enrollee Records, Interior/OS
Youth Conservation Corps (YCC) Recruitment Files, Interior/OS
Youth Conservation Corps (YCC) Research File, Interior/OS
Antitrust Divison
Board of Immigration Appeals
Bureau of Prisons
Civil Division
Civil Rights Division
Criminal Division
Drug Enforcement Administration
FBI
The Immigration and Naturalization Service Index System
Land and Natural Resources Division
Law Enforcement Administration
Office of the Deputy Attorney General
Office of Legal Counsel
Office of Legislative Affairs
Office of Management and Finance
Office of the Pardon Attorney
Office of the Solicitor General
Tax Division
U.S. Attorneys' Office
U.S. Board of Parole
U.S. Marshals Service
Watergate Special Prosecution

U.S. Department of Justice

Following is a list of the agencies and subagencies of the U.S. Department of Justice, with their abbreviations:

Justice   Department of Justice
DEA   Drug Enforcement Administration
FBI   Federal Bureau of Investigation
INS   Immigration and Naturalization Service
LEAA   Law Enforcement Assistance Administration
WSPF   Watergate Special Prosecution Force

Office of the Deputy Attorney General

For information about any Deputy Attorney General system of records, write to the following address and identify the system of interest: Office of the Deputy Attorney General, Department of Justice, 10th St. and Constitution Ave., NW, Washington, DC 20530, (202) 633-2000.

Following is a list of the files maintained by the Department of Justice. Anyone interested in obtaining additional information from any of these files should contact the appropriate agency head or the Office of the Deputy Attorney General, 10th St. and Constitution Ave., NW, Washington, DC 20530.

Appointed Assistant United States Attorneys Personnel System
Assistant United States Attorney Applicant Records System
Declassification Review Index
Financial Disclosure Statements
Freedom of Information Act Index System
Freedom of Information Appeals Index
Freedom of Information Original Request Index
Honor Program Applicant System
Master Index File of Names

Presidential Appointee Candidate Records System
Presidential Appointee Records System
Special Candidates for Presidential Appointments Records System
Summer Intern Program Records System
United States Judge and Department of Justice Presidential Appointee Records
United States Judges Records System

Antitrust Division

INDEX DEFENDANTS IN PENDING AND TERMINATED ANTITRUST CASES

Individual defendants in pending and terminated criminal and civil cases brought by the United States under the antitrust laws.

For information about any Antitrust Division system of records, write to the following address, identifying the system of interest: Assistant Attorney General, Antitrust Division, Department of Justice, 10th St. and Constitution Ave., NW, Washington, DC 20530, (202) 633-2401.

Following is a list of the files maintained by the Antitrust Division. Anyone interested in obtaining additional information from any of these files should contact the appropriate agency head, or the Office of the Deputy Attorney General, 10th St. and Constitution Ave., NW, Washington, DC 20530.

Antitrust Caseload Evaluation System (ACES)—Time Reporter
Antitrust Division Expert Witness File
Computerized Document Retrieval System—"Tire Cases," (CDRS-Tire Cases)
Computerized Document Retrieval System—United States v. International Business Machines (CDRS-IBM)

Congressional Correspondence Log File
Statements by Antitrust Division Officials (ATD Speech File)

Bureau of Prisons

For information about any Bureau of Prisons system of records, write to the following address, stating which system of records is of interest: Director, Bureau of Prisons, 320 1st Street, NW, Washington, DC, (202) 724-3250.

CUSTODIAL AND SECURITY RECORD SYSTEM

Current and former inmates under the custody of the attorney general. The major part of this system is exempt from this requirement under 5 U.S.C. 552a (j).

FEDERAL TORT CLAIMS ACT RECORD SYSTEM

Current and former inmates under the custody of the attorney general. The major part of this system is exempt from this requirement under 5 U.S.C. 552a (j).

FREEDOM OF INFORMATION ACT RECORD SYSTEM

Current and former inmates under the custody of the attorney general. The major part of this system is exempt from this requirement under 5 U.S.C. 552a (j).

INMATE ADMINISTRATIVE REMEDY RECORD SYSTEM

Current and former inmates under the custody of the attorney general. The major part of this system is exempt from this requirement under 5 U.S.C. 552a (j).

INMATE CENTRAL RECORDS SYSTEM

Current and former inmates under the custody of the attorney general. The major part of this system is exempt from this requirement under 5 U.S.C. 552a (j).

INMATE PHYSICAL AND MENTAL HEALTH RECORD SYSTEM

Current and former inmates under the custody of the attorney general. The major part of this system is exempt from this requirement under 5 U.S.C. 552a (j).

INMATE SAFETY AND ACCIDENT COMPENSATION RECORD SYSTEM

Current and former inmates under the custody of the attorney general. The major part of this system is exempt from this requirement under 5 U.S.C. 552a (j).

Following is a list of the remaining files maintained by the Bureau of Prisons. Anyone interested in obtaining additional information from any of these files should contact the appropriate agency head, or the Office of the Deputy Attorney General, 10th St. and Constitution Ave., NW, Washington, DC 20530.

Industrial Inmate Employment Record System
Inmate Commissary Accounts Record System

Civil Division

CIVIL DIVISION CASE FILE SYSTEM

Any and all parties involved in the cases handled by the Civil Division.

Assistant Attorney General, Civil Division, Department of Justice, 10th St. and Constitution Ave., NW, Washington, DC 20530 (202) 633-3301.

Civil Rights Division

For information on any Civil Rights Division system of records write to the following, identifying the system of records of interest: Assistant Attorney General, Civil Rights Division, Department of Justice, Washington, DC 20530, (202) 633-2151.

CENTRAL CIVIL RIGHTS DIVISION INDEX FILE AND ASSOCIATED RECORDS

Persons referred to in potential or actual cases and matters of concern to the Civil Rights Division and correspondents on subjects directed or referred to the Civil Rights Division.

FILES ON CORRESPONDENCE RELATING TO CIVIL RIGHTS MATTERS FROM PERSONS OUTSIDE THE DEPARTMENT OF JUSTICE

Persons communicating in written form, including complaints, requests for information or action, or expressions of opinion regarding civil rights matters.

FILES ON EMPLOYMENT CIVIL RIGHTS MATTERS REFERRED BY THE EQUAL EMPLOYMENT OPPORTUNITY COMMISSION

Persons seeking employment or employed by a state or political subdivision of a state who have filed charges alleging discrimination in employment with the Equal Employment Opportunity Commission (hereinafter EEOC) which have resulted in a determination by EEOC that there is probable cause to believe that such discrimination has occurred, and attempts by EEOC at conciliation have failed.

RECORDS OBTAINED BY OFFICE OF SPECIAL LITIGATION CONCERNING RESIDENTS OF CERTAIN STATE INSTITUTIONS

Individuals who are residents of state operated or supported institutions for mentally and physically handicapped persons, juveniles, and the aged, if such institutions have been the subject of litigation or investigation involving the Civil Rights Division. Information may also pertain to other individuals who are not receiving but may be entitled to forms of educational, habilitative, or rehabilitative care under state or federal law.

Additional Files

Following is a list of the remaining files maintained by the Civil Division. Anyone interested in obtaining additional information from any of these files should contact the appropriate agency head, or the Office of the Deputy Attorney General, 10th St. and Constitution Ave., NW, Washington, DC 20530.

Civil Rights Division Employees Travel Reporting and Control System
Files of Applications for the Position of Attorney with the Civil Rights Division
Files of Federal Programs Section, Civil Rights Division
Files of Pending Applications for Clerical or Research Analyst Positions with the Civil Rights Division
Registry of Names of Interested Persons Desiring Notification of Submissions Under Section 5 of the Voting Rights Act

Criminal Division

For information about any Criminal Division system of records, write to the following address and identify the system of records of interest: Assistant Attorney General, Criminal Division, Department of Justice, 10th St. and Constitution Ave., NW, Washington, DC 20530, (202) 633-2601.

CENTRAL CRIMINAL DIVISION INDEX FILE AND ASSOCIATED RECORDS

Persons referred to in potential or actual cases and matters of concern to the Criminal Division and correspondents on subjects directed or referred to the Criminal Division.

CRIMINAL DIVISION WITNESS SECURITY FILE

Persons who are potential or actual witnesses and/or informants, relatives, and associates of those individuals.

FILE OF NAMES CHECKED TO DETERMINE IF THOSE INDIVIDUALS HAVE BEEN THE SUBJECT OF AN ELECTRONIC SURVEILLANCE

Grand jury witnesses, defendants, and potential defendants in criminal cases and their attorneys. A part of this system is exempted from this requirement under 5 U.S.C. 552a (j) (2).

GENERAL CRIMES SECTION, CRIMINAL DIVISION, CENTRAL INDEX FILE AND ASSOCIATED RECORDS

Persons referred to in potential or actual cases and matters of concern to the general crimes section, Criminal Division, and correspondents on subjects directed or referred to the Criminal Division. The major part of this system is exempted from this requirement under 5 U.S.C. 552a (j) (2), (k) (1), or (k) (2).

INFORMATION FILE ON INDIVIDUALS AND COMMERCIAL ENTITIES KNOWN OR SUSPECTED OF BEING INVOLVED IN FRAUDULENT ACTIVITIES

Individuals involved in actual or suspected fraudulent activities and their victims.

NARCOTIC AND DANGEROUS DRUG WITNESS SECURITY PROGRAM FILE

Persons who are potential or actual witnesses and/or informants, relatives, and associates of those individuals in narcotic and dangerous drug cases.

ORGANIZED CRIME AND RACKETEERING INFORMATION SYSTEM

Persons who have been prosecuted or who are under investigation for potential or actual criminal prosecution as well as persons allegedly involved in organized criminal activity and those alleged to be associated with the subject.

ORGANIZED CRIME AND RACKETEERING SECTION, GENERAL INDEX FILE AND ASSOCIATED RECORDS

Persons who have been prosecuted or are under investigation for potential or actual criminal prosecution as well as persons allegedly involved in organized criminal activity and those alleged to be associated with the subject.

ORGANIZED CRIME AND RACKETEERING SECTION, INTELLIGENCE AND SPECIAL SERVICES UNIT, INFORMATION REQUEST SYSTEM

Individuals making inquiries of the intelligence and special services unit data sources, unit personnel processing those inquiries, intelligence analysts assigned to the strike forces, and those individuals about whom such inquiries are made.

RECORDS ON PERSONS WHO HAVE OUTSTANDING AND UNCOLLECTED FEDERAL CRIMINAL FINES OR FEDERAL BOND FORFEITURES

Persons who have outstanding and uncollected federal criminal fines or federal bond forfeitures whose address is presently unknown or was, at one time or another.

REGISTRATION FILES OF INDIVIDUALS WHO HAVE
KNOWLEDGE OF, OR HAVE RECEIVED INSTRUCTION
OR ASSIGNMENT IN, ESPIONAGE, COUNTERESPION-
AGE, OR SABOTAGE SERVICE, OR TACTICS OF A
FOREIGN GOVERNMENT OR OF A FOREIGN POLIT-
ICAL PARTY

Persons who have knowledge of, or who have received instruction or assignment in, espionage, counterespionage, or
sabotage service or tactics of a foreign government or of a
foreign political party.

REQUESTS TO THE ATTORNEY GENERAL FOR AP–
PROVAL OF APPLICATIONS TO FEDERAL JUDGES
FOR ELECTRONIC INTERCEPTIONS

Individuals who have been the subject of requests by federal investigative agencies for electronic surveillance.

REQUESTS TO THE ATTORNEY GENERAL FOR AP-
PROVAL OF APPLICATIONS TO FEDERAL JUDGES
FOR ELECTRONIC INTERCEPTIONS IN NARCOTIC
AND DANGEROUS DRUG CASES

Individuals who have been the subject of requests by federal investigative agencies for electronic surveillance.

THE STOCKS AND BONDS INTELLIGENCE CONTROL
CARD FILE SYSTEM

Individuals, and their known associates, who are actual,
potential, or alleged violators, of statutes dealing with
stocks, bonds, and other securities.

Additional Files

Following is a list of the remaining files maintained by the
Criminal Division. Anyone interested in obtaining additional
information from any of these files should contact the appropriate agency head, or the Office of the Deputy Attorney General, 10th St. and Constitution Ave., NW, Washington, DC 20530.

Index to Names of Attorneys Employed by the Criminal
    Division, U.S. Department of Justice, Indicating the
    Subject of the Memoranda on Criminal Matters They
    Have Written
Name Card File on Criminal Division Personnel Authorized
    to Have Access to the Central Criminal Division Records
Name Card File on Department of Justice Personnel Auth-
    orized to Have Access to Classified Files of the Depart-
    ment of Justice
Organized Crime and Racketeering Section File Check Out
    System
Inspector General Investigative System
Law Enforcement Education System
Personnel System
Public Information System

Drug Enforcement Administration

ADDICTS/ABUSERS SYSTEM

Persons arrested for any crime whom the arresting officer
suspects are either addicted to narcotics or chronically
abusing narcotics.

Chief, Statistical and Data Services Divisions; Drug Enforcement Administration, 1405 I Street, NW, Washington,
DC 20537 (202) 633-1263.

AUTOMATED INTELLIGENCE RECORDS (PATH-
FINDER I) PROPOSED SYSTEM

Known and suspected drug traffickers and associates.

Assistant Administrator for Intelligence, Drug Enforcement Administration, Department of Justice, 1405 I
Street, NW, Washington, DC 20537, (202) 633-1071.

DEA/FAA TRANS-BORDER FLIGHT PLAN REPORTING
SYSTEM (PROPOSED)

Known and suspected air narcotic traffickers and pilots.

Director, El Paso Intelligence Center, 4110 Rio Bravo,
El Paso, TX 79902, (915) 543-7255.

DEFENDANT DATA SYSTEM

Persons arrested for drug law violations by federal law enforcement officials.

Chief, Statistical and Data Services Division, Drug Enforcement Administration, 1405 I Street, NW, Washington, DC
20537, (202) 633-1263.

DOMESTIC INTELLIGENCE DATA BASE

Persons involved or suspected of involvement in illicit
manufacturing and trafficking in controlled substances.

Assistant Administrator for Intelligence, Drug Enforcement Administration, Department of Justice, 1405 I Street,
NW, Washington, DC 20537, (202) 633-1071.

INTERNATIONAL INTELLIGENCE DATA BASE

Known and suspected drug traffickers.

Assistant Administrator for Intelligence, Drug Enforcement Administration, Department of Justice, 1405 I
Street, NW, Washington, DC 20537, (202) 633-1071.

INVESTIGATIVE REPORTING AND FILING SYSTEM

Drug offenders, persons suspected of drug offenses, confidential informants, defendants, witnesses, nonimplicated
persons with pertinent knowledge of some circumstance or
aspect of a case or suspect. These are pertinent references
of fact developed by personal interview or third-party interview and are recorded as a matter for which a probable
need for recall will exist. In the regulatory portion of the

system, records are maintained on the following categories of individuals: Individuals registered with DEA under the Comprehensive Drug Abuse Prevention and Control Act of 1970; responsible officials of business firms registered with DEA; employees of DEA registrants who handle controlled substances or occupy positions of trust related to the handling of controlled substances; applicants for DEA registration and their responsible employees.

Assistant Administrator for Enforcement, Drug Enforcement Administration, Department of Justice, 1405 I Street, NW, Washington, DC 20537, (202) 633-1151.

REGISTRATION STATUS/INVESTIGATION RECORDS

Individuals who have a Controlled Substances Act registration number under their personal name and who have had some action taken against their license or registration.

Assistant Administrator for Enforcement, Drug Enforcement Administration, Department of Justice, 1405 I Street, NW, Washington, DC 20537, (202) 633-1151.

SECURITY FILES

DEA personnel; cooperating individuals and informants; drug traffickers and suspected drug traffickers; individuals who might discover DEA investigations or undercover operations by chance.

Assistant Administrator for Intelligence, Drug Enforcement Administration, Department of Justice, 1405 I Street, NW, Washington, DC 20537, (202) 633-1071.

SEMI-AUTOMATED NARCOTICS TRAFFICKER PROFILES (KISS)

Known and suspected drug traffickers.

Assistant Administrator for Intelligence, Drug Enforcement Administration, Department of Justice, 1405 I Street, NW, Washington, DC 20537, (202) 633-1071.

SPECIALIZED AUTOMATED INTELLIGENCE FILES (NIMROD)

Known and suspected drug traffickers.

Assistant Administrator for Intelligence, Drug Enforcement Administration, 1405 I Street, NW, Washington, DC 20537, (202) 633-1071.

SYSTEM TO RETRIEVE INFORMATION FROM DRUG EVIDENCE (STRIDE)

Defendants and suspected violators.

Chief, Forensic Sciences Division, Drug Enforcement Administration, 1405 I Street, NW, Washington, DC 20537, (202) 633-1211.

Additional Files

Following is a list of the remaining files maintained by the Drug Enforcement Administration. Anyone interested in obtaining additional information from any of these files should contact the appropriate agency head, or the Office of the Deputy Attorney General, 10th St. and Constitution Ave., NW, Washington, DC 20530.

Air Intelligence Program
Congressional Correspondence File
Controlled Substances Act Registration Records (CSA)
DEA Applicant Investigations (DAI)
Drug Enforcement Administration Accounting System (DEAAS)
Drug Theft Reporting System (DTR)
Freedom of Information Request Files
Grants of Confidentiality Files (GCF)
Medical Records
Office of Internal Security Records
Operations Files
Source Registry Narcotics (SRN/1)
Training Files

Federal Bureau of Investigation

For information about any FBI system of records, write to the following address, indicating system of interest: Director, Federal Bureau of Investigation, J. Edgar Hoover Building, 10th St. and Pennsylvania Ave., NW, Washington, DC 20535, (202) 324-3444.

ELECTRONIC SURVEILLANCE (ELSUR) INDICES

Individuals who have been the targets of direct electronic surveillance coverage by the FBI, who have participated in conversations monitored by an FBI electronic installation, or who have owned, leased, or licensed premises on which the FBI has conducted an electronic surveillance.

THE "FBI CENTRAL RECORDS SYSTEM" CONTAINING INVESTIGATIVE, PERSONNEL, ADMINISTRATIVE, APPLICANT, AND GENERAL FILES

Individuals who relate in any manner to official FBI investigations including, but not limited to suspects, victims, witnesses, and close relatives and associates that are relevant to an investigation; applicants for and current and former personnel of the FBI and persons related thereto that are considered relevant to an applicant investigation, personnel inquiry, or persons related to personnel matters; applicants for and appointees to sensitive positions in the United States government and persons related thereto that are considered relevant to the investigation; individuals who are the subject of unsolicited information, who offer unsolicited information, request assistance, and make inquiries concerning record material, including general correspondence, contacts with other agencies, businesses, institutions, clubs, the public, and the news media; individuals associated with administrative operations or services including pertinent functions, contractors and pertinent persons related thereto.

IDENTIFICATION DIVISION RECORDS SYSTEM

Individuals fingerprinted as a result of arrest or incarceration by federal, state, or local law enforcement agencies; persons fingerprinted as a result of federal employment applications, military service, alien registration and naturalization purposes, and individuals desiring to have their fingerprints placed on record with the FBI for personal identification purposes.

NATIONAL CRIME INFORMATION CENTER (NCIC)

Wanted persons: Individuals for whom federal warrants are outstanding; individuals who have committed or have been identified with an offense which is classified as a felony or serious misdemeanor under the existing penal statutes of the jurisdiction originating the entry, and felony or misdemeanor warrant has been issued for the individual with respect to the offense which was the basis of the entry; probation and parole violators meeting the foregoing criteria; individuals for whom a "Temporary Felony Warrant" has been entered. Individuals who have been charged with serious and/or significant offenses. *Missing persons*: Persons of any age who are missing and who are under proven physical/mental disability or are senile, thereby subjecting themselves or others to personal and immediate danger; persons of any age who are missing under circumstances indicating that their disappearance was not voluntary; persons of any age who are in the company of another person under circumstances indicating that their physical safety is in danger; persons who are declared unemancipated as defined by the laws of their state of residence and who do not meet any of the entry criteria set forth above.

Following is a list of the remaining files maintained by the FBI. Anyone interested in obtaining additional information from any of these files should contact the appropriate agency head, or the Office of the Deputy Attorney General, 10th St. and Constitution Ave., NW, Washington, DC 20530.

Bureau Mailing List
FBI Automated Payroll System
Personnel Information Network System (PINS)
Routine Correspondence Handled by Preprinted Form
Routine Correspondence Prepared Without File Yellow

Immigration and Naturalization Service

AGENCY INFORMATION CONTROL RECORD INDEX

United States citizens, resident and nonresident aliens named in documents classified for national security reasons and individuals referenced in documents classified for national security reasons.

Associate Commissioner, Management, Immigration and Naturalization Service, 425 I St., NW, Washington, DC 20536, (202) 633-3182.

ALIEN ADDRESS REPORTS (FORM I-53), 1975 AND SUBSEQUENT YEARS

Aliens who filed reports.

Associate Commissioner, Management, Immigration and Naturalization Service, 425 I St., NW, Washington, DC 20536, (202) 633-3182; or nearest district office.

ALIEN ENEMY INDEX

Alien enemies who were interned during World War II; Americans of Japanese ancestry (nisei) who returned to Japan and, during World War II, either accepted employment by the Japanese government or became naturalized in Japan.

Associate Commissioner, Management, Immigration and Naturalization Service, 425 I St., NW, Washington, DC 20536, (202) 633-3182.

AUTOMOBILE DECAL PARKING IDENTIFICATION FOR EMPLOYEES

Current service employees of INS who have the privilege of parking their cars on government premises, and who have a decal for their cars for parking identification.

COMPASSIONATE CASES SYSTEM

Employees of the service.

Associate Commissioner, Management, Immigration and Naturalization Service, 425 I St., NW, Washington, DC 20536, (202) 633-3182; or regional offices.

CENTRALIZED INDEX (MASTER INDEX)

Aliens lawfully admitted for permanent residence, and United States citizens; and individuals who are under investigation, were investigated in the past, or who are suspected of violating the criminal or civil provisions of treaties, statutes, executive orders and presidential proclamation administered by the Immigration and Naturalization Service, and witnesses and informants having knowledge of such violations.

Associate Commissioner, Management, Immigration and Naturalization Service, 425 I St., NW, Washington, DC 20536, (202) 633-3182.

CONGRESSIONAL MAIL UNIT

Aliens lawfully admitted for permanent residence and United States citizens named in correspondence received including, but not necessarily limited to: (a) employees and past employees, (b) federal, state and local officials, and (c) members of the general public; aliens lawfully admitted for permanent residence and United States citizens named in reports or correspondence received, as individuals investigated in the past or under active investigations for, or suspected of violations of, the criminal or civil provisions of statutes enforced by the service, including presidential proclamations and executive orders relating thereto, and witnesses and informants having knowledge of violations.

Associate Commissioner, Management, Immigration and Naturalization Service, 425 I St., NW, Washington, DC 20536, (202) 633-3182.

DOCUMENT VENDORS AND ALTERERS INDEX (SERVICE DOCUMENTS)

Aliens lawfully admitted for permanent residence and United States citizens.

Associate Commissioner, Management, Immigration and Naturalization Service, 425 I Street, NW, Washington, DC 20536, (202) 633-3182.

ENFORCEMENT BRANCH INDICES—GROUP I

Group I includes aliens lawfully admitted for permanent residence, and citizens who are in a position to know or learn of, and assist in locating aliens illegally in the United States. Aliens lawfully admitted for permanent residence, and citizens who are former or present members of an organization subversive in nature, whether foreign or domestic, and are willing to appear as government witnesses to testify as to their knowledge of an individual's membership therein, or as to the nature, aims, and purpose of the organization, or as to the identification, publication, distribution, and authenticity of the literature of such organization, or are in possession of information relative to such organization or on specific individuals and are willing to cooperate with the Immigration and Naturalization Service, or who, although they have not been members of subversive organizations, are in possession of information relating to such organizations or members thereof, and are willing to cooperate with the Service on a continuing basis. Aliens lawfully admitted for permanent residence, and citizens who are known or suspected of being professional arrangers, transporters, harborers, or smugglers of aliens, who operate or conspire to operate with others to facilitate the surreptitious entry of an alien over a coastal or land border of the United States and witnesses having knowledge of such matters. Aliens lawfully admitted for permanent residence and citizens who are known or suspected of being habitual or notorious criminals, immorals, narcotics violators, or racketeers, or subversive functionaries or leaders. Aliens lawfully admitted for permanent residence, and citizens who are known, or believed, to be engaged in fraud opera-

tions involving the preparation and submission of visa petitions and other applications for service benefits, or the preparation and submission of applications for immigrant visas and/or Department of Labor certifications, or the filing of false United States birth registrations for alien children to enable parents who are immigrant visa applicants to evade the labor certification requirements or to enable such children to pose as citizens.

Associate Commissioner, Management, Immigration and Naturalization Service, 425 I St., NW, Washington, DC 20536, (202) 633-3182.

ENFORCEMENT BRANCH INDICES—GROUP II

For information contained in the following Group II files, request should be made to:

Associate Commissioner, Management, Immigration and Naturalization Service, 425 I St., NW, Washington, DC 20536, (202) 633-3182; regional offices; or the Border Patrol.

AIR DETAIL OFFICE INDEX SYSTEM

United States citizens and aliens lawfully admitted for permanent residence who are pilots and/or owners of private aircraft and who have engaged in flying between the United States and foreign countries; pilots, owners, and associates, including United States citizens and aliens lawfully admitted for permanent residence who engage in, or are suspected of being engaged in, illegal activity, such as alien smuggling or entry without inspection.

ANTI-SMUGGLING INFORMATION CENTERS FOR THE CANADIAN BORDER AND MEXICAN BORDER

Citizens and aliens lawfully admitted for permanent residence who are smugglers or transporters of illegal aliens or who are suspects in the violation of statutes relating to smuggling and transporting illegal aliens.

BORDER PATROL ACADEMY INDEX SYSTEM

United States citizens who are students in attendance at the Border Patrol Academy; former students who have attended the academy; and officers attending advanced training classes at the academy.

BORDER PATROL SECTORS GENERAL INDEX

United States citizens who are past or present employees of the service; United States citizens and aliens lawfully admitted for permanent residence who are classified as law violators; witnesses, contacts, informants, members of the general public; and federal, state, county, and local offices.

FRAUDULENT DOCUMENT CENTER INDEX

United States citizens and/or aliens lawfully admitted for permanent residence who are categorized as members of the general public, notaries public, state, and local birth registration officials and employees, immigration law violators, vendors of documents, donors of documents, midwives, and witnesses.

ENFORCEMENT BRANCH INDICES—GROUP III (Associate Commissioner, Enforcement)

Aliens lawfully admitted for permanent residence and citizens of the United States named in correspondence received, including but not necessarily limited to: (a) employees and past employees; (b) federal, state, and local officials; and (c) members of the general public; aliens lawfully admitted for permanent residence and citizens of the United States named in documents, reports, or correspondence received as individuals under investigation, or investigated in the past, or suspected of violation of the criminal or civil provisions of the statutes enforced by the Service, including presidential executive orders and proclamations relating thereto, and witnesses and informants having knowledge of violations.

Associate Commissioner, Enforcement, Immigration and Naturalization Service, 425 I St., NW, Washington, DC 20536 (202) 633-3182.

EMERGENCY REASSIGNMENT INDEX

Employees of the service.

Associate Commissioner, Management, Immigration and Naturalization Service, 425 I St., NW, Washington, DC 20536, (202) 633-3182; or regional offices, district offices, suboffices, and border patrols.

EXAMINATIONS BRANCH INDEXES

Aliens lawfully admitted for permanent residence and United States citizens and individuals who are violators or suspected violators of the criminal or civil provisions of statutes enforced by the service.

Associate Commissioner, Management, Immigration and Naturalization Service, 425 I St., NW, Washington, DC 20536, (202) 633-3182.

EXTENSION TRAINING PROGRAM ENROLLEES

Service employees, and other federal agency employees enrolled in extension training program courses.

Associate Commissioner, Management, Immigration and Naturalization Service, 425 I St., NW, Washington, DC 20536, (202) 633-3182.

FINANCE SECTION INDEXES

Individuals who are indebted to the United States government for goods, services, or benefits or for administrative fines and assessments; employees who have received travel advances or overpayments from the United States govern-

ment, who are in arrears in their accounts, or who are liable for damage to government property, vendors who have furnished supplies, material, equipment, and services to the government; employees, witnesses, and special deportation attendants who have performed official travel; and employees or other individuals who have a valid claim against the government.

Associate Commissioner, Management, Immigration and Naturalization Service, 425 I St., NW, Washington, DC 20536, (202) 633-3182, or nearest regional office.

FREEDOM OF INFORMATION CORRESPONDENCE CONTROL INDEX

Individuals who request, under the Freedom of Information Act, access to, or copies of, records maintained by the service.

Associate Commissioner, Management, Immigration and Naturalization Service, 425 I St., NW, Washington, DC 20536, (202) 633-3182, or any appropriate Service office.

HEALTH RECORDS SYSTEM

Persons in central Washington office who need health services or who require emergency treatment.

Associate Commissioner, Management, Immigration and Naturalization Service, 425 I St., NW, Washington, DC 20536, (202) 633-2000.

INTELLIGENCE INDEX

Aliens who have been lawfully admitted to the United States for permanent residence, and United States citizens who have, or who are suspected of having, violated the criminal or civil provisions of the statutes enforced by the service.

Associate Commissioner, Management, Immigration and Naturalization Service, 425 I St., NW, Washington, DC 20536, (202) 633-3182; or nearest regional office.

MICROFILMED MANIFEST RECORDS

Aliens lawfully admitted for permanent residence to the United States, and United States citizens.

Associate Commissioner, Management, Immigration and Naturalization Service, 425 I St., NW, Washington, DC 20536, (202) 633-3182.

NATURALIZATION AND CITIZENSHIP DOCKET CARDS

Aliens lawfully admitted for permanent residence and citizens of the United States, and other individuals seeking benefits under Title III of the Immigration and Nationality Act of 1952, as amended.

PERSONAL DATA CARD SYSTEM

Employees and former employees of the service.

Associate Commissioner, Management, Immigration and Naturalization Service, 425 I St., NW, Washington, DC 20536, (202) 633-3182; or regional offices.

EXAMINER'S DOCKET LISTS OF PETITIONERS FOR NATURALIZATION

Petitioners for naturalization and beneficiaries.

MASTER DOCKET LIST OF PETITIONERS FOR NATURALIZATION PENDING ONE YEAR OR MORE

Petitioners for naturalization and beneficiaries.

District offices or Associate Commissioner, Management, Immigration and Naturalization Service, 425 I St., NW, Washington, DC 20536, (202) 633-3182.

PERSONAL INVESTIGATIONS

Employees, former employees, other government agency employees designated to perform immigration functions, witnesses, informants, and certain persons having contact with service operations.

Associate Commissioner, Management, Immigration and Naturalization Service, 425 I St., NW, Washington, DC 20536, (202) 633-3182.

PROPERTY ISSUED TO EMPLOYEES

Employees of the service who have been issued property and have in addition signed for receipt of the property on Form G-570.

Associate Commissioner, Management, Immigration and Naturalization Service, 425 I St., NW, Washington, DC 20536, (202) 633-3182; or regional or district office.

SECURITY SYSTEM

United States citizens and aliens lawfully admitted for permanent residence to the United States who are currently employed with the Service who have been cleared for access to documents and materials classified in the interest of national security.

Associate Commissioner, Management, Immigration and Naturalization Service, 425 I St., NW, Washington, DC 20536, (202) 633-3182.

WHITE HOUSE AND ATTORNEY GENERAL CORRESPONDENCE CONTROL INDEX

Citizens and aliens lawfully admitted for permanent residence to the United States who are named in correspondence received, including, but not necessarily limited to: (a) employees and past employees of the Service; (b) federal, state and local officials; and (c) members of the general public.

Associate Commissioner, Management, Immigration and Naturalization Service, 425 I St., NW, Washington, DC 20536, (202) 633-3182.

Additional Files

Following is a list of the remaining files maintained by the Immigration and Naturalization Service. Anyone interested in obtaining additional information from any of these files should contact the appropriate agency head, or the Office of the Deputy Attorney General, 10th St. and Constitution Ave., NW, Washington, DC 20530.

Decisions of the Board of Immigration Appeals
Roster of Organizations and Their Accredited Representatives Recognized by the Board of Immigration Appeals

Land and Natural Resources Division

DOCKET CARD SYSTEM

Persons, associations, or corporations whose names may appear in the case name or subject name of a matter coming to the attention of the Land and Natural Resources Division for possible litigation.

Assistant Attorney General, Land and Natural Resources Division, Department of Justice, 10th and Constitution Ave., NW, Washington, DC 20530, (202) 633-2701.

Additional Files

Following is a list of the remaining files maintained by the Land and Natural Resources Division. Anyone interested in obtaining additional information from any of these files should contact the appropriate agency head, or the Office of the Deputy Attorney General, 10th St. and Constitution Ave., NW, Washington, DC 20530.

Appraisers File
Congressional Correspondence File

Office of Legal Counsel

For information about any Office of Legal Counsel system of records, write to the following address, identifying the system of records of interest: Assistant Attorney General, Office of Legal Counsel, Department of Justice, 10th St. and Constitution Ave., NW, Washington, DC 20530, (202) 633-2041.

Additional Files

Following is a list of the files maintained by the Office of Legal Counsel. Anyone interested in obtaining additional

information from any of these files should contact the appropriate agency head, or the Office of the Deputy Attorney General, 10th St. and Constitution Ave., NW, Washington, DC 20530.

Attorney Assignment Reports
Citizens Mail Index

Office of Legislative Affairs

For information about any OLA system of records, write to the following address, identifying the system of records of interest: Assistant Attorney General, Office of Legislative Affairs, Department of Justice, 10th St. and Constitution Ave., NW, Washington, DC 20530, (202) 633-2141.

Additional Files

Following is a list of the files maintained by the Office of Legislative Affairs. Anyone interested in obtaining additional information from any of these files should contact the appropriate agency head, or the Office of the Deputy Attorney General, 10th St. and Constitution Ave., NW, Washington, DC 20530.

Citizen Correspondence File
Congressional Committee Chairman Correspondence File
Congressional Correspondence File

Office of the Solicitor General

For information about any Office of the Solicitor General system of records, including Attorney Assignment Reports, write to the following address, identifying the system of records of interest: Solicitor General, Department of Justice, 10th St. and Constitution Ave., NW, Washington, DC 20530, (202) 633-2201.

Office of the Pardon Attorney

NEWS RELEASE, DOCUMENT, AND INDEX SYSTEM

Defendants in civil and criminal actions brought by the Department of Justice for which news releases were issued; current and former employees of the Department of Justice on which news releases and biographical information were prepared.

Director of Public Information, Department of Justice, 10th St. and Constitution Ave., NW, Washington, DC 20530, (202) 633-2028.

Additional Files

The following files are maintained by the Office of the Pardon Attorney department. Anyone interested in obtaining

additional information should contact the appropriate agency head or the Office of the Deputy Attorney General, 10th St. and Constitution Ave., NW, Washington, DC 20530.

Executive Clemency Files

Information on executive clemency, including pardon, commutation, remission of fine, and reprieve. Requests for discretionary releases of records contained in the file system considered in accordance with the guidelines in CFR 1.6, which governs disclosure of such information. Requests should be made in writing to: Privacy Act Request, Office of the Pardon Attorney, U.S. Department of Justice, Constitution Ave. and 10th St., Washington, DC 20530.

U.S Board of Parole

DOCKET, SCHEDULING, AND CONTROL

Current and former inmates under the custody of the attorney general who have become eligible for parole. Former inmates include those presently under supervision as parolees or mandatory releases and those against whom a revocation warrant has been issued.

Attorney-Management Analyst, U.S. Board of Parole, 320 First St., NW, Room 342, Washington, DC 20537, (202) 724-7567; or regional director at appropriate location. The attorney (legal counsel) general has exempted this system from compliance with the provisions of Subsection (d), under the provisions of Subsection (j).

FREEDOM OF INFORMATION ACT RECORD SYSTEM

Current and former inmates under the custody of the attorney general, including former inmates under supervision.

General Counsel, U.S. Board of Parole, 320 First St., NW, Washington, DC 20537, (202) 724-7567.

INMATE AND SUPERVISION FILES

Current and former inmates under the custody of the attorney general. Former inmates include those presently under supervision as parolees or mandatory releasees.

Attorney-Management Analyst, U.S. Board of Parole, 320 First St., NW, Room 342, Washington, DC 20537, (202) 633-2000; or regional director at appropriate location. The attorney general has exempted this system from compliance with the provisions of Subsection (d) under the provisions of Subsection (j).

LABOR AND PENSION CASE, LEGAL FILE, AND GENERAL CORRESPONDENCE SYSTEM

All applicants for exemptions under 29 U.S.C. 504 and 29 U.S.C. 1111, all persons litigating with the U.S. Board of

Parole, all persons corresponding with the board on subjects not amenable to being filed in an inmate or supervision file identified by an individual, and all legislators inquiring about constituents.

Attorney-Management Analyst, U.S. Board of Parole, 320 First St., NW, Room 342, Washington, DC 20537, (202) 724-7567.

Additional Files

Following is a list of the remaining files maintained by the U.S. Board of Parole. Anyone interested in obtaining additional information from any of these files should contact the appropriate agency head, or the Office of the Deputy Attorney General, 10th St. and Constitution Ave., NW, Washington, DC 20530.

Office Operation and Personnel System
Statistical, Educational, and Developmental System
Workload Record, Decision Result, and Annual Report
   System

Law Enforcement Assistance Administration

CIVIL RIGHTS INVESTIGATIVE SYSTEM

Complaints of discrimination by individuals affected by the agency program for which the agency has compliance responsibility, grantees, subgrantees, contractors, subcontractors, employees, and applicants.

Office of Civil Rights Compliance, Law Enforcement Assistance Administration, Department of Justice, 633 Indiana Ave., NW, Washington, DC 20531, (202) 633-2284.

Additional Files

Following is a list of the remaining files maintained by the Law Enforcement Assistance Administration. Anyone interested in obtaining additional information from any of these files should contact the appropriate agency head, or the Office of the Deputy Attorney General, 10th St. and Constitution Ave., NW, Washington, DC 20530.

Congressional Correspondence System
Federal Advisory Committee Membership Files
Financial Management System
Grants Management Information System
Organized Crime Information Management System
Organized Crime and Racketeering Section Intelligence and
   Special Services Unit Visitor Pass System
Registration and Propaganda Files under the Foreign Agents
   Registration Act of 1938, as Amended
Weekly Statistical Report
Witness Immunity Records

Office of Management and Finance

CONTROLLED SUBSTANCES ACT NONPUBLIC RECORDS

Persons who have been convicted for the first time of violating Section 404 (a) of the Controlled Substances Act (Public Law 91-513), i.e., persons who have knowingly or intentionally possessed a controlled substance except as authorized by the act.

Drug Enforcement Administration under Chief Counsel, Justice of Management Division, Freedom of Information Division, Department of Justice, 1405 I Street, NW, Washington, DC 20537, (202) 633-5236.

INTER-DIVISIONAL INFORMATION SYSTEM (IDIS) (A NONOPERATIONAL, DEACTIVATED SYSTEM)

Individuals who were allegedly involved or connected with civil disturbances or other activities.

Director, Information Systems Staff, Department of Justice, Office of Management and Finance, 10th St. and Constitution Ave., NW, Washington, DC 20530, (202) 633-3925.

Civil Rights Division, Freedom of Information Act. Each agency has a freedom of information office. Each one must be contacted individually.

Additional Files

Following is a list of the remaining files maintained by the Office of Management and Finance. Anyone interested in obtaining additional information from any of these files should contact the appropriate agency head, or the Office of the Deputy Attorney General, 10th St. and Constitution Ave., NW, Washington, DC 20530.

Background Investigation Check-Off Card (OMF-154)
Data Index System for Classified Documents (DIS)
Department of Justice Controlled Parking Records
Department of Justice Payroll System
Directory of Organization, Functions, and Staff for Office
   of Management and Finance
EEO (Equal Employment Opportunity) Volunteer Representative Roster
Employee Clearance Record
Employee Locator File
Employee Time Distribution Record
Executive Biography
Interim Performance Appraisal Record
Justice Data Services Center Tape Library System
Justice Data Services Center Utilization Data
Legal and General Administration Accounting System
   (LAGA)
Security Clearance Information System (SCIS)

Tax Division

TAX DIVISION CENTRAL CLASSIFICATION CARDS, INDEX DOCKET CARDS, AND ASSOCIATED RECORDS

Persons referred to in potential or actual cases and matters of concern to the Tax Division under the internal revenue laws.

Assistant Attorney General, Tax Division, Department of Justice, 10th St. and Constitution Ave., NW, Washington, DC 20530, (202) 633-2901.

Additional Files

Following is a list of the remaining files maintained by the Tax Division department. Anyone interested in obtaining additional information from any of these files should contact the appropriate agency head, or the Office of the Deputy Attorney General, 10th St. and Constitution Ave., NW, Washington, DC 20530.

Files of Applications for the Position of Attorney with the Tax Division
Freedom of Information Request Files

U.S. Attorneys' Offices

For addresses of U.S. Attorneys' district offices, see pp. 114-117.

ADMINISTRATIVE FILES

Office personnel (present and past); expert professionals whose services are used by the office; applicants for office positions; witnesses in court proceedings; prisoners-in-custody; defendants; debtors; vendors; citizens making inquiries; members of local and state bar associations.

Administrative officer/assistant for the U.S. Attorney for each district.

CITIZEN COMPLAINT FILES

Individuals who have been charged with federal and District of Columbia code violations; those individuals who are currently under investigation for violations of federal and District of Columbia code; those individuals about whom complaints have been made or upon whom investigations were conducted, but no prosecution was initiated; and complainants.

Chief, Misdemeanor Trial Section, U.S. Attorney's Office, Superior Court Division, Building B, 4th & E Sts., NW, Washington, DC (202) 724-6143.

CIVIL CASE FILES

Individuals being investigated in anticipation of civil suits; individuals involved in civil suits; defense counsel(s); information sources; individuals relevant to the development of civil suits.

Administrative officer/assistant for the U.S. Attorney for each district.

CONSUMER COMPLAINTS

Individuals who have been charged with federal and District of Columbia code violations; individuals who are currently under investigation for violations of federal and District of Columbia codes; individuals upon whom investigations were conducted, but no prosecution was initiated; complainants.

Chief, Fraud Division, U.S. Attorney's Office, U.S. District Court, 3rd St. & Constitution Ave., NW, Washington, DC 20001, (202) 633-4904.

CRIMINAL CASE FILES

Individuals charged with violations; individuals being investigated for violations; defense counsel(s); information sources; individuals relevant to development of criminal cases; individuals investigated, but prosecution declined; individuals referred to in potential or actual cases and matters of concern to a U.S. Attorney's Office.

Administrative officer/Assistant, for the U.S. Attorney for each district.

KLINE—DISTRICT OF COLUMBIA AND MARYLAND—STOCK AND LAND FRAUD INTERRELATIONSHIP FILING SYSTEM

Individuals who have been charged with federal and District of Columbia code violations; individuals who are currently under investigation for violations of federal and District of Columbia codes; individuals upon whom investigations were conducted but no prosecution was initiated.

Chief, Fraud Division, U.S. Attorney's Office, U.S. District Court, 3rd St. & Constitution Ave., NW, Washington, DC 20001, (202) 633-4904.

MAJOR CRIMES DIVISION INVESTIGATIVE FILES

Individuals who have been charged with federal and District of Columbia code violations; individuals who are currently under investigation for violations of federal and District of Columbia codes; individuals upon whom investigations were conducted, but no prosecution was initiated; other informants.

Chief, Major Crimes Division, U.S. Attorney's Office, U.S. District Court, 3rd St. & Constitution Ave., NW, Room 4400, Washington, DC 20001, (202) 633-1704.

PROSECUTOR'S MANAGEMENT INFORMATION SYSTEM (PROMIS)

Individuals who have been charged with criminal violations; individuals who are currently under investigation for criminal violations; individuals upon whom criminal investigations were conducted, but no prosecution was initiated; and all witnesses and arresting police officers.

Administrative Assistant, U.S. Attorney, U.S. District Court, 3rd St. & Constitution Ave., NW, Room 3602-A, Washington, DC 20001, (202) 633-4920.

U.S. ATTORNEY, DISTRICT OF COLUMBIA SUPERIOR COURT DIVISION, CRIMINAL FILES, INCLUDING BUT NOT LIMITED TO THE FOLLOWING SUBSYSTEMS: (A) CRIMINAL FILE FOLDER (USA-S1), (B) CRIMINAL FILE FOLDER (USA-33), (C) CRIMINAL DOCKET CARD (USA-T7), AND (D) INDEX

Individuals who have been charged with criminal violations; individuals who are currently under investigation for criminal violations; individuals upon whom criminal investigations were conducted, but no prosecution was initiated.

Administrative Officer, U.S. Attorney's Office, Superior Court Division, Room 108, Building B, 4th & F Sts., NW, Washington, DC 20001, (202) 633-1714.

U.S. Attorneys' Office Locations

Alabama, N
200 Federal Building
1800 Fifth Avenue North
Birmingham, AL 35203

Alabama, M
P.O. Box 197
Montgomery, AL 36101

Alabama, S
P.O. Drawer E
Mobile, AL 36601

Alaska
P.O. Box 680
Anchorage, AK 99510

Arizona
P.O. Box 1951
Tucson, AZ 85702

Arkansas, E
P.O. Box 1229
Little Rock, AR 72203

Arkansas, W
P.O. Box 1524
Fort Smith, AR 72901

California, N
450 Golden Gate Avenue
San Francisco, CA 94102

California, E
2058 Federal Building & Court House
650 Capitol Mall
Sacramento, CA 95814

California, C
312 N. Spring Street
Los Angeles, CA 90012

California, S
U.S. Court House, Annex A
325 West F Street
San Diego, CA 92101

Canal Zone
Box 2090
Balboa, CZ

Colorado
323 U.S. Court House
P.O. Box 3615
1961 Stout Street
Denver, CO 80202

Connecticut
Post Office Building
141 Church Street
New Haven, CT 06507

Delaware
5001 New Federal Building
9th & King Streets
Wilmington, DE 19801

District of Columbia
Room 3600 – E U.S. Court House
3rd St. & Constitution Ave., NW
Washington, DC 20001

Florida, N
P.O. Box 12313
Pensacola, FL 32501

Florida, M
P.O. Box 600
Jacksonville, FL 32201

Florida, S
300 Ainsley Building
14 NE 1st Avenue
Miami, FL 33132

Georgia, N
P.O. Box 912
Atlanta, GA 30301

Georgia, M
P.O. Box U
Macon, GA 31202

Georgia, S
P.O. Box 2017
Augusta, GA 30903

Guam
P.O. Box Z
Agana, GU 96910

Hawaii
P.O. Box 654
Honolulu, HI 96809

Idaho
Room 698 Federal Building
Box 037, 550 W. Fort Street
Boise, ID 83702

Illinois, N
Room 1500 South
Everett McKinley Dirksen Building
219 S. Dearborn Street
Chicago, IL 60604

Illinois, E
P.O. Box 226
East St. Louis, IL 62202

Illinois, S
P.O. Box 375
Springfield, IL 62705

Indiana, N
P.O. Box 327
Fort Wayne, IN 46801

Indiana, S
Room 246
Federal Building & U.S. Court House
Ohio & Meridian Streets
Indianapolis, IN 46204

Iowa, N
P.O. Box 1138
Sioux City, IA 51102

Iowa, S
113 U.S. Court House
Des Moines, IA 50309

Kansas
P.O. Box 2098
Wichita, KS 67201

Kentucky, E
P.O. Box 1490
Lexington, KY 40501

Kentucky, W
U.S.P.O. & Court House Building
Sixth and Broadway
Louisville, KY 40202

Louisiana, E
500 St. Louis Street
New Orleans, LA 70130

Louisiana, M
Federal Building & U.S. Court House
Room 130, 707 Florida Street
Baton Rouge, LA 70801

Louisiana, W
P.O. Box 33
Shreveport, LA 71161

Maine
Federal Court House
156 Federal Street
Portland, ME 04112

Maryland
405 U.S. Court House
Fayette & Calvert Streets
Baltimore, MD 21202

Massachusetts
1107 John W. McCormack
P.O. & Court House
Boston, MA 02109

Michigan, E
817 Federal Building
231 Lafayette
Detroit, MI 48226

Michigan, W
544 Federal Building & U.S. Court House
110 Michigan Avenue, NW
Grand Rapids, MI 49502

Minnesota
596 U.S. Court House
110 S. 4th Street
Minneapolis, MN 55401

Mississippi, N
P.O. Drawer 886
Oxford, MS 38655

Mississippi, S
P.O. Box 2091
Jackson, MS 39205

Missouri, E
Room 402
1114 Market Street
St. Louis, MO 63101

Missouri, W
549 U.S. Court House
811 Grand Avenue
Kansas City, MO 64106

Montana
P.O. Box 1478
Billings, MT 59101

Nebraska
P.O. Box 1228
Omaha, NE 68101

Nevada
Box 16030
Las Vegas, NV 89101

New Hampshire
Federal Building
Concord, NH 03301

New Jersey
P.O. Box 330
Newark, NJ 07101

New Mexico
P.O. Box 607
Albuquerque, NM 87105

New York, N
P.O. Box 1258
Federal Building
Syracuse, NY 13201

New York, S
U.S. Court House Annex
One St. Andrew's Plaza
New York, NY 10007

New York, E
U.S. Court House
225 Cadman Plaza East
Brooklyn, NY 11201

New York, W
502 U.S. Court House
Buffalo, NY 14202

North Carolina, E
P.O. Box 26897
Raleigh, NC 27611

North Carolina, M
P.O. Box 1858
Greensboro, NC 27402

North Carolina, W
P.O. Box 132
Asheville, NC 28802

North Dakota
P.O. Box 2505
Fargo, ND 58102

Ohio, N
Room 400
U.S. Court House
Cleveland, OH 44114

Ohio, S
200 Federal Building
85 Marconi Boulevard
Columbus, OH 43215

Oklahoma, N
Room 460, U.S. Court House
333 West Fourth Street
Tulsa, OK 74103

Oklahoma, E
P.O. Box 1009
Muskogee, OK 74401

Oklahoma, W
Room 4434
U.S. Court House & Federal Office Building
Oklahoma City, OK 73102

Oregon
P.O. Box 71
Portland, OR 97207

Pennsylvania, E
Room 4042, U.S. Court House
9th & Market Streets
Philadelphia, PA 19107

Pennsylvania, M
U.S.P.O. Building
Room 426
Scranton, PA 18501

Pennsylvania, W
633 U.S.P.O. & Court House
7th Avenue & Grant Street
Pittsburgh, PA 15219

Puerto Rico
P.O. Box 3391
San Juan, PR 00904

Rhode Island
P.O. Box 1401
Providence, RI 02901

South Carolina
151 U.S. Court House
Columbia, SC 29201

South Dakota
231 Federal Building & U.S. Court House
400 S. Phillips Avenue
Sioux Falls, SD 57102

Tennessee, E
201 U.S.P.O. & Court House Building
Knoxville, TN 37902

Tennessee, M
P.O. Box 800
Nashville, TN 37202

Tennessee, W
1058 Federal Office Building
167 North Main Street
Memphis, TN 38301

Texas, N
310 U.S. Court House
10th at Lamar
Fort Worth, TX 76102

Texas, S
P.O. Box 61129
Houston, TX 77061

Texas, E
P.O. Box 1049
Tyler, TX 75701

Texas, W
P.O. Box 1701
San Antonio, TX 78296

Utah
200 P.O. & Court House
350 South Main Street
Salt Lake City, UT 84101

Vermont
P.O. Box 10
Rutland, VT 05701

Virgin Islands
P.O. Box 1441
St. Thomas, VI 00801

Virginia, E
Box 749
Alexandria, VA 22313

Virginia, W
P.O. Box 1709
Roanoke, VA 24008

Washington, E
Box 1494
Spokane, WA 99210

Washington, W
P.O. Box 1227
Seattle, WA 98111

West Virginia, N
P.O. Box 591
Wheeling, WV 26003

West Virginia, S
Room 4006 Federal Building
500 Quarrier Street
Charleston, WV 25301

Wisconsin, E
361 Federal Building
517 East Wisconsin Avenue
Milwaukee, WI 53202

Wisconsin, W
P.O. Box 112
Madison, WI 53701

Wyoming
P.O. Box 668
Cheyenne, WY 82001

Following is a list of the remaining files maintained by the U.S. Attorney's Office. Anyone interested in obtaining additional information from any of these files should contact the appropriate agency head, or the Office of the Deputy Attorney General, 10th St. and Constitution Ave., NW, Washington, DC 20530.

Assistant U.S. Attorney Applicant Files
Citizen Correspondence Files
Evaluation Reports by Regional Assistant Directors
Freedom of Information Act Files
Security Clearance Forms for Grand Jury Reporters

United States Marshals Service

For information about any United States Marshals Service system of records, write to the named official at the following address, identifying the system of interest: U.S. Marshals Service, Department of Justice, 10th St. and Constitution Ave., NW, Washington, DC 20530, (202) 285-1111.

UNITED STATES MARSHALS SERVICE PRISONER COORDINATION SYSTEM

Prisoners taken into U.S. Marshal custody.

Associate Director for Operations.

WARRANT-INFORMATION SYSTEM

Individuals for whom federal warrants have been issued.

Associate Director for Operations.

Additional Files

Following is a list of the remaining files maintained by the United States Marshals Service. Anyone interested in obtaining additional information from any of these files should contact the appropriate agency head, or the Office of the Deputy Attorney General, 10th St. and Constitution Ave., NW, Washington, DC 20530.

Special Deputy File
Special Detail System
United States Marshals Service Badge and Credentials File
United States Marshals Service Internal Inspection System
United States Marshals Service Training Files
Witness Security Files Information System

Watergate Special Prosecution Force

WATERGATE SPECIAL PROSECUTION FORCE INVESTIGATIVE AND PROSECUTORY FILES—WSPF 1

Persons referred to in potential or actual cases and matters of concern to the Watergate Special Prosecution Force and correspondents on subjects directed or referred to the Watergate Special Prosecution Force.

WATERGATE SPECIAL PROSECUTION FORCE AUTOMATED INVESTIGATION FILES—WSPF 2

Persons referred to in potential or actual cases and matters of concern to the Watergate Special Prosecutor's Office.

Watergate Special Prosecutor, Department of Justice, 1425 K St., NW, Washington DC 20005.

WATERGATE SPECIAL PROSECUTION FORCE TRAVEL FILE—WSPF 3

Persons who are retained by the Watergate Special Prosecution Force as staff, consultants, or experts.

Watergate Special Prosecutor, Department of Justice, 1425 K St., NW, Washington, DC 20005.

U.S. Department of Labor

Following is a list of the agencies and subagencies of the Department of Labor, with their abbreviations.

BLS Bureau of Labor Statistics
DOL Department of Labor
ESA Employment Standards Administration
FCCO Federal Contract Compliance Office
Manpower Manpower Administration
OSHA Occupational Safety and Health Administration
W and H Wage and Hour Division

Note: LMRDA in the following entries is an abbreviation for *Labor Management Reporting and Disclosure Act.*

BONDING VIOLATIONS FILE

Persons investigated with respect to violations of bonding requirements of LMRDA (Section 502).

Associate Solicitor, Division of Labor-Management Laws, Office of the Solicitor, Department of Labor, 200 Constitution Ave., NW, Washington, DC 20210, (202) 523-8607.

CONFLICT OF INTEREST FILE

Those persons from whom reports may be required under Section 202 of the LMRDA are those allegedly having conflicts of interest who must file reports.

Associate Solicitor, Division of Labor-Management Law, Office of the Solicitor, Department of Labor, 200 Constitution Ave., NW, Washington, DC 20210, (202) 523-8607.

EMPLOYMENT STANDARDS WATER POLLUTION/ WATER SAFETY ANTI-DISCRIMINATION FILES

Individuals filing complaints against employers on account of discharge or other acts of discrimination by reason of exercise of protected rights under the Federal Water Pollution Prevention and Control Act and the Safe Drinking Water Act of 1974.

Wage-Hour Administrator, Employment Standards Administration, New Department of Labor Building, Room S3502, 200 Constitution Ave., NW, Washington, DC 20210, (202) 523-8305.

EXEMPLARY REHABILITATION CERTIFICATION PROGRAM FILE

Ex-servicemen and ex-servicewomen with less-than-honorable discharges from the United States armed forces.

Manpower Administration, U.S. Employment Service (METR), Department of Labor, Washington, DC 20213, (202) 523-6318.

EX-OFFENDER'S APPLICATION FILE

Persons convicted of crimes identified under Section 504 of the LMRDA who have applied for relief from the U.S. Board of Parole to serve as union officers or labor relations consultants.

Associate Solicitor, Division of Labor-Management Laws, Office of the Solicitor, Department of Labor, 200 Constitution Ave., NW, Washington, DC 20210, (202) 523-8607.

FALSIFIED REPORTS FILE

Persons suspected or prosecuted for violation of Section 209, LMRDA, falsifying required reports.

Associate Solicitor, Division of Labor-Management Laws, Office of the Solicitor, Department of Labor, 200 Constitution Ave., NW, Washington, DC 20210, (202) 523-8607.

FEDERAL TORT CLAIMS ACT (FTCA)

Claimants under Federal Tort Claims Act.

Associate Solicitor, Division of Employee Benefits, N2716, New Department of Labor Building, 200 Constitution Ave., NW, Washington, DC 20210, (202) 523-7625.

GENERAL INVESTIGATIONS FILE

Employees, applicants, contractors, subcontractors, grantees, sub-grantees, claimants, and individuals threatening DOL employees.

Director of Audit and Investigations, OASA, Department of Labor, 200 Constitution Ave., NW, Washington, DC 20210, (202) 523-8666.

LMSE INDEX CARDS DIVISION OF ENFORCEMENT

Union officers, individuals investigated, and individuals interviewed.

System Manager, LMSE, Department of Labor, 200 Constitution Ave., NW, Room N5408, Washington, DC 20216, (202) 523-6414.

MANPOWER ADMINISTRATION INVESTIGATORY FILE

Named plaintiffs/complainants in court and administrative proceedings involving the Manpower Administration, and individual subjects of an administrative investigation under Manpower Administration programs.

Associate Solicitor for Manpower, Room N2101, Department of Labor, 200 Constitution Ave., NW, Washington, DC 20210, (202) 523-6128;

OFFICE OF FEDERAL CONTRACT COMPLIANCE PROGRAMS COMPLAINT FILE

Individuals filing complaints of discrimination.

Director, Office of Federal Contract Compliance Programs, Department of Labor, 200 Constitution Ave., NW, Washington, DC 20210, (202) 523-9475.

OFFICE OF FEDERAL CONTRACT COMPLIANCE PROGRAMS INTERNAL COMPLAINT FILE

Individuals filing complaints of discrimination.

Director, Office of Federal Contract Compliance Programs, Room N3402, 200 Constitution Ave., NW, Washington, DC 20210, (202) 523-9475.

OFFICE OF FEDERAL CONTRACT COMPLIANCE PROGRAMS VETERANS' COMPLAINT FILES

Disabled veterans, recently discharged veterans.

Leader, Veteran's Task Force, Room N4418, New Department of Labor Building, 200 Constitution Ave., NW, Washington, DC 20210, (202) 376-6550.

OFFICE OF WORKERS' COMPENSATION PROGRAMS, BLACK LUNG ANTIDISCRIMINATION FILES

Individuals filing complaints against employers on account of discharge or other acts of discrimination by reason of a pneumoconiosis disease.

Associate Director, Division of Coal Mine Workers' Compensation, Office of Workers' Compensation Programs, Employment Standards Administration, Department of Labor, 200 Constitution Ave., NW, Washington, DC 20210, (202) 523-6692.

PENSION BONDING VIOLATIONS FILE

Person suspected of violating the bonding requirements of the Welfare and Pension Plans Disclosure Act (since repealed), Section 13.

Associate Solicitor, Division of Labor-Management Laws, Office of the Solicitor, Department of Labor, 200 Constitution Ave., NW, Washington, DC 20210, (202) 523-8607.

PENSION EMBEZZLEMENT FILE

Persons suspected of theft or embezzlement from employee welfare and pension benefit plans, 18 U.S.C. 664.

Associate Solicitor, Division of Labor-Management Laws, Office of the Solicitor, Department of Labor, 200 Constitution Ave., NW, Washington, DC 20210, (202) 523-8607.

VETERANS' REEMPLOYMENT RIGHTS COMPLAINT FILE

Veterans or rejectees from military service; reservists or national guard personnel.

Associate Solicitor for General Legal Services, Room N2458, 200 Constitution Ave., NW, Washington, DC 20210, (202) 523-8286, Regional Solicitor's Office.

Additional Files

Following is a list of remaining files maintained by the Department of Labor. Anyone interested in obtaining information from any of these files should contact the appropriate agency head or the Office of the Secretary, U.S. Department of Labor, 200 Constitution Ave., NW, Washington, DC 20210.

Administrative Information System Financial Master File
Attendance, Leave, and Payroll File
Budget and Position Control
Budget Position Control System
Bureau of Apprenticeship and Training, Field Service Staff Budget and Position Control File
Bureau of Apprenticeship and Training, Foreign Nationals Individual Program File
Bureau of Apprenticeship and Training, National Industry Promotion File
Characteristics of the Insured Unemployed File
Comprehensive Employment and Training Act (Paragraph 416 (b)) (CETA)
DOL Accident Reports
Employee Address File
Employee Locator Card File
Employers of the Year Award File
Employment Standards Public Inquiry File
Freedom of Information Act Appeals
Handicapped American of the Year Award File
Health Unit Employee Medical Records
Immigration and Rehabilitation Certification Program File
Job Corps Mainstream and Placement File
Job Corps Mainstream and Placement Reports File
Labor-Management Relations—Inquiries from Congressmen and Private Citizens
LMSA Case Opening and Closing Reports
Migrant Worker File
Military Personnel and Civilian Employees Claims Act
Occupational Injury and Illness Reporting File
OEBS—Division of Enforcement; Case Files
OEBS—Executive Secretary/Advisory Council on Employee Welfare and Pension Benefit Plans
Office of Federal Contract Compliance Programs Handicapped Worker Complaint File

Office of Statistical Operations and Processing, Staff Utilization File
Office of Workers' Compensation Programs, Black Lung Benefit Claim File
Office of Workers' Compensation Programs, Black Lung Benefit Payments File
Office of Workers' Compensation Programs, Black Lung Claimant Information File
Office of Workers' Compensation Programs, Black Lung Medical Treatment Records File
Office of Workers' Compensation Programs, Black Lung Profile Beneficiaries File
Office of Workers' Compensation Programs, Black Lung Service Payments File
Office of Workers' Compensation Programs, Black Lung X-Ray Interpretations File
Office of Workers' Compensation Programs, Federal Employees' Compensation Act Chargeback File
Office of Workers' Compensation Programs, Federal Employees' Compensation Act File
Office of Workers' Compensation Programs, Longshore and Harbor Workers' Compensation Act File
1 Percent Employee-Employer Sample File
Organizational Interference File
Organizational Operating Pattern File
OVRR Correspondence Files
Physician of the Year Award File
Position Classification File
Rehabilitation and Counseling File
Staff Utilization File
Trainee Characteristic File
Wage-Hour Sheltered Workshop File
WIN II Characteristics File

U.S. Department of State

BERLIN DOCUMENT CENTER RECORDS

Individuals associated with the former government, organizations, or party apparatus of the Third Reich, who are now United States citizens or lawfully admitted resident aliens.

Director, Foreign Affairs Document and Reference Center, Room 1239, Department of State, 2201 C St., NW, Washington, DC 20520, (202) 632-0394; or the director, Berlin Document Center.

Request for information should contain: Individual's name, date, and place of birth; current mailing address and zip code; signature; and a brief description of the circumstances, with approximate dates, which give the individual cause to believe that the Berlin Document Center might have records pertaining to him or her.

COORDINATOR FOR THE COMBATTING OF TERRORISM RECORDS

American citizens involved in terrorist incidents.

Director, Foreign Affairs Document and Reference Center, Room 1239, Department of State, 2201 C St., NW, Washington, DC 20250, (202) 632-0394.

The individual must specify that he wishes the records of the Office of the Coordinator for Combatting Terrorism to be checked. Request for information should contain: Individual's name, date and place of birth, current mailing address, signature, a brief description of the circumstances, including the approximate dates, which give the individual cause to believe that the Office of the Coordinator for the Combatting of Terrorism might have records pertaining to him or her.

COUNSELOR SERVICE AND ASSISTANCE RECORDS

Individuals assisted by the Office of Special Consular Services or by consular officers overseas who are the subject of requests concerning welfare and whereabouts; who have received financial assistance; who have been repatriated; who have received emergency medical assistance; who have been detained or arrested overseas; who have required notarial and documentation services; about whom judicial assistance has been requested; who have died overseas and whose estate has had to be settled; who have claimed interests in property abroad; who are living overseas and who receive federal benefits; American seamen.

Director, Foreign Affairs Document and Reference Center, Room 1239, Department of State, 220 C St., NW, Washington, DC 20520, (202) 632-0394.

The individual must specify that he wishes the records of the Office of Special Consular Services to be checked. Request for information should contain: Individual's name, date and place of birth, current mailing address, signature, a brief description of the circumstances, including the location (city and country) and the approximate dates, which give the individual cause to believe that the Office of Special Consular Services have records pertaining to him or her.

EQUAL EMPLOYMENT OPPORTUNITY RECORDS

Employees who have filed formal or informal complaints alleging discrimination; minority and women applicants for employment.

Director, Foreign Affairs Document and Reference Center, Room 1239, Department of State, 2201 C St., NW, Washington, DC 20250, (202) 632-0394.

The individual must specify that he wishes the records of the Office of Equal Employment Opportunity to be checked. Request for information should contain: Individual's name, date and place of birth, current mailing address and zip code, signature, and the approximate date upon which the individual filed a formal or informal complaint alleging discrimination or requested other services from the Office of Equal Employment Opportunity.

EXTRADITION RECORDS

Individuals charged with or convicted of an extraditable crime who have fled to or from the United States and whose return is sought by state or federal law enforcement agencies or by a foreign country; individuals whose return is sought by deportation when they are in another country illegally.

Director, Foreign Affairs Document and Reference Center, Room 1239, Department of State, 2201 C St., NW, Washington, DC 20250, (202) 632-0394.

The individual must specify that he wishes the record of the Office of the Legal Adviser to be checked. Request for information should contain: Individual's name, date and place of birth, current mailing address and zip code, signature, and the countries to and from which he or she was extradited and the approximate date.

FOREIGN ASSISTANCE INSPECTION RECORDS

Members of Congress who have corresponded with the Office of the Inspector General of Foreign Assistance (IGA) or received reports or memoranda from IGA; present and former employees or contractors of the Agency for International Development, Overseas Private Investment Corporation, Inter-American Foundation, Peace Corps, Department of State, Department of Defense, or the Department of Agriculture alleged to have violated laws or agency regulations in connection with programs for which IGA has oversight responsibility.

Director, Foreign Affairs Document and Reference Center, Room 1239, Department of State, 2201 C St., NW, Washington, DC 20520, (202) 632-0394.

The individual must specify that he wishes the records of the Office of the Inspector General of Foreign Assistance to be checked. Request for information should contain: Individual's name, date and place of birth, current mailing address and zip code, signature, and a brief description of circumstances, including approximate dates, which give the individual cause to believe that the Office of the Inspector General of Foreign Assistance might have records pertaining to him.

FOREIGN SERVICE GRIEVANCE BOARD RECORDS

Foreign Service personnel of the Department of State, the Agency for International Development (AID), and the U.S.

Information Agency (USIA) who have filed a grievance with the Foreign Service Grievance Board.

Director, Foreign Affairs Document and Reference Center, Room 1239, Department of State, 2201 C St., NW, Washington, DC 20520, (202) 632-0394.

The individual must specify that he wishes the records of the Foreign Service Grievance Board to be checked. Request for information should contain: Individual's name, date and place of birth, current mailing address and zip code, signature, and the approximate date upon which the individual filed a formal grievance with the Foreign Service Grievance Board.

LEGAL CASE MANAGEMENT RECORDS

Individuals who have filed administrative grievances and equal employment opportunity complaints; individuals involved in disciplinary proceedings; individuals involved in alleged criminal activity or activity in violation of regulations; individuals who have sued the Department of State or any officials, or who have raised administrative and management questions which require legal analysis.

Director, Foreign Affairs Document and Reference Center, Room 1239, Department of State, 2201 C St., NW, Washington, DC 20520, (202) 632-0394.

The individual must specify that he or she wishes the records of the Office of the Legal Adviser to be checked. Request for information should contain: Individual's name, date and place of birth, present mailing address and zip code, signature, and brief description of the circumstances, including the approximate dates, which give the individual cause to believe that the Office of the Legal Adviser might have records pertaining to him or her.

PASSPORT RECORDS

Individuals who have applied for the issuance, amendment, extension or renewal of United States passports; individuals who have been issued passports or had passports amended, extended, renewed, limited, revoked, or denied. Individuals who have applied to have births overseas reported as births overseas of United States citizens; individuals for whom Consular Reports of Birth Abroad of United States citizens or Certifications of Birth have been issued. Individuals who have applied at American diplomatic or consular posts for registration as United States citizens; individuals who have been so registered; and individuals who have been issued Certificates or Cards of Registration and Identity as United States citizens. Individuals for whom the Department of State has issued Certificates of Loss of Nationality of the United States. Individuals who have applied at American diplomatic or consular posts for issuance of Certificates of Witness to Marriage; and individuals who have been issued Certificates of Witness to Marriage. Individuals who are not or may not be entitled under passport laws and regulations to issuance or possession of United States passports or other documentation or service.

Director, Foreign Affairs Document and Reference Center, Room 1239, Department of State, 2201 C St., NW, Washington, DC 20520, (202) 632–0394.

The individual must specify that he wishes the records of the Passport Office to be checked. Request for information should contain: Individual's name, date and place of birth, current mailing address and zip code, and signature.

PERSONAL PROPERTY CLAIMS

Employees of the Department of State, the Agency for International Development, and the United States Information Agency who have filed claims for loss of personal property.

Director, Foreign Affairs Document and Reference Center, Room 1239, Department of State, 2201 C St., NW, Washington, DC 20520, (202) 632–0394.

The individual must specify that he wishes the records of the Office of Personal Property Claims to be checked. Request for information should contain: Individual's name, date and place of birth, current mailing address and zip code, signature, and the approximate date of the claim.

SECURITY RECORDS

Employees and former employees of the Department of State; applicants for department employment who have been or are presently being investigated; contractors working for the department; recipients of cultural grants; individuals requiring access to the official Department of State premises who have undergone or are undergoing security clearance; individuals involved in matters of passport and visa fraud, munitions control, unauthorized access to classified information; alien prospective spouses of American personnel of the Department of State; individuals whose activities have a potential bearing on the security of departmental or Foreign Service operations. In addition, security files contain information needed to provide protective services for the Secretary of State and visiting foreign dignitaries and heads of state, and to protect the department's official premises. There are also information copies of investigations of individuals conducted abroad at the request of federal agencies; documents and reports furnished to the department by other agencies, concerning individuals whose activities the other agencies believe may have a bearing on United States foreign policy interests.

Director, Foreign Affairs Document and Reference Center, Room 1239, Department of State, 2201 C St., NW, Washington, DC 20520, (202) 632–0394.

Request for information should contain: Individual's name, date and place of birth, current mailing address and zip code, and signature.

Additional Files

Following is a list of the remaining files maintained by the Department of State. Anyone interested in obtaining information from any of these files should contact the Department of State, 2201 C Street, NW, Washington, DC 20520.

Biographic Register Records
Board of Appellate Review Records
Board of the Foreign Service Records
Confidential Statement of Employment and Financial
  Interests Records
Congressional Correspondence Records
Congressional Travel Records
Contractors Records
Cryptographic Clearance Records
Educational and Cultural Exchange Program Records
External Research Records
Fine Arts Records
Foreign Service Employee Locator/Notification Records
Foreign Service Institute Records
Intelligence and Research Records
International Conference Delegates Records
International Organizations Records
Labor Attaches Records
Law of the Sea Records
Legal Adviser Personnel Records
Media Correspondents Records
Media Personnel Records
Medical Records
Munitions Control Records
Overseas Records (and U.S. Missions to International
  Organizations)
Personality Cross-Reference Index to the Secretariat Automated Data Index
Personality Index to the Central Foreign Policy Records
Personnel Payroll Records
Personnel Records
Personnel Travel Records
Privacy Act Requests Records
Protocol Records
Public Affairs Applicants Records
Public Affairs Records
Senior Personnel Appointments Records
Translators and Interpreters Records
Vendor Records
Visa Records

U.S. Department of Transportation

Following is a list of the agencies and subagencies of the U.S. Department of Transportation, with their abbreviations.

CG	Coast Guard
DOT	Department of Transportation
FAA	Federal Aviation Administration
FHA	Federal Highway Administration
FRA	Federal Railroad Administration
NHTSA	National Highway Traffic Safety Administration
SLSD	Saint Lawrence Seaway Development Corporation
UMTA	Urban Mass Transportation Administration

Office of the Secretary

ALLEGATIONS OF INFRINGEMENT OF UNITED STATES PATENTS DOT/OST

An individual who believes that an agency of DOT is infringing upon a United States patent owned by the individual.

Department of Transportation, Office of the Secretary, Office of the General Counsel, Office of Patent Counsel, Room 10424, 400 7th St., SW, Washington, DC 20590.

DISCRIMINATION COMPLAINT INVESTIGATIVE FILES DOT/OST

Complaints of discrimination by employees of, and applicants to, the DOT. Complaints of discrimination by individuals affected by departmental programs for which the DOT has compliance responsibility.

Director of Civil Rights, Office of the Secretary, 400 7th St., SW, Washington, DC 20590.

FILES RELATING TO PERSONNEL HEARINGS DOT/OST

Certain employees of the Office of the Secretary who have availed themselves of the opportunity for a hearing in certain personnel matters.

Department of Transportation, Office of the Secretary, Office of the General Counsel, Room 10428, Washington, DC 20590.

SECRETARIAT INFORMATION RETRIEVAL SYSTEM (SIRS) DOT/OST

Individuals who write, or are referred in writing by a second party, to the secretary, deputy secretary, deputy undersecretary, deputy undersecretary for budget and program review, and their immediate offices. Individuals who are the subject of an action requiring approval or action by one of the forenamed, such as appeal actions, training, awards, foreign travel, promotions, selections, grievances, and discipline.

Office of the Executive Secretary, Office of the Secretary, 400 7th St., SW, Washington, DC 20590.

Additional Files

Following is a list of the remaining files maintained by the DOT. Anyone interested in obtaining information from any of these files should contact the appropriate agency head, or the Office of the Secretary, Department of Transportation, 400 7th St., SW, Washington, DC 20590.

Active Duty Military Payroll System DOT/CG
Adjudication and Settlement of Claims System DOT/CG
Aircraft Registration System DOT/FAA

Airman Certification System DOT/FAA
Allotment System (Military) DOT/CG Commandant (G-FP)
Appointment of Trustee or Guardian for Mentally Incompetent Personnel DOT/CG
Auxiliary Management Information System (AUXMIS) DOT/CG
Aviation Medical Certification System DOT/FAA
Aviation Medical Examiner System DOT/FAA
Basic Supervisory Personnel Records DOT/CG
Biographical Statement DOT/CG
Centralized Reserve Pay and Retirement System DOT/CG
Chemical Transportation Industry Advisory Committee DOT/CG
Civilian Payroll System DOT/CG
Closed Out Military Pay Record System DOT/CG
Coast Guard Family Housing DOT/CG
Coast Guard Motor Vehicle Operator Permit DOT/CG
Coast Guard Personnel Security Program DOT/CG
Coast Guard Reserve Personnel Mobilization System DOT/CG
Coast Guard Welfare DOT/CG
Contract and Real Property File System DOT/CG
Custody and Safekeeping of Savings Bonds DOT/CG
Defense Mobilization Emergency Record System DOT/FAA
Detainee's Log DOT/CG
Drug and Alcohol Abuse Prevention Program Record System DOT/CG
Employee Health Record System DOT/FAA
Enlisted Personnel Record System DOT/CG
Enlisted Recruiting Selection Record System DOT/CG
Equal Employment Opportunity Minority/Female Statistical Reporting System DOT/FAA
Federal Aviation Administration Employee Payable System DOT/FAA
FICA Wage and Tax System for Military Pay DOT/CG
General Aviation Aircraft Accident System DOT/FAA
General Aviation Medical Accident System DOT/FAA
Medical Exemptions – Public Dockets DOT/FAA
Merchant Vessel Casualty Reporting System DOT/CG
Merchant Vessel Documentation System (Manual and Automated)
Military Training and Education Records DOT/CG
Motor Vehicle Operator/Examiner System DOT/FAA
Motorboat Registration DOT/CG
Nonappropriated Funds System (NAFA) DOT/CG
Officer, Enlisted, and Recruiter Selection Test File DOT/CG
Officer Selection and Appointment System DOT/CG
Official Officer Service Records DOT/CG
Official Coast Guard Reserve Service Record DOT/CG
Outside Employment of Active Duty Coast Guard Personnel DOT/CG
Pending Legislation (Employee's) – Private Relief and Public/Private Laws (Employee's) Private Relief DOT/FAA
Personnel Management Information System (PMIS) DOT/CG
Petitions for Exemptions (Other than Medical Exemption) – Public Dockets DOT/FAA
Petitions for Rulemaking – Public Dockets DOT/FAA
Physical Disability Separation System DOT/CG

Physiological Training System DOT/FAA
Port Security Card System DOT/CG
Psychological Support for Air Traffic Controller Health Program and Air Traffic Controller Applicant Screening System DOT/FAA
Registered/Applicant Pilot Eligibility Folder DOT/CG
Representatives of The Administrator DOT/FAA
Request for Remission of Indebtedness DOT/CG
Reserve Master Personnel File (Automated) DOT/CG
Reserve Pay and Points System (Automated) DOT/CG
Retired Pay and Personnel System DOT/CG
Statement of Employment and Financial Interest Record System DOT/CG
System Error Reporting Program DOT/FAA
Travel and Transportation of Household Effects DOT/CG
Uniformed Services Identification and Privilege Card Record System DOT/CG
USCG Military Personnel Health Record System DOT/CG
U.S. Merchant Seamen's Records
U.S. Public Health Services (USPHS) Commissioned Officer Corps Staffing and Recruitment Files DOT/CG
Working Level Files for Employees Assigned Overseas DOT/FAA
Working Level Personnel Folder System DOT/FAA

Office of the Secretary

Applications for Employment with Office of Pipeline Safety Operations (OPSO) DOT/OST
Applications for U.S. Government Motor Vehicle Operator's Identification Card (Government Drivers License) DOT/OST
Board for Correction of Military Records (BCMR) DOT/OST
Citizens' Advisory Committee on Transportation Quality DOT/OST
Confidential Statement of Employment and Financial Interests DOT/OST
Contract Information System DOT/OST
Departmental Advisory Committee Files DOT/OST
Departmental Personnel Management Information System DOT/OST
Employee Management Files DOT/OST
Employment Applications Files DOT/OST
Executive Team Cadre Listings for Continuity of Operations Plan of the Office of the Secretary DOT/OST
Funds Management Records DOT/OST
Garnishment Files DOT/OST
General Employee Records System DOT/OST
General Investigations Record System DOT/OST
General Personnel Management Files DOT/OST
Identification Media Record System DOT/OST
Individual Personal Interests in Intellectual Property DOT/OST
Information Systems Division Project Management System DOT/OST
Informational Work Folders on Employees of the Office of Pipeline Safety Operations DOT/OST
Management Personnel File
National Defense Executive Reserve (NDER) File DOT/OST

Operating Management Personnel File DOT/OST
Parking Permit Application File DOT/OST
Parking Permit Management System DOT/OST
Payroll Management System DOT/OST
Personnel Convenience Files DOT/OST
Personnel Data Working Files DOT/OST
Personnel Management Convenience Files DOT/OST
Personnel Management Operating Record System DOT/OST
Personnel Records DOT/OST
Personnel Security Record System DOT/OST
Planning Officials for Emergency Functions DOT/OST
Records of Confirmation Proceedings Requirements for
    Proposed Executive Appointments to the Department of
    Transportation DOT/OST
Safety Management Information System (SMIS) DOT/OST
Security Management Records DOT/OST
TAD-60, Personnel Operating Management File DOT/OST
TCI Personnel Convenience Files DOT/OST
Technical Pipeline Safety Committee DOT/OST
Telephone Directory and Locator System DOT/OST
Time and Attendance Report (FHWA Form 320 (7-73)) for
    the Office of Emergency Transportation DOT/OST
Transportation Research Activities Information Service
    (TRAIS) DOT/OST
Transportation Research Information Service on Lint
    (TRIS-On-Line) DOT/OST
Travel and Transportation Management File DOT/OST
Unsolicited Contract or Research and Development Pro-
    posals Embodying Claims of Proprietary Rights DOT/OST
Visit Control Records System DOT/OST

Coast Guard and Federal Aviation Authority

ADMINISTRATIVE ACTION AND LEGAL ENFORCEMENT SYSTEM DOT/CG

Individuals against whom FAA has taken administrative action or legal enforcement action for violation of certain federal aviation regulations; individuals or companies holding Federal Aviation Administration certificates; persons charged with violating FAA regulations; persons allegedly violating FAA regulations; applicants who have been denied airman medical certificates; persons denied certificates or allegedly violating FAA regulations who have appealed to the National Transportation Safety Board (NTSB) or the courts.

For official agency legal enforcement action records: Chief, Statistics and Dockets Section, Enforcement Division, Office of Chief Counsel, FAA, 800 Independence Ave., SW, Washington, DC 20591, (202) 426-3364; or regional counsel and flight standards offices in the region of occurrence or the chief of the field office that made the charge. For administrative action records: Chief, Safety Data Branch, Aeronautical Center, Oklahoma City, OK 73125, (405) 686-4391; and flight standard office and regional counsel in the region of occurrence.

CIVIL AVIATION SECURITY SYSTEM DOT/FAA

Hijackers, potential hijackers, extortionists, terrorists, and other individuals who have been involved or might be involved in crimes against civil aviation.

Chief, Operations Liaison Staff, ACS-20, Civil Aviation Security Service, FAA, 800 Independence Ave., SW, Washington, DC 20591, (202) 426-8038; and regional air transportation security organizations.

CLAIMS AND LITIGATION DOT/CG

Individuals, corporations, insurance companies, estate administrators.

Office of Chief Counsel, U.S. Coast Guard Headquarters, Washington, DC 20590, (202) 426-1616; Commandant (G-CMA), U.S. Coast Guard Headquarters, Washington, DC 20590, (202) 426-2390.

COAST GUARD MILITARY DISCRIMINATION COMPLAINTS DOT/CG

Coast guard military personnel.

Commandant (G-CMA), U.S. Coast Guard Headquarters, Washington, DC 20590, (202) 426-2390.

COAST GUARD SUPPLEMENT TO THE MANUAL OF COURTS-MARTIAL INVESTIGATIONS DOT/CG

Military and civilian employees of the coast guard and other individuals who may be involved in any coast guard investigation.

Commandant (G-CMA), U.S. Coast Guard Headquarters, Washington, DC 20590, (202) 426-2390.

COMPLAINTS OF DISCRIMINATION DOT/CG

Civilian employees (including nonappropriated funds employees), applicants for employment.

Commandant (G-CMA), U.S. Coast Guard Headquarters, Washington, DC 20590, (202) 426-2390.

DISCRIMINATION COMPLAINT FILES DOT/FAA

FAA employees, applicants for FAA employment, and members of the public who are directly or indirectly involved in a discrimination complaint filed with FAA.

Director, Office of Civil Rights, ACR-1 FAA, 800 Independence Ave., SW, Washington, DC 20591, (202) 426-3254, and regional and center civil rights offices.

ENVIRONMENTAL LITIGATION FILES DOT/FAA

Litigants, witnesses, plaintiff's attorneys, FAA attorneys, and Department of Justice attorneys.

Chief, Environmental Staff, Office of Chief Counsel, FAA, 800 Independence Ave., SW, Washington, DC 20591, (202) 426-3924.

INTELLIGENCE AND SECURITY INVESTIGATIVE CASE SYSTEM DOT/CG

U.S. Coast Guard military personnel, merchant marine personnel, port and dock workers, and persons under investigation for violations of laws and regulations administered by the coast guard.

Commandant (G-CMA), U.S. Coast Guard Headquarters, Washington, DC 20590, (202) 426-2390.

INVESTIGATION OF VIOLATIONS OF MARINE SAFETY LAWS OR REGULATIONS DOT/CG

Persons who have violated or who are suspected of violating marine safety or related laws or regulation including the report of violation and supporting documents.

Commandant (G-CMA), U.S. Coast Guard Headquarters, Washington, DC 20590, (202) 426-2390.

INVESTIGATIVE RECORD SYSTEM DOT/FAA

Current and former applicants for FAA employment; current and former FAA employees; individuals considered for access to classified information or restricted areas and/or security determinations as contractors, employees of contractors, experts, instructors, and consultants to federal programs; aircraft owners, flight instructors, pilots, mechanics, designated FAA representatives, other individuals certified by FAA, individuals involved in tort claims against the FAA.

The FAA Investigative Record System is decentralized and requests for such records should be directed to the appropriate system manager as follows:

- For the Washington metropolitan area, excluding eastern region jurisdiction: Director of Investigations and Security, 800 Independence Ave., SW, Washington, DC 20591, (202) 426-3520.

- For the geographical area under the jurisdiction of the various regions: Chief, Air Transportation Security Division, of the appropriate region.

- For the jurisdiction of the National Aviation Facilities Experimental Center (NAFEC): Chief, Air Transportation Security Division, NAFEC, Atlantic City, NJ 08405.

- For the jurisdiction of the Aeronautical Center: Chief, Investigations and Security Division, Aeronautical Center, Oklahoma City, OK 73126.

LEGAL ASSISTANCE CASE FILE SYSTEM DOT/CG

Clients of officers assigned to render legal assistance regarding the personal affairs of coast guard military members.

Commandant (G-CMA), U.S. Coast Guard Headquarters, Washington, DC 20590, (202) 426-2390.

LITIGATION AND CLAIMS FILES WITH DOCKET SHEET AND CARD CATALOGUE INDEX FOR CROSS REFERENCE DOT/FAA

Litigants, claimants, witnesses, plaintiff's attorneys, FAA attorneys, and Department of Justice attorneys.

Chief, Litigation Division, Office of Chief Counsel, FAA, 800 Independence Ave., SW, Washington, DC 20591, (202) 426-3661.

MARINE POLLUTION CASE FILES DOT/CG

Owner/operator and/or person in charge of a vessel or a facility, or other persons found in violation of marine environmental protection regulations.

Commandant (G-CMA), U.S. Coast Guard Headquarters, Washington, DC 20590, (202) 426-2390.

Request for information must be signed by the individual.

MASTER CHIEF PETTY OFFICER OF THE COAST GUARD INDIVIDUAL GRIEVANCE AND CORRESPONDENCE FILE DOT/CG

Enlisted coast guard personnel who have filed a grievance or requested information through the master chief petty officer of the coast guard (at headquarters) or the senior enlisted advisors at field units.

Commandant (G-CMA), U.S. Coast Guard Headquarters, Washington, DC 20590, (202) 426-2390.

NON-JUDICIAL PUNISHMENT REPORT DOT/CG

Coast guard military personnel who have been subject to nonjudicial punishment proceedings under Article 15 of the Uniform Code of Military Justice.

Commandant (G-CMA), U.S. Coast Guard Headquarters, Washington, DC 20590, (202) 426-2390.

PERSONAL AFFAIRS RECORD SYSTEM TAX COAST GUARD MILITARY PERSONNEL DOT/CG

Active duty and retired coast guard military personnel who have been subject to damage arising out of domestic relations, disputes, alleged personal indebtedness, and claims of alleged paternity.

Commandant (G-CMA), U.S. Coast Guard Headquarters, Washington, DC 20590, (202) 426-2390.

POLICE WARRANT FILE AND CENTRAL FILES DOT/FAA

Individuals failing to pay violation notices and individuals involved in situations requiring a police report; individuals cited for parking and traffic violations; individuals having criminal records.

Director, Metropolitan Washington Airport Service, Washington National Airport Hangar 9, Washington, DC 20001, (202) 557-1155; Chief of Investigation and Security Division, Aeronautical Center, Oklahoma City, Oklahoma 73125, (405) 686-2212.

PORT SAFETY REPORTING SYSTEM INDIVIDUAL VIOLATION HISTORIES DOT/CG

Master, operators, owners, agents, shippers, charterers and/or pilots of commercial vessels, barges, dock, and waterside facilities reported for violations of United States port safety regulations.

Commandant (G-CMA), U.S. Coast Guard Headquarters, Washington, DC 20590, (202) 426-2390.

PUGET SOUND VESSEL TRAFFIC SYSTEM REGULATIONS VIOLATIONS DOT/CG

Masters and/or pilots found in violation of Puget Sound Vessel Traffic System regulations.

Commanders, 13th Coast Guard District, Federal Building, 915 2nd Ave., Seattle, WA 98174, (206) 399-5078.

RECORDS OF TRIAL: SPECIAL, GENERAL, AND SUMMARY COURTS-MARTIAL DOT/CG

Any individual who is tried by court-martial in the coast guard.

Chief Counsel, U.S. Coast Guard Headquarters, Washington, DC 20590, (202) 426-1616; Commandant (G-CMA), U.S. Coast Guard Headquarters, Washington, DC 20590, (202) 426-2390.

RECREATIONAL BOATING LAW ENFORCEMENT CASE FILES DOT/CG

Owners/operators of vessels found in violation of federal recreational boating laws or regulations.

Commandant (G-CMA), U.S. Coast Guard Headquarters, Washington, DC 20590, (202) 426-2390.

TORT CLAIMS AND PERSONAL PROPERTY CLAIMS RECORD SYSTEM DOT/FAA

Tort and property claimants who have filed claims against the government or FAA.

Regional and center counsels.

Federal Highway Administration (FHWA)

ACCOUNTS RECEIVABLE DOT/FHWA

Individuals indebted to the Federal Highway Administration.

Chief, General Ledger & Funds Control Section, Office of Fiscal Services, Federal Highway Administration, 400 7th St., SW, Washington, DC 20590, (202) 426-0622.

FHWA MOTOR CARRIER SAFETY PROPOSED CIVIL AND CRIMINAL ENFORCEMENT CASES DOT/FHWA

Officers, agents, or employees of motor carriers, including drivers who have been the subject of investigation for motor carrier safety regulation violations.

Regional Counsel, Federal Highway Administration, Room 1625, George H. Fallon Federal Office Building, 31 Hopkins Plaza, Baltimore, MD 21201, (301) 962-2482.

INVESTIGATIONS CASE FILE SYSTEM DOT/FHWA

Any individual, including Federal Highway Administration (FHWA) employees, state and other political subdvision personnel, contractors and contractor employees who were the subjects of investigation based on allegations of wrongdoing relating to the federal aid highway program.

Office of Program Review and Investigations, Federal Highway Administration, Room 4203, Nassif Building, 400 7th St., SW, Washington, DC 20590, (202) 426-0620.

Additional Files

Following is a list of the remaining files maintained by the Federal Highway Administration. Anyone interested in obtaining information from any of these files should contact the appropriate agency head, or the Office of the Secretary, Department of Transportation, 400 7th St., SW, Washington, DC 20590.

Application for U.S. Government Motor Vehicle Operator's Identification Card (U.S. Government Drivers License) DOT/FHWA
Driver Accident Record Cross-Reference File DOT/FHWA
Driver Waiver File DOT/FHWA
Employee Utilization (Monthly Report) DOT/FHWA
Medals of Honor File DOT/FHWA
Memorandum of Monthly Performance of Keypunch Operators DOT/FHWA
Motor Carrier Accident File—Property & Passenger DOT/FHWA
Occupational Safety and Health Accident Reporting System DOT/FHWA
Payroll Administration DOT/FHWA
Travel Advance File DOT/FHWA
Travel Voucher—Change of Duty Station DOT/FHWA
University and Industry Programs Coding and Filing System DOT/FHWA

National Highway Traffic Safety Administration

ALCOHOL SAFETY ACTION PROJECTS (ASAP) DOT/NHTSA

Vehicle operators having committed alcohol-related driving violations.

Chief, Demonstration Management Division, ODPP, TSP, NHTSA, 400 7th St., SW, Washington, DC 20590.

CIVIL PENALTY ENFORCEMENT FILES DOT/NHTSA

Persons (corporate or individual) against whom civil penalties are sought or contemplated for violations of NHTSA-administered statutes.

Office of Chief Counsel, NHTSA, Room 5219, 400 7th St., SW, Washington, DC 20590.

DEBARRED BIDDERS LIST DOT/NHTSA

Various individuals who have committed offenses which require that they be barred from bidding or employment with the federal government.

Director, Office of Contracts and Procurement, NHTSA, 400 7th St., SW, Washington, DC 20590.

DEBT COMPLAINT FILE DOT/NHTSA

Employees of the NHTSA on whom the agency has received contacts of creditors' indebtedness.

Director, Office of Personnel Management, Room 5306, Nassif Building, 400 7th St., SW, Washington, DC 20590.

DRINKING DRIVER TRACKING SYSTEM DOT/NHTSA

Persons arrested while driving under the influence of alcohol.

Department of Transportation, National Highway Traffic Safety Administration, Room 5301 N48-30, 400 7th St., SW, Washington, DC 20590.

EEO COUNSELING PROGRAM AND DISCRIMINATION COMPLAINT FILE DOT/NHTSA

NHTSA personnel or those seeking clerical or professional employment with NHTSA.

Room 5312, DOT Headquarters Building, Washington, DC 20590.

FEDERAL MOTOR VEHICLE SAFETY STANDARDS (FMVSS) COMPLIANCE DOT/NHTSA

Complaints about, or individuals suspected of, violation of FMVSS.

Associate Administrator, MVP, NHTSA, 400 7th St., SW, Washington, DC 20590.

HABITUAL OFFENDER ANALYSIS FILE DOT/NHTSA

Individuals certified as habitual offenders in North Carolina in the calendar year 1973, pursuant to Section 20-220-Section 20-231, General Statutes of North Carolina.

National Highway Traffic Safety Administration, Room 5301 N48-30, 400 7th St., SW, Washington, DC 20590.

INVESTIGATIONS OF ALLEGED MISCONDUCT OR CONFLICT OF INTEREST DOT/NHTSA

Name of individual, state, or contractor.

National Highway Traffic Safety Administration, Room 5238, N48-01, 400 7th St., SW, Washington, DC 20590, Attention: Associate Administrator for Administration.

INVESTIGATIONS AND SECURITY DOT/NHTSA

NHTSA employee security violations.

National Highway Traffic Safety Administration, 400 7th St., SW, Washington, DC 20590.

NATIONAL DRIVER REGISTER DOT/NHTSA

Persons who have had their driver licenses denied, withdrawn, revoked or suspended as reported by state or territorial driver licensing authorities.

Room 3214, Trans Point Building, Second and V Sts., SW, Washington, DC.

Requests for information should include: Individual's full legal name, other names used (such as nicknames, professional names, or maiden name, if any), date of birth, place of birth (city, state, or foreign country), sex, height, weight, color of eyes, and Social Security account number and/or driver's license number. (Provision of the Social Security account number is voluntary.) In addition, although not mandatory, it would help to more positively identify any records the agency may have concerning the inquirer if the following information is included: The reason the license was withdrawn or denied, the date of the action, and the state which took the action. Individuals requesting information through a personal visit should have at least two means of positive identification. For mailed inquiries the foregoing identification elements should be included in the form of a notarized affidavit and addressed to System Manager, Room 3214, Trans Point Building, Second and V Sts., SW, Washington, DC. A form for this purpose will be provided by the National Driver Register upon request. Use of this form is optional.

RHODE ISLAND SPECIAL ADJUDICATION FOR ENFORCEMENT (SAFE) DOT/NHTSA

Persons charged with traffic violations; persons who have had motor vehicle accidents; persons who have had driver licenses suspended.

National Highway Traffic Safety Administration, Room 5301-N48-30, 400 7th St., SW, Washington, DC 20590, Attention: Director, Office of Contracts and Procurement.

VEHICLES DEFECT PROGRAM FILE
(PROPOSED) DOT/NHTSA

Owners of vehicles suspected of having safety related defects.

Executive Vice President, Connecticut Motor Club, 2276 Whitney Ave., Hamden, CT 06518.

Additional Files

Following is a list of the remaining files maintained by the NHTSA. Anyone interested in obtaining information from any of these files should contact the appropriate agency head, or the Office of the Secretary, Department of Transportation, 400 7th St., SW, Washington, DC 20590.

Active Contract Run DOT/NHTSA
Alcohol Behavior Research DOT/NHTSA
College Station/Young Problem Driver Improvement Program/TDIP Driving Record File DOT/NHTSA
Contract Grievance Records DOT/NHTSA
Cooperative Agreement Number DOT-HS-5-01057 Motor Vehicle Diagnostic Inspection Investigation DOT/NHTSA
Cost Effectiveness Study of Breakaway and Non-Breakaway Poles Including Signs and Light Standards along Highways DOT/NHTSA
D.C. Motor Vehicle Diagnostic Inspection Demonstration Project DOT/NHTSA
Diagnostic Demonstration Project DOT/NHTSA
Diagnostic Inspection Demonstration DOT/NHTSA
Docket DOT/NHTSA
Dynamic Sled Tests of Human Volunteer Subjects DOT/NHTSA
Emergency Medical Information System DOT/NHTSA
Experts and Consultants List DOT/NHTSA
General Public Correspondence
General Public Inquiries DOT/NHTSA
Government Driver Licenses DOT/NHTSA
Highway Safety Literature Personal Author File DOT/NHTSA
Hotline-Call Report System DOT/NHTSA
Idaho Traffic Records System Accident Component—Drive Component DOT/NHTSA
In-Depth Accident Investigation DOT/NHTSA
Injuries, Illnesses, Motor Vehicle Accidents and Property Damages DOT/NHTSA
Manpower Training File DOT/NHTSA
Medical Records and Research Data DOT/NHTSA
Motor Vehicle Accident and Claim Reporting System, Federal Register Identifier: GSA/FSS-6 DOT/NHTSA
Motor Vehicle Defects DOT/NHTSA
Motor Vehicle and Motor Vehicle Equipment Report DOT/NHTSA
National Highway Safety Advisory Committee Membership/ Nominee Files DOT/NHTSA
National Motor Vehicle Safety Advisory Council Membership/Nominee Files DOT/NHTSA
Odometer Rollback DOT/NHTSA
Offerors Data Bank DOT/NHTSA

Offerors Mailing List DOT/NHTSA
Restraint System Effectiveness Study DOT/NHTSA
Safety Related Defects Interviews and Vehicle Disablement Study DOT/NHTSA
Special Adjudication for Enforcement (SAFE) DOT/NHTSA
Statement of Employment and Financial Interest DOT/NHTSA
Subjects for Accident Avoidance Skill Training and Performance Testing DOT/NHTSA
Survey of Recreational Vehicle Suspensions DOT/NHTSA
Temporary Exemption Petitions DOT/NHTSA
Vendor Edit Table Listing (Employees) DOT/NHTSA
Volunteer Pool DOT/NHTSA
Youth Highway Safety Advisory Committee DOT/NHTSA

St. Lawrence Seaway Development Corporation

CLAIMANTS UNDER FEDERAL TORT
CLAIMS ACT DOT/SLS

Persons who make claims against the corporation.

General Counsel, St. Lawrence Seaway Development Corporation, P.O. Box 520, Massena, NY 13662.

Additional Files

Following is a list of the remaining files maintained by the St. Lawrence Seaway Development Corporation. Anyone interested in obtaining information from any of these files should contact the appropriate agency head, or the Office of the Secretary, Department of Transportation, 400 7th St., SW, Washington, DC 20590.

Biographical Files DOT/SLS
Data Automation Program Records DOT/SLS
Emergency Operating Records (Vital Records) DOT/SLS
Employees' Compensation Records DOT/SLS
Personnel Convenience Files DOT/SLS
Safety Management Information System DOT/SLS
Vehicle Operator Identification DOT/SLS

Transportation Systems Center

LEGAL COUNSEL INFORMATION FILES DOT/TSC

TSC employees involved in legal matters.

Department of Transportation, Transportation Systems Center, Office of Legal Counsel/Code 140, Kendall Square, Cambridge, MA 02142.

Additional Files

Following is a list of the remaining files maintained by the Transportation Systems Center. Anyone interested in obtaining information from any of these files should contact the appropriate agency head, or the Office of the Secretary, Department of Transportation, 400 7th St., SW, Washington, DC 20590.

Automated Management Information Systems DOT/TSC
Automated Manpower Distribution System DOT/TSC
Automated Payroll/Personnel/Communications/Security
  System DOT/TSC
Automated Personnel Skills Reporting System DOT/TSC
Automated Planning System DOT/TSC
Bi-Weekly Personnel Status Report DOT/TSC
Blood Donor Information File DOT/TSC
Combined Federal Campaign Information DOT/TSC
Employee Payroll – Manpower Distribution System
  DOT/TSC
Employee Travel Records DOT/TSC
Health Unit Employee Medical Records DOT/TSC
Minority Information Files DOT/TSC
Occupational Safety & Health Reporting System
  DOT/TSC
Personnel Management Convenience Files DOT/TSC
Stand-By Personnel Information DOT/TSC

Urban Mass Transportation Administration

Additional Files

Following is a list of the remaining files maintained by the
Urban Mass Transportation Administration and the Federal
Railroad Administration. Anyone interested in obtaining
additional information from any of these files should contact the appropriate agency head of the Federal Railroad
Administration, 400 Seventh St., SW, Washington, DC
20590, (202) 426-4000.

Urban Mass Transportation Administration

Blood-Donor File DOT/UMTA
Minority Recruitment File DOT/UMTA

Personnel Convenience Files DOT/UMTA
UMTA-Sponsored Reports, Author File DOT/UMTA

Federal Railroad Administration

Alaska Railroad Examination of Operating Personnel
  DOT/FRA
Alaska Railroad Personnel and Pay Management Informa-
  tion System DOT/FRA
Alaska Railroad Security and Freight Claims Investigatory
  Files DOT/FRA
Application for Operator's (Vehicle) Identification Card
  DOT/FRA
Confidential Statement of Employment and Financial
  Interest DOT/FRA
Department of Transportation
Employee Travel Records DOT/FRA
Occupational Safety and Health Reporting System
  DOT/FRA
Office of Chief Counsel Internal Personal Data File
  DOT/FRA
Office of Policy and Program Development Internal Work
  Reference File DOT/FRA
Office of Research and Development Internal Work
  Reference File DOT/FRA
Office of Safety Past Employees Files DOT/FRA
Office of Safety Personnel Convenience File DOT/FRA
Personnel and Pay Management Information System
  DOT/FRA
Regional Personnel Convenience Files DOT/FRA
Transportation Test Center Employee Service Record File
  DOT/FRA
Travel Advance Records DOT/FRA
Work Measurement System DOT/FRA

U.S. Department of the Treasury

Following is a list of the agencies and subagencies of the Department of the Treasury, with abbreviations:

Treasury	*Treasury Department*
AT and F	Bureau of Alcohol, Tobacco, and Firearms
Customs	Customs Service
Comptroller	Comptroller of the Currency
ESO	Economic Stabilization Office (temporary)
FLETC	Federal Law Enforcement Training Center
FS	Fiscal Service
IRS	Internal Revenue Service
Mint	Bureau of the Mint

OFFICE OF THE SECRETARY

CIVIL LITIGATION RECORDS TREASURY/OS

Persons who are parties, plaintiff or defendant, in civil litigation with the Treasury Department.

Exempt system.

CLAIMANT, DISBURSING TREASURY/OS

Claimants for disbursements by the United States.

Administrative Officer, Office of the General Counsel, Department of Treasury, 1500 Pennsylvania Ave., NW, Washington, DC 20220, (202) 566-2093.

CORRESPONDENCE FILES AND RECORDS ON EMPLOYEE COMPLAINTS AND/OR DISSATISFACTION TREASURY/OS

Former or current department employees.

Assistant Director of Personnel, Employee Relations and Services, Department of the Treasury, Room 2425, Main Treasury Building, Washington, DC 20220, (202) 566-8083.

DISBARMENTS TREASURY/OS

Individuals formerly eligible to practice before the Internal Revenue Service but now disbarred from such practice.

Exempt system.

EEO COMPLAINT PROCESSING SYSTEM TREASURY/OS

Applicants for employment and aggrieved employees who have filed formal equal employment opportunity complaints against the department and its bureaus.

Director, Office of Equal Opportunity Program, Department of the Treasury, 15th St. and Pennsylvania Ave., NW, Washington, DC 20220, (202) 376-0744.

Request for information should contain: Individual's name, the date he or she filed a formal complaint, the bureau against whom the complaint was filed, and if known, the date the complaint was closed.

EEO COUNSELOR COMPLAINT FILES TREASURY/OS

Individuals alleging discrimination related to employment with the Office of the Secretary and who have been assigned to a counselor for informal counseling.

Equal Employment Opportunity Officer, Office of the Secretary, Department of the Treasury, Main Treasury Building, Room 4406, Washington, DC 20220, (202) 376-0744.

EMPLOYEE GRADE COMPLAINT FILE TREASURY/OS

Employees of the Treasury Department.

Deputy Director of Personnel, Department of the Treasury, 15th St. and Pennsylvania Ave., Washington, DC 20220, (202) 566-2703.

FOREIGN ASSETS CONTROL ENFORCEMENT RECORDS TREASURY/OS

Individuals who have engaged in unlicensed financial, commercial, or other transactions which are prohibited under regulations administered by the Office of Foreign Assets Control; individuals who have made any unlicensed importation of prohibited merchandise from a foreign country which is a "designated country" under regulations administered by the Office of Foreign Assets Control; individuals who have made an unlicensed remittance of funds or exportation of goods to a "designated country" or national thereof, or to a "specially designated national"; individuals who have otherwise violated any Treasury ruling, license, or regulation issued under or pursuant to the Trading with the Enemy Act or the United Nations Participation Act; individuals suspected of having engaged in activities or transactions which violated statutes or regulations administered by the controls; individuals who have applied for Foreign Assets Control Licensing when there is reason to suspect the truth of statements contained in an individual's application; individuals who have or are suspected of misuse or misappropriation of blocked property.

Proposed exempt system.

FOREIGN ASSETS CONTROL LEGAL FILES TREASURY/OS

Individuals who have corresponded with (or been the subject of correspondence) regarding legal matters and regulations administered by the Office of Foreign Assets Control; individuals who have been criminally prosecuted, or involved in civil litigation (as plaintiff or defendant) with the United States, in matters involving statutes and/or regulations administered by the Office of Foreign Assets Control.

Administrative Officer, Room 3006, Department of the Treasury, 1500 Pennsylvania Ave., NW, Washington, DC 20220, (202) 566-2093.

FOREIGN ASSETS CONTROL LITIGATION FILES TREASURY/OS

Individuals who have been criminally prosecuted, or involved in civil litigation (as plaintiff or defendant) with the United States, in matters which involve statutes and/or regulations which are administered by the Office of Foreign Assets Control.

Written requests should be made to: Office of Foreign Assets Control, Department of the Treasury, Washington, DC 20220, (202) 376-0395. Personal visits may be made to: Office of Foreign Assets Control, 1331 G St., NW, Room 504, Washington, DC 20220.

INTERNATIONAL CRIMINAL POLICE ORGANIZATION (INTERPOL) CRIMINAL INVESTIGATIVE RECORDS TREASURY/OS

Individuals who have been convicted or are subjects of a criminal investigation with international aspects; specific missing persons; specific deceased persons in connection with death notices; certain weapons, motor vehicles, artifacts, etc., stolen and/or involved in crime which may or may not be associated with an individual; certain victims of criminal violations in the United States or abroad.

Exempt system.

INVENTORY TREASURY/OS

Attorneys, certified public accountants, and enrolled agents about which alleged misconduct in their practice before the Internal Revenue Service is being reviewed and evaluated.

Exempt system.

MERIT SYSTEM COMPLAINTS TREASURY/OS

Employees who have a basis for believing that civil service personnel laws or rules are being violated, and the matter is not appropriate for the grievance or appeals procedure.

Proposed for exemption.

PHYSICAL SECURITY INFORMATION SYSTEM TREASURY/OS

Treasury Department officials who actually classify a document using a national security classification, i.e., top secret, secret, or confidential; department officials by name and position title, who have been delegated the authority to downgrade and declassify national security information and material; department officials by name and position title, who have been delegated the authority for original classification of national security information and material as confidential; employees who are responsible for valid security violations regarding the handling of classified information or material; department officials who communicated or transferred classified information or material to an unauthorized person; department and contractor personnel, employed in the metropolitan Washington, DC, area, who utilized the building pass system for the main Treasury and annex buildings; department officials who have used an unnecessary national security classification, an over or under national security classification, or failed to assign the proper downgrading and declassification schedule, or improperly applied national security classification markings. It also includes any national security classification action by any official not authorized in writing to exercise appropriate classification or exemption authority or the improper delegation of such.

Assistant Director for Physical Security, Office of Administrative Programs, Room 313, 1625 I St., NW, c/o Main Treasury Mailroom, Washington, DC 20220, (202) 376-0763.

PRESENT SUSPENSIONS FROM PRACTICE BEFORE THE INTERNAL REVENUE SERVICE

Attorneys, certified public accountants, and enrolled agents who have offered their consent to voluntary suspension from practice before the Internal Revenue Service or who have been suspended from such practice after due notice and opportunity for hearing.

Exempt system.

REGISTER OF DOCKETED CASES AND APPLICANT APPEALS TREASURY/OS

Individuals against whom complaints have been filed with the Office of Director of Practice pursuant to Title 31, CFR, Subpart C, Section 10.54, for alleged violation of the regulations governing practice before the Internal Revenue Service and individuals who have appealed to the Director of Practice the denials of their application for enrollment to practice before the Internal Revenue Service.

Office of Director of Practice, Department of the Treasury, 1500 Pennsylvania Ave., NW, Washington, DC 20220, (202) 376-0767.

TREASURY ENFORCEMENT COMMUNICATIONS SYSTEM (TECS) TREASURY/OS

Individuals who have been convicted or are subjects of a criminal investigation with international aspects; specific missing persons; specific deceased persons in connection with death notices; certain weapons, motor vehicles, artifacts, etc., stolen and/or involved in crime which may or may not be associated with an individual; certain victims of criminal violation in the United States or abroad.

Exempt system.

Additional Files

Following is a list of the remaining files maintained by the Office of the Secretary. Anyone interested in obtaining information from any of these files should contact the Secretary, Department of the Treasury, 1500 Pennsylvania Ave., NW, Washington, DC 20220, (202) 566-2533.

Abandoned Enrollment Applications Treasury/OS
Accounting for Investment Credit File, Office of the Assistant Secretary for Tax Policy Treasury/OS
Affirmative Action Plan; Employment of Handicapped Individuals, Treasury/OS

Annual Performance Rating and Annual Performance Analysis Treasury/OS
Applicant Appeal Files Treasury/OS
Appointment at above the Minimum Rate of the Grade Files Treasury/OS
Assistant Secretary, Personnel Administrative Files Treasury/OS
Attorney Books Treasury/OS
Attorneys Past and Present Treasury/OS
Automated Directory System Treasury/OS
Banks' Affirmative Action Files Treasury/OS
Bilateral Development Program Office Personnel File Treasury/OS
Buildings Management Employee Folder Treasury/OS
Buildings Management Staffing and Recruitment File Treasury/OS
CD 11/4 Gold Licenses Treasury/OS
Centralized Automated System for Reporting Employment Statistics in the Department of the Treasury (REST) Treasury/OS
Chief Counsel for Revenue Sharing Personnel Treasury/OS
Closed Files Containing Derogatory Information about Individuals' Practice Before the Internal Revenue Service and Files of Attorneys and Certified Public Accountants Formerly Enrolled to Practice Treasury/OS
Combined Applicant/Applicant Correspondence File Treasury/OS
Confidential Statements of Employment and Financial Interests, Personnel Division, Office of the Secretary Treasury/OS
Contractors File Treasury/OS
Contracts and Research Proposals Treasury/OS
Daily Bindery Log, Reproduction Branch Treasury/OS 00.198
Daily Work Log, Reproduction Branch Treasury/OS 00.199
Derogatory Information (No Action) Treasury/OS
Detailed Employee Files Treasury/OS
Directory File of Reporters on Treasury Foreign Exchange and Foreign Currency Forms Treasury/OS
Disabled Veterans Statistical Report Treasury/OS
Employee Inventions Treasury/OS
Employee Locator Record Treasury/OS
Employee Promotion Information Treasury/OS
Employee Record Cards Treasury/OS
Employment Applications Treasury/OS
Energy Policy Office Administrative File Treasury/OS
EOTA FOI Request/Appeals Files Treasury/OS
Executive Inventory Files Treasury/OS
FAC 1950 Census of Blocked Chinese Assets Treasury/OS
FAC 1964 Census of Blocked Cuban Assets Treasury/OS
FAC 1970 Census of Blocked Chinese Assets Treasury/OS
FOL Compliance File, Office of the Assistant Secretary for Tax Policy Treasury/OS
Foreign Assets Control Administrative Records Treasury/OS
Foreign Assets Control General Correspondence Files Treasury/OS

Foreign Assets Control Licensing Records Treasury/OS

Foreign Assets Control Mailing List Treasury/OS

Freedom of Information Requests for Office of Secretary and Other Department Records Treasury/OS

General Correspondence File Treasury/OS

General Counsel Personnel File Treasury/OS

Gifts to the United States Treasury/OS

IFI and USG Officials Connected with IFI Annual Meetings or Project Inspection Trips Treasury/OS

Library Circulation Control Records Treasury/OS

Management Analysis Division (MAD) Personnel Working Files Treasury/OMO

Monthly Production Report, Reproduction Branch Treasury/OS 00.200

OASIA Correspondence Files Treasury/OS

OASIA Invitation Lists Treasury/OS

OASIA Time Cards Listed on Form 2384 Treasury/OS

OIDB Employee and Employee Candidate Files Treasury/OS

OMO Management Consultants File Treasury/OS

Office of Computer Science, Work Assignment, and Control Form Treasury/OS

Office of Debt Analysis, Actuarial Valuation System, Treasury/OS

Office of Debt Analysis, General Correspondence Treasury/OS

Office of Trade Finance Correspondence Files Treasury/OS

Office of Trade Finance, Home Addresses, and Telephone Number File Treasury/OS

ORS Auditors' Address File Treasury/OS

ORS Compliance Division Employee File Treasury/OS

ORS Contractors' File Treasury/OS

ORS Governors' Address File Treasury/OS

ORS Governors and Governors Authorized Representatives List Treasury/OS

Office of Revenue Sharing, Intergovernmental Relations Division Mailing List Treasury/OS

ORS Leave Records Treasury/OS

ORS Personnel Records Treasury/OS

ORS Public Affairs Personnel File Treasury/ORS

ORS Senate, House and Governors' Address File Treasury/OS

ORS State Attorney Generals' Records Treasury/OS

Overtime Records, Reproductive Branch Treasury/OS 00.201

Parking Permit Application Treasury/OS

Payroll, Time and Attendance Records Treasury/OS

Personnel: General Counsels, Deputy General Counsels, and Assistant General Counsels Treasury/OS

Personnel Files Treasury/OS

Personnel and Payroll Data: Transaction Lists; Employee Service Record Report; Leave Without Pay Report; Employee Information List; Comprehensive Payroll Listing; Alphabetical Locator List Treasury/OS

Personnel; Recruitment, Personnel; Evaluations Treasury/OS

Personnel Security Files Treasury/OS

Personnel Security Files and Indices Treasury/OS

Planning and Evaluation Division Employee Locator Card Copy and Information Sheet File Treasury/OS

Planning and Evaluation Division Employee Personnel File Treasury/OS

Printing Procurement Charge Ticket, Printing Procurement Treasury/OS 00.202

Private Relief Bill System Treasury/OS

Private Relief Tax Bill Files Office of the Assistant Secretary for Tax Policy Treasury/OS

Public Correspondence Treasury/OS

Reference Letters—Special Assignments Branch, Office of the Secretary of the Treasury

Resigned Enrolled Agents (Action Pursuant to 31 CFR, Section 10:55(b) Treasury/OS

Roster of Former Enrollees Treasury/OS

Roster of Office of the Secretary Employees Treasury/OS

Scheduled Annual Leave Records Treasury/OS

Security Clearance Index Card File, Security Branch, Office of the Secretary of the Treasury Treasury/OS

Sign-In Sheet, Reproduction Branch Treasury/OS

Spanish Speaking Informal Application File (S.F. 171) Treasury/OS

Special Personnel Working Files, Office of the Assistant Secretary for Tax Policy Treasury/OS

State Attorney Generals Records (ORS) Treasury/OS

Summer Employees Listing Treasury/OS

Tax Court Judge Applicants Treasury/OS

Time and Attendance Cards Treasury/OS

Timecards Treasury/OS

Travel Records Treasury/OS

Treasury Emergency Preparedness Information Program. The Information System of this Program Contains the Following Information Records Which are Subject to this Inventory: Emergency Executive Teams Lists, Alert Notification Procedures, Federal Emergency Assignee Identification Treasury/OS

Treasury Foreign Currency (TFC) Reporters Treasury/OS

Treasury Foreign Exchange (TFEX) Reporters Treasury/OS

Treasury Payroll/Personnel Information System (To be Implemented Approximately January 1977 to July 1978) Treasury/OS

Upward Mobility Program; Counseling Application Treasury/OS

Wage Case Files Treasury/OS

Weekly Activity Report, Printing Procurement Branch Treasury/OS

Written Amendment Exception Files Treasury/OS

BUREAU OF ALCOHOL, TOBACCO, AND FIREARMS

ADMINISTRATIVE RECORD SYSTEM TREASURY/ATF

Present employees of the Bureau of ATF; former employees of the Bureau of ATF; claimants against the Bureau of ATF.

Privacy Act Request, Bureau of Alcohol, Tobacco, and Firearms, 1200 Pennsylvania Ave., NW, Washington, DC 20226, (202) 566-7118.

CRIMINAL INVESTIGATION REPORT SYSTEM TREASURY/ATF

Criminal offenders or alleged criminal offenders acting alone or in concert with other individuals and suspects who have been or are under investigation for a violation or suspected violation of laws enforced by the bureau; criminal offenders or alleged criminal offenders acting alone or in concert with individuals who have been referred to the bureau by other law enforcement agencies, governmental units, and the general public; informants; persons who come to the attention of the bureau in the conduct of criminal investigations; persons who have been convicted of a crime punishable by imprisonment for a term exceeding one year and who have applied for relief from disabilities under federal law with respect to the acquisition, receipt, transfer, shipment, or possession of firearms and explosives and whose disability was incurred by reason of such conviction; victims of crimes; witnesses.

Privacy Act Request, Bureau of Alcohol, Tobacco, and Firearms (Disclosure Branch), 1200 Pennsylvania Ave., NW, Washington, DC 20026, (202) 566-7118.

Additional Files

Following is a list of the remaining files maintained by the Bureau of Alcohol, Tobacco, and Firearms. Anyone interested in obtaining information from any of these files should contact the Secretary, Department of the Treasury, 1500 Pennsylvania Ave., NW, Washington, DC 20220, (202) 566-2533.

Correspondence Record System Treasury/ATF
Fiscal Record System Treasury/ATF
Freedom of Information Requests Treasury/ATF
Internal Security Record System Treasury/ATF
Personnel Record System Treasury/ATF
Regulatory Enforcement Record System Treasury ATF
Technical and Scientific Services Record System
    Treasury/ATF

BUREAU OF ENGRAVING AND PRINTING

For information about any BEP system, write to the following address, identifying the system of interest: Superintendent, Management Services Division, Bureau of Engraving and Printing, 14th and C Sts., SW, Washington, DC 20228, (202) 447-0261. Attention: Privacy Law Information.

COUNSELING RECORDS TREASURY/BEP

Employees whose actions or conduct warrants counseling.

DEBT FILES (EMPLOYEES) TREASURY/BEP

Employees on whom debt complaints are received.

EMPLOYEE ARREST RECORD TREASURY/BEP

Employees who have been arrested.

INFORMAL EEO COMPLAINT PROCESSING RECORDS TREASURY/BEP

Employees who register informal equal employment opportunity complaints.

RECORDS OF DISCRIMINATION COMPLAINTS TREASURY/BEP

Employees who have initiated discrimination complaints.

TORT CLAIMS (AGAINST THE UNITED STATES) TREASURY/BEP

Individuals and/or organizations making claim for money damage against the United States for injury to or loss of property, or personal injury, or death caused by the neglect or wrongful act or omission of a Bureau of Engraving and Printing employee while acting within the scope of their office or employment.

Additional Files

Following is a list of the remaining files maintained by the Bureau of Engraving and Printing. Anyone interested in obtaining information from any of these files should contact the Secretary, Department of the Treasury, 1500 Pennsylvania Ave., NW, Washington, DC 20220, (202) 566-2533.

Accident and Safety Report Treasury/BEP
Civilian Employee Claim File Treasury/BEP
Compensation Claims Treasury/BEP
Continuation of Pay Record Treasury/BEP
Departmental Integrated Personal Services System
    (DIPS) Treasury/BEP
Emergency Contact Records Treasury/BEP
Employee Index File Treasury/BEP
Employee Locator Record Treasury/BEP
Employee Seniority List Treasury/BEP
Employee Suggestions Treasury/BEP
Employee's Daily Production Record Treasury/BEP
Employee's Health Unit Daily Report Treasury/BEP
Employees Home Contact File Treasury/BEP
Freedom of Information Requests Treasury/BEP
Guard Uniform Control Account Treasury/BEP
Identification Files Treasury/BEP
Industrial Truck Licensing Records Treasury/BEP
Investigative Files Treasury/BEP
Monthly Equal Employment Opportunity Activity
    Report Treasury/BEP
Motor Vehicle Licensing Records Treasury/BEP
Parking Program Records Treasury/BEP
Payroll Records Treasury/BEP
Payroll Statistical Data Treasury/BEP
Personal Protective Equipment File Treasury/BEP

Personnel Movement Control Record Treasury/BEP
Personnel Progress and Achievement Record Treasury/BEP
Personnel Security Files and Indices Treasury/BEP
Petition of Election Treasury/BEP
Project REST (Reporting Employment Statistics in
    Treasury), Minority Statistics Treasury/BEP
Reemployment Information Record Treasury/BEP
Retention Register Treasury/BEP
Roster of Bureau of Engraving and Printing
    Employees Treasury/BEP
Time and Attendance Record Treasury/BEP
Union Dues Allotments Treasury/BEP
Union Index Treasury/BEP
Unscheduled Absence Record Treasury/BEP
Work Performance Records Treasury/BEP

BUREAU OF GOVERNMENT FINANCIAL OPERATIONS

For information about any GFO system of records, write or call the following official, indicating the system of interest: Special Assistant (P.A.), Bureau of Government Financial Operations, Department of the Treasury, Room 600, Treasury Annex No. 1, Pennsylvania Ave. and Madison Pl., NW, Washington, DC 20226, (202) 566-8707.

Additional Files

Following is a list of the remaining files maintained by the Bureau of Government Financial Operations. Anyone interested in obtaining information from any of these files should contact the Secretary, Department of the Treasury, 1500 Pennsylvania Ave., NW, Washington, DC 20220, (202) 566-2533.

Administrative Records Treasury/GFO
Check Issue Records for Regular Recurring Benefit
    Payments Treasury/GFO
Claims and Inquiry Records on Treasury Checks, U.S.
    Currencies, and International Claimants Treasury/GFO
Freedom of Information Requests Treasury/GFO
GFO Personnel Records Treasury/GFO
Identification Files on Individuals Cashing Treasury Checks
    at the U.S. Treasury Treasury/GFO
Individual Retirement Cards, SF2806 Treasury/GFO
Payroll and Pay Administration Treasury/GFO
Personnel Security Records Treasury/GFO
Postal Savings Deposits Treasury/GFO
Precomplaint Counseling and Complaint Activities
    Treasury/GFO
Records of Accountable Officers' Authority with Treasury
    Treasury/GFO

BUREAU OF THE MINT

EMPLOYEES, FORMER EMPLOYEES, AND VISITORS, OCCUPATIONAL SAFETY AND HEALTH, ACCIDENT AND INJURIES RECORDS: AND CLAIMS FOR INJURIES OR DAMAGE COMPENSATION RECORDS TREASURY/MINT

Bureau of the Mint employees, former employees, and visitors to mint offices and facilities, reporting accidents and injuries occurring on federal government property or in areas immediately adjacent to government property, for which potential liability exists due to local laws.

Safety Officer, Bureau of the Mint, Department of the Treasury, Warner Building, 501 13th St., NW, Washington, DC 20220, (202) 376-0592; Safety Officer, United States Mint, Independence Mall, Philadelphia, PA 19106, (215) 597-4435; Safety Manager, United States Mint, 320 West Colfax Ave., Denver, CO 80204, (303) 837-3404; Safety Manager, United States Assay Office, 155 Hermann St., San Francisco, CA 94102, (415) 556-5663; Safety Manager, United States Assay Office, 32 Old Slip St., New York, NY 10005, (212) 264-1722; Safety Manager, United States Bullion Depository, West Point, NY 10996, (914) 938-4011; Safety Manager, United States Bullion Depository, Fort Knox, KY 40121, (502) 624-4520; Safety Manager, United States Old Mint, 88 Fifth St., San Francisco, CA 94103, (415) 556-6514.

EQUAL EMPLOYMENT OPPORTUNITY (EEO) COMPLAINT COUNSELING RECORDS TREASURY/MINT

Employees and applicants for employment at the Bureau of the Mint.

EEO Officer, Bureau of the Mint, Department of the Treasury, Warner Building, 501 13th St., NW, Washington, DC 20220, (202) 376-0493; EEO Officer, United States Mint, Independence Mall, Philadelphia, PA 19106, (215) 597-2365; EEO Officer, United States Mint, 320 West Colfax Ave., Denver, CO 80204, (303) 837-3658; EEO Officer, United States Assay Office, 32 Old Slip St., New York, NY 10005, (212) 264-1729; EEO Officer, United States Assay Office, 155 Hermann St., San Francisco, CA 94102, (415) 556-6175; EEO Officer, United States Old Mint, 88 Fifth St., San Francisco, CA 94103, (415) 556-4434; EEO Officer, United States Bullion Depository, Fort Knox, KY 40121, (502) 624-2545.

EXAMINATION REPORTS OF COINS FORWARDED TO MINT FROM U.S. SECRET SERVICE TREASURY/MINT

Individuals from whom the Secret Service has seized coins suspected to be counterfeit or altered.

This system is proposed for exemption.

GRIEVANCES, UNION/AGENCY NEGOTIATED TREASURY/MINT

Employees and former employees of the Bureau of the Mint.

For current and former employees: Personnel Officer, Bureau of the Mint, Department of the Treasury, 15th St. & Pennsylvania Ave., NW, Washington, DC 20220, (202) 376-0555; Personnel Officer, U.S. Mint, Independence Mall, Philadelphia, PA 19106, (215) 597-4988; Personnel Officer, U.S. Mint, 320 Colfax Ave., Denver, CO 80204, (303) 837-4951; Personnel Officer, U.S. Assay Office, 155 Hermann St., San Francisco, CA 94102, (415) 556-7866; Personnel Officer, U.S. Assay Office, 32 Old Slip St., New York, NY 10005, (212) 264-0617; Personnel Officer, U.S. Old Mint, 88 Fifth St., San Francisco, CA 94103, (415) 556-7866; Officer-in-Charge, U.S. Bullion Depository, Fort Knox, KY 40121, (502) 624-3454; Administrative Officer, West Point Bullion Depository, West Point, NY 10996, (914) 938-4011.

INVESTIGATORY FILES ON THEFT OF MINT PROPERTY TREASURY/MINT

Mint employees and members of public suspected of the theft of government property.

This system is proposed for exemption.

Additional Files

Following is a list of the remaining files maintained by the Bureau of the Mint. Anyone interested in obtaining information from any of these files should contact the Secretary, Department of the Treasury, 1500 Pennsylvania Ave., NW, Washington, DC 20220, (202) 566-2533.

Applicant and Information Forms for Great Plaza Parking Permits Treasury/Mint
Applicants for Selection for the Current Annual Assay Commission, and Members of Former Commissions Treasury/Mint
Cash Receivable Accounting Information System Treasury/Mint
Confidential Statements of Financial Interest Treasury/Mint
Current Employee Security Identification Record Treasury/Mint
Employee and Former Employee Travel and Training Accounting Information System Treasury/Mint
Employee Payroll, Personnel and Time and Attendance History Automated Recording System; Departmental Integrated Personal Services System (DIPS) Treasury/Mint
Employee-Supervisor Performance, Evaluation, Counseling and Time and Attendance Records Treasury/Mint
General Correspondence Treasury/Mint
Numismatic Coin Operations System (NUCOS) Records; Customer Mailing List and Order Processing Records for Coin Sets, Medals, and Numismatic Items Treasury/Mint

Purchases, Sales, Exchanges, and Assays of Precious Metals Treasury/Mint
Redemption of Uncurrent or Multilated Coins Treasury/Mint

COMPTROLLER OF THE CURRENCY

For information about any Comptroller of the Currency system, write to the following address, indicating the system of interest: Special Assistant for Public Affairs, Comptroller of the Currency, Sixth Floor, 490 E. L'Enfant Plaza, SW, Washington, DC 20219, (202) 447-0154.

CONSUMER COMPLAINT INDEX TREASURY/COMPTROLLER

Complainants.

CONSUMER COMPLAINT INDEX TREASURY/COMPTROLLER

Persons filing complaints with regional offices against national banks.

CONSUMER COMPLAINT INDEX TREASURY/COMPTROLLER

Individuals who lodge complaints against national banks.

CONSUMER COMPLAINT INDEX TREASURY/COMPTROLLER

Employees.

CONSUMER COMPLAINT LETTER FILE TREASURY/COMPTROLLER

Persons who file complaints against banks.

FEDERAL BUREAU OF INVESTIGATION REPORT CARD INDEX TREASURY/COMPTROLLER

Persons who have been involved in or associated with unlawful activity respecting national banking associations. The Department of Justice has exempted this system.

FORMAL COMPLAINT REPORTS TREASURY/COMPTROLLER

Employees filing formal complaints of discrimination because of race, color, religion, age, or sex.

INFORMATION FILE ON INDIVIDUALS AND
COMMERCIAL ENTITIES KNOWN OR SUSPECTED
OF BEING INVOLVED IN FRAUDULENT ACTIVITIES
TREASURY/COMPTROLLER

Individuals and entities involved in actual or suspected fraudulent activities. The Department of Justice has exempted this system.

PRECOMPLAINT COUNSELING AND COMPLAINT
ACTIVITIES TREASURY/COMPTROLLER

Employees seeking services of equal employment opportunity counselors.

Additional Files

Following is a list of the remaining files maintained by the Comptroller of the Currency. Anyone interested in obtaining information from any of these files should contact the Secretary, Department of the Treasury, 1500 Pennsylvania Ave., NW, Washington, DC 20220, (202) 566-2533.

Accident Report Treasury/Comptroller
Active Personnel File Treasury/Comptroller
Address Card—CC-6020-01 Treasury/Comptroller
Address Card File Treasury/Comptroller
Addressograph Plates Treasury/Comptroller
ADP Time and Attendance Reports
    Treasury/Comptroller
Annual Employee Leave Record Treasury/Comptroller
Annual Leave Request Treasury/Comptroller
Application for Employment Treasury/Comptroller
Application for Travel Advance Form CC-6042-17
    Treasury/Comptroller
Attendance and Leave Records of Comptroller of
    the Currency Employees Treasury/Comptroller
Attorneys File Treasury/Comptroller
Automobile Authorizations Treasury/Comptroller
Bank Files Treasury/Comptroller
Bank Organizers and Proposed Officer Files (Listed by
    Name of Bank) Treasury/Comptroller
Bond Issue Listing Treasury/Comptroller
Civil Defense Card Control Register Treasury/Comptroller
Civil Defense Card Register Treasury/Comptroller
Civil Defense Card Control Sheet—CC-6020-08
    Treasury/Comptroller
Comprehensive History of Employees Master Files
    Treasury/Comptroller
Comprehensive Listing of Employee Master File Form
    TUS 404, Treasury/Comptroller
Comprehensive Listing of Employees Treasury/
    Comptroller
Computer Leave Balance Printout Treasury/Comptroller
Computer List of Travel Advances Treasury/Comptroller
Computer Printout, Series E Bond
    Subscribers Treasury/Comptroller
Daily Absentee Reports of Comptroller of the
    Currency Employees Treasury/Comptroller

"E" Bond List Treasury/Comptroller
Educational Record File Treasury/Comptroller
Employee Annual Leave Record Cards
    Treasury/Comptroller
Employee Annual and Sick Leave Record
    (T&A) Treasury/Comptroller
Employee Compensation Treasury/Comptroller
Employee Comprehensive Listing Treasury/Comptroller
Employee Identification Card Register
    Treasury/Comptroller
Employee Index Treasury/Comptroller
Employee Leave Treasury/Comptroller
Employee Locator Map Treasury/Comptroller
Employee Mailing Labels Treasury/Comptroller
Employee Mailing List Treasury/Comptroller
Employee Management and Planning, Employee
    Relations, Incentive Awards, Performance Evaluation
    Treasury/Comptroller
Employee Parking Permit and Space No.
    Treasury/Comptroller
Employee Payroll Records Treasury/Comptroller
Employee Reference File Treasury/Comptroller
Employee Relations Treasury/Comptroller
Employee Residence Treasury/Comptroller
Employee Time Cards Copies Treasury/Comptroller
Employee Vehicle Authorization CC-6042-22
    Treasury/Comptroller
Employees I.D. Pin Register Treasury/Comptroller
Employees I.D. Register Treasury/Comptroller
Employment Applications Treasury/Comptroller
Employment Applications Files Treasury/Comptroller
Employment Applications Under Competitive
    Appointment Basis Treasury/Comptroller
Evaluation Cards Treasury/Comptroller
Examination Failures Treasury/Comptroller
Examiner Authorization Certificate Treasury/Comptroller
Examiner Identification Card Register
    Treasury/Comptroller
Examiner Identification Register Treasury/Comptroller
Financial and Biographical Reports of Organizers
    of New National Banks Treasury/Comptroller
Form TUS 404 Comprehensive, History of Employee
    Master File Treasury/Comptroller
Form TUS 430 Computer, Leave Balance Printout
    Treasury/Comptroller
Government Transportation Requests
    Treasury/Comptroller
Greater Cleveland Federal Campaign
    Treasury/Comptroller
History of Employee-Master File TUS 404
    Treasury/Comptroller
Identification Card Register Treasury/Comptroller
Identification Pin Control Register Treasury/Comptroller
Inactive Personnel Files Treasury/Comptroller
Inventory Control Cards Treasury/Comptroller
Inventory Control of Property Treasury/Comptroller
Inventory Control Records Treasury/Comptroller
Inventory Control Sheets Treasury/Comptroller
Inventory of Identification Cards and Pins
    Treasury/Comptroller

Inventory (Property) Control Card Treasury/Comptroller
Investigation Files/Employee Reference File
     Treasury/Comptroller
Job Applicants (Active) Treasury/Comptroller
Job Application File Treasury/Comptroller
Job Application Forms Treasury/Comptroller
Job Applications Treasury/Comptroller
Leave Applications
List of E Bonds Treasury/Comptroller
List of Travel Advances Treasury/Comptroller
Mailing List Master Sheet Treasury/Comptroller
Mailing Plates Treasury/Comptroller
Monthly List of Travel Advances Treasury/Comptroller
Monthly Outstanding Report of Travel Advances
     Treasury/Comptroller
Parking Space Applications Treasury/Comptroller
Payroll Roster Treasury/Comptroller
Personnel Directory Treasury/Comptroller
Personnel Files (Current Employees) Treasury/Comptroller
Personnel Files (Former Employees) Treasury/Comptroller
Personnel Notebook Treasury/Comptroller
Personnel Records (Active) Treasury/Comptroller
Personnel Records (Inactive) Treasury/Comptroller
Picket Identification Card, Control Sheet—CC-6020-09
     Treasury/Comptroller
Pocket Identification Card Control Register
     Treasury/Comptroller
Public Files Treasury/Comptroller
Regional Advisory Committee Treasury/Comptroller
Regional Telephone Log Treasury/Comptroller
Salary Cards Treasury/Comptroller
Telephone Log Treasury/Comptroller
Time and Attendance Records Treasury/Comptroller
Time and Attendance Report Form TUS 430
     Treasury/Comptroller
Time and Leave Register Treasury/Comptroller
TR Index Treasury/Comptroller
Transportation Request Treasury/Comptroller
Travel Advance Files Treasury/Comptroller
Travel Advance Listing Treasury/Comptroller
Travel Expense Voucher Treasury/Comptroller
Travel and Expense Vouchers Form CC-6040-03
     Treasury/Comptroller
Travel and Expense Vouchers Form CC-6042-03
     Treasury/Comptroller
Travel and Per Diem Vouchers Treasury/Comptroller
Travel Voucher Files Treasury/Comptroller
Visitor and Telephone Logs, Persons Calling or
     Visiting Regional Office Treasury/Comptroller
Weekly Examiner Itinerary Treasury/Comptroller
Weekly Itineraries Treasury/Comptroller
Weekly Itinerary Form CC-1427-0X Treasury/Comptroller

CUSTOMS SERVICE

Unless otherwise noted, all requests for information concerning records systems maintained by the United States Customs Service should be addressed to the regional commissioner of the region in which the records are located, or to the Director, Entry Procedures and Penalties Division, Office of Regulations and Rulings, U.S. Customs Service Headquarters, 1301 Constitution Ave., NW, Washington, DC 20229, (202) 566-5761. Where the request is not presented in person, it should be accompanied by a notarized statement executed by the requester asserting identity and stipulating the requester's understanding that knowingly or willingly seeking or obtaining access to records about another person under false pretenses is punishable by a fine up to $5000.

ACCEPTABLE LEVEL OF COMPETENCE, NEGATIVE DETERMINATION TREASURY/CUSTOMS

Any employee of U.S. Customs Service Region I, who receives a negative determination regarding acceptable level of competence.

ACCOUNTS RECEIVABLE TREASURY/CUSTOMS

File on individuals and corporations that owe the Customs Service money.

ACCOUNTS RECEIVABLE FILES TREASURY/CUSTOMS

All individuals incurring Customs obligations (duties, taxes, fines, and penalties).

ARREST/SEIZURE/SEARCH REPORT AND NOTICE OF PENALTY FILE TREASURY/CUSTOMS

Persons who are suspected of attempting to smuggle, or who have smuggled, merchandise or contraband into the United States; individuals who have undervalued merchandise upon entry into the United States; vessels and aircraft found to be in violation of Customs laws.

ATTORNEY CASE FILE TREASURY/CUSTOMS

Persons who are parties in litigation with the United States government or subunits, or employees or officers thereof, in matters which affect or involve the U.S. Customs Service.

BANKRUPT PARTIES-IN-INTEREST TREASURY/CUSTOMS

Individuals indebted to U.S. Customs Service.

BOARDING REPORT TREASURY/CUSTOMS

All suspect vessels and/or boats that information has been received on indicating unlawful or suspicious activity requiring a Customs search.

CASE AND COMPLAINT FILE TREASURY/CUSTOMS

Any individual initiating a court case or against whom a court case is brought; any individual involved in a personnel action, either initiating a grievance, discrimination complaint, or unfair labor practice complaint against the U.S. Customs Service or against whom a disciplinary or other adverse action is initiated; claimants or potential claimants under the Federal Tort Claims Act; individuals involved in accidents with U.S. Customs Service employees; U.S. Customs Service employees involved in accidents; persons seeking relief from fines, penalties, and forfeitures, and restoration of proceeds from the sale of seized and forfeited property; requesters under the Freedom of Information Act.

CASE FILES (REGIONAL COUNSEL–REGION V) TREASURY/CUSTOMS

Employees who have filed adverse actions, equal employment opportunity complaints, and grievances within Region V; employees who have filed tort claims under the Military Personnel and Civilian Employees' Claim Act; employees of the regional counsel's staff with regard to travel, training, evaluations, and other related personnel records; and applications for employment submitted to the Office of the Regional Counsel by prospective employees; individuals not employed by the agency who have filed equal employment opportunity complaints; individuals who have filed tort claims under the Federal Tort Claims Act, or tort claims filed under the Small Claims Act; individuals who have outstanding customs bills submitted for collection; individuals, corporations, partnerships, and proprietorships that have filed supplemental petitions on fines, penalties, and forfeitures within Region V; individuals, corporations, partnerships, and proprietorships which criminal case reports are prepared pending litigation and prosecution for violation of 19 U.S.C. 1305, 18 U.S.C. 542, 18 U.S.C. 545, 18 U.S.C. 549, 18 U.S.C. 1001, 18 U.S.C. 496, and 18 U.S.C. 371; individuals, corporations, partnerships and proprietorships that have filed supplemental petitions submitted in civil and technical violations for 19 U.S.C. 592, 19 U.S.C. 1448, 19 U.S.C. 1584, irregular deliveries, shortages and overages; and miscellaneous civil and technical violations.

CLAIMS ACT FILE TREASURY/CUSTOMS

Current or former Customs employees who have filed or may file claims under the Military Personnel and Civilian Employees' Claim Act of 1964 for damage to or loss of personal property incident to their service.

CLAIMS CASE FILE TREASURY/CUSTOMS

Parties who have filed claims for damage or injury against the government, or against whom the government has a claim for damage or injury in matters which affect or involve the U.S. Customs Service; private individuals or government employees who are involved in the incident which gave rise to the claim.

CLAIMS FILES (REGION VIII) TREASURY/CUSTOMS

Private persons filing claims under the Federal Tort Claims Act for property damage or personal injury allegedly caused by a wrongful or negligent act or omission on the part of a Customs Service employee while acting within the scope of his employment; current or former customs employees filing claims under the Military Personnel and Civilian Employees' Claim Act of 1964 for damage to or loss of personal property incident to their service; individuals against whom the government may have a claim for property damage caused by a wrongful or negligent act of omission on the part of the individual.

CLAIMS FOR AUTOMOBILE ACCIDENTS TREASURY/CUSTOMS

Persons involved in automobile accidents for which the Customs Service is pursuing collection.

CLAIMS (RECEIVABLE AND PAYABLE) TREASURY/CUSTOMS

Persons who have presented claims for payment by the U.S. Customs Service or a person involved in debts due the Customs Service.

COLLECTION FILE TREASURY/CUSTOMS

Individuals against whom the Customs Service has asserted monetary claims and maintains collection efforts, principally for damages done to government property.

COMPLAINTS AGAINST CUSTOMS PERSONNEL TREASURY/CUSTOMS

Present and past employees of the Patrol Division and U.S. Customs Service.

COMPLAINTS AGAINST CUSTOMS PERSONNEL TREASURY/CUSTOMS

Individuals who have lodged complaints against Customs personnel.

CONGRESSIONAL AND PUBLIC CORRESPONDENCE FILE TREASURY/CUSTOMS

Persons sending letters of complaint or making written inquiries concerning Customs inspectional activities and procedures.

COURT CASE FILE TREASURY/CUSTOMS

Persons who are parties in litigation with the United States government or subunits or employees or officers thereof, in matters which affect or involve the U.S. Customs Service.

COURT CASE FILES (REGION VIII)
TREASURY/CUSTOMS

Persons who are parties in litigation with the U.S. government or subunits or employees or officers thereof, in matters which affect or involve the U.S. Customs Service.

COURT DOCKET RECORDS SYSTEM
TREASURY/CUSTOMS

Persons either suing or being sued by the Customs Service in civil actions for damages; for recovery or enforcement of obligations to the Customs Service, including duties, tort claims, fines, penalties, forfeitures, seizures; for reversal of adverse personnel actions and any other proceeding in U.S. District Courts and U.S. Circuit Courts of Appeal, involving the Customs Service and/or officers and employees of the U.S. Customs Service in their official capacity, or persons accused of violation of laws enforced by the Customs Service.

CUSTOMS FUGITIVE PROGRAM
TREASURY/CUSTOMS

Persons for whom an outstanding arrest warrant exists.

DISCIPLINARY ACTION AND RESULTING
GRIEVANCE OR APPEAL CASE FILE
TREASURY/CUSTOMS

Customs employees on whom disciplinary action is pending or has occurred.

EEO COMPLAINT FILE TREASURY/CUSTOMS

Customs employees and applicants for Customs positions who make allegations of discriminatory job treatment based on sex, religion, race or national origin, color, or age.

EEO COMPLAINTS PROCESSING
TREASURY/CUSTOMS

Employees with applicants for employment who have filed discrimination complaints with equal employment opportunity counselors.

EQUAL EMPLOYMENT OPPORTUNITY PROGRAM
TREASURY/CUSTOMS

Customs employees with a grievance or complaint filed under Part 713 of the Federal Personnel Manual on discrimination complaint procedure.

EQUAL OPPORTUNITY COMPLAINT PROCESSING
RECORDS SYSTEM TREASURY/CUSTOMS

Employees of Customs Region V (New Orleans) who file equal opportunity complaints.

EQUAL OPPORTUNITY DISCRIMINATION
COMPLAINT CASE FILE TREASURY/CUSTOMS

Government and private industry employees, including present and former Customs Service employees, who have filed formal and informal complaints alleging discrimination on the part of the Customs Service or its officers or employees in violation of the Equal Employment Opportunity Act of 1972.

EQUAL OPPORTUNITY INFORMAL DISCRIMINATION
COMPLAINT FILES TREASURY/CUSTOMS

Government and private industry employees, including present and former Customs Service employees and applicants for jobs, who filed informal complaints alleging discrimination on the part of the Customs Service or its officers or employees in violation of the Equal Employment Opportunity Act of 1972.

FEDERAL TORT CLAIMS ACT FILE
TREASURY/CUSTOMS

Private persons filing claims under the Federal Tort Claims Act.

FILM LIBRARY OF SEIZURES TREASURY/CUSTOMS

Individuals arrested for suspected smuggling activities.

FINES, PENALTIES, AND FORFEITURE CONTROL
AND INFORMATION RETRIEVAL SYSTEM
TREASURY/CUSTOMS

Individuals and/or businesses that have been fined, penalized, or have forfeited merchandise because of violations of Customs and/or related laws or breaches of bond conditions.

FINES, PENALTIES, AND FORFEITURE RECORDS
TREASURY/CUSTOMS

Individuals and firms that have been administratively charged with violations of Customs laws and regulations and other laws and regulations enforced by the Customs Service.

FINES, PENALTIES, AND FORFEITURE RECORDS
(HEADQUARTERS) TREASURY/CUSTOMS

Persons who have been administratively charged with violating Customs and related laws and regulations, and persons who have applied for awards of compensation for providing information regarding such violations.

FINES, PENALTIES, AND FORFEITURES
(SUPPLEMENTAL PETITIONS) TREASURY/CUSTOMS

Any person requesting further relief from the regional commissioner after having a petition acted on by the district director from any fine, penalty, forfeiture, or claim for liquidated damages incurred under the provisions of any law administered by the Customs Service.

FINES, PENALTIES, AND FORFEITURES FILES (SUPPLEMENTAL PETITIONS) TREASURY/CUSTOMS

Individuals who have filed supplemental petitions for relief from fines, penalties, and forfeitures assessed for violations of the laws and regulations administered by Customs.

FINES, PENALTY, AND FORFEITURE (FP&F) RECORDS SYSTEM TREASURY/CUSTOMS

Persons seeking relief from fines, penalties, and forefeitures incurred for alleged violations of the laws enforced by the U.S. Customs Service, and/or restoration of proceeds from the sale of seized and forfeited property.

INFORMATION AND INVESTIGATIVE REPORTS FROM OTHER FEDERAL AGENCIES TREASURY/CUSTOMS

Individuals on whom information has been received indicating unlawful or suspicious activity.

INFORMATION RECEIVED FILE TREASURY/CUSTOMS

Persons who are believed to be involved in activities which constitute, or may develop into, possible violation of Customs and related laws.

INFORMATION RECEIVED FILE (PATROL DIVISION–NEW ORLEANS, LA) TREASURY/CUSTOMS

Individuals on whom information has been received indicating unlawful or suspicious activity.

INFORMATION RECEIVED (MOIR) FILE TREASURY/CUSTOMS

All persons who have been found or are suspected of being in violation of Customs or other governmental agency regulations or laws.

INTELLIGENCE LOG TREASURY/CUSTOMS

Persons who are believed to be involved in activities which constitute, or may develop into, possible violation of Customs and related laws.

INVESTIGATIONS RECORD SYSTEM TREASURY/CUSTOMS

Individuals who may bear some necessary relevance to investigations conducted within the scope of authority of the Office of Investigations, U.S. Customs Service. The categories include but are not limited to: Known violators of Customs laws; convicted violators of Customs and/or drug laws in the United States and foreign countries; fugitives with outstanding warrants, federal or state; suspect violators of Customs or other related laws; victims of violations of the Customs or related laws.

JUSTICE COURT CASE FILE TREASURY/CUSTOMS

Persons who are in litigation with the United States government or subunits or employees or officers thereof, in matters which affect or involve the Customs Service.

JUSTICE COURT CASE FILE TREASURY/CUSTOMS

Persons who are parties in litigation with the U.S. government or agencies or employees or officers thereof, in matters which affect or involve the Customs Service.

JUSTICE DEPARTMENT CASE FILE TREASURY/CUSTOMS

Persons who are parties in litigation with the United States government or subunits or employees or officers thereof, in matters which affect or involve the Customs Service.

LABORATORY REPORT CARD TREASURY/U.S. CUSTOMS

Persons from whom suspected narcotics or dangerous drugs have been seized by Customs officials in the region served by the Chicago laboratory when the seizure in question was submitted to the laboratory for analysis.

LIQUIDATED DAMAGE CASES: PRIOR VIOLATORS TREASURY/CUSTOMS

Prior violators of Customs laws; e.g., customhouse brokers, individual Treasury/Customs violators, liquidated damage cases only.

LITIGATION ISSUE FILES TREASURY/CUSTOMS

Parties in litigation before the U.S. Customs Court (or subunits or employees or officers thereof), and other individuals with knowledge of the issues in controversy.

LOOKOUT NOTICE TREASURY/CUSTOMS

Suspected violators of laws enforced by customs.

NARCOTICS IMPORTERS TREASURY/CUSTOMS

Individuals and companies importing dangerous drugs.

NARCOTICS SUSPECT FILE TREASURY/CUSTOMS

Known violators of federal narcotics laws; suspected violators of federal narcotics laws; associated or known and suspected violators; informants and other persons of interest to patrol officers in the performance of their duties.

NARCOTICS VIOLATOR FILE TREASURY/CUSTOMS

Persons who have been found in possession of any controlled substance within the Buffalo, NY, district.

NON-DISCIPLINARY GRIEVANCE CASE FILES TREASURY/CUSTOMS

Customs employees who have nondisciplinary grievances pending or completed.

NOTIFICATION OF PERSONNEL MANAGEMENT DIVISION WHEN AN EMPLOYEE IS PLACED UNDER INVESTIGATION BY THE OFFICE OF INTERNAL AFFAIRS TREASURY/CUSTOMS

Customs employees who are suspected of misconduct.

PATROL INFORMATION DATA SYSTEM TREASURY/CUSTOMS

Customs violators, suspects, known narcotic violators; business names; suspect vessels, aircraft, and vehicles. The Commissioner of Customs pursuant to 5 U.S.C. 552a (j) and/or (k) has proposed to exempt this system of records from certain requirements of 5 U.S.C. 552a.

PATROL OFFICERS CASE FILE TREASURY/CUSTOMS

Known criminal and civil violators of federal, state, and local laws, statutes, and ordinances; suspected criminal and civil violators of federal, state, and local laws, statutes, and ordinances; associates of known and suspected violators of federal, state, and local laws, statutes, and ordinances; other persons of interest to patrol officers in the performance of their duties. This system is exempted.

PENALTY CASE FILE TREASURY/CUSTOMS

Individuals who have submitted supplemental petitions in relation to penalties, claims for liquidated damages, or forfeitures of property which are being processed by the U.S. Customs Service, Region I, and which have been referred to the Regional Commissioner of Customs, Region I.

PERSONAL SEARCH—NEGATIVE (DISTRICT PATROL—NEW ORLEANS, LA, AND MOBILE, AL) TREASURY/CUSTOMS

Individuals indicating unlawful or suspicious activity that might result in a Customs violation.

PERSONAL SEARCH FILE TREASURY/CUSTOMS

Persons on whom personal searches are performed at the various ports of entry.

PERSONNEL ACTION RECORDS SYSTEM TREASURY/CUSTOMS

Persons employed by the Treasury Department, Customs Service who either initiate a grievance, discrimination complaint, or unfair labor practice complaint against the Customs Service or an officer or employee thereof, or who have a disciplinary or other adverse action initiated against them by the Customs Service in Region IX.

PERSONNEL CASE FILE TREASURY/CUSTOMS

Current or former Customs Service employees against whom disciplinary action has been proposed or taken, who have filed grievances, and who have filed complaints under the Equal Opportunity (EO) Program, in most cases where administrative proceedings have been instituted.

PERSONNEL CASE FILE TREASURY/CUSTOMS

Current or former Customs Service employees against whom disciplinary action has been proposed or taken, who have filed grievances, and who have filed complaints under the Equal Opportunity (EO) Program, in most cases where administrative proceedings have been instituted.

PERSONNEL CASE FILES (REGION VIII) TREASURY/CUSTOMS

Current or former Customs Service employees against whom disciplinary action has been proposed or taken, who have filed grievances, and who have filed complaints under the Equal Opportunity (EO) Program, in most cases where administrative proceedings have been instituted.

SEARCH, ARREST, AND SEIZURE REPORT TREASURY/CUSTOMS

Persons who have or may have violated a law of the United States.

SEARCH, ARREST, AND SEIZURE REPORTING SYSTEM TREASURY/CUSTOMS

Violators of Customs and related laws apprehended by Customs officers.

SEIZURE FILE TREASURY/CUSTOMS

Ship's masters, ship's crew members, longshoremen, vessels, private aircraft, private vessels, and individuals from whom seizures have been made, or upon whom memoranda of information have been received.

SEIZURE REPORT FILE TREASURY/CUSTOMS

Individuals to whom prohibited merchandise is addressed.

SUSPECT FILE TREASURY/CUSTOMS

Individuals on whom suspect information is received by patrol headquarters.

SUSPECT FILE TREASURY/CUSTOMS

Persons in whom the Customs Service is interested from a law enforcement point of view.

SUSPECT PERSONS INDEX TREASURY/CUSTOMS

Persons suspected of violation of Customs laws.

TELEPHONE ANALYSIS PROGRAM (TELAN)
TREASURY/CUSTOMS

Telephone numbers of known and suspected violators of Customs and other laws.

TELEVISION SYSTEM TREASURY/CUSTOMS

Persons involved in incidents related to search and subsequent disturbance while entering the United States from Mexico.

TEMPORARY IMPORTATION UNDER BOND (TIB)
DEFAULTER CONTROL SYSTEM
TREASURY/CUSTOMS

Individuals who have been denied TIB privileges because of failure to pay outstanding liquidated damages.

TEMPORARY IMPORTATION VIOLATION RECORD
TREASURY/CUSTOMS

Persons making importations against temporary importation bonds.

THEFT INFORMATION SYSTEM (TIS)
TREASURY/CUSTOMS

Individuals who are suspected of, or who have been arrested for, thefts from international commerce.

TORT CLAIMS ACT FILE TREASURY/CUSTOMS

Private persons filing claims under the Federal Tort Claims Act for property damage or personal injury allegedly caused by a wrongful or negligent act or omission on the part of a Customs Service employee acting within the scope of the employee's duties.

TORT CLAIMS ACT FILE TREASURY/CUSTOMS

Private persons who have filed or may file claims under the Federal Tort Claims Act for property damage or personal injury allegedly caused by a wrongful or negligent act or omission on the part of a Customs Service employee acting within the scope of the employee's duties.

TORT CLAIMS ACT FILE TREASURY/CUSTOMS

Private persons filing claims under the Federal Tort Claims Act for property damage or personal injury allegedly caused by a wrongful or negligent act or omission on the part of Customs Service employee acting within the scope of the employee's duties.

TORT CLAIMS ACT FILE TREASURY/CUSTOMS

All individuals presenting claims of damage to personal property resulting from Customs activities.

TORT CLAIMS FILE TREASURY/CUSTOMS

All individuals filing tort claims and correspondence relating thereto.

TORT CLAIM RECORDS SYSTEM
TREASURY/CUSTOMS

Claimants under the Federal Tort Claims Act.

TORT CLAIMANTS SYSTEM TREASURY/CUSTOMS

Individuals filing tort claims against the Customs Service.

TREASURY ENFORCEMENT COMMUNICATIONS
SYSTEM (TECS) TREASURY/CUSTOMS

Known violators of U.S. Customs laws; convicted violators of Customs and/or drug laws in the United States and foreign countries; fugitives with outstanding warrants, federal or state; suspected violators of customs or other related laws; victims of Customs law violations.

TREASURY ENFORCEMENT COMMUNICATIONS
SYSTEM CARD FILE TREASURY/CUSTOMS

Suspected violators of Customs or other laws.

UNCOLLECTIBLE CHECKS FILE
TREASURY/CUSTOMS

Passengers or crews of vessels or aircraft, brokers, importers, or other individuals involved principally in the uncollectible payment of duties.

VESSEL IDENTIFICATION REPORT
TREASURY/CUSTOMS

All suspect vessels and/or boats on which information has been received indicating unlawful or suspicious activity.

VESSEL VIOLATION PROFILE SYSTEM
TREASURY/CUSTOMS

Masters associated, in the capacity of ship's agent or representative, with vessels in actual or suspected violation of Customs and related laws.

VIOLATION INDEX FILE TREASURY/CUSTOMS

Individuals and/or vessels for which civil penalty cases have been made.

VIOLATORS CARD FILE TREASURY/CUSTOMS

Persons or firms who have violated any law administered by the Customs Service within the Norfolk, VA, district.

VIOLATOR'S CASE FILES TREASURY/CUSTOMS

Individuals involved in smuggling, filing false invoices, documents, or statements; violators of Customs bonds.

VIOLATORS FILE TREASURY/CUSTOMS

Violators and alleged violators of Customs regulations and law; associates of violators and alleged violators; individuals, business firms, and groups suspected of violating customs regulations and laws. Individuals and firms regulated by the Customs Service and those having routine business with the Customs Service. Regional Director of Investigations, Customhouse, 6 World Trade Center, New York, NY 10048, (212) 466-5817.

WAREHOUSE VIOLATION RECORD TREASURY/CUSTOMS

Persons making importations against their warehouse proprietor's bond.

WARNINGS TO IMPORTERS IN LIEU OF PENALTY TREASURY/CUSTOMS

Individuals and firms in violation of Customs laws.

Additional Files

Following is a list of the remaining files maintained by the Customs Department. Anyone interested in obtaining information from any of these files should contact the Secretary, Department of the Treasury, 1500 Pennsylvania Ave., NW, Washington, DC 20220, (202) 566-2533.

Accident and Injury Report File Treasury/Customs
Accident Reports Treasury/Customs
Accounts Payable Voucher File Treasury/Customs
Accounts Receivable Correspondence and Follow-Up
    Treasury/Customs
Accounts Receivable Treasury/Customs
Acting Customs Inspector (Excepted) Treasury/Customs
Acting Customs Officer (Excepted) Treasury/Customs
Advice Requests (Legal) (Region VIII) Treasury/Customs

Aircraft Ownership File Treasury/Customs
Aircraft Registers Treasury/Customs
Aircraft Sanctioned List Treasury/Customs
Aircraft and Yacht Arrival Notice Treasury/
    Customs
Applicant Supply File Treasury/Customs
Applicants File Treasury/Customs
Authorization to Perform Travel Treasury/Customs
Automated Customs Air Fleet Management Reporting
    System (CAMS) Treasury/Customs
Automated Merchandise Processing System (AMPS)
    Liquidation File Treasury/Customs
Background-Record File of Non-Customs Employees
    Treasury/Customs
Badge and Gun Report Treasury/Customs
Badge Number File Treasury/Customs
Baggage Declaration Treasury/Customs
Baggage Declaration File on Local Residents of the
    Virgin Islands, Treasury/Customs
Bills Issued Files Treasury/Customs
Biographical Files (Headquarters) Treasury/Customs
Biographical Information File Treasury/Customs
Boat Automated Management System (BAMS)
    Treasury/Customs
Boat Owners Mailing List Treasury/Customs
Cargo Security File Treasury/Customs
Cargo Security Record System Treasury/Customs
CARNET Information System Treasury/Customs
Carrier File Treasury/Customs
Certificates of Clearance Treasury/Customs
Community Leader Treasury/Customs
Confidential Source Identification File Treasury/Customs
Confidential Statements of Employment and
    Financial Interests Treasury/Customs
Congressional and Employment Correspondence
    Treasury/Customs
Container Station Operator File Treasury/Customs
Cooperating Individual Files Treasury/Customs
Correspondence Log for the Classification and Value
    Division Treasury/Customs
Counseling Reports Treasury/Customs
Credit Card File Treasury/Customs
Crew Declarations File Treasury/Customs
Crew List File Treasury/Customs
Currency Declaration File (IRS Form 4790)
    Treasury/Customs
Currency and Monetary Instrument Report System
    (CMIR) Treasury/Customs
Customhouse Brokers Examination Records
    Treasury/Claims
Customhouse Brokers File, Chief Counsel
    Treasury/Customs
Customhouse Brokers, Headquarters Records
    Treasury/Customs
Customhouse Brokers Records Treasury/Customs
Customhouse Brokers Records (Headquarters)
    Treasury/Customs
Customs Licensing and Identification Program
    (Proposed) Treasury/Customs

Custom Patrol Officer (CPO) Daily Activity Reporting System Treasury/Customs
Customs Officer Badge Inventory Treasury/Customs
Disclosure of Information File Treasury/Customs
Disclosure of Information Request Files (Region VIII) Treasury/Customs
Dock Passes Treasury/Customs
Drivers License File Treasury/Customs
Duty Assessment by Account (DABA), Interest Persons List Treasury/Customs
Employee Debts Treasury/Customs
Employee Relations Case Files Treasury/Customs
Employee Relocation Allowances Treasury/Customs
Equipment Record File Treasury/Customs
Equipment Record Treasury/Customs
Exit Interview Treasury/Customs
Federal and New York State Licenses for Commercial Importation of Alcoholic Beverages Treasury/Customs
Firearms Qualification Certificate Record Treasury/Customs
Firearms Qualification Records Treasury/Customs
Florida Boat Registration File Treasury/Customs
Former Employees Treasury/Customs
Freedom of Information Requests Treasury/Customs
Full-Field Investigation—Active and Completed Log Treasury/Customs
Government Employees' Drivers License File Treasury/Customs
Handicapped Employee File Treasury/Customs
I.D. Cards Treasury/Customs
Identification Cards (CF 3135) File Treasury/Customs
Immediate Delivery Violation Record Treasury/Customs
Import Specialist Activities Investigation Referrals Treasury/Customs
Import Specialist Activities Laboratory Samples Treasury/Customs
Import Specialist Activities Seminars Treasury/Customs
Import Specialist Activities 220 Visits, Region IX Treasury/Customs
Importer Name and Address Record System Treasury/Custom
Importers, Brokers, Carriers, Individuals, and Sureties Master Files, Treasury/Customs
Importer Name and Address Record System
Injury Notice Treasury/Customs
Inspector Training Quarterly Checklist Forms and Inspector Correspondence Course Enrollment Forms (CF-66) Treasury/Customs
Internal Security File Treasury/Customs
Internal Security Records System Treasury/Customs
Investigations Program Analysis Treasury/Customs
Investigative Program Analysis Treasury/Customs
Legal Case Inventory System Treasury/Customs
List of Vessel Agents Employees Treasury/U.S. Customs
Locator Cards ¡Treasury/Customs
Mail Entry Protest Treasury/Customs
Mail Protest Treasury/Customs
Mail Protest File Treasury/Customs

Merit Promotion Plan Case Files Treasury/Customs
Military Declarations File: DD Form 1252, Unaccompanied Articles Arriving from Foreign DD Form 1854, Military Customs Declarations, Treasury/Customs
Military Personnel and Civilian Employees' Claim Act File Treasury/Customs
Motor Vehicle Accident Reports Treasury/Customs
Motor Vehicle Operator's Identification Card Treasury/Customs
Motor Vehicle Operator's Identification Card and Records Treasury/Customs
Operations Officer's (Classification and Value) Work Accomplishments Treasury/Customs
Operator Identification File Treasury/Customs
Optional Retirement List Treasury/Customs
Organization (Customs) and Automated Position Management System (COAPMS) Treasury/Customs
Outside Employment Requests Treasury/Customs
Overtime Earnings Treasury/Customs
Overtime Earnings Daily Log Book Treasury/Customs
Overtime Earnings Record Customs Warehouse Officers Treasury/Customs
Overtime File Treasury/Customs
Overtime Log Treasury/Customs
Overtime Reports Treasury/Customs
Parking Permit File Treasury/Customs
Parking Permits File (New York Region) Treasury/Customs
Parking Space File (Los Angeles Region) Treasury/Customs
Passengers' Declarations File Treasury/Customs
Patrol Division Daily Activity Report Treasury/Customs
Patrol Officer Activity Listing Treasury/Customs
Payroll Administration/Problems Treasury/Customs
Payroll Record of Employees Not Covered by the Automated System Treasury/Customs
Payroll Report Treasury/Customs
Personal Search (Negative) Treasury/Customs
Personal Search New York District (Negative Results) Treasury/Customs
Personal Search—Negative (District Director—Mobile, Alabama) Treasury/Customs
Personnel Files of Customs Employees Treasury/Customs
Personnel/Payroll System Treasury/Customs
Personnel Records System, Office of Regional Counsel, Region IX Treasury/Customs
Preclearance Costs Treasury/Customs
Private Aircraft Inspection Reporting System (PAIRS) Treasury/Customs
Private Yacht Inspection Reporting System Treasury/Customs
Property Assigned to Employee Treasury/Customs
Property File Treasury/Customs
Property File—Non-Expendable Treasury/Customs
Protest Inventory System Treasury/Customs
Receipt for Property Assigned Treasury/Customs
Reclassification Requests Treasury/Customs
Regulatory Audits of Customhouse Brokers Treasury/Customs

Reimbursable Assignment System Treasury/Customs

Restoration of Forfeited Annual Leave Cases
Treasury/Customs

Resumes of Professional Artists Treasury/Customs

Revocation of I.S. Privileges and "Cash Basis Only"
for Reimbursable Services List Treasury/Customs

Sanction List Treasury/Customs

Service Records of Former Employees
Treasury/Customs

Set Off Files Treasury/Customs

Skills Inventory Records Treasury/Customs

Supervisory Notes and SF 7B Files
Treasury/Customs

Time and Attendance and Leave Records
Treasury/Customs

Training and Career Individual Development Plans
Treasury/Customs

Training Records Treasury/Customs

Travel Advance File Treasury/Customs

Travel Advances Treasury/Customs

Travel Payment System Treasury/Customs

Uniform Allowance Treasury/Customs

Uniform Allowance File Treasury/Customs

Uniform Allowances–Unit Record Treasury/Customs

Unscheduled Overtime Report (Customs Form 31)
Treasury/Customs

Valuable Shipped Under the Government Losses in
Shipment Act Treasury/Customs

Vehicle Microfiche Files Treasury/Customs

Warehouse Proprietor Files Treasury/U.S. Customs

Work Hour Records of Employees Treasury/
Customs

Workman's Compensation and Job-Related Injury File
Treasury/Customs

INTERNAL REVENUE SERVICE

In requesting information from any IRS system of records,
see pp. 155-162.

ACTS: C TREASURY/IRS–RETURNS COMPLIANCE PROGRAMS (RCP)

Taxpayers who may be delinquent in filing or paying federal
taxes. This system of records may not be accessed for purposes of determining whether the system contains a record
pertaining to a particular individual.

ALPHABETICAL NAME FILE AND INDEX, INTELLIGENCE DIVISION TREASURY/IRS

Informants; subjects of information items; subjects of intelligence investigations; subjects of special interest to the
Justice Department; racketeers and associates; subjects of
field queries; and foreign bank account holders. This system of records may not be accessed for purposes of determining whether the system contains a record pertaining to a
particular individual.

APPEALS, GRIEVANCES, AND COMPLAINTS RECORDS, ADMINISTRATION TREASURY/IRS

Applicants for federal employment, current and former federal employees, agencies, and annuitants who appeal a determination made by an official of an agency or the Civil Service
Commission to the Civil Service Commission, a board established to adjudicate appeals, or an agency. District director for each district whose records are to be searched;
service center director for each service center whose records are to be searched; regional commissioner for each
regional office whose records are to be searched: Director,
Personnel Division, IRS, 1111 Constitution Ave., NW, Washington, DC 20224, (202) 566-3161; Assistant Commissioner
(Administration), IRS, 1111 Constitution Ave., NW, Washington, DC 20224, (202) 566-3016; regional counsel for
each region whose records are to be searched; IRS, 1111
Constitution Ave., NW, Washington, DC 20224, (202) 376-
0662; Director, Disclosure Division, IRS, 1111 Constitution
Ave., NW, Washington, DC 20224, (202) 566-4263; the
National Office of Chief Counsel, or other appropriate
official.

ASSAULT AND THREAT INVESTIGATION FILES INSPECTION TREASURY/IRS

Persons who attempt to interfere with the administration of
the internal revenue laws through threats, assaults, or forcible
interference of any officer or employee while discharging the
official duties of his position. This system of records may
not be accessed for purposes of determining whether the
system contains a record pertaining to a particular individual.

AUDIT UNDERREPORTER CASE FILE, ACTS: A TREASURY/IRS

Recipients of income who appear not to have declared on
their income tax returns (Forms 1040 and 1040A) all income paid to them in the tax year under study. This system
of records may not be accessed for purposes of determining
whether the system contains a record pertaining to a particular individual.

BRIBERY INVESTIGATION FILES, INSPECTION TREASURY/IRS

Employees or former employees of the Treasury Department, and taxpayers and non-IRS persons whose alleged
criminal actions may affect the integrity of the service. This
system of records may not be accessed for purposes of determining whether the system contains a record pertaining
to a particular individual.

CHIEF COUNSEL CRIMINAL TAX CASE FILES. Each
regional counsel office, each branch regional counsel office,
and the national office maintain one of these systems.

The information in this notice applies to all 38 systems.)
TREASURY/IRS

Taxpayers and related parties against whom tax-related criminal recommendations have been made; taxpayers and related parties under investigation for criminal tax-related violations who have corresponded with the regional counsel's office; taxpayers and related parties on whom advice has been requested concerning investigation for tax-related offenses; potential witnesses in criminal tax investigations; investigative subjects in connection with Organized Crime Drive, Strike Force, Narcotics Project, or HUD projects. This system of records may not be accessed for purposes of determining whether the system contains a record pertaining to a particular individual, as it is exempt under 5 U.S.C. 552z(j) (2).

CHIEF COUNSEL GENERAL LEGAL SERVICES CASE FILES TREASURY/IRS. (Each of the seven regional counsel offices and the national office does or will maintain a general legal services case file system. The information in this notice applies to all eight systems.)

Persons involved in litigation, actions, investigations, or cases falling within the jurisdiction of the general legal services function including persons who have caused service of subpoenas, summonses, or other judicial process directed to an officer or employee of the Treasury Department in an official capacity; who are parties in personnel matters, as well as discrimination and labor management relations matters, of the Internal Revenue Service, Chief Counsel's Office, or, in some instances, other agencies in the Treasury Department; who are parties in practitioner actions under the jurisdiction of the Director of Practice or the Joint Board of Actuaries; who are parties in procurement matters and under the Federal Claims Collection Act; who are parties in litigation or administrative claims involving the Federal Tort Claims Act, the Military Personnel and Civilian Employee Compensation Act, relief of accountable officers for loss of government funds, rewards, acts of officers or employees acting within the scope of their employment, or official acts of officers or employees not directly relating to federal tax issues but relating to the Internal Revenue Service; who are parties in miscellaneous matters referred to the General Legal Service Division; who are the subjects of investigations made by the Internal Services Division; who have filed petitions for the remission or mitigation of forfeitures or who are otherwise directly involved as parties in forfeiture matters, judicial or administrative; who have corresponded regarding a matter under consideration within the General Legal Services Division. This system of records may not be accessed for purposes of determining whether the system contains a record pertaining to a particular individual, as the records are exempt under 5 U.S.C. 552a(d) (5) and/or (k) (2).

CHIEF COUNSEL GENERAL LITIGATION CASE FILES TREASURY/IRS. (Each regional counsel office, each branch regional counsel office, and the national office maintain one of these systems. The information in this notice applies to all 38 systems.)

Taxpayers or other individuals involved in matters referred to the general litigation function including, taxpayers with outstanding tax liabilities or with potential outstanding tax liabilities; persons from whom information is being sought (summons); persons requesting information (disclosure); present or former Internal Revenue Service employees who are being or may be sued in connection with their duties or who have been called upon to testify in private litigation; persons who are or may be liable to the United States on nontax claims; persons who have submitted offers in compromise of federal taxes; persons who have corresponded regarding a matter under consideration within the general litigation section. Most of the records in this system may not be accessed for purposes of determining if the records pertain to a particular individual, as the records are exempt under 5 U.S.C. 552a(d) (5) and/or (k) (2). Individuals who wish to determine whether the system contains any records pertaining to themselves which are not exempt may address inquiries to the regional counsel of the region in which the records are located or the Director of the Disclosure Division in the case of national office records.

CHIEF COUNSEL INTERPRETATIVE DIVISION CASE FILES TREASURY/IRS

Taxpayers concerning whom legal issues have been referred to the Interpretative Division for opinion. Director, Disclosure Division, IRS, 1111 Constitution Ave., NW, Washington, DC 20224, (202) 566-4263.

CHIEF COUNSEL REFUND LITIGATION DIVISION CASE FILES TREASURY/IRS

Taxpayers who have filed suits for refunds of federal taxes; persons who have corresponded regarding a matter under consideration within the Refund Litigation Division. This system of records may not be accessed for purposes of determining whether the system contains a record pertaining to a particular individual, as the records are exempt under 5 U.S.C. 552a(d) (5) and/or (k) (2).

CHIEF COUNSEL TAX COURT CASE FILES TREASURY/IRS. (Each regional counsel office and the national office maintain one of these systems. The information in this notice applies to all 38 systems.)

Taxpayers who have filed petitions with the tax court; taxpayers upon whom the issuance of a statutory notice is or was contemplated whose case has been referred to the tax court function; taxpayers who are the subject of formal or informal advisory opinions during the investigative stage of the case or while under administrative processing; persons who have corresponded regarding a matter under consideration within the tax court function. Most of the records in this system may not be accessed for purposes of determining whether the records pertain to a particular individual as the records are exempt under 5 U.S.C. 552a(d) (5) and/or (k) (2). An individual who wishes to determine whether the system contains any records pertaining to himself which are not exempt may address inquiries to the regional counsel of the region in which the records are located or in the case of national office records, Director, Disclosure Division, IRS, 1111 Constitution Ave., NW, Washington, DC 20224, (202) 566-4263.

COLLECTION CASE FILE, ACTS: A TREASURY/IRS

Recipients of income who appear not to have filed income-tax returns (Forms 1040 or 1040A) for the tax year in which that income was paid to them. This system of records may not be accessed for purposes of determining whether the system contains a record pertaining to a particular individual.

COMPLIANCE PROGRAMS AND PROJECTS FILES TREASURY/IRS

Taxpayers who may be involved in tax evasion schemes or areas of noncompliance grouped by industry, occupation, or financial transactions, i.e., return preparers, political contributions, corporate kickbacks. This system of records may not be accessed for purposes of determining whether the system contains a record pertaining to a particular individual.

CONTROLLED ACCOUNTS—OPEN AND CLOSED, INTELLIGENCE DIVISION TC 910/TC 914 TREASURY/IRS

Subjects and potential subjects of criminal tax investigation. District director for each district whose records are to be searched.

CORRESPONDENCE FILES INQUIRIES ABOUT ENFORCEMENT ACTIVITIES TREASURY/IRS

Individuals for whom tax liabilities exist, individuals who have made a complaint or inquiry relative to an internal revenue tax matter, or individuals for whom a third party is interceding relative to an internal revenue tax matter. District director for each district whose records are to be searched. This system may contain some records which are exempt from the notification provisions of the Privacy Act. Requesters will not be advised of the existence of records exempt from the notification provisions.

DAMAGE AND INJURY CLAIMS FILES SYSTEM TREASURY/IRS

Internal Revenue Service employees and private individuals acting as claimants against the Service; private parties against which the Service has a claim. For National Office—Safety Management Officer, Protective Programs Branch, Facilities Management Division, IRS, 1111 Constitution Ave., NW, Washington, DC 20224, (202) 566-3111. For regional offices—Chief, Facilities Management Branch, appropriate regional office.

DEFUNCT SPECIAL SERVICE STAFF FILE BEING RETAINED BECAUSE OF CONGRESSIONAL DIRECTIVE, ACTS: C TREASURY/IRS

Individuals suspected of violating the internal revenue laws. Assistant Commissioner (ACTS), IRS, 1111 Constitution Ave., NW, Washington, DC 20224, (202) 566-6353.

DELINQUENCY PREVENTION PROGRAMS, ACTS: C TREASURY/IRS

Taxpayers having a history of federal tax delinquency. This system of records may not be accessed for purposes of determining whether the system contains a record pertaining to a particular individual.

DISCLOSURE TO DEPARTMENT OF JUSTICE, COMPLIANCE TREASURY/IRS

Individuals alleged or suspected by U.S. Attorneys or by attorneys of the Department of Justice to have violated, or to be connected with violations of, federal laws other than the Internal Revenue Code (included are individuals who have initiated legal actions against the federal government, or who are connected with such actions); individuals identified by the Assistant Attorney General, Criminal Division, as being strike force targets, as persons connected with organized crime activities, or under investigation for other purposes by his office; individuals of interest to the Internal Security Division and the Criminal Division of the Department of Justice who were under investigation for national security reasons; individuals alleged or suspected by attorneys of the Department of Justice and U.S. Attorneys to have violated or to be connected with violations of the narcotics laws (this includes requests from the Bureau of Customs prior to the transfer of that agency's narcotics activities to the Department of Justice); individuals identified by the Attorney General as being of interest to the Watergate Special Prosecution Force, or individuals whose tax matters have been referred by the service to that office for investigation; individuals alleged by the Internal Revenue Service to have violated, or to be connected with violations of, federal laws other than the Internal Revenue Code; individuals alleged or suspected by attorneys of the Department of Justice to have violated, or to be connected with violations of, laws administered by the Department of Housing and Urban Development. This system of records may not be accessed for purposes of determining whether the system contains a record pertaining to a particular individual.

DISCLOSURE TO EXECUTIVE DEPARTMENTS AND CONGRESSIONAL COMMITTEES, COMPLIANCE TREASURY/IRS

Individuals who are under investigation or of interest to an executive department (other than the Department of Justice or U. S. Attorneys) and congressional committees, and for whom tax information has been requested under 26 U.S.C. 6103 and regulations issued pursuant thereto. This system of records may not be accessed for purposes of determining whether the system contains a record pertaining to a particular individual.

DISCLOSURE INVESTIGATION FILES, INSPECTION TREASURY/IRS

Internal Revenue Service employees who have allegedly disclosed confidential tax information; state and local government employees who have allegedly disclosed confidential federal tax information; tax return preparers who have allegedly disclosed confidential federal tax information. This system of records may not be accessed for purposes of determining whether the system contains a record pertaining to a particular individual.

DISCRIMINANT FUNCTION FILE (DIF), ACTS: A TREASURY/IRS

Individuals whose Forms 1040 and 1040A have a DIF score higher than a cutoff score determined by the Audit Division, indicating high audit potential. The DIF Score is the computation of audit potential, based on formulas prescribed by the Audit Division. This system of records may not be accessed for purposes of determining whether the system contains a record pertaining to a particular individual.

ELECTRONIC SURVEILLANCE FILE, INTELLIGENCE DIVISION TREASURY/IRS

Subjects of electronic surveillance; individuals who have been subjects of queries by other agencies. This system of records may not be accessed for purposes of determining whether the system contains a record pertaining to a particular individual.

ENROLLMENT AND PRACTICE FILES TREASURY/IRS

Practitioners authorized to practice before the IRS under Treasury Department Circular No. 230; applicants for enrollment to practice before the IRS; applicants to take the written examination preparatory for enrollment to practice before the IRS; enrolled agents whose authorizations to practice before the IRS have terminated (disbarment, suspension, resignation, etc.); return preparers. District director for each district whose records are to be searched or the Director, Audit Division, National Office, if national office records are to be searched.

FILE OF PERSONS MAKING THREATS OF FORCE OR FORCIBLE ASSAULTS, ACTS: C TREASURY/IRS

Individuals who have or may threaten or assault collection activity personnel. This system of records may not be accessed for purposes of determining whether the system contains a record pertaining to a particular individual.

FORM 2209, COURTESY INVESTIGATIONS, ACTS: C TREASURY/IRS

Taxpayers on whom a delinquent account or delinquency or other investigation is or was located in one IRS district office, but the individual is now living or has assets located in the jurisdiction of another IRS district office. This system of records may not be accessed for purposes of determining whether the system contains a record pertaining to a particular individual.

FORM 2990—MISCELLANEOUS INVESTIGATIONS, ACTS: C TREASURY/IRS

Taxpayers on whom an investigation has been initiated for purposes of securing information necessary for Federal Tax Administration purposes. This system of records may not be accessed for purposes of determining whether the system contains a record pertaining to a particular individual.

INFORMATION GATHERING AND RETRIEVAL SYSTEM, INTELLIGENCE DIVISION TREASURY/IRS

Potential subjects of criminal tax investigations; associates of subjects. This system of records may not be accessed for purposes of determining whether the system contains a record pertaining to a particular individual.

INFORMATION INDEXING SYSTEM, INTELLIGENCE DIVISION TREASURY/IRS

Potential subjects of criminal tax investigations. This system of records may not be accessed for purposes of determining whether the system contains a record pertaining to a particular individual.

INFORMATION ITEMS, INTELLIGENCE DIVISION TREASURY/IRS

Taxpayers about whom the Internal Revenue Service has received information alleging a violation of laws within the IRS jurisdiction. This system of records may not be accessed for purposes of determining whether the system contains a record pertaining to a particular individual.

INTERNAL CONTROL RECORDS FOR CHIEF COUNSEL LEGAL FILES TREASURY/IRS

Taxpayers who file petitions, suits for refund, requests for revenue rulings, and those who have had other matters pending before the Office of Chief Counsel. Most of the records in this system may not be accessed for purposes of determining whether the records pertain to a particular individual as the records are exempt under 5 U.S.C. 552a(d) (5) and/or (k) (2). An individual who wishes to determine whether the system contains any records pertaining to himself which are not exempt may address inquiries to the Director, Disclosure Division, IRS, 1111 Constitution Ave., NW, Washington, DC 20224, (202) 566-4263.

IRS AND TREASURY EMPLOYEE DELINQUENCY, ACTS: C TREASURY/IRS

IRS and Treasury employees who are shown on the master file as delinquent in meeting federal tax requirements. This system of records may not be accessed for purposes of determining whether the system contains a record pertaining to a particular individual.

LIEN FILES (OPEN AND CLOSED), ACTS: C TREASURY/IRS

Taxpayers on whom federal tax liens have been filed. Individuals seeking to determine if the system of records contains a record pertaining to themselves may address inquiries to the district director for each district whose records are to be searched.

LITIGATION CASE FILES, ACTS: C TREASURY/IRS

Taxpayers on whom federal tax assessments have been made but against whom litigation has been initiated or is being considered by the government or who have instituted suits against the government. This system of records may not be accessed for purposes of determining whether the system contains a record pertaining to a particular individual.

MISCELLANEOUS INFORMATION FILE, INSPECTION TREASURY/IRS

Employees and former employees of the Internal Revenue Service, tax practitioners (attorneys, certified public accountants, enrolled persons, return preparers), alleged tax violators, persons whose actions or alleged actions indicate a threat to IRS employees, facilities, or the integrity of the tax system, confidential informants, and reputed members of organized crime. Assistant Commissioner, Inspection, IRS, 1111 Constitution Ave., NW, Washington, DC 20224, (202) 566-4656.

MULTIPLE REFUND FILE, ACTS: A TREASURY/IRS

Tax return preparers or other individuals who prepare possibly fraudulent, bogus, or otherwise illegal returns, and preparers who use their own address as the taxpayer's address. This system of records may not be accessed for purposes of determining whether the system contains a record pertaining to a particular individual.

NATIONAL REGISTER, INTELLIGENCE DIVISION TREASURY/IRS

Subjects of open investigations and potential Special Enforcement Program subjects. This system of records may not be accessed for purposes of determining whether the system contains a record pertaining to a particular individual.

ONE HUNDRED PERCENT PENALTY CASES, ACTS: C TREASURY/IRS

Individuals against whom federal tax assessments have been made or are being considered as a result of their being deemed responsible for payment of unpaid corporation withholding taxes and Social Security contributions. This system of records may not be accessed for purposes of determining whether the system contains a record pertaining to a particular individual.

OPEN AND CLOSED NARCOTICS TRAFFICKERS FILES TREASURY/IRS

Taxpayers suspected of being involved as middle or upper echelon narcotics traffickers and whose returns have been or will be examined. This system of records may not be accessed for purposes of determining whether the system contains a record pertaining to a particular individual.

PENALTY CASE FILE ACTS: A TREASURY/IRS

Taxpayers who have had substantial penalties assessed to their accounts. Director of the Internal Revenue Service Center servicing the area in which the individual resides.

POTENTIAL REFUND LITIGATION CASE FILES, ACTS: A TREASURY/IRS

Taxpayers who have indicated to the service that they may file suit against the service for a refund. Director of the Internal Revenue Service Center servicing the area in which the individual resides.

PROJECT FILES, INTELLIGENCE DIVISION TREASURY/IRS

Potential subjects of criminal tax investigations. This system of records may not be accessed for purposes of determining whether the system contains a record pertaining to a particular individual.

RECORD 21, RECORD OF SEIZURE AND SALE OF REAL PROPERTY, ACTS: C TREASURY/IRS

Individuals against whom tax assessments have been made and whose real property was seized and sold to satisfy their tax liability, also name and address of purchaser; District director of each district whose records are to be searched.

RECORDS BEING MAINTAINED AT THE REQUEST OF CONGRESSIONAL COMMITTEES, ACTS: C TREASURY/IRS

Individuals who have previously been the subject of collection case assignments and/or individuals who have been identified as potential tax delinquents; includes former sensitive case files and various returns compliance files which are not normally retained. This system of records may not be accessed for purposes of determining whether the system contains a record pertaining to a particular individual.

RECORDS AND INFORMATION RETRIEVAL ACTIVITY COMPUTER AND MICROFILM RECORDS TREASURY/IRS

Taxpayers who initiated suits for refund in district courts or the court of claims; taxpayers who have filed petitions with the United States Tax Court; taxpayers who have requested rulings from the Service in those cases in which the request has been referred to the Office of Chief Counsel for a legal opinion; taxpayers who have been involved in litigation concerning the collection of taxes; taxpayers whose cases were the subject of technical advice, and memoranda to the solicitor general, and similar advisory memoranda. Most of the records in this system may not be accessed for purposes of determining whether the records pertain to a particular individual as the records are exempt under 5 U.S.C. 552a(d) (5) and/or (k) (2). An individual who wishes to determine whether the system contains records pertinent to himself which are not exempt may address inquiries to the Director, Disclosure Division, IRS, 1111 Constitution Ave., NW, Washington, DC 20224, (202) 566-4263.

RUNAWAY PARENTS LIST TREASURY/IRS

Parents who have deserted families on public assistance. Inquiries should be addressed to the service center whose records are to be searched.

SECURITY CLEARANCE FILES SYSTEM TREASURY/IRS

Employees of the Internal Revenue Service requiring a security clearance, having their security clearance cancelled or transferred, and individuals who have violated IRS security regulations. Chief, Protective Programs Branch, Facilities Management Division, IRS, 1111 Constitution Ave., NW, Washington, DC 20224, (202) 566-9868.

SECURITY VIOLATIONS, ADMINISTRATION TREASURY/IRS

Violators of IRS security regulations. Chief, Facilities Management Branch, Service Center, at center servicing the area in which the individual resides.

SEIZED PROPERTY RECORDS, ACTS: C TREASURY/IRS

Taxpayers whose property has been seized for subsequent sale by IRS to satisfy tax liabilities. Director of the Internal Revenue Service Center servicing the area in which the individual resides.

SPECIAL INQUIRY (COMPLAINT) INVESTIGATION FILES, INSPECTION—TREASURY/IRS

Employees or former employees of the Treasury Department and the Internal Revenue Service; non-employees whose alleged criminal actions may affect the integrity of the Internal Revenue Service. Assistant Commissioner, Inspection, IRS, 1111 Constitution Ave., NW, Washington, DC 20224, (202) 566-4656.

TAX SHELTER PROGRAM FILES TREASURY/IRS

Taxpayers who may be abusing the tax laws through the use of tax shelters. District director for each district whose records are to be searched. This system of records may contain some records which are exempt from the notification provisions of the Privacy Act. Requesters will not be advised of the existence of records exempt from the notification provisions.

TDI (TAXPAYER DELINQUENCY INVESTIGATION) FILES, ACTS: C TREASURY/IRS

Taxpayers believed to be delinquent in filing federal tax returns. This system of records may not be accessed for purposes of determining whether the system contains a record pertaining to a particular individual.

TESTIMONY OF IRS EMPLOYEES IN NONTAX MATTERS, COMPLIANCE TREASURY/IRS

Individuals who are parties to criminal or civil nontax litigation. This system of records may not be accessed for purposes of determining whether the system contains a record pertaining to a particular individual.

TORT INVESTIGATION FILES, INSPECTION TREASURY/IRS

Employees of the Department of the Treasury and non-federal employees involved in accidents on property under Department of the Treasury jurisdiction or with Department of the Treasury employees. Assistant Commissioner,

Inspection, IRS, 1111 Constitution Ave., NW, Washington, DC 20224, (202) 566-4656.

TREASURY ENFORCEMENT COMMUNICATIONS SYSTEM (TECS), INTELLIGENCE DIVISION TREASURY/IRS

Fugitives; subjects of open Special Enforcement Program investigations; subjects of open Narcotics Traffickers Program investigations; subjects of interest to Special Enforcement Program. This system of records may not be accessed for purposes of determining whether the system contains a record pertaining to a particular individual.

TREASURY/IRS INTELLIGENCE DIVISION, INFORMATION AND CORRESPONDENCE FILES, INTELLIGENCE DIVISION TREASURY/IRS

Subjects of correspondence which has been referred to or processed by the Intelligence Division; other individuals of interest to, or who have had contact with, the Intelligence Division; individuals potentially dangerous to service personnel; service personnel who have been threatened or who have provided armed escort. This system of records may not be accessed for purposes of determining whether the system contains a record pertaining to a particular individual.

UNIT LEDGER CARDS, ACTS: A TREASURY/IRS

Taxpayers who have accounts with the Internal Revenue Service which are not compatible with normal master file processes, e.g., penalties, transferee assessments, termination assessments, excise protest accounts, RMF overflow accounts, culpable and nonpetitioning spouses, Forms 1042, 1040-NR, 926, 5330, 4720, 990-AR (Penalty), and any pre-ADP returns. Director of the Internal Revenue Service Center servicing the area in which the individual resides.

Addresses

Inquiries under Treasury/IRS systems should be addressed to the office whose records are to be searched. The titles and addresses of the systems managers are as follows:

National Office Internal Revenue Service

Assistant Commissioner (Public Affairs)
Assistant Commissioner (Accounts, Collection and
  Taxpayer Service)
Assistant Commissioner (Administration)
Assistant Commissioner (Compliance)
Assistant Commissioner (Employee Plans and
  Exempt Organizations)
Assistant Commissioner (Inspection)
Assistant Commissioner (Planning and Research)
Assistant Commissioner (Technical)
Chief Counsel

The address for all of the above systems managers is 1111 Constitution Avenue, NW, Washington, DC 20224.

Regional Office, Internal Revenue Service

Central Region:

REGIONAL COMMISSIONER
Internal Revenue Service
550 Main Street
Cincinnati, OH 45202

REGIONAL INSPECTOR
Internal Revenue Service
550 Main Street
Cincinnati, OH 45202

DISTRICT DIRECTOR
Internal Revenue Service
550 Main Street
Cincinnati, OH 45202

DISTRICT DIRECTOR
Internal Revenue Service
1240 East 9th Street
Cleveland, OH 44199

DISTRICT DIRECTOR
Internal Revenue Service
U.S. Post Office and Courthouse Building
Detroit, MI 48226

DISTRICT DIRECTOR
Internal Revenue Service
U.S. Post Office and Courthouse Building
Indianapolis, IN 46204

DISTRICT DIRECTOR
Internal Revenue Service
313 Post Office Building
Louisville, KY 40202

DISTRICT DIRECTOR
Internal Revenue Service
425 Juliana Street
Parkersburg, WV 26101

DIRECTOR
Internal Revenue Service Center
Central Region
Cincinnati, OH 45298

Mid-Atlantic Region:

REGIONAL COMMISSIONER
Internal Revenue Service
2 Penn Center Plaza
Philadelphia, PA 19102

REGIONAL INSPECTOR
Internal Revenue Service
Room 300, 1315 Walnut Street
Philadelphia, PA 19107

DISTRICT DIRECTOR
Internal Revenue Service
Federal Building
31 Hopkins Plaza
Baltimore, MD 21201

DISTRICT DIRECTOR
Internal Revenue Service
970 Broad Street
Newark, NJ 07102

DISTRICT DIRECTOR
Internal Revenue Service
600 Arch Street
Philadelphia, PA 19108

DISTRICT DIRECTOR
Internal Revenue Service
1000 Liberty Avenue
Pittsburgh, PA 15222

DISTRICT DIRECTOR
Internal Revenue Service
400 North 8th Street
Richmond, VA 23240

DISTRICT DIRECTOR
Internal Revenue Service
800 Delaware Avenue
Wilmington, DE 19801

DIRECTOR
Internal Revenue Service
Mid-Atlantic Region
11601 Roosevelt Boulevard
Philadelphia, PA 19155

Midwest Region:

REGIONAL COMMISSIONER
Internal Revenue Service
1 Wacker Drive
Chicago, IL 60606

REGIONAL INSPECTOR
Internal Revenue Service
Suite 646
35 East Wacker Drive
Chicago, IL 60601

DISTRICT DIRECTOR
Internal Revenue Service
115 4th St. SE
Aberdeen, SD 57401

DISTRICT DIRECTOR
Internal Revenue Service
230 S. Dearborn Street
Chicago, IL 60604

DISTRICT DIRECTOR
Internal Revenue Service
Federal Building
210 Walnut Street
Des Moines, IA 50309

DISTRICT DIRECTOR
Internal Revenue Service
653 Second Avenue, North
Fargo, ND 58102

DISTRICT DIRECTOR
Internal Revenue Service
517 East Wisconsin Avenue
Milwaukee, WI 53202

DISTRICT DIRECTOR
Internal Revenue
Federal Office Building
106 South 15th Street
Omaha, NE 68102

DISTRICT DIRECTOR
Internal Revenue Service
U.S. Court and Custom House
1114 Market Street
St. Louis, MO 63101

DISTRICT DIRECTOR
Internal Revenue Service
Federal Building and Court House
316 North Robert Street
St. Paul, MN 55101

DISTRICT DIRECTOR
Internal Revenue Service
325 West Adams St.
Springfield, IL 62704

DIRECTOR
Internal Revenue Service
Midwest Region
2306 East Bannister Road
Kansas City, MO 64170

North-Atlantic Region:

REGIONAL COMMISSIONER
Internal Revenue Service
120 Church Street
New York, NY 10007

REGIONAL INSPECTOR
Internal Revenue Service
26 Federal Plaza (14th Floor)
New York, NY 10007

DISTRICT DIRECTOR
Internal Revenue Service
68 Sewall Street
Augusta, ME 04330

DISTRICT DIRECTOR
Internal Revenue Service
John F. Kennedy Federal Building
Boston, MA 02203

DISTRICT DIRECTOR
Internal Revenue Service
Clinton Ave. and N. Pearl St.
Albany, NY 12207

DISTRICT DIRECTOR
Internal Revenue Service
120 Church Street
New York, NY 10007

DISTRICT DIRECTOR
Internal Revenue Service
111 W. Huron Street
Buffalo, NY 14202

DISTRICT DIRECTOR
Internal Revenue Service
11 Elmwood Avenue
Burlington, VT 05401

DISTRICT DIRECTOR
Internal Revenue Service
450 Main Street
Hartford, CT 06103

DISTRICT DIRECTOR
Internal Revenue Service
Federal Building
80 Daniel Street
Portsmouth, NH 03801

DISTRICT DIRECTOR
Internal Revenue Service
130 Broadway
Providence, RI 02903

DIRECTOR
Internal Revenue Service Center
North-Atlantic Region
310 Lowell Street
Andover, MA 01812

DIRECTOR
Internal Revenue Service Center
North-Atlantic Region
1040 Waverly Avenue
Holtsville, NY 11799

Southeast Region:

REGIONAL COMMISSIONER
Internal Revenue Service
275 Peachtree Street, NE
Atlanta, GA 30303

DISTRICT DIRECTOR
Internal Revenue Service
2121 8th Avenue, North
Birmingham, AL 35203

DISTRICT DIRECTOR
Internal Revenue Service
901 Sumter Street
Columbia, SC 29201

DISTRICT DIRECTOR
Internal Revenue Service
320 Federal Place
Greensboro, NC 27401

DISTRICT DIRECTOR
Internal Revenue Service
301 North Lamar Street
Jackson, MS 39202

DISTRICT DIRECTOR
Internal Revenue Service
Federal Office Building
400 West Bay Street
Jacksonville, FL 32202

DISTRICT DIRECTOR
Internal Revenue Service
801 Broadway
Nashville, TN 37203

DIRECTOR
Internal Revenue Service Center
Southeast Region
4800 Bufford Highway
Chamblee, GA 30006

DIRECTOR
Internal Revenue Service Center
Southeast Region
3131 Democrat Road
Memphis, TN 38110

Southwest Region:

REGIONAL COMMISSIONER
Internal Revenue Service
7839 Churchill Way
Dallas, TX 75251

DISTRICT DIRECTOR
Internal Revenue Service
517 Gold Avenue, SW
Albuquerque, NM 87101

DISTRICT DIRECTOR
Internal Revenue Service
300 E. 8th Street
Austin, TX 78701

DISTRICT DIRECTOR
Internal Revenue Service
301 W. 21st St.
Cheyenne, WY 82001

DISTRICT DIRECTOR
Internal Revenue Service
1100 Commerce Street
Dallas, TX 75202

DISTRICT DIRECTOR
Internal Revenue Service
1050 17th Street
Denver, CO 80202

DISTRICT DIRECTOR
Internal Revenue Service
700 W. Capitol Ave.
Little Rock, AR 72201

DISTRICT DIRECTOR
Internal Revenue Service
600 South Street
New Orleans, LA 70130

DISTRICT DIRECTOR
Internal Revenue Service
200 NW 4th Street
Oklahoma City, OK 73102

DISTRICT DIRECTOR
Internal Revenue Service
412 S. Main Street
Wichita, KS 67202

DIRECTOR
Internal Revenue Service Center
Southwest Region
3651 S. Interregional Highway
Austin, TX 78740

Western Region:

REGIONAL COMMISSIONER
Internal Revenue Service
525 Market Street
San Francisco, CA 94105

REGIONAL INSPECTOR
Internal Revenue Service
540 5th Avenue
Anchorage, AK 99501

DISTRICT DIRECTOR
Internal Revenue Service
550 West Fort Street
Boise, ID 83702

DISTRICT DIRECTOR
Internal Revenue Service
W. 6th St. and Park Ave.
Helena, MT 59601

DISTRICT DIRECTOR
Internal Revenue Service
335 Merchant St.
Honolulu, HI 96813

DISTRICT DIRECTOR
Internal Revenue Service
300 N. Los Angeles Street
Los Angeles, CA 90012

DISTRICT DIRECTOR
Internal Revenue Service
230 N. 1st Avenue
Phoenix, AZ 85025

DISTRICT DIRECTOR
Internal Revenue Service
319 S.W. Pine Street
Portland, OR 97204

DISTRICT DIRECTOR
Internal Revenue Service
300 Booth Street
Reno, NV 89502

DISTRICT DIRECTOR
Internal Revenue Service
465 S. 4th St. East
Salt Lake City, UT 84111

DISTRICT DIRECTOR
Internal Revenue Service
450 Golden Gate Avenue
San Francisco, CA 94102

DISTRICT DIRECTOR
Internal Revenue Service
6th & Lenora Building
Seattle, WA 98121

DIRECTOR
Internal Revenue Service Center
Western Region
1160 W. 1200 South Street
Ogden, UT 84401

DIRECTOR
Internal Revenue Service Center
Western Region
5045 East Butler Avenue
Fresno, CA 93730

Chief Counsel and Regional Counsel Offices

National Offices

ADMINISTRATIVE SERVICES DIVISION
Office of Chief Counsel
Internal Revenue Service
1111 Constitution Avenue, NW
Washington, DC 20224

CRIMINAL TAX DIVISION
Office of Chief Counsel
Internal Revenue Service
1111 Constitution Avenue, NW
Washington, DC 20224

DISCLOSURE DIVISION
Office of Chief Counsel
Internal Revenue Service
1111 Constitution Avenue, NW
Washington, DC 20224

GENERAL LEGAL SERVICES DIVISION
Office of Chief Counsel
Internal Revenue Service
1111 Constitution Avenue, NW
Washington, DC 20224

GENERAL LITIGATION DIVISION
Office of Chief Counsel
Internal Revenue Service
1111 Constitution Avenue, NW
Washington, DC 20224

INTERPRETATIVE DIVISION
Office of Chief Counsel
Internal Revenue Service
1111 Constitution Avenue, NW
Washington, DC 20224

LEGISLATION AND REGULATIONS DIVISION
Office of Chief Counsel
Internal Revenue Service
1111 Constitution Avenue, NW
Washington, DC 20224

REFUND LITIGATION DIVISION
Office of Chief Counsel
Internal Revenue Service
1111 Constitution Avenue, NW
Washington, DC 20224

TAX COURT LITIGATION DIVISION
Office of Chief Counsel
Internal Revenue Service
1111 Constitution Avenue, NW
Washington, DC 20224

CHIEF COUNSEL
Associate Chief Counsels, or Assistant Chief Counsel
Office of Chief Counsel
Internal Revenue Service
1111 Constitution Avenue, NW
Washington, DC 20224

Regional Counsel Offices

North-Atlantic Region:

REGIONAL COUNSEL'S OFFICE
IRS
North-Atlantic Region
26 Federal Plaza
12th Floor
New York, NY 10007

Branch Regional Counsel Offices

REGIONAL COUNSEL'S OFFICE
IRS
100 Summer Street
17th Floor
Boston, MA 02109

REGIONAL COUNSEL'S OFFICE
IRS
Mid-Atlantic Region
Room 464
2 Penn Center Plaza
Philadelphia, PA 19102

REGIONAL COUNSEL'S OFFICE
IRS
Room 1117 Federal Building
31 Hopkins Plaza
Baltimore, MD 21201

REGIONAL COUNSEL'S OFFICE
IRS
Ninth Floor
970 Broad Street
Newark, NJ 07102

REGIONAL COUNSEL'S OFFICE
IRS Federal Building
Room 726
100 Liberty Avenue
Pittsburgh, PA 15222

REGIONAL COUNSEL'S OFFICE
IRS
2018 Federal Building
8th and Marshall Streets
Richmond, VA 23240

REGIONAL COUNSEL'S OFFICE
IRS
Room 422
Universal Building, North
1875 Connecticut Avenue, NW
Washington, DC 20009

Southeast Region:

Regional Counsel Office

REGIONAL COUNSEL'S OFFICE
IRS
Southeast Region
Federal Office Building
275 Peachtree Street, NE
Atlanta, GA 30303
Mailing Address: P.O. Box 1074,
Atlanta, GA 30301

Branch Regional Counsel Offices

REGIONAL COUNSEL'S OFFICE
IRS
Room 1624
2121 8th Avenue, North
Birmingham, AL 35203

REGIONAL COUNSEL'S OFFICE
IRS
Room 509

320 Federal Place
Greensboro, NC 27401

REGIONAL COUNSEL'S OFFICE
IRS
Box 35027 Federal Building
400 West Bay Street
Jacksonville, FL 32202

REGIONAL COUNSEL'S OFFICE
IRS
Room 1502
Federal Office Building
51 SW First Avenue
Miami, FL 33130

REGIONAL COUNSEL'S OFFICE
IRS
703 U. S. Court House Building
801 Broadway
Nashville, TN 37203

Central Region:

REGIONAL COUNSEL'S OFFICE
IRS
Central Region
7510 Federal Office Building
500 Main Street
Cincinnati, OH 45202
Mailing Address: P.O. Box 2059
Cincinnati, OH 45201

Branch Regional Counsel Offices

REGIONAL COUNSEL'S OFFICE
IRS
1620 Williamson Building
215 Euclid Avenue
Cleveland, OH 44114

REGIONAL COUNSEL'S OFFICE
IRS
2300 Cadillac Tower Building
Detroit, MI 48226

REGIONAL COUNSEL'S OFFICE
IRS
Room 508, New Federal Building
575 North Pennsylvania Street
Indianapolis, IN 46204

REGIONAL COUNSEL'S OFFICE
IRS
Room 579, Federal Office Building
Louisville, KY 40202

Midwest Region:

REGIONAL COUNSEL'S OFFICE
IRS
Midwest Region
Everett McKinley Dirksen Building
22nd Floor, South
219 S. Dearborn Street
Chicago, IL 60604

Branch Regional Counsel Offices

REGIONAL COUNSEL'S OFFICE
IRS
Federal Office Building
911 Walnut Street
Kansas City, MO 64106

REGIONAL COUNSEL'S OFFICE
IRS
Continental Plaza
735 West Wisconsin Avenue
Sixth Floor
Milwaukee, WI 53233

REGIONAL COUNSEL'S OFFICE
IRS
Room 3101
U.S. Post Office & Court House
215 North 17th Street
Omaha, NE 68102

REGIONAL COUNSEL'S OFFICE
IRS
1114 Market Street
St. Louis, MO 63101

REGIONAL COUNSEL'S OFFICE
IRS
Room 572
Federal Building & U.S. Court House
140 East Fourth Street
St. Paul, MN 55101

Southwest Region:

REGIONAL COUNSEL'S OFFICE
IRS
Southwest Region
Room 12D27
1100 Commerce Street
Dallas, TX 75202

Branch Regional Counsel Offices

REGIONAL COUNSEL'S OFFICE
IRS
20th Floor
1050 17th Street
Denver, CO 80202

REGIONAL COUNSEL'S OFFICE
IRS
Room 8102
515 Rusk Avenue
Houston, TX 77002

REGIONAL COUNSEL'S OFFICE
IRS
Room 845
Federal Office Building
600 South Street
New Orleans, LA 70130

REGIONAL COUNSEL'S OFFICE
200 Northwest 4th Street
Oklahoma City, OK 73102

Western Region:

REGIONAL COUNSEL'S OFFICE
IRS
Western Region
Two Embarcadero Center
Suite 900
San Francisco, CA 94111

Branch Regional Counsel Offices

REGIONAL COUNSEL'S OFFICE
IRS
300 North Los Angeles Street
Los Angeles, CA 90012

REGIONAL COUNSEL'S OFFICE
IRS
319 Pine St.
Portland, OR 97204

REGIONAL COUNSEL'S OFFICE
IRS
Security Center Building
Suite 1214
222 North Central Avenue
Phoenix, AZ 85003

REGIONAL COUNSEL'S OFFICE
IRS
915 Second Avenue
Seattle, WA 98134

REGIONAL COUNSEL'S OFFICE
465 S. 4th East
Salt Lake City, UT 84111

Additional Files

Following is a list of the remaining files maintained by the Internal Revenue Service. Anyone interested in obtaining information from any of these files should contact the Secretary, Department of the Treasury, 1500 Pennsylvania Ave., NW, Washington, DC 20220, (202) 566–2533.

Accident Investigation Files System Administration
    Treasury/IRS
Accident Reporting Files System Treasury/IRS
Acquired Property Records, ACTS: C Treasury/IRS
Actuary Mailing File (AMF), ACTS: A Treasury/IRS
Adjustment and Payment Tracer Files, ACTS;
    C Treasury/IRS
Airway Use Tax Registrant, Data, ACTS:
    A Treasury/IRS
Annual Listing of Undelivered Refund Checks, ACTS:
    A Treasury/IRS
Appellate Case Files Treasury/IRS
Appellate Conferee Inventory and Unit Time Report,
    Form 2568 Treasury/IRS
Appellate Division Case Data Source Document,
    Form 3564 Treasury/IRS
Appraisal and Valuation Files Treasury/IRS
Artist File, Assistant Commissioner (TECHNICAL)
    Treasury/IRS
Audit Administrative File Treasury/IRS
Audit Control File, ACTS: A Treasury/IRS
Audit Information Management System (AIMS)
    Treasury/IRS
Biographical Files, Public Affairs Treasury/IRS
By-Line Files, Public Affairs Treasury/IRS
Card Index File of Erroneous Refunds (ACTS)
    Treasury/IRS
Case Management and Time Reporting System,
    Intelligence Division Treasury/IRS
Chief Counsel Disclosure Division Case Files
    Treasury/IRS
Chief Counsel General Administrative Systems. Each of the
    37 Regional Counsel Offices and Branch Regional
    Counsel Offices, each of the 9 Divisions in the National
    Office, the Office of the Chief Counsel, the 2 Offices of
    the Associate Chief Counsels, and the Office of the
    Assistant Chief Counsel Maintain a General Admin-

istrative System. (This notice applies to all 50 of these
    systems.) Treasury/IRS
Classification and Audit Selection Files Treasury/IRS
Collateral Files, ACTS: C Treasury/IRS
Collateral Files and Competent Authority Requests
    Treasury/IRS
Collateral and Information Requests System
    Treasury/IRS
Combined Account Number File, ACTS:
    A Treasury/IRS
Conduct Investigation Files, Inspection Treasury/IRS
Confidential Informants, Intelligence Division
    Treasury/IRS
Coordinated Examinations of Large Cases Program
    Treasury/IRS
Correspondence Control and Records, Assistant
    Commissioner (Technical) Treasury/IRS
Correspondence Files Treasury/IRS
Correspondence Files Audit Treasury/IRS
Correspondence Files and Correspondence Control
    Files Treasury/IRS
Data on Foreign Corporations Treasury/IRS
Digest Room Files Containing Briefs and Digests of Docu-
    ments Generated Internally or by the Department of Justice
    Relating to the Administration of the Revenue Laws
    Treasury/IRS
Disclosure Staff Control Card System, Compliance
    Treasury/IRS
Driver Licensing Files System Treasury/IRS
Economic Stabilization Program Closed Case Files
    Treasury/IRS
Economic Stabilization Program Special Correspondence
    Files Treasury/IRS
Emergency Preparedness Cadre Assignments and
    Alerting Rosters Files System Treasury/IRS
Employee Accountability for Personal Property and
    Miscellaneous Items Treasury/IRS
Employee Activity Records, Administration Treasury/IRS
Employee Administrative Files, Tax Administration,
    Advisory Services Division Treasury/IRS
Employee Plans/Exempt Organizations, Employee Plans/
    Exempt Organizations Assignment Record
    (Form M-6209) Treasury/IRS
Employee Plans/Exempt Organizations, Reports of
    Significant Matters in EP/EO (M-5945) Treasury/IRS
Employee Recruiting Files Maintained by the
    Administrative Services Division Treasury/IRS
Employer Inquiry Look-Up for TDA Inquiries,
    ACTS: A Treasury/IRS
Enrollee Applicant Investigation Files; Inspection Treasury/IRS
Enrollee Charge Investigation Files, Inspection
    Treasury/IRS
Executive Resources Information System Treasury/IRS
Expert Witness and Fee Appraiser Files, Assistant
    Commissioner (Technical) Treasury/IRS
Experts in Economic Assistance Examinations
    Treasury/IRS
Expropriation of Property by Cuban Government
    Treasury/IRS

File of Freedom of Information Act Correspondence, Compliance Treasury/IRS

Financial Statements File Treasury/IRS

Foreign Stock Ownership File Treasury/IRS

Form 1042 Index Register, ACTS: A Treasury/IRS

Form 1042 Name Directory, ACTS: A Treasury/IRS

Form 1042S Index by Name of Recipient, ACTS: A Treasury/IRS

Forms Filed by U.S. Citizens or Residents Relating to Foreign Companies, ACTS: Treasury/IRS

General Personnel Records (Official Personnel Folder and Records Related Thereto), Administration Treasury/IRS

General Training Records, Administration Treasury/IRS

Highway Use Tax Audit Program Treasury/IRS

Identification Media Files System for Employees Treasury/IRS

Identity of Taxpayers Using ADP Accounting Records and the Evaluation Thereof Treasury/IRS

IDRS Security Profile System, ACTS: A Treasury/IRS

IRS Employee Delinquency Notice List, ACTS: A Treasury/IRS

Index Card Retrieval System Treasury/IRS

Individual Account Number File, ACTS: A Treasury/IRS

Individual Income Tax Returns, Statistics of Income Treasury/IRS

Individual Master File (IMF), ACTS: A Treasury/IRS

Individual Master File Change and Adjustment Document File, ACTS: A Treasury/IRS

Individual Master File (IMF) Microfilm Retention Register, ACTS: A Treasury/IRS

Individual Master File (IMF) 608 and 388 Microfilm Retention Register, ACTS: A Treasury/IRS

Individual Returns Files, ACTS: A Treasury/IRS

Intelligence Clips, Public Affairs Treasury/IRS

Interest Equalization Tax Forms File, ACTS: A Treasury/IRS

Internal Revenue Service Employees' Returns Control Files Treasury/IRS

International Enforcement Program Files Treasury/IRS

Joint Compliance Program, Intelligence Division Treasury/IRS

Labor Management Relations Records, Administration Treasury/IRS

Land Trust Files, Intelligence Division Treasury/IRS

Legal Case Files of the Chief Counsel, Deputy Chief Counsel, Associate Chief Counsels, Assistant Chief Counsels, and Their Staff Assistants Treasury/IRS

Lists of Prospective Bidders at Internal Revenue Sales of Seized Property, ACTS: C Treasury/IRS

Management Files Maintained by Administrative Services Division and the Assistant Chief Counsel Other than the Civil Service Commission's Official Personnel Files Treasury/IRS

Manual Accounting Index of Uncollectible Accounts Treasury/IRS

Married Taxpayers Filing Separately File Treasury/IRS

Medical Records, Administration Treasury/IRS

Miscellaneous Forms Files, ACTS: A Treasury/IRS

Motor Vehicle Registration and Entry Pass Files System Treasury/IRS

Offer in Compromise (OIC) File, ACTS: C Treasury/IRS

Overseas Compliance Projects System

Parking Space Application and Assignment Treasury/IRS

Payroll/Personnel System, Administration Treasury/IRS

Personal Data on Official Contracts, Tax Administration Advisory Services Division Treasury/IRS

Personnel Identification Files System for Service Centers Treasury/IRS

Personnel Investigation Records, Administration Treasury/IRS

Personnel Research and Test Validation Records, Administration Treasury/IRS

P.O.W.-M.I.A. Reference File, ACTS: A Treasury/IRS

Pre-Employment Tax Check for Executive Departments, Compliance, Treasury/IRS

Project Files for the Uniformed Application of Laws as a Result of Technical Determinations and Court Decisions, Treasury/IRS

Project Personnel, Intelligence Division Treasury/IRS

Property Pass for Government Property Treasury/IRS

Public Speaking and Other Public Appearances, Public Affairs Treasury/IRS

Record of Government Books of Transportation Requests Treasury/IRS

Recruiting, Examining, and Placement Records, Administration, Treasury/IRS

Reference Index Digest Cards, Assistant Commissioner (Technical) Treasury/IRS

Reference Records of the Library in the Office of Chief Counsel Treasury/IRS

Relocated Witnesses, Intelligence Division Treasury/IRS

Reports of Significant Matters (Form M5945), Assistant Commissioner (Technical) Treasury/IRS

Request and Submittal File for Technical Advice, Assistance, Determination or Coordination Treasury/IRS

Requests for Printed Tax Materials Including Lists, Administration Treasury/IRS

Residual Master File (RMF), ACTS: A Treasury/IRS

Residual Master File Change and Adjustment Document File, ACTS: A Treasury/IRS

Residual Master File (RMF) Microfilm Retention Register, ACTS: A Treasury/IRS

Residual Master File (RMF) Transaction, Codes 608 and 388 Microfilm Retention Register, ACTS: A Treasury/IRS

Residual Returns Files, ACTS: A Treasury/IRS

Retirement, Life Insurance, and Health Benefits Records System, Administration Treasury/IRS

Return of Initial Excise Taxes on Private Foundations, Foundation Managers, and Disqualified Persons File, ACTS: A Treasury/IRS

Schedules of Collections and Schedules of Canceled Checks, Administration Treasury/IRS

Scholarship Program Cost Record, Administration
Treasury/IRS
Secret Service Details, Intelligence Division Treasury/IRS
Security, Background, and Character Investigation
Files, Inspection, Treasury/IRS
Social Security Administration's Daily Search File
(SSA DSF), ACTS: A Treasury/IRS
Special Agent Skills Inventory, Intelligence
Division Treasury/IRS
St. Louis District Office and Other Selected Economic
Stabilization Program Closed Case Files Treasury/IRS
Statistics of Income Individual Selection Sheet,
ACTS: A Treasury/IRS
Strike Force Disclosure Authorization List,
Intelligence Division Treasury/IRS
Strike Force Treasury/IRS
Subject Files, Public Affairs Treasury/IRS
Subsidiary Accounting Files, ACTS: A Treasury/IRS
System for Controlling Returns in Inventory and
Production Data (SCRIP) Treasury/IRS
Tax Case Files, Public Affairs Treasury/IRS
Tax Collection Waiver Form 900 Files, ACTS:
C Treasury/IRS
Taxpayer Service Correspondence System Treasury/IRS
Tax Practitioner, Extension-of-Time Card File,
ACTS: A Treasury/IRS
Tax Practitioner Files, Intelligence Division
Treasury/IRS
Tax Practitioner Mail File, ACTS: A Treasury/IRS
Tax Termination File, Intelligence Division Treasury/IRS
TDA (Taxpayer Delinquent Accounts), ACTS:
C Treasury/IRS
Technical Information Release Mailing List, Public
Affairs Treasury/IRS
Tentative Carryback Allowance File, ACTS:
A Treasury/IRS
Transferee Files, ACTS: C Treasury/IRS
Travel Expense Record, Administration Treasury/IRS
Unidentified Remittance File, ACTS: A Treasury/IRS
Wage and Information Document (WAID) File,
ACTS: A Treasury/IRS

U.S. SECRET SERVICE

For information concerning any individual files, request
should be made to: Staff Assistant, Freedom of Information
& Privacy Acts, U.S. Secret Service, 1800 G St., NW, Room
908, Washington, DC 20223, (202) 535-5798.

ADMINISTRATIVE OPERATIONS INFORMATION SYSTEM TREASURY/USSS

Individuals who are now or were Secret Service employees;
individuals, contractors, and vendors, etc., who are presently doing or previously did business with the Secret Service; claimants against the service under the Federal Tort
Claims Act and the Military Personnel and Civilian Employees' Claims Act.

PROTECTION INFORMATION SYSTEM TREASURY/USSS

Individuals who have been or are currently the subject of a
criminal investigation by the Secret Service or another law enforcement agency for the violation of certain criminal statutes
relating to the protection of persons or the security of properties; individuals who are the subjects of investigative records
and reports supplied to the Secret Service by federal, state,
and local law enforcement agencies, foreign and domestic;
other governmental agencies; private institutions and individuals for evaluation by the Secret Service in connection
with the performance by that agency of its authorized protective functions; individuals who are the subjects of noncriminal protective and background investigations by the
Secret Service and other law enforcement agencies where the
evaluation of such individuals, in accordance with criteria
established by the Secret Service, indicates a need for such
investigations; individuals who are granted ingress to and
egress from areas secured by the Secret Service, the Executive
Protective Service, or to areas in close proximity to persons
protected by the Secret Service, including but not limited
to invitees, passholders, tradesmen, law enforcement, maintenance and service personnel; individuals who have attempted
or solicited unauthorized entry into areas secured by the
Secret Service; individuals who have sought an audience or
contact with persons protected by the Secret Service or who
have been involved in incidents or events which relate to the
protective functions of the Secret Service; individuals who are
witnesses, protectees, complainants, informants, suspects,
defendants, fugitives, released prisoners, and correspondents
who have been identified by the Secret Service or from
information supplied by other law enforcement agencies,
governmental units, private institutions, and members of the
general public in connection with the performance by the
Secret Service of its authorized protective functions.

TREASURY/USSS CRIMINAL INVESTIGATION INFORMATION SYSTEM

Individuals who have been or are currently the subject of a
criminal investigation by the Secret Service in connection
with the performance by that agency of its authorized criminal investigative functions; individuals who are payees,
registered owners or endorsers of stolen or lost obligations
and other securities of the United States; individuals who
are witnesses, complainants, informants, suspects, defendants, fugitives, released prisoners, correspondents, organized
crime figures, and victims of crimes who have been identified
by the Secret Service in the conduct of criminal investigations or by information supplied by other law enforcement
agencies, government units, and the general public.

TREASURY/USSS FINANCIAL MANAGEMENT INFORMATION SYSTEM

Individuals who are now, or were previously, Secret Service

employees; individuals, contractors, vendors, etc., who are presently doing business with or previously did business with the Secret Service; individuals who are involved in or were previously involved in tort claims with the Secret Service; individuals who are or previously were involved in payments (accounts receivable) with the Secret Service; individuals who have been recipients of awards.

TREASURY/USSS LEGAL COUNSEL RECORD SYSTEM

Individuals who have filed administrative claims involving an employee of the Secret Service; any individual who is involved in litigation against the Secret Service; individuals who have filed a petition for remission of forfeiture of equipment that was seized from them during an investigation and/or arrest by the Secret Service.

Additional Files

Following is a list of the remaining files maintained by the U.S. Secret Service. Anyone interested in obtaining information from any of these files should contact the Secretary, Department of the Treasury, 1500 Pennsylvania Ave., NW, Washington, DC 20220, (202) 566-2533.

Freedom of Information Request System Treasury/USSS
Non-Criminal Investigation Information System
    Treasury/USSS

Public Affairs Record System Treasury/USSS
Training Information System Treasury/USSS

Additional Treasury Files

Some additional offices within the Department of the Treasury that maintain minor files are:

BUREAU OF THE PUBLIC DEBT

Personnel and Administrative Records Treasury/BPD
United States Savings-Type Securities Treasury/BPD
United States Securities (Other than Savings-Type
    Securities) Treasury/BPD

FEDERAL LAW ENFORCEMENT TRAINING CENTER

FLETC Confidential Financial Records Treasury/FLETC
FLETC Payroll System Treasury/FLETC
FLETC Trainee Records Treasury/FLETC

U.S. SAVINGS BONDS DIVISION

Savings Bonds Employee Records System Treasury/USSBD
Savings Bonds Sales Promotion/Volunteer Record System
    Treasury/USSBD
Savings Bonds Sales Record System Treasury/USSBD

ACTION

CLASSIFIED DOCUMENT SECURITY VIOLATION FILE ACTION/AF

Any ACTION employee responsible for using or taking care of classified documents.

Chief, Facilities and Property Management Division, Administrative Service Division/ACTION, 806 Connecticut Ave., NW, Washington, DC 20525, (202) 254-8105.

DISCRIMINATION COMPLAINT FILE

Any employee or applicant for employment who has filed a complaint of discrimination against ACTION.

Director, Equal Employment Opportunity, ACTION, 806 Connecticut Ave., NW, Washington, DC 20525, (202) 254-5940.

EMPLOYEES INDEBTEDNESS FILES ACTION/AF

Present and former ACTION employees on whom correspondence has been received to the effect that they have failed to honor a debt.

Chief, Labor and Employee Relations Division, Office of Personnel Management/ACTION, 806 Connecticut Ave., NW, Washington, DC 20525, (202) 254-5940.

GRIEVANCE, APPEAL, AND ARBITRATION ACTION/AF

Any individual involved in a grievance or grievance appeal or who has filed a complaint with the Department of Labor, Federal Labor Relations Council, Federal Mediation and Conciliation Services, or similar organizations.

Chief, Labor and Employee Relations Division, Office of Personnel Management/ACTION, 806 Connecticut Ave., NW, Washington, DC 20525, (202) 254-5940.

Additional Files

Following is a list of the remaining files maintained by ACTION. Anyone interested in obtaining information from any of these files should contact the Director, ACTION, 806 Connecticut Ave., NW, Washington, DC 20525, (202) 254-3120.

Accounts Receivable (Collection of Debts Record and Claims Record), ACTION/AF
ACTION Employees Occupational Injury and Illness Reports ACTION/AF
ACTION Travel Files ACTION/AF
Combined Domestic and International Volunteer Applicant System ACTION/ORC
Conflict of Interest Records ACTION/GN
Congressional Files System ACTION/CA
Contractors and Consultants Records File ACTION/IO
Data Entry Statistics of Keypunch Operators ACTION/AF
Domestic Full-Time Volunteer Census Master File ACTION/DO
Domestic Full-Time Volunteer Legal File ACTION/DO
Domestic Full-Time Volunteer Personnel File ACTION/DO
Domestic and International Volunteer Security Files
Domestic Program Applicant Medical Record
Domestic Volunteer Appeal File ACTION/AF
Domestic Volunteer Applicant Psychiatric Report System ACTION/AF
Domestic Volunteer Medical File and Medical Claims ACTION/DO
Domestic Volunteer Payroll Record ACTION/AF
Domestic Volunteers Status Change System
Employee Payroll Records ACTION/AF
Employee Reemployment and Repromotion Priority Consideration Files ACTION/AG

Employee Travel File ACTION/DO
Employee Unofficial Personnel Files
Former Peace Corps Volunteer Medical Records
ACTION/IO
Legal Files Staff and Applicants (A-Z) ACTION/GN
Legal Files Volunteers and Applicants (A-Z) ACTION/GN
Management Union Records System ACTION/AF
National Advisory Council File
Office of the Director Personnel Records ACTION/OD
Overseas Health Records ACTION/IO
Overseas Staff Correspondence Files ACTION/IO
Overseas Staff Personnel Records
Peace Corps Applicant and Trainee Medical History
ACTION/AF
Peace Corps Applicant File for Period 1963 to June, 1974
ACTION/ORC
Peace Corps Applicant Record System ACTION/IO
Peace Corps Medical Evacuation/Administrative
System ACTION/IO
Peace Corps Medical Evacuation Cards ACTION/IO
Peace Corps Property Records ACTION/IO
Peace Corps Trainee and Volunteer Personnel and
Pay Records ACTION/AF
Peace Corps Volunteer Authorized Storage File
ACTION/AF

Peace Corps Volunteer Death Files ACTION/IO
Peace Corps Volunteer Emergency Leave Records
Peace Corps Volunteer Extension/Transfer/
Reenrollment Files ACTION/IO
Peace Corps Volunteer Financial Records ACTION/IO
Peace Corps Volunteer Personnel and Payroll System
(Computer System) ACTION/AF
Peace Corps Volunteer Program Correspondence
System ACTION/IO
Peace Corps Volunteer Termination/Consultation
System ACTION/IO
Performance Evaluation File ACTION/AF
Personal Service Contracts Records ACTION/AF
Regional Peace Corps Personnel Records ACTION/IO
Regional Volunteer Correspondence Files ACTION/IO
Staff Security Files
Staff and Volunteer Household Storage File
ACTION/AF
Talent Bank ACTION/AF
Theft of Employee Property File ACTION/AF
Travel Authorization File ACTION/AF
United Nations Volunteer System ACTION/IO
Volunteer Applicants Record System ACTION/ORC
Voucher Payment Record and Schedules of Payments
File ACTION/AF

Administrative Conference of the United States

Requests for any files maintained by this agency should be made to: Executive Secretary, Administrative Conference of the United States, 2120 L St. NW, Washington, DC 20037, (202) 254-7020.

Consultants' Contracts and Correspondence Files ACUS
Council Membership and Correspondence Files ACUS

Mailing List for Press Releases, Newsletters, Annual Reports, and General Information ACUS
Membership and Correspondence Files ACUS
Pay and Pay-Related Records (Payroll, Travel, Attendance, Leave) ACUS
Personnel Records ACUS

Advisory Commission on Intergovernmental Relations

Requests for any files maintained by this agency should be made to: Executive Director, Advisory Commission on Intergovernmental Relations, Suite 2000, Vanguard Building, 1111 Twentieth St., NW, Washington, DC 20575, (202) 653-5640.

Audience Mailing Lists ACIR
Financial Accounts ACIR
Official Personnel Files ACIR
Secondary Personnel Records ACIR

Advisory Committee on Federal Pay

Requests for any files maintained by this agency should be made to: ACFP Administrative Assistant, Room 101, 1016 16th St., NW, Washington, DC 20036, (202) 653-6193.

General Financial Records ACFP
Payroll Records ACFP

Agency for International Development

For information about most AID systems of records, write to the following address, identifying the system of records of interest: Office of Personnel Management (SER/PM), Privacy Liaison Officer, Agency for International Development, 515 22nd St., NW, Washington, DC 20037, (202) 632-9608.

CLAIMS RECORDS

Employees who have filed claims against the agency and employees against whom the agency has filed a claim.

CRIMINAL LAW ENFORCEMENT RECORDS

Present and former employees of the agency and of the Overseas Private Investment Corporation in furtherance of an investigation for suspected violation of criminal laws; present and former employees of contractors used by the agency and individuals involved or associated with such employees; individuals investigated at the request of another federal agency. Exempt system.

EMPLOYEE RELATIONS RECORDS

Any AID employee or employee of another federal agency assigned to AID under a participating agency service agreement who has filed a complaint, grievance, or appeal; has been subject of an alimony or child support claim; has been listed as a prisoner of war or missing in action; or has a medical problem affecting his or her employment. Exempt system.

EMPLOYEES EQUAL EMPLOYMENT OPPORTUNITY COMPLAINT INVESTIGATIVE RECORDS

Employees of AID who have filed a discrimination complaint. Exempt system.

LITIGATION RECORDS

Foreign Service employees, civil service employees, and personal services contractors. Exempt system.

PERSONNEL SECURITY AND SUITABILITY INVESTIGATORY RECORDS

Present and former employees, including full and part-time, "when actually employed" (WAE), "without compensation" (WOC), intermittent experts and consultants; current and former applicants for employment; Americans currently or formerly employed under contract; applicants for contract; certain contractors and contractor personnel. Individual names not included in the above categories are also cross-indexed in security files when significantly involved in security-related investigations; and individuals currently and formerly employed under participating agency service agreements (PASA) or interagency personnel act (IPA) or other authority. Exempt system.

Additional Files

Following is a list of the remaining files maintained by the Agency for International Development. Anyone interested in obtaining additional information from any of these files should contact the appropriate agency head or the Agency for International Development, International Bank for Reconstruction and Development, 1818 H Street, NW, Washington, DC 20433 (202) 477-1234.

Attendance and Leave Reporting Records
Awards and Incentives Records
Civil Service Employee Office Personnel Records
Congressional Relations, Inquiries and Travel Records
Emergency Case File

Employee Automated Records
Employee Conduct and Discipline Records
Employee-Owned or Leased Property Records
Employee Use of U.S. Government Owned or Leased
    Property Records
Employees Payroll Records
Executive Assignment Records
Foreign Service Employee Personnel Records

Foreign Service Personnel Evaluation Records
Medical Clearance and Health Records
Orientation and Training Records
Position Classification Records
Privacy Act Implementation Records
Public Information Records
Recruiting, Examining, and Placement Records
Travel and Transportation Records

American Battle Monuments Commission

Requests for any files maintained by this agency should be made to: Director, American Battle Monuments Commission, 4CO14, Forrestal Building, Washington, DC 20314, (202) 693-6067.

Conflict of Interest Files ABMC
General Financial Records ABMC
Informal Personnel Files ABMC
Official Personnel Records ABMC

Board for International Broadcasting

For information about any BIB system of records, write to the following address, stating which system of records are of interest: Special Assistant to the Executive Director, Board for International Broadcasting, Suite 430, 1030 15th St., NW, Washington, DC 20005, (202) 254–8040.

General Financial Records BIB
General Personnel Files BIB
Payroll Records BIB

Central Intelligence Agency

For information about any CIA system of records, write to the following address, identifying the system(s) of records of interest: Privacy Act Coordinator, Central Intelligence Agency, Washington, DC 20505, (703) 351-1100.

CONGRESSIONAL LIAISON RECORDS

Matters of Liaison with congressional offices filed in the name of the member of the office involved.

EMPLOYEE GRIEVANCE FOLDERS

Employee grievances, generally filed by IG case number assigned by office of inspector general.

EQUAL EMPLOYMENT OPPORTUNITY COMPLAINANT RECORDS

Current or former contract, staff, or detailed military personnel of the agency as well as applicants for employment.

LEGAL SUBJECT RECORDS

Agency employees, defectors, individual plaintiffs in litigation cases, individuals asserting claims against CIA, contractors and consultants, authors, journalists, and other individuals who become involved in legal relationships or matters with CIA.

LIAISON CONTACT FILES

Federal civilian and military personnel with whom various agency personnel conduct liaison.

SECURITY ANALYSIS RECORDS

Any individual who comes to the attention of the agency because of a counterintelligence interest that concerns agency personnel or agency security.

SECURITY RECORDS

Applicants, staff and contract employees, former employees, consultants, contractors, military detailees, individuals of security interest, persons of substantive affiliation with or service to the agency, and persons on whom the agency has conducted an investigation.

Academic Relations File
Agency Training Record
Applicant Files
Applications Division Tracking System
Briefing Program File
Career Trainee Files
Central Badge System
CIA Authors File
Clinical and Psychiatric Files (Applicants)
Clinical and Psychiatric Files (Employees)
Computer Access File
Consultant and Independent Contractor Records
Cryptographic Access File
Current Employees and Former Employees (Official Personnel Files and Records Related Thereto)
Directorate of Operations Records System
Equipment and Supplies Accountability Records
External Training Files
Financial Records
Foreign Map Sources Files
Freedom of Information Act Requesters
Guest Speakers
Intelligence in Public Literature File
Language Learning Center Student Files
Language Qualifications Register
Library Open Literature Ready Reference File
Logistics Security Clearance Records
Manpower Control System
Medical Facilities and Physicians

Modern Language Aptitude Test Scores (MLAT)
Occupational Accident Report Records
Off-Campus Instructor Applicant Files
Office of Joint Computer Support Training and Skills
  Inventory
Parking Permit Files
Personal Property Claim Records
Polygraph Files
Privacy Act Requesters
Private Attorney Panel

Professors and Placement Officers of Selected Colleges
Prospective Contributors for the Collection of Foreign
  Intelligence
Psychological Test Data Files
Publications about CIA
Security Duty Office Event Reports
Soviet-U.S. Contacts File
Special Clearance System
Supplemental Personnel (Soft) Files
Vehicle Operators File

Civil Aeronautics Board

CONSUMER COMPLAINT RECORDS AND FILES CAB

Individuals who as consumers address complaints or requests for assistance to the CAB concerning services provided or offered in air transportation, and persons against whom such complaints or requests are directed.

Office of Information, Civil Aeronautics Board, 1825 Connecticut Ave., NW, Washington, DC 20428, (202) 673-5990.

Request for information should contain: Individual's return address, printed or typewritten name, and signature.

Additional Files

Following is a list of the remaining files of the CAB. For information concerning any of these files, contact the Secretary, Civil Aeronautics Board, 1825 Connecticut Ave., NW, Washington, DC 20428, (202) 673-5068.

Agreements Between Carriers for Performance of Services by Specified Persons CAB

Applications by Air Carriers for Approval of the Holding by their Officers and Directors of Similar Positions in Certain Other Carriers and Businesses CAB

Correspondence Between Civil Aeronautics and Persons Outside the Board CAB

Employee Payroll and Leave and Attendance Records and Files CAB

Employee Reports of Financial Interests and Employment CAB

Employee Travel Records and Files CAB

Investigatory Material Compiled for Law Enforcement Purposes CAB

Mailing Lists of Persons Requesting CAB Informational, Technical, or Statistical Material CAB

Members of Congress Biographical Information and Correspondence, CAB

Procurement Records and Files CAB

Property Accountability Records CAB

Commission of Fine Arts

Requests for any files maintained by this agency should be
made to: Secretary, Commission of Fine Arts, 708 Jackson
Place, NW, Washington, DC 20006, (202) 566-1066.

Members of the Commission of Fine Arts and the Board of
    Architectural Consultants for Old Georgetown CFA
Personnel Administration CFA

Commission on Civil Rights

APPEALS, GRIEVANCES, AND COMPLAINTS (STAFF)

Applicants for federal employment, current and former employees, agencies, and annuitants who appeal a determination made by the commission.

Office of General Counsel, U.S. Commission on Civil Rights, 1121 Vermont Ave., NW, Room 600, Washington, DC 20425, (202) 254-6606.

COMPLAINTS

Records are maintained by the name of the person filing the complaint and by the name of the person or organization against whom the complaint is filed.

General Counsel, U.S. Commission on Civil Rights, 1121 Vermont Ave., NW, Washington, DC 02425, (202) 254-6606.

OTHER EMPLOYEE PROGRAMS: EQUAL EMPLOYMENT OPPORTUNITY, TROUBLED EMPLOYEE, AND UPWARD MOBILITY

Equal employment opportunity; all employees of the commission. Troubled employee program; employees with personal problems which detract from job effectiveness (alcoholism, drug abuse, mental stress, etc.). Upward mobility; clerical employees who are eligible for entry into the program or who are participating in the program.

General Counsel, U.S. Commission on Civil Rights, 1121 Vermont Ave., NW, Washington, DC 20425, (202) 254-6758.

Additional Files

Following is a list of the remaining files maintained by the Commission on Civil Rights. For information concerning any of these files contact the Office of the General Counsel, U.S. Commission on Civil Rights, 1121 Vermont Ave., NW, Room 600, Washington, DC 20425, (202) 254-6606.

Applications for Employment
Commission Projects
Information on Commissioners, Staff, and State Advisory
    Committee Members, Past and Present
Personnel Records
Resource and Consultant
State Advisory Committee Project Files
Travel, Payroll, Time and Attendance of Commissioners,
    Staff Consultants, and State Advisory Committee Members

Committee for Purchase from the Blind and Other Severely Handicapped

Requests for any files maintained by the committee should be made to: Executive Director, 2009 14th St., N., Suite 610, Arlington, VA 22201, (804) 557-1145.

General Financial Records for Committee for Purchase from the Blind and Other Severely Handicapped CBH-2

General Personnel File for Committee for Purchase from the Blind and Other Severely Handicapped CBH-1

Payroll Records for Committee for Purchase from the Blind and Other Severely Handicapped CBH-3

Commodity Futures Trading Commission

COMPLAINT REGISTER AND COMPLAINT INDICES, CFTC

Persons alleged to have violated or suspected of having violated the Commodity Exchange Act or the rules and regulations adopted thereunder; persons lodging complaints with the commission.

Privacy Unit, Commodity Futures Trading Commission, 1120 Connecticut Ave., NW, Washington, DC 20036, (202) 254-8630.

DOCKET FILES, CFTC ·

Parties and persons involved in any CFTC proceeding.

Privacy Unit, Commodity Futures Trading Commission, 1120 Connecticut Ave., NW, Washington, DC 20036, (202) 254-8630.

EXEMPTED INVESTIGATORY RECORDS, CFTC

Individuals whom the staff of the commission has reason to believe have violated, are violating, or are about to violate the Commodity Exchange Act and the rules, regulations, and orders promulgated thereunder; individuals whom the staff of the commission has reason to believe may have information concerning violations of the Commodity Exchange Act and the rules, regulations, and orders promulgated thereunder; individuals involved in investigations authorized by the commission concerning the activities of members of the commission or its employees, based upon formal complaint or otherwise; individuals filing Form 4-R (registration as an associated person) or Form 94 (biographical information questionnaire) in connection with an application for registration with the commission.

Personnel Officer, Commodity Futures Trading Commission, 1120 Connecticut Ave., NW, Washington, DC 20036, (202) 254-3275.

INVESTIGATION FILES, CFTC

Individuals whom the staff of the commission has reason to believe have violated, are violating, or are about to violate the Commodity Exchange Act and the rules, regulations and orders promulgated thereunder, or the rules and regulations of any board of trade designated as a contract market; individuals whom the staff of the commission has reason to believe may have information concerning violations of the Commodity Exchange Act and the rules, regulations, and orders promulgated thereunder, or the rules and regulations of any board of trade designated as a contract market; individuals involved in investigations authorized by the commission concerning the activities of members of the commission or its employees, based upon formal complaint or otherwise.

Privacy Unit, Commodity Futures Trading Commission, 1120 Connecticut Ave., NW, Washington, DC 20036, (202) 254-8630.

LITIGATION FILES, CFTC

Persons or firms against whom the commission has issued a complaint based on violations of the Commodity Exchange Act or the rules and regulations promulgated thereunder.

Privacy Unit, Commodity Futures Trading Commission, 1120 Connecticut Ave., NW, Washington, DC 20036, (202) 254-8630.

LITIGATION FILES-OGC, CFTC

Parties involved in litigation with the commission or including, but not limited to: administrative proceedings before the commission; injunctive actions brought by the commission; other federal court cases to which the commission is a party. Litigation in which the commission is participating as a micus curiae; other cases involving issues of concern to the commission, including those brought by other law enforcement and regulatory agencies and those brought by private parties.

Privacy Unit, Commodity Futures Trading Commission, 1120 Connecticut Ave., NW, Washington, DC 20036, (202) 254-8630.

LOGBOOK ON SPECULATIVE LIMIT VIOLATIONS CFTC

Record of all individuals who have exceeded speculative limits in a particular fiscal year.

Privacy Unit, Commodity Futures Trading Commission, 1120 Connecticut Ave., NW, Washington, DC 20036, (202) 254-8630.

SUBPOENA FILE, CFTC

Individuals who have been subpoenaed by the commission.

Privacy Unit, Commodity Futures Trading Commission, 1120 Connecticut Ave., NW, Washington, DC 20036, (202) 254-8630.

VIOLATION FOLLOW-UP FILES, CFTC

Persons who have had criminal, civil, or administrative action taken against them, or who have been sent compliance or warning letters regarding violations of the Commodity Exchange Act or the rules and regulations thereunder.

Privacy Unit, Commodity Futures Trading Commission, 1120 Connecticut Ave., NW, Washington, DC 20036, (202) 254-8630.

Additional Files

Following is a list of the remaining files maintained by the Commodity Futures Trading Commission. For information concerning any of these files, contact the Privacy Unit, Commodity Futures Trading Commission, 1120 Connecticut Ave., NW, Washington, DC 20036, (202) 254-8630.

Correspondence Files CFTC
Employee Leave, Time, and Attendance CFTC
Employee Personnel Records CFTC
Employee Travel Records CFTC
Employee Records Maintained by the National Finance
    Center/USDA CFTC
Employment Applications CFTC
Exempted Employee Background Investigation Material
    CFTC
Fitness Files CFTC
Fitness Investigations CFTC
Interpretation Files OGC, CFTC
Large Trader Report Files CFTC
Petitions and Rulings
Registration of Commodity Pool Operators CFTC
Registration of Commodity Trading Advisors CFTC
Registration and Fitness of Associated Persons CFTC
Registration of Floor Brokers CFTC
Registration of Futures Commission Merchants CFTC
Stipulation of Compliance File CFTC

Community Services Administration

For information about any CSA system of records, write to the Privacy Act reviewing officer at the address given.

INSPECTION REPORTS ON GRANTEES, CONTRACTORS, AND CSA EMPLOYEES—CSA

Employees of CSA, grantees, contractors and consultants who have been or are being investigated in complaints alleging misfeasance, malfeasance, and nonfeasance.

REGIONAL OFFICES

Region I
John F. Kennedy Federal Building
Boston, MA 02203

Region II
25 Federal Plaza
32nd Floor
New York, NY 10007

Region III
Gateway Building
3535 Market Street
Philadelphia, PA 19104

Region IV
730 Peachtree Street, NE
Atlanta, GA 30308

Region V
300 South Wacker Drive
24th Floor
Chicago, IL 60606

Region VI
1200 Main Street
Dallas, TX 75202

Region VII
911 Walnut Street
Kansas City, MO 64106

Region VIII
Federal Building
1961 Stout Street
Denver, CO 80202

Region IX
100 McAllister Street
San Francisco, CA 94102

Region X
Arcade Plaza Building
1321 Second Avenue
Seattle, WA 98101

Additional Files

Following is a list of the remaining files maintained by the Community Services Administration. Anyone interested in obtaining additional information from any of these fields should contact the appropriate agency head or the Community Services Administration, 1200 Nineteenth Street, NW, Washington, DC 20506, (202) 254-5590.

Employee Applicants for Upward Mobility Program CSA
Employee Attendance, Leave, and Payroll Records, CSA
Employee Employment History CSA
Employee and Personnel System CSA
Employees of CSA and Other Government Agencies and Invited Travelers' Travel Records CSA
Equal Employment Opportunity System CSA
Federal Employee Compensation Act System CSA
Federal Motor Vehicle Accident Reporting System CSA
Freedom of Information Act Requests for Records CSA

Consumer Product Safety Commission

ACCIDENT REPORTS (IN-DEPTH) CPSC

Victims of consumer product-related injuries on which specific epidemiologic data is needed in order to analyze and correct product hazards.

Director, Bureau of Epidemiology, Room 332, 5401 Westband Ave., Washington, DC 20207, (202) 492-6440.

CLAIMS, CPSC

CPSC employees sustaining property damage incident to service; CPSC employees involved in situations where personal injury or property damage results from wrongful or negligent acts of employees acting within the scope of their employment; claimants sustaining injury or property damage due to CPSC employee actions.

Present and former employees: Director, Office of Administration–Resource Utilization, Consumer Product Safety Commission, 5401 Westband Ave., Washington, DC 20207, (202) 492-6775. Others: Office of the Secretary, Consumer Product Safety Commission, 1750 K St., NW, Suite 1025, Washington, DC 20207, (202) 634-7700.

EMPLOYEE DISCRIMINATION COMPLAINT AND INVESTIGATION FILE CPSC

Commission employees and others who have filed complaints of discrimination based on race, color, religion, sex, national origin, or age.

Present and former employees: Director, Office of Resource Utilization, Consumer Product Safety Commission, 5401 Westband Ave., Washington, DC 20207, (202) 492-6775. Others: Office of the Secretary, Consumer Product Safety Commission, 1750 K St., NW, Suite 1025, Washington, DC 20207, (202) 634-7700.

LABOR MANAGEMENT RELATIONS FILES, CPSC

CPSC employees involved in union activity, whether in the capacity of an officer or a rank-and-file employee utilizing the grievance machinery.

Present and former employees: Director, Office of Resource Utilization, Consumer Product Safety Commission, 5401 Westband Ave., Washington, DC 20207, (202) 492-6775. Others: Office of the Secretary, Consumer Product Safety Commission, 1750 K St., NW, Suite 1025, Washington, DC 20207, (202) 634-7700.

Additional Files

Following is a list of the remaining files maintained by the Consumer Product Safety Commission. For information concerning any of these files contact the Secretary, Consumer Product Safety Commission, 1750 K St., NW, Suite 1025, Washington, DC 20207, (202) 634-7700.

Advisory Committee Application CPSC
Consumer Volunteer Roster CPSC
Employee Biographies CPSC
Employee Career Development CPSC
Employee Executive Development Program Record CPSC
Employee Financial Interest Statements CPSC
Employee Merit Promotion Program CPSC
Employee Motor Vehicle Operators and Accident Report Records CPSC
Employee Outside Activity Notice CPSC
Employee Payroll, Leave, and Travel Records CPSC
Employee Personal Data File CPSC
Employee Relations Files CPSC
Employee Upward Mobility Counseling Files CPSC
Job Applicant Files CPSC
Upward Mobility Program Training Records CPSC

Council on Wage and Price Stability

Requests for any files maintained by the Council on Wage and Price Stability should be made to: Administrative Officer, Council on Wage and Price Stability, Room 3235, New Executive Office Building, 726 Jackson Place, NW, Washington, DC 20006, (202) 456-7850.

Correspondence Records CWPS
Personnel Records CWPS

Defense Manpower Commission

Requests for files maintained by the Defense Manpower Commission should be made to: Director of Administration, Defense Manpower Commission, 1111 18th St., NW, Suite 300, Washington, DC 20036, (202) 695-0643.

General Financial Records Defense Manpower Commission
General Personnel Records
Payroll Records Defense Manpower Commission

U.S. Energy Research and Development Administration

U.S. ENERGY RESEARCH AND DEVELOPMENT ADMINISTRATION (ERDA) has Privacy Act administration officers at the following addresses. Check specific systems of records for applicable locations:

Headquarters
Washington, DC 20545

Albuquerque Operations Office
P.O. Box 5400
Albuquerque, NM 87115

Bartlesville Energy Research Center
P.O. Box 1398
Bartlesville, OK 74003

Chicago Operations Office
9800 South Cass Avenue
Argonne, IL 60439

Grand Forks Energy Research Center
University Station
Grand Forks, ND 58201

Idaho Operations Office
550 2nd Street
Idaho Falls, ID 83401

Laramie Energy Research Center
P.O. Box 3395
University Station
Laramie, WY 82070

Morgantown Energy Research Center
P.O. Box 880
Morgantown, WV 26505

Nevada Operations Office
P.O. Box 14100
Las Vegas, NV 89114

Oak Ridge Operations Office
P.O. Box E
Oak Ridge, TN 37830

Pittsburgh Energy Research Center
4800 Forbes Avenue
Pittsburgh, PA 15213

Richland Operations Office
P.O. Box 550
Richland, WA 99352

San Francisco Operations Office
1333 Broadway, Wells Fargo Building
Oakland, CA 94616

Savannah River Operations Office
P.O. Box A
Aiken, SC 29801

DISCRIMINATION COMPLAINT FILES ERDA

Each ERDA employee, ERDA contractor employee, or assigned facilities contractor employee who has filed a written complaint of discrimination based on race, religion, national origin, or sex with ERDA or with another federal agency which has referred the complaint to ERDA.

U.S. ERDA, Privacy Act Administration Officer's mail addresses in: Washington, DC; Albuquerque, NM; Bartlesville, OK; Argonne, IL; Grand Forks, ND; Idaho Falls, ID; Laramie, WY; Morgantown, WV; Las Vegas, NV; Oak Ridge, TN; Pittsburgh, PA; Richland, WA; Oakland, CA; and Aiken, SC.

Request for information should contain: Individual's full name, and time period.

ERDA CONTRACTOR EMPLOYEE INSURANCE CLAIMS ERDA

Claimants under workmen's compensation insurance; third-party claimants against ERDA contractors.

U.S. ERDA, Privacy Act Administration Officer's mail address in Washington, DC.

Request for information should contain: Individual's full name and time period.

INVESTIGATIVE FILES ERDA

Current and former ERDA and contractor employees who are subjects of investigations, and individuals involved in miscellaneous investigative matters.

U.S. ERDA, Privacy Act Administration Officer's mail addresses in: Washington, DC; Albuquerque, NM; Bartlesville, OK; Argonne, IL; Grand Forks, ND; Idaho Falls, ID; Laramie, WY; Morgantown, WV; Las Vegas, NV; Oak Ridge, TN; Pittsburgh, PA; Richland, WA; Oakland, CA; and Aiken, SC.

Request for information should contain: Individual's full name, identity and address of employer, and dates of employment.

LABOR STANDARDS COMPLAINTS AND GRIEVANCE FILES ERDA

Current and former contractor employees.

U.S. ERDA, Privacy Act Administration Officer's mail addresses in: Washington, DC; Albuquerque, NM; Bartlesville, IL; Idaho Falls, ID; Oak Ridge, TN; Richland, WA; and Oakland, CA.

Request for information should contain: Name of contractor, union, individual name, and time period.

LEGAL OFFICE–CLAIMS, LITIGATIONS, CRIMINAL VIOLATIONS, PATENTS, AND OTHER LEGAL FILES ERDA

ERDA-related debtors and bankrupts; radiation, tort, and patent claimants; claimants with respect to employees compensation and workmen's compensation claims; radiation injury and other personal injury claims; injured parties, litigants, and complaints generally; inventors; those against whom claims have been filed; persons suspected of violating criminal law.

U.S. ERDA, Privacy Act Administration Officer's mail addresses in: Washington, DC; Albuquerque, NM; Bartlesville, OK; Argonne, IL; Grand Forks, ND; Idaho Falls, ID; Laramie, WY; Morgantown, WV; Las Vegas, NV; Oak Ridge, TN; Pittsburgh, PA; Richland, WA; Oakland, CA; and Aiken, SC.

Request for information should contain: Individual's full name, approximate date of event, place of origin, category of record, and cognizant office.

Additional Files

Following is a list of the remaining files maintained by ERDA. Anyone interested in obtaining additional information from any of these files should contact the appropriate agency head or the Federal Communications Commission, 1919 M Street, NW, Washington, DC 20554.

Alien Visits and Participation ERDA

Applications and Reference Checks for Overseas Employment with International Atomic Energy Agency (IAEA) ERDA

Census of High Energy Physicists ERDA

Clearance Board Cases Administrative Review and Personnel ERDA

Compensation for Contractor Employees (25,000 Dollars or More) ERDA

Consultants to ERDA Contractors–Directory of ERDA

Employee and Visitor Access Control Record ERDA

Employment and Financial Interests ERDA

ERDA Personnel Applicant Records ERDA

ERDA Personnel Appraisal and Development Records ERDA

ERDA Personnel/General Employment Records (Addendum to the U.S. Civil Service Commission Federal Register Notice of Records Reporting CSC–General Personnel Records, Official Personnel Folder and Related Records) ERDA

ERDA Personnel–Supervisor Records ERDA

ERDA Technology Training Program–Skill Training at Technician Level ERDA

FHA–Insured Loans (Certificates of Eligibility) ERDA

Firearms Qualifications Record ERDA

Foreign Travel ERDA

Government Drivers License File ERDA

Investigations Pertaining to Violations of Law and Losses of Security Interest ERDA

Medical History System ERDA and Contractor Employees ERDA

Nationwide Traineeship Reporting System ERDA

Nuclear Qualification Examination Records (For Personnel to Be Assigned to Ships, Shipyards, and Prototypes) ERDA

Occupational and Industrial Health, and Safety Records ERDA

Payroll and Leave ERDA

Payroll and Pay-Related Data for Employees of Terminated Contractors ERDA

Personnel Assurance Records ERDA

Personnel Radiation Exposure Information ERDA

Personnel Records of Former and Present Contractor Employees ERDA

Personnel Security Clearance Files ERDA

Security Correspondence File ERDA

Security Education and/or Infraction Reports ERDA

Special Access Authorization for Categories of Classified Information, ERDA

Statistical Analysis Using Personnel Security Questionnaire (Mancuso Study) ERDA

Travel Files ERDA

Weapons Data and Weapons Program Facilities Access to, ERDA

Environmental Protection Agency

INSPECTION BRANCH REPORTS, EPA

EPA employees, or persons, or firms under contract to EPA or receiving grants from EPA suspected of having committed illegal or unethical acts.

Chief, Inspection Branch, Security and Inspection Division, EPA, 401 M St., SW, Washington, DC 20460, (202) 245-3090.

Additional Files

Following is a list of the remaining files maintained by the EPA. For information concerning any of these files contact the Director, Environmental Protection Agency, 401 M St., SW, Washington, DC 20460.

General Personnel Records EPA
Health Unit and Stress Lab Medical Records EPA
Payroll System (Departmental Integrated Payroll System; Payroll Accounting Master File; and Detail History File) EPA
Personnel Security File System EPA
Security Computer Program System EPA
Travel Voucher Folders, Advance Cards, and Payee Files EPA

Equal Employment Opportunity Commission

CHARGE OF DISCRIMINATION CASE FILES—EEOC

Any aggrieved individuals who charge that an unlawful employment practice within the meaning of Title VII of the Civil Rights Act of 1964, as amended, has been committed by an employer, employment agency, labor organization, or joint labor-management apprenticeship committee.

District director of the field office where charge was filed.

Additional Files

Following is a list of the remaining files maintained by the EEO Commission. For information concerning any of these files contact the Director, Equal Employment Opportunity Commission, 2401 E St., NW, Washington, DC 20506.

Affirmative Action Plan Employee Data EEOC
Attorney Referral List EEOC
Commissioners' Biographical File EEOC
Correspondence File EEOC
Employee Alcoholism and Drug Abuse Records EEOC
Employee Pay and Leave Records EEOC
Employee Productivity Listing EEOC
Employee Travel Records EEOC
Labor-Management Negotiated Agreements EEOC
Officials' Biographical File EEOC
Voluntary Programs Skills Bank EEOC

Export-Import Bank of the United States

To request information or access to records in any Eximbank system of records, contact: Vice President, Administration, 811 Vermont Ave., NW, Washington, DC 20571, (202) 566-2117.

EIB PERSONNEL RECORDS

Eximbank employees, applicants, consultants, advisory committee members and former employees who have been dismissed, retired, transferred, and/or resigned from the Eximbank.

EIB EQUAL EMPLOYMENT OPPORTUNITY, GRIEVANCE

Eximbank employee filing a grievance.

Additional Files

Following is a list of the remaining files maintained by Eximbank. Anyone interested in obtaining information from any of these files should contact the Export-Import Bank of the United States, 811 Vermont Ave., NW, Washington, DC 20571.

EIB Applicant File, SF-171's and Resumes
EIB Biographical Sketches on Eximbank Employees and Advisory Committee Members
EIB Confidential Statement of Employment and Financial Interest
EIB Driver's License File
EIB Earnings and Tax Statement

EIB Employee Records (Relocation Site)
EIB Financial Assistance Request for (Under Federal Employee Training Act)
EIB Financial Organization, Credit to Account (Checking)
EIB Financial Organization, Credit to Account (Savings)
EIB Garage Space Application
EIB Immunization Request
EIB Passport Request File
EIB Payroll Certification
EIB Payroll Change Slip, SF-1126
EIB Payroll Coding Sheet, Magnetic Tape
EIB Payroll Control Manual
EIB Payroll Information Employee
EIB Payroll Listing
EIB Payroll Master Record
EIB Performance Appraisals
EIB Periodic Step Increase File
EIB Personnel Action, Notification SF-50
EIB Personnel Files
EIB Personnel Listing
EIB Personnel Roster
EIB Personnel Security Correspondence
EIB Position Description File
EIB Referrals for Non-Career Assignments
EIB Retirement Record Cards
EIB Savings Bond Authorization
EIB Savings Bond File
EIB Tax Exemption Certificate
EIB Time and Attendance Card
EIB Travel Advance Application
EIB Travel Ledger
EIB Visa Request File

Farm Credit Administration

For information about any FCA system of records, write to the following address, indicating the system of interest: Director, Administrative Division, Farm Credit Administration, 490 L'Enfant Plaza, SW, Washington, DC 20578, (202) 755-2130.

Biographical Files, FCA
Congressional Correspondence File FCA
Employee Attendance, Leave, and Payroll Records FCA
Employee Reports of Financial Interests and
   Employment FCA
Employee Travel and Vendor Voucher Files FCA

Farm Credit Bank Personnel Records FCA
Federal Land Bank Loans FCA
Financial Management Records FCA
Former Employee Records FCA
Freedom of Information Requests FCA
General Personnel Records FCA
Group Accident Insurance Records FCA
Procurement Records FCA
Production Credit Association Loans FCA
Property Accountability Records FCA
Public Information Requests File FCA
Upward Mobility Skills Survey FCA

Federal Communications Commission

ALLEGED VIOLATORS FILE (EX PARTE RULES)
FCC/OGC

Individuals alleged to have violated the commission's *ex parte* rules.

General Counsel, 1919 M St., NW, Washington, DC 20554, (202) 632-7020.

ALLEGED VIOLATORS FILE (UNITED STATES DISTRICT COURT ENFORCEMENT ACTION) FCC/OGC

Any person allegedly violating the Communications Act, certain specified federal statutes, treaties, FCC rules, and FCC orders.

General Counsel, 1919 M St., NW, Washington, DC 20554, (202) 632-7020.

ALPHABETICAL COMPLAINT AND INQUIRY
FILE FCC/CCB

Individuals who have made complaints or inquiries.

Chief, Common Carrier Bureau, 1919 M St., NW, Washington, DC 20554 (202) 632-6910.

AMATEUR AND CITIZEN LICENSE FEES,
REFUNDED OR UNCOLLECTED FCC/SSRSB

Applicant who was issued a refund by Gettysburg field office or Washington, DC office; applicant whose check was returned by bank for such things as insufficient funds, account closed, or payment stopped.

Chief, Safety and Special Private Radio Services Bureau, 2025 M St., NW, Washington, DC 20554, (202) 632-6940.

ATTORNEY MISCONDUCT FILES FCC/OGC

Any attorney who appears in a representative capacity before the FCC and who is being charged with attorney misconduct.

General Counsel, 1919 M St., NW, Washington, DC 20554, (202) 632-7020.

COMMUNICATIONS INTERCEPTION—SECTION
605 FCC/OGC

Anyone against whom a complaint is registered.

General Counsel, 1919 M St., NW, Washington, DC 20554, (202) 632-7020.

COMPLAINTS AGAINST BROADCAST STATIONS,
LICENSEES, OFFICERS, EMPLOYEES FCC/BCB

Individual broadcast licensees, partners, owners; directors and officers of corporate licensees; employees of broadcast stations.

Chief, Broadcast Bureau, 1919 M St., NW, Washington, DC 20554, (202) 632-6460.

CONVICTED FELON LICENSEES AND
SUSPENSIONS FCC/OGC

Individual licensees and former licensees who have been suspended.

General Counsel, 1919 M St., NW, Washington, DC 20554, (202) 632-7020.

EMPLOYEE COMPLAINT ADJUDICATION FCC/OGC

Any commission employee who is the subject of a complaint investigation involving internal personnel actions or activities.

General Counsel, Room 614, 1919 M St., NW, Washington, DC 20554, (202) 632-7020.

EMPLOYMENT DISCRIMINATION COMPLAINTS AGAINST COMMON CARRIERS FCC/CCB

All individuals who send complaint letters to the FCC concerning alleged employment discrimination by common carriers.

Chief, Common Carrier Bureau, 1919 M St., NW, Washington, DC 20554, (202) 632-6910.

LICENSEES OR UNLICENSED PERSONS OPERATING RADIO EQUIPMENT IMPROPERLY FCC/SSRSB

Licensees operating under Parts 81, 83, 87, 89, 91, 93, 95 and 97 of the rules in violation of the commission rules or the Communications Act of 1934; unlicensed persons operating radio equipment.

Chief, Safety and Special Private Radio Services Bureau, 2025 M St., NW, Washington, DC 20554, (202) 632-6940.

PARTIES INVOLVED IN CURRENT LITIGATION BEFORE FEDERAL COURTS FCC/OGC

Any person who is a captioned party of record in an appeal from or petition for review of a commission action, or other court filing.

General Counsel, 1919 M St., NW., Washington, DC 20554, (202) 632-7020.

PARTIES WITH PENDING CIVIL CASES BEFORE ANY DISTRICT COURT THAT AFFECT THE COMMISSION FCC/OGC

Any individual who has a miscellaneous case before any district court that involves the commission.

General Counsel, 1919 M St., NW, Washington, DC 20554, (202) 632-7020.

PRIVATE OR CIVIL INJURY CLAIMANTS FCC/OGC

Any individual who files a tort claim against the commission or commits a tort against a commission employee.

General Counsel, 1919 M St., NW, Washington, DC 20554, (202) 632-7020.

VIOLATORS FILE (RECORDS KEPT ON INDIVIDUALS WHO HAVE BEEN SUBJECTS OF FCC FIELD ENFORCEMENT ACTIONS) FCC/FOB

Individuals who have been subjects of FCC field enforcement actions (monitoring, inspection, investigation) for violations of radio law, FCC rules and regulations, or international radio treaties.

Chief, Field Operations Bureau, 1919 M St., NW, Washington, DC 20554, (202) 632-6980.

Additional Files

Following is a list of the remaining files maintained by the FCC. For information concerning any of these files contact the Director, Federal Communications Commission, 1919 M St., NW, Washington, DC 20554.

Activity Reporting System FCC/OED
Alcoholism and Drug Abuse Case Files FCC/OED
Alien Rights under Section 310 of the Communications Act FCC/OGC
Applicant for Position FCC/CCB
Applicant for Position FCC/COMM
Applicant Position FCC/CTB
Application and License File FCC/SSRSB
AT&T Witness File FCC/CCB
Attorney Applicants File FCC/OGC
Broadcast Station Ownership Interest File FCC/BCB
Conflicts of Interest by Commission Employees and Prospective Employees FCC/OGC
Contracts for Personal Services FCC/CCB
Contracts for Personal Services FCC/OGC
Correspondence Associated with Docketed Matters FCC/CCB
Docket History Cards FCC/OED
Employee Activity Report FCC/BCB
Employee Activity Report FCC/CTB
Employee Activity Report FCC/OALJ
Employee Activity Report FCC/OCE
Employee Activity Report FCC/SSRSB
Employee Claims for Reimbursement FCC/OGC
Employee Records FCC/BCB
Employee Records FCC/CB
Employee Records FCC/COMM
Employee Records FCC/CTB
Employee Records FCC/FOB
Employee Records FCC/OALJ
Employee Records FCC/OCE
Employee Records FCC/OGC
Employee Records FCC/OOR
Employee Records FCC/OPP
Employee Records FCC/RB
Employee Records FCC/SSRSB
Employee Relations Case File FCC/OED
Employee Travel Records FCC/SSRSB
Experimental Radio Station Licensee File FCC/OCE
Financial Disclosures by Employees FCC/OED
Index of Commission Agenda Items FCC/OED
National Industry Advisory Committee (NIAC) Membership FCC/OED
Pay, Leave, and Travel Records FCC/OED
Personnel Investigations of Employees FCC/OED

Personnel Investigations of Members of Advisory Committee Maritime Communications Subcommittee, National Industry Advisory Committee), FCC/OED

Project Management of the Data Automation Division FCC/OED

Public Land Mobile Radio Operators File FCC/CCB

Radio Operator Records FCC/FOB

Recess and Interim Appointments of Employees FCC/OGC

Staff Travel Records FCC/CCB

Staff Travel Records FCC/CTB

Staff Travel Records FCC/OALJ

State and Operational Areas Emergency Communications Committee FCC/OED

Witness Appearance Request Files FCC/OGC

Federal Deposit Insurance Corporation

For information about any FDIC system of records, write to the following address, indicating the system of interest:

Executive Secretary, Records Unit, FDIC, 550 17th St., NW, Washington, DC 20429, (202) 389-4486.

BANK IRREGULARITY RECORD SYSTEM FDIC

Directors, officers, and employees of FDIC-insured state nonmember banks who have been involved in reported irregularities at such banks, customers of FDIC-insured state nonmember banks, and other individuals, who have been involved in reported irregularities at such banks. Request for information should contain a notarized statement attesting to the identity of the inquirer.

BOARD OF DIRECTORS' ACTIONS SYSTEM FDIC

Individuals who have been subject to administrative actions by the FDIC board of directors.

CONSUMER COMPLAINT AND INQUIRY RECORDS FDIC

Consumers who have filed complaints or inquiries concerning unfair trade practices by FDIC-insured state nonmember banks.

LEGAL COMPLIANCE AND ENFORCEMENT RECORDS FDIC

Directors or officers of FDIC-insured state nonmember banks who have been the subject of an indictment, information, or complaint for a felony involving dishonesty or breach of trust; directors or officers of FDIC-insured state nonmember banks who are suspected of committing violations of law, rule, or regulation, or of a final cease-and-desist order, or of committing acts, omissions, or practices constituting a breach of fiduciary duty; individuals who have sought FDIC consent to serve as an officer, director, or employee of an FDIC-insured state nonmember bank after having been convicted of a crime involving dishonesty or breach of trust. Request for information should contain: Individual's full name and the name of the bank with which he was associated. Request must include a notarized statement attesting to the individual's identity.

Additional Files

Following is a list of the remaining files maintained by the FDIC. Anyone interested in obtaining information from any of these files should contact the Federal Deposit Insurance Corporation, 550 17th St., NW, Washington, DC 20429.

Attorney–Legal Intern Applicant System FDIC
Employee Confidential Statements of Employment and Financial Interests FDIC
Employee Education System FDIC
Examiner Training and Education Records FDIC
Graduate Fellowship Applications FDIC
Payroll and Employee Financial Records FDIC
Savings Bond Payroll Deduction Systems FDIC
Travel Voucher System FDIC

Federal Election Commission

FEC COMPLIANCE ACTIONS

Persons who have filed complaints and persons complained about. Exempt system.

Following is a list of the files maintained by this agency. For information concerning any of these files, contact the Director, Federal Election Commission, 1325 K St., NW, Washington, DC 20463.

Certification for Primary Matching Funds and for Election Campaign Funds

FEC Advisory Opinion Requests and Public Comment
FEC Audits and Investigations
FEC Correspondence
FEC Meetings and Telephone Communications
FEC Personnel
FEC Registration of Political Committees and Designations by Candidates
FEC Reports of Contributions and Expenditures
FEC Rulemaking and Public Comment
Payments for Presidential Nominating Conventions

Federal Energy Administration

ACCOUNTS RECEIVABLE FINANCIAL (ACCOUNTING) SYSTEM

Debtors owing money to the agency, including employees, former employees, business firms, general public, and institutions.

Director of Administration, Federal Energy Administration, 12th St. and Pennsylvania Ave., NW, Washington, DC 20461, (202) 252-5942.

EQUAL OPPORTUNITY (EO) COMPLAINT FILES, FEA

Employees and applicants for employment with the FEA filing complaints under Federal Personnel Manual (FPM) No. 713.

Director, Office of Equal Opportunity, Federal Energy Administration, Old Post Office Building, 12th St. and Pennsylvania Ave., NW, Washington, DC 20461, (202) 252-2218.

INVESTIGATIVE REPORT RECORDS

FEA employees, past and present, who have been the subject of an FEA investigation.

Office Director, Inspections, Office of Security Inspections, FEA, Old Post Office Building, Room 323, 12th St. and Pennsylvania Ave., NW, Washington, DC 20461, (301) 353-5106.

Additional Files

Following is a list of the remaining files maintained by the FEA. For information concerning any of these files contact:

Director, Federal Energy Administration, Old Post Office Building, 12th St. and Pennsylvania Ave., NW, Washington, DC 20461.

Accounts Payable Financial (Accounting) System
Advisory Committee Management Office, Office of the Administrator, Resume and Mailing List File
Confidential Statements of Employment and Financial Interest
Congressional Files Federal Energy Administration/Office of Congressional Affairs
Employee Applications for Motor Vehicle Operators Card
Employee Assistance Program (Alcohol and Drug Abuse Program)
Employee Carpool Parking Applications and Assignments for the Federal Building, Federal Energy Administration
Employee Travel Records (Domestic and Foreign)—Financial (Accounting) System
FEA Medical Records
FEA Personnel Records and Management Information System
Freedom of Information Act Requests for Records
Intergovernmental Personnel Act Contracts (IPA)
Mailing Lists for Requestors of Energy Related Information Sent Out Periodically and on a Monthly Basis
Minority Group Data File
Payroll System (Departmental Integrated Personnel System)
Personnel Security Records
Project Conserve (Homeowners Information)
Records of Oral Communications with Persons from Outside FEA
Training Records System, Office of Training and Development, FEA Forms 34, 35, Course Evaluation Form, Accounting Records, and Central Personnel Data File (CPDF) Quarterly Training Report

Federal Home Loan Bank Board

Unless another address is given for information concerning any files, contact listed officials at the following address: Federal Home Loan Bank Board, 320 First St., NW, Washington, DC 20552.

DEPOSITORS/ACCOUNT HOLDERS IN DEFAULTED ASSOCIATIONS

Every individual with an account in a defaulted association.

Receivership Agent, Midwestern Office Receiverships, Federal Savings and Loan Insurance Corporation, 1001 West Roosevelt Boulevard, Westchester, IL 60153; Insurance Settlement Office, Federal Savings and Loan Insurance Corporation, 1001 West Roosevelt Boulevard, Westchester, IL 60153; Manager, Scottsdale Office, Federal Savings and Loan Insurance Corporation, 6370 North Scottsdale Road, Scottsdale, AZ 85252; Receivership Manager, Northwest Guaranty Receivership, Federal Savings and Loan Insurance Corporation, 1100 Tower Building, Seattle, WA 98101.

Request for information should contain: Individual's name, name of institution where account was held, account number, and the name of the record system.

DISCRIMINATION COMPLAINT SYSTEM

Any current or former agency employee or applicant who files a formal complaint of discrimination based on race, color, religion, sex, national origin, or age.

Equal Employment Opportunity Officer, (202) 377-6579.

Request for information should contain: Individual's name, Social Security account number, date of birth, period of employment and office of employment (including location), and name of record system.

EMPLOYEE RELATIONS FILE

Individual employees against whom allegations have been made.

Employee Relations Officer, Personnel Management Division, (202) 377-6060.

Request for information should contain: Individual's name, Social Security account number, date of birth, office of employment of the person making the inquiry, and name of the record system.

FBI INVESTIGATORY RECORDS COPY FILE

Persons under investigation by the Federal Bureau of Investigation. Exempt system under 5 U.S.C. 552(J) or (K).

REMOVAL AND PROHIBITIONS FILE

Officers and directors of federally chartered savings-and-loan associations and state-chartered insured institutions.

Secretary to the Board, Director, Compliance Division, Office of the General Counsel, (202) 377-6250.

Request for information should contain: Sufficient information to establish the identity of the individual involved in the proceedings, including the institutional association, and approximate date of board action.

SUSPENSION FILE

Officers and directors of federally chartered savings-and-loan associations and state-chartered insured institutions.

Secretary to the Board, (202) 377-6250.

Request for information should contain: Sufficient information to establish the identity of the individual involved, including name, institutional association, and approximate date of board action.

Additional Files

Following is a list of remaining files maintained by the Federal Home Loan Bank Board. Anyone interested in obtaining information from these files should contact the Federal Home Loan Bank Board, 320 First St., NW, Washington, DC 20552.

Asset Management System
Assignment History of Examiners
Biographical File of Federal Home Loan Bank Directors
Biographies and Photographs
Candidates for Appointed Directorships of Federal Home
    Loan Banks
Candidates for Employment

District Bank Officers' Biography File
District Bank Officers' Salary Cards
Employee Locator File
Employee Service Records Cards (SF-7)
Form 587 File—Training Request, Authorization, Notice of
    Completion of Training
Home Owners' Loan Corporation Home Loan Records
    (HOLC)
Internal Office Personnel Files
Manpower/Budget System
Office of Examinations and Supervision Training Records
Office of the Secretary, Card Files
Payroll
Payroll Personnel
Prospective Organizer of Federal Savings and Loan
    Association File
Statements of Employment and Financial Interests
Training Log Book
Travel Records
Upward Mobility Program (Career Development)

Federal Maritime Commission

For information concerning any FMC system of records, write to the following address, indicating the records of interest: Assistant Managing Director, Federal Maritime Commission, 1100 L St., NW, Washington, DC 20573, (202) 523-5800.

Abolished and Cancelled Position Description File FMC
Chronological Journal File FMC
Confidential Statement of Employment and Financial Interests FMC
Correspondence and Communication File FMC
Correspondence Course on Traffic and Transportation Management FMC

Current and Active Position Description File FMC
Desk Audit File FMC
Individual Licensed Independent Ocean Freight Forwarders File FMC
Merit Promotion Program File FMC
Non-Attorney Practitioner File FMC
Official Personnel Folder FMC
Personnel Security File FMC
Reading File FMC
Special Training Agreement File FMC
Training Purchase Order File FMC
Travel Orders/Vouchers File FMC

Federal Mediation and Conciliation Service

For information concerning any Federal Mediation and Conciliation Service system of records, contact: Director of Administration, Federal Mediation and Conciliation Service, Washington, DC 20427, (202) 653-5333.

Agency Internal Personnel Records
Agency Pay Records
Agency Personnel Security Records
Arbitrator Personal Data File

Federal Power Commission

APPEALS, GRIEVANCES, AND COMPLAINTS
RECORDS, FPC (THIS RECORDS SYSTEM
SUPPLEMENTS THE APPEALS, GRIEVANCES, AND
COMPLAINTS RECORDS SYSTEM OF THE CIVIL
SERVICE COMMISSION.)

Applicants for FPC employment, current and former FPC
employees, agencies, and annuitants who appeal a determination made by an official of the FPC or the Civil Service
Commission to the Civil Service Commission, a board
established to adjudicate appeals, or to the FPC.

Equal employment opportunity complaints records: Executive Director, Federal Power Commission, 825 North
Capitol St., NE, Washington, DC 20426, (202) 357-8300.
All other appeals, grievances, and complaints: Director, Office of Personnel Programs, Federal Power Commission, 825
North Capitol St., NE, Washington, DC 20426, (202) 275-
4080.

Additional Files

Following is a list of the remaining files maintained by the
FPC. For information contact: Secretary of the Federal
Power Commission, 825 North Capitol St., NE, Washington,
DC 20426, (202) 357-8400.

Applications for Interlocking Directorates under the
    Federal Power Act Maintained in the Public Files FPC
Applications for Interlocking Directorates under the
    Federal Power Act Maintained under Security FPC
Biographical Material on Chairmen, Vice Chairmen, Com-
    missioners, Secretaries, and Assistant Secretaries of the
    Federal Power Commission FPC

Biographical Material on Key Staff Members of the Federal
    Power Commission FPC
Blood Donor Records FPC
Claims by Employees for Losses of Personal Property FPC
Committee Memberships and Assignments FPC
Computer Usage Production Statistics for the Office of
    Regulatory Information Systems FPC
Congressional Correspondence File Maintained in the
    Bureau of Power FPC
Congressional Correspondence File Maintained in the
    Office of the General Counsel FPC
Correspondence File Maintained in the Bureau of
    Natural Gas FPC
Data Operator Performance Statistics for the Office of
    Regulatory Information Systems FPC
Data Sources within Regulated Industries FPC
Employee Conduct Records FPC
Mailing List for Information Concerning Applications for
    Interlocking Directorates FPC
Mailing List for Information Concerning Electric Adequacy
    and Reliability FPC
Mailing List for Information Concerning Energy
    Consumption and Demand FPC
Mailing List for Official Publications FPC
Mailing List for Press Releases FPC
Pay and Pay-Related Records (Payroll, Travel, Attendance,
    Leave) FPC
Personnel Investigations Records (Security and Suitability)
    FPC (Note: This record system supplements the
    Personnel Investigations Records System of the Civil
    Service Commission.)
Personnel Records (General) FPC
Recruiting, Examining, Promotion, and Placement
    Records FPC
Retirement, Life Insurance, and Health Benefits
    Records FPC
Time Distribution Reports FPC

Federal Reserve System

For information concerning the systems of records identified below, contact: Director of Personnel, Board of Governors, Federal Reserve System, 20th and Constitution, NW, Washington, DC 20551, (202) 452-3660.

FRB—ADVERSE INFORMATION AND ACTION, DISCIPLINARY, OUTSIDE BUSINESS ACTIVITY AND FINANCIAL RESPONSIBILITY RECORDS

Current and former board employees (including special employees) and annuitants who are involved in an adverse action; board officials providing annual financial responsibility statements; employees who suffer a withholding of a progress step increase; employees who file an outside business activity application; and those employees who have creditors contacting the board relative to credit problems.

FRB-EEO DISCRIMINATION COMPLAINT FILE

Applicants for board employment, current and former board employees, and annuitants who file a complaint of discrimination or appeal a determination made by an official of the board relating to equal employment opportunities.

Additional Files

Following is a list of the remaining files maintained by the Federal Reserve System. Anyone interested in obtaining in-

formation from any of these files should contact the Federal Reserve System, 20th St. and Constitution Ave., NW, Washington, DC 20551.

Biographical File of Federal Reserve Personnel FRB
Consultant File FRB
General File on Board Members FRB
General File of Examiners and Assistant Examiners at
    Federal Reserve Banks, FRB
General Files of Federal Reserve Agents, Alternates, and
    Representatives at Federal Reserve Banks FRB
General File of Federal Reserve Bank and Branch Directors,
    FRB
General Personnel Records FRB
Leave Records FRB
Medical Records FRB
Official General Files FRB
Payroll FRB
Personnel Background Investigation Reports FRB
Recruiting and Placement Records FRB
Regulation Ownership Reports FRB
Regulation G Reports FRB

Federal Trade Commission

For information about any FTC system of records, write to the following address, indicating the system of interest: Privacy Act Request, Office of the Secretary, Federal Trade Commission, 6th St. and Pennsylvania Ave., NW, Washington, DC 20580, (202) 523-3582.

CLAIMANTS UNDER FEDERAL TORT CLAIMS AND MILITARY PERSONNEL AND CIVILIAN EMPLOYEES' CLAIMS ACT FTC

Individuals who have claimed reimbursement from FTC under Federal Tort Claims Act and Military Personnel and Civilian Employees' Claims Act.

COMMISSION MINUTES FTC

Individual respondents and proposed respondents in commission proceedings and investigations, individuals requesting advisory opinions, and those subject to commission disciplinary proceedings and commission orders.

COMPLAINT CARDS, DALLAS REGIONAL OFFICE FTC

Individuals who have filed complaints or requested information.

CONGRESSIONAL INQUIRY FILES, DALLAS REGIONAL OFFICE FTC

Constituents who have written their congressional representative for aid in resolving consumer problems, and members of Congress.

CONSUMER COMPLAINT FILES, ATLANTA REGIONAL OFFICE FTC

Members of the general public.

CONSUMER COMPLAINT FILES, CLEVELAND REGIONAL OFFICE FTC

Individual consumers who filed a complaint.

CONSUMER COMPLAINT FILES, DIVISION OF MARKETING PRACTICES: BUREAU OF CONSUMER PROTECTION FTC

Individuals filing complaints or requesting information.

CONSUMER COMPLAINT FILES, LOS ANGELES REGIONAL OFFICE FTC

Consumer complaint letters and forms relating to companies, practices, and individuals in the Los Angeles office area.

CONSUMER COMPLAINT FILES, NEW ORLEANS REGIONAL OFFICE FTC

Complainants.

CONSUMER COMPLAINT LETTERS, SEATTLE REGIONAL OFFICE FTC

Those persons who direct a consumer complaint or request for assistance or information to the Seattle regional office, FTC, or those forwarding a complaint from a consumer such as a member of the media or federal, state, or local agency.

CONSUMER REDRESS LISTS, COMPLIANCE DIVISION: BUREAU OF CONSUMER PROTECTION, FTC

Consumers entitled to redress pursuant to commission or court order. Request for information should contain: Name of the firm or proceeding.

DISCIPLINARY ACTION INVESTIGATORY FILES FTC

FTC personnel, counsel for parties under investigatory or adjudicatory proceedings, and others participating in FTC matters, subject to investigation for possible improper or unethical conduct.

INVESTIGATIONAL, LEGAL, AND PUBLIC RECORDS FTC

Respondents, proposed respondents, and others in commission investigations and law enforcement proceedings; parties requesting formal advisory opinions. Request for information should contain: Name of the party subject to the investigation or adjudicatory proceeding.

LITIGATION INFORMATION MANAGEMENT SYSTEM FOR INVESTIGATIONS, RULE-MAKING, ADJUDICATORY PROCEEDINGS FTC

Individual respondents, witnesses, informants, and interested parties in certain selected, complex investigations, or rule-making or adjudicatory proceedings; individuals submitting comments or named in records obtained in the course of such investigations or proceedings. Request for information should contain: Name of the party subject to the investigation or adjudicatory proceedings.

PRELIMINARY INVESTIGATION FILES FTC

Respondents and corespondents in preliminary investigations. Request for information should contain: Name of the party subject to the investigation or adjudicatory proceeding, bureau (and division, if possible) or regional office conducting the investigation.

PUBLIC CONTACT REPORT SYSTEM, ATLANTA REGIONAL OFFICE FTC

Individual members of the public who file complaints or request information either by telephone or in person concerning matters believed to be of interest to or within the jurisdiction of the FTC.

Additional Files

Following is a list of the remaining files maintained by the FTC. Anyone interested in obtaining information from any of these files should contact the Federal Trade Commission, 6th St. and Pennsylvania Ave., NW, Washington, DC 20580.

Basis Computerized System, Bureau of Competition FTC
Biographies of Commissioners and Key Staff Members FTC
Call for Comment Mailing List FTC
Consultant Files, Division of National Advertising; Bureau of Consumer Protection FTC
Consumer and Industry Correspondence Files, Division of Special Statutes; Bureau of Consumer Protection FTC
Consumer Mailing List, Los Angeles Regional Office FTC
Correspondence with Compliance Division, Bureau of Consumer Protection, Concerning Parties Subject to Commission Orders FTC
Correspondence with Members of Congress and Agency Officials FTC
Counseling Records FTC
Financial Management System FTC
Financial Statements of Commissioners-Elect FTC
General Correspondence Records FTC
General Personnel Records (Official Personnel Folder and Records Related Thereto): Duplicate Personnel Files and Automated Records FTC
Internal Assignment Tracking System, Office of General Counsel FTC
Page Count Sheet Tabulation, Dallas Regional Office FTC
Payroll Processing System FTC
Public Information Mailing List FTC
Public Information Mailing List, Boston Regional Office FTC
Public Information Mailing List, Dallas Regional Office, FTC
Public Information Mailing List, New Orleans Regional Office FTC
Unofficial Personnel Records FTC

Foreign Claims Settlement Commission of the United States

For information about any FCSC system of records, write to the following address, indicating the system of interest: Executive Director, Foreign Claims Settlement Commission, 1111 20th St., NW, Washington, DC 20579, (202) 382-3137.

BULGARIA, CLAIMS AGAINST (1st Program) FCSC

U.S. nationals who suffered certain property losses or damages in Bulgaria prior to August 9, 1955.

BULGARIA, CLAIMS AGAINST (2nd Program) FCSC

U.S. nationals who suffered property losses in Bulgaria between August 9, 1955, and July 2, 1963.

CHINA, CLAIMS AGAINST COMMUNIST FCSC

U.S. nationals who suffered property losses, death, and disability in mainland China arising since October 1, 1949.

CORRESPONDENCE (INQUIRIES CONCERNING CLAIMS IN FOREIGN COUNTRIES) FCSC

U.S. nationals suffering losses in foreign countries, inquiries from members of Congress.

CUBA, CLAIMS AGAINST FCSC

U.S. nationals who suffered property losses, death, and disability in Cuba since January 1, 1959.

CZECHOSLOVAKIA, CLAIMS AGAINST FCSC

U.S. nationals who suffered property losses in Czechoslovakia after January 1, 1945.

EAST GERMANY, REGISTRATION OF CLAIMS AGAINST FCSC

U.S. nationals who suffered certain property losses in East Germany.

FEDERAL REPUBLIC OF GERMANY, QUESTIONNAIRE INQUIRIES FORM FCSC

Individuals suffering losses in East European countries, including West Germany.

HUNGARY, CLAIMS AGAINST (1st Program) FCSC

U.S. nationals who suffered certain property losses or damages in Hungary prior to August 9, 1955.

HUNGARY, CLAIMS AGAINST (2nd Program) FCSC

U.S. nationals who suffered certain property losses or damages in Hungary between August 9, 1955, and March 6, 1973.

INDEXES OF CLAIMANTS (ALPHABETICAL) FCSC

Individuals who filed claims for compensation under the statutes administered by the Foreign Claims Settlement Commission.

ITALY, CLAIMS AGAINST (1st Program) FCSC

U.S. nationals who suffered property losses attributable to Italian military action arising out of World War II.

ITALY, CLAIMS AGAINST (2nd Program) FCSC

U.S. nationals who suffered certain property losses attributable to military action arising out of World War II, including deceased U. S. nationals; persons who did not file under the 1st Italian Claims Program.

MICRONESIA, CLAIMS ARISING IN FCSC

Inhabitants of Micronesia, including U.S. nationals, who suffered damages to property, disability, and death arising out of World War II and arising during the period from the dates of the securing of the various islands of Micronesia to July 1, 1951.

PANAMA, CLAIMS AGAINST FCSC

U.S. nationals who suffered loss of property in Panama as a result of a judgment of the Supreme Court of Panama on October 20, 1931, nullifying title to certain land in Panama.

POLAND, REGISTRATION OF CLAIMS FCSC

U.S. nationals who suffered property losses in Poland due to nationalization or other taking of such property.

POLAND, CLAIMS AGAINST FCSC

U.S. nationals who suffered property losses in Poland due to nationalization or other taking of such property.

RUMANIA, CLAIMS AGAINST (1st Program) FCSC

U.S. nationals who suffered certain property losses or damages in Rumania prior to August 9, 1955.

RUMANIA, CLAIMS AGAINST (2nd Program) FCSC

U.S. nationals who suffered certain property losses in Rumania between August 9, 1955, and March 30, 1960.

SOVIET UNION, CLAIMS AGAINST FCSC

U.S. nationals suffering loss of property in the Soviet Union prior to November 16, 1933, and claims by individuals based upon liens acquired with respect to property in the United States assigned to United States government by the Soviet government under the Latvinov Assignment of November 16, 1933.

YUGOSLAVIA, CLAIMS AGAINST (1st Program) FCSC

U.S. nationals who suffered property losses in Yugoslavia prior to July 19, 1948.

YUGOSLAVIA, CLAIMS AGAINST (2nd Program) FCSC

U.S. nationals who suffered losses in Yugoslavia that occurred between July 19, 1948, and November 5, 1964.

Additional Files

Following is a list of the remaining files maintained by the FCSC. Anyone interested in obtaining any information from these files should contact the Foreign Claims Settlement Commission of the United States, 1111 20th St., NW, Washington, DC 20579.

Certification of Awards FCSC
Civilian Internees (Vietnam) FCSC
Correspondence (General) FCSC
General Financial Records FCSC
General Personnel Files FCSC
Payroll Records FCSC
Prisoners of War (Vietnam) FCSC
Rosters of Prisoners of War and Civilian Internees FCSC

General Services Administration

DISCIPLINARY ACTION AND APPEAL AND GRIEVANCE FILES GSA/OAD

GSA employees who may be or who have been subjects of disciplinary action, and employees who have filed appeals or grievances.

Director of Personnel, General Services Administration, 18th & F Sts., NW, Washington, DC 20405, (202) 566-3098.

DISCRIMINATION COMPLAINT FILE, GSA/OCR

Employees or applicants for employment who consult an equal employment opportunity counselor concerning allegations of discrimination.

Director of Civil Rights, General Services Administration, 18th & F Sts., NW, Washington, DC 20405, (202) 566-1264.

EMPLOYEE DRUG ABUSE (INCLUDING ALCOHOLISM) FILES GSA/OAD

Employees who have been suspected of or known to have, drug abuse problems.

Director of Personnel, General Services Administration, 18th & F Sts., NW, Washington, DC 20405, (202) 566-3098.

GENERAL LAW FILES, GSA/OGC. (THIS NOTICE COVERS 21 UNIQUE SYSTEMS OF RECORDS INVOLVING RELATED SUBJECT MATTER.)

Each of the 21 systems covers one or more of the following categories of individuals: GSA employees, past and present; other agency employees, members of the public (including individuals, corporations, and firms); witnesses in regulatory proceedings; persons who have made Freedom of Information and Privacy Act requests and persons about whom such requests have been made; persons involved in litigation with GSA; grievants under collective bargaining agreements; appellants.

Director, Office of Administration, General Services Administration, 18th & F Sts., NW, Washington, DC 20405, (202) 566-1212.

INCIDENT REPORTING SYSTEM GSA/PBS

Individuals who were the source of an initial complaint or an allegation that a crime has taken place; witnesses having information or evidence relating to any side of an investigation; possible and actual suspects in the criminal situation that is subject of an investigation; material developed on subjects of investigation, both those whose identity is known and those who are unknown; sources of information, sources of evidence. (The identity of these individuals may be confidential as well as the subject matter they contribute. These files contain information vital to the outcome of administrative procedures, and civil and criminal cases. Much of this information is subject to the Jencks Act, the Freedom of Information Act, and the Privacy Act.)

Assistant Commissioner for Federal Protective Service Management, General Services Administration, Room 2042, 18th & F Sts., NW, Washington, DC 20405, (202) 566-0887.

LABOR-MANAGEMENT RELATIONS FILES GSA/OAD

Employees who are union officials or are in an exclusively recognized unit; employees who have filed grievances under the negotiated grievance procedure.

Director of Personnel, General Services Administration, 18th & F Sts., NW, Washington, DC 20405, (202) 566-0398, or appropriate regional director of personnel.

MOTOR VEHICLE ACCIDENT AND CLAIM
REPORTING SYSTEM GSA/FSS

Operators of government motor vehicles, third parties, and witnesses involved in accidents.

Director, Motor Equipment Management Division, Federal Supply Service, Crystal Mail Building 4, Washington, DC 20406, (202) 557-1327.

Additional Files

Following is a list of the remaining files maintained by this agency. For information concerning any file, contact: Administrator, General Services Administration, 18th & F Sts., NW, Washington, DC 20405, (202) 566-1212.

Accountability and Property Inventory Systems GSA/FSS
Application and Physical Fitness Evaluation for Motor
    Vehicle Operators
Attorney Evaluations, GSA/OGC
Attorney Placement, GSA/OGC. (This notice covers 5
    unique systems of records of related subject matter.)
Authors Files, GSA/NARS
Biographical Sketches, GSA/Region 9
Cataloging Action Master File—Work Measurement System,
    GSA/FSS
Classified Control Files, GSA/ADTS
Computer Access Code Assignments, GSA/FPA
Conference and Related Activities Files, GSA/NARS
Confidential Statements of Employment and
    Financial Interests, GSA/OGC
Congressional Files, GSA/ADTS
Credentials (includes passes and licenses) GSA/OAD
Disbursement and Accounts Payable Files, GSA/OAD
Discretionary Supervisor Files, GSA/ADTS
Distribution Lists, GSA/FPS
Donors of Historical Materials Files, GSA/NARS
Emergency Assignment System, GSA/FPA
Emergency Notification Files, GSA/ADTS
Employee Appraisal Files GSA/OAD
Employee Benefits Files GSA/OAD
Employee Credit Reports GSA/OAD
Employee Directories, GSA/FPA
Employee Payroll and Time and Attendance
    Reporting System
Employee Related Files GSA/FMPO
Employee Related Files GSA/FSS
Employee Related Files GSA/NARS
Employee Related Files GSA/OCR
Employee Related Files GSA/PBS
Employee Related Files GSA/Region 2
Employee Related Files GSA/Region 3
Essential Residence Telephone Service GSA/OAD
Financial Management Files GSA/ADTS
Foreign Gift Records GSA/FSS
Fund-Raising Campaigns File GSA/OAD
General Personnel Files. (This notice covers 21 unique sys-
    tems of records involving related subject matter.)

General Staffing Information Maintained by the Central
    Office, Office of Personnel and Personnel Offices of
    GSA, GSA/OAD
GSA/NARS Addresses of Locations, Telephone Numbers,
    and Business Hours
Hazardous Materials Exposure History System GSA/FSS
Incentive Awards Files GSA/OAD
Intergovernmental Management Trainee Association
    Records GSA/OAD
Inventory Management and Buyer Workload Automated
    Systems GSA/FSS
Investigation and Personnel Security Case Files GSA/OAD
Key Personnel Directory and Key Contact Card GSA/FSS
Key Personnel and Essential Residence Telephone Directory
Listing of Physicians GSA/OAD
Mailing List Files GSA/NARS
Mandatory Review of Classified Documents/Request
    Files, GSA/NARS
Manpower and Payroll Statistics System (MAPS)
National Defense Executive Reserve (NDER) Personnel and
    Management Information System GSA/FPA
National and Regional Archives Advisory Council Files
    GSA/NARS
Occupational Health and Injury Files GSA/OAD
Office-Level Employee Records GSA/FPA
Office Personnel Files GSA/OAD
Official Employee Records GSA/FPA
Personal Property Disposal Work Measurement
    System GSA/FSS
Personnel Administrative Files, GSA/ADTS
Personnel Roster GSA/FPA
Potential Employees Referred by Members of the Legislative
    and Executive Branches and Other Sources
Processing and Records Files GSA/OAD
Project Control, Assignment, and Reporting Systems,
    GSA/FSS
Project Management Information System GSA/FPA
Property Inventory System GSA/FPA
Quality Control Automated Management System GSA/FSS
Records Related to Trainee Programs in GSA, GSA/OAD
Records Relating to the Assignment, Promotion, and
    Retirement Activities for Executives within General
    Services Administration
Records Relating to Career and Executive Development,
    GSA/OAD
Records Relating to Compensation and Classification
    Activities Within GSA, GSA/OAD
Records Relating to Formal Training of GSA Employees,
    GSA/OAD
Records Relating to Staffing Activities of FSA, GSA/OAD
Reference Request Files GSA/NARS
Regional Administrator's Official Correspondence File
    GSA/Region 2
Regional Administrator's Official Correspondence File
    GSA/Region 9
Researcher Application Files GSA/NARS
Resource Interruption Monitoring System GSA/FPA
Restricted and Classified Records/Access Authorization
    Files, GSA/NARS

Roster of GSA Officials (GSA Form 2177) GSA/OAD
Security Management System GSA/FPA
Space Management and Employee Information,
   Automated Systems GSA/PBS
Special Personnel Studies and Reports GSA/OAD
Staffing Reporting System GSA/OAD
Standards of Conduct Files GSA/OAD
Supply Distribution Work Measurement System GSA/FSS

Test Material GSA/OAD
Travel System GSA/OAD
Vehicle and Motor Pool Services and Operations
   System GSA/FSS
Workload Measurement Files GSA/ADTS
Work Measurement, Performance, and Analysis Systems
   GSA/FSS
Work Record Systems GSA/FSS

Inter-American Foundation

For information concerning any files maintained by the Inter-American Foundation, contact: President, Inter-American Foundation, 1515 Wilson Blvd., Rosslyn, VA 22209, (703) 841-3810.

Conflict of Interest Files IAF
Foundation Fellowship Program Files IAF
Informal Personnel Files IAF
Inter-American Foundation–General Financial Records IAF
Travel Records IAF

Interstate Commerce Commission

CASE STATUS SYSTEM (FORMAL CASE CONTROL), ICC

Administrative law judges and attorney-advisers who have been assigned to work on cases before the commission, parties of record and parties to be advised of all proceedings.

Chief, Section of System Development, Room B0411, Interstate Commerce Commission, 12th St. & Constitution Ave., NW, Washington, DC 20423, (202) 275-7538.

CONSUMER COMPLAINT SYSTEM, ICC

Letters received from consumers and/or shippers regarding the operation of the ICC or carriers subject to its regulations.

Public Information Officer, Interstate Commerce Commission, 12th St. & Constitution Ave., NW, Washington, DC 20423, (202) 275-7252.

INVESTIGATIVE AND ENFORCEMENT RECORDS, CROSS-INDEXED, ICC (EXEMPT)

Individual, corporation, partnership, or sole proprietorship subject to enforcement actions being taken by the Interstate Commerce Commission as a result of preliminary investigations.

Assistant Director, Bureau of Enforcement, Interstate Commerce Commission, 12th St. & Constitution Ave., NW, Washington, DC 20423, (202) 275-7612.

PRELIMINARY INVESTIGATIVE FILES, ICC

Suspected violators of the Interstate Commerce Act or ICC orders or regulations.

Director, Bureau of Operations, Room 7115, Interstate Commerce Commission, 12th St. & Constitution Ave., NW, Washington, DC 20423, (202) 275-7849, or Regional Managers, or Officers in Charge.

Following is a list of the remaining files maintained by the ICC. For information concerning any file, contact: Security, Interstate Commerce Commission, 12th St. & Constitution Ave., NW, Washington, DC 20423, (202) 275-7032.

Automated Personnel and Payroll System ICC
Correspondence and Management Control ICC
Employee Travel Records ICC
Health Unit Medical Records ICC
ICC Employee Parking Permit Applications for Carpools ICC
ICC Identification System File ICC
National Defense Executive Reserve Files ICC
Operating Personnel Files (Nonpermanent Records) ICC

Joint Board for the Enrollment of Actuaries

For information about any JBEA system of records, write to the following address, identifying the system of interest: Executive Director, Joint Board for the Enrollment of Actuaries, c/o Department of the Treasury, 15th St. & Pennsylvania Ave., NW, Washington, DC 20220, (202) 566-2000.

CHARGE CASE INVENTORY FILES JBEA

Individuals enrolled to perform actuarial services under Employee Retirement Income Security Act (ERISA) with respect to whom derogatory information has been received.

Application Files JBEA
Denied Applications JBEA
Enrollment Files JBEA
Enrollment Roster JBEA
General Correspondence File JBEA
General Information JBEA
Suspension and Termination Files JBEA
Suspension and Termination Roster JBEA

Marine Mammal Commission

For information about any MMC system of records, write to the following address, identifying the system of interest:

Executive Director, Marine Mammal Commission, 1625 I St., NW, Room 307, Washington, DC 20006, (202) 653-6237.

Applications for Permits to Take or Import Marine Mammals or to Import Marine Mammal Products for Purposes of Scientific Research or Public Display MMC

General Financial Records MMC

Payroll Records MMC

Personnel Files on Current, Past and Prospective Employees and Members of the Marine Mammal Commission and Its Committee of Scientific Advisors MMC

Research Proposals and Contracts MMC

National Aeronautics and Space Administration

EQUAL OPPORTUNITY RECORDS NASA

Complainants and applicants.

Assistant Administrator for Equal Opportunity Programs, National Aeronautics and Space Administration, Washington, DC 20546, (202) 755-3714.

Following are the remaining files maintained by NASA. For information concerning any of these files, contact: Administrator, National Aeronautics and Space Administration, Washington, DC 20546, (202) 755-3918.

Aircraft Crewmember Qualifications and Performance Records NASA
Biographical Records for Public Affairs NASA
Exchange Records on Individuals NASA
Executive Development Records NASA
Government Motor Vehicle Operators Permit Records NASA

GSFC Civil Defense Training Survey Records NASA
GSFC Radiation Safety Committee Records NASA
History Archives Biographical Collection NASA
Inspections Division Case Files NASA
JSC Exchange Activities Records NASA
KSC Radiation Training and Experience Summary NASA
KSC USAEC Occupational External Radiation Exposure History for Nuclear Regulatory Commission Licenses NASA
MSFC Federal Housing Administration (FHA) 809 Housing Program NASA
Payroll System NASA
Security Records System NASA
Special Personnel Records NASA
Standards of Conduct Counseling Case Files NASA
System of Medical Records NASA
WSTF Federal Housing Administration (FHA) 809 Housing Program NASA

National Credit Union Administration

EQUAL EMPLOYMENT OPPORTUNITY GRIEVANCE AND DISCRIMINATION COMPLAINT RECORDS, NCUA

Employees who have filed a grievance or formal complaint of discrimination under the Equal Employment Opportunity Act.

Security Officer, National Credit Union Administration, 2025 M St., NW, Washington, DC 20456, (202) 357-1235.

FEDERAL EMPLOYEE SECURITY INVESTIGATIONS CONTAINING ADVERSE INFORMATION, NCUA

Employees on whom a routine CSC security investigation has been conducted, the results of which contain adverse information.

Security Officer, National Credit Union Administration, 2025 M St., NW, Washington, DC 20456, (202) 357-1235.

INVESTIGATIVE REPORTS INVOLVING POSSIBLE FELONIES AND/OR VIOLATIONS OF FEDERAL CREDIT UNION ACT

Credit union employees who have misused or are suspected of having misused trust placed in them by credit unions, with subsequent investigation and/or prosecution; credit union members involved or suspected of involvement in felonies or infractions under the Federal Credit Union Act; individuals involved in robberies, burglaries, and other crimes against credit unions. Information in this system only rarely includes names or other identifiers for suspected perpetrators.

Security Officer, National Credit Union Administration, 2025 M St., NW, Room 4306, Washington, DC 20456, (202) 357-1235.

Additional Files

Following is a list of the remaining files maintained by NCUA. For information concerning any file, contact: Director, National Credit Union Administration, 2025 M St., NW, Washington, DC 20456, (202) 357-1100.

Intergovernmental Personnel Act Records, NCUA
Loan Management Records System, NCUA
Member Account Records of Federally Insured Credit Unions Closed for Involuntary Liquidation, NCUA
Minority Group Designator System (MGD), NCUA
New Examiner Training Files, NCUA
Payroll Records System, NCUA
Promotion Qualification Ranking List of Career NCUA Examiners, by Pay Grade, NCUA
Region I Regional Office Staff Development/Correspondence Records, NCUA
Region II Regional Office Staff Development/Correspondence Records, NCUA
Region III Regional Office Staff Development/Correspondence Records, NCUA
Region IV Regional Office Staff Development/Correspondence Records, NCUA
Region V Regional Office Staff Development/Correspondence Records, NCUA
Region VI Regional Office Staff Development/Correspondence Records, NCUA
Security Clearance Records Concerning NCUA Personnel Who Occupy Critical Sensitive Positions
Trusteed Account Records System, NCUA
Verified Employee Mailing List, NCUA

National Foundation of the Arts and the Humanities

For information concerning any file maintained by this agency, contact: Director, National Foundation on the Arts and the Humanities, 2401 E St., NW, Washington, DC 20506, (202) 634-6369.

Consultants, NFAH
Contracts, NFAH

Employee Payroll and Leave and Attendance Records and Files, NFAH
Equal Employment Opportunity Case File, NFAH
Grant Applications, NFAH/NEA
Grants to Individuals NFAH/NEA
Grants to Individuals and Institutions NFAH
Personnel Records NFAH

National Labor Relations Board

FEDERAL TORT CLAIMS ACT–CLAIMANTS, NLRB

Individuals filing claims under the Federal Tort Claims Act.

Chief, Security and Safety Branch, NLRB, 1717 Pennsylvania Ave., NW, Washington, DC 20570, (202) 254-9177.

GRIEVANCES, APPEALS, AND COMPLAINTS RECORDS, NLRB

Current and former NLRB employees.

Employee's supervisors or those employees under supervision of the General Counsel: General Counsel, NLRB, 1717 Pennsylvania Ave., NW, Washington, DC 20570, (202) 254-9150. For those employees under supervision of the NLRB: Solicitor, NLRB, 1717 Pennsylvania Ave., NW, Washington, DC 20570, (202) 254-9110.

PREFILING COMMUNICATIONS, NLRB

Persons who have sought assistance regarding possible institution of an unfair labor practice, representation, or other civil action or proceeding before the National Labor Relations Board.

General Counsel, NLRB, 1717 Pennsylvania Ave., NW, Washington, DC 20570; or appropriate regional director, officer-in-charge, or resident officer of the agency office where the individual sought, or was referred to for, assistance.

Additional Files

Following is a list of the remaining files maintained by the NLRB. For information concerning any file, contact: Chairman, NLRB, 1717 Pennsylvania Ave., NW, Washington, DC 20570, (202) 254-9266.

Accounting Records–Financial NLRB
Applicant Files for Attorney and Field Examiner Positions, General Counsel's Staff, NLRB
Biographical Data File–Presidential Appointees, NLRB
Employment and Performance Appraisals, Attorneys and Field Examiners, General Counsel's Staff NLRB
Evaluations and Promotion Appraisals of Field Clericals NLRB
Health Maintenance Program Records NLRB
Occupational Injury and Illness Records NLRB
Pay Records–Retirement NLRB
Payroll–Data Processing File NLRB
Payroll–Finance Records NLRB
Performance Appraisals–Attorneys, Board Members' Staffs, Office of Solicitor, NLRB
Program Measurement System Report NLRB
Promotion Appraisals Washington–Clericals and Nonlegal Professionals, NLRB
Time and Attendance Records NLRB

National Science Foundation

For information about any NSF system of records, contact: NSF Privacy Act Officer, National Science Foundation, 1800 G Street, NW, Washington, DC 20550.

EMPLOYEE GRIEVANCE AND APPEALS FILE

NSF employees

Additional Files

Following is a list of the remaining files maintained by the NSF. Anyone interested in obtaining information from any of these files chould contact the National Science Foundation Privacy Officer, National Science Foundation, 1800 G Street, NW, Washington, DC 20550.

Applicants to Committee on the Challenges of Modern Society Fellowship Programme (NATO)
Applicants for Employment
Application and Account for Advance of Funds (SF 1038)
Confidential Statement of Employment and Financial Interests
Congressional Contact Files
Doctorate Records File
Earnings and Tax Statement (W-2)
Employees Locator Record Card
Employee's Payroll Jacket
Equal Employment Opportunity Case File

Fellowship Payroll
Fellowship and Traineeship Filing System
Grants to Individuals
Health Service Medical Records
Individuals Retirement Record (SF 2806)
Intergovernmental Personnel Act Assignment Agreements
Manpower Management Subsystem
Medical Examination Records for Service in Antarctica
Minority Applicants for Employment
Nominees for and Recipients of the National Medal of Science
NSF Payroll System
NSF Staff Biography
Official Passports
Personnel Security Control Cards
Presidential Internships in Science and Engineering
Principal Investigator/Project Director Files
Principal Investigator/Project Director Subsystem
Reviewer, Consultant, and Panelist Files
Reviewer/Panelist Information Subsystem. (Note: This system differs from NSF System No. 30 in that system 39 is used to collect information concerning reviewers used by Foundation offices, whereas No. 30 is used as an aid in the selection of reviewers.)
Science Education Applicant Information Subsystem
Separated Employees Service Record (SF 7)
Student Science Training Program Participant Information
Time and Attendance Reports

National Security Council

For information about any NSC system of records, write to the following address, identifying the system of interest: Staff Secretary, National Security Council, Old Executive Office Building, Washington, DC 20506, (202) 395-3440.

Agency Personnel Records and Files NSC
Central Research Index NSC

NSC Correspondence Files NSC
NSC Meetings Registry NSC
Presidential Advisory Files NSC
Presidential Contact File NSC
Presidential Correspondence Files NSC

National Transportation Safety Board

EQUAL EMPLOYMENT OPPORTUNITY COMPLAINT RECORDS NTSB

Employees of the board or job applicants who file complaints of discrimination with the board.

Director of Equal Employment Opportunity, National Transportation Safety Board, 800 Independence Ave., SW, Washington, DC 20594, (202) 472-6166.

Additional Files

Following is a list of the remaining files maintained by the NTSB. For information concerning any of these files, contact: Director of Administration, Office of the General Manager, National Transportation Safety Board, 800 Independence Ave., SW, Washington, DC 20594, (202) 472-6111.

Privacy Act Request Records NTSB
Security Records NTSB
Travel Records of Employees NTSB

Nuclear Regulatory Commission

For information about any NRC system of records, write to the following address, identifying the system of interest: Public Affairs, Office of U.S. Nuclear Regulatory Commission, Washington, DC 20555, (301) 492-7715.

EMPLOYEE APPEALS, GRIEVANCES, AND COMPLAINTS RECORDS NRC

Applicants for NRC employment, current and former NRC employees, and annuitants who have filed complaints or initiated grievance or appeal proceedings as a result of a determination made by the NRC, the Civil Service Commission, or a board or other entity established to adjudicate such grievances and appeals.

EQUAL EMPLOYMENT OPPORTUNITY RECORDS FILES NRC

Applicants for NRC employment and current and former NRC employees who have filed a complaint of discrimination with the Office of Equal Employment Opportunity or the Equal Employment Opportunity officer. Pursuant to 5 U.S.C. 552a(k) (5), the commission has exempted portions of this system of records from 5 U.S.C. 552a(c) (3), (d), (e) (1), (e) (4) (G), (H), and (I), and (f). The exemption rule is contained in Section 9.95 of the NRC regulation (10 CFR 9.95).

OFFICE OF INSPECTOR AND AUDIT INDEX FILE AND ASSOCIATED RECORDS NRC

Individuals referred to in potential or actual cases and matters of concern to the Office of Inspector and Auditor and correspondents on subjects directed or referred to the Office of Inspector and Auditor. Pursuant to 5 U.S.C. 552a (k)(1) and (5), the commission has exempted portions of

this system of records from 5 U.S.C. 552a(c)(3), (d), (e) (1), (e) (4) (G), (H), and (I), and (f). The exemption rule is contained in Section 9.95 of the NRC regulation (10 CFR 9.95).

PROTECTION SUPPORT FILES AND ASSOCIATED RECORDS NRC

Persons including present or former NRC employees, NRC consultants, NRC contractors, licensees, other government agency personnel and actual or suspected violators of laws relating to the NRC's activities.

Additional Files

Following is a list of the remaining files maintained by the NRC. Anyone interested in obtaining information from any of these files should contact the Nuclear Regulatory Commission at the address given above.

Advisory Committee on Reactor Safeguards (ACRS) Correspondence Index and Associated Records NRC
Appointment and Promotion Certificate Records NRC
Biographical Information Records NRC
Byproduct Material License Records NRC
Central Personnel Security Clearance Index NRC
Conflict of Interest Files NRC
Contracts Records Files NRC
Development and Advancement for Regulatory Employees (DARE) Records—NRC
Division of Administrative Operations Workload Assignment and Production Records NRC
Division of Technical Review Employee Work Schedule File NRC
Employee Locator Records Files NRC

Facility Operator Licensees Records File
(10 CFR Part 55) NRC
Freedom of Information Act (FOIA) and Privacy Act Requests Records NRC
Government Motor Vehicle Operators License File NRC
Incentive Awards File NRC
Information Security Files and Associated Records NRC
Mailing Lists NRC
Medical Records NRC
National Standards Committee Membership Files NRC
Occupational Injuries and Illness Reports NRC
Official Personnel Training Records Files NRC
Official Travel Records NRC
Payroll Accounting Records NRC

Personnel Performance Appraisals NRC
Personnel Research and Test Validation Records NRC
Personnel Security Files and Associated Records NRC
Photo Badge Request File NRC
Principal Correspondence File NRC
Radiation Exposure Information and Reports System (REIRS) Files NRC
Recruiting, Examining and Placement Records NRC
Regulatory Management System (RMS) Records Files
(Manpower Module Only) NRC
Secretariat Records Facility Files NRC
Source and Special Nuclear Material Administrative
Management Records NRC
Standards Development Greenbook Task File NRC

Occupational Safety and Health Review Commission

For information concerning any file maintained by OSAHRC write to the following address, identifying the file of interest: Chief Judge, OSAHRC, 1825 K St., NW, Washington, DC 20006, (202) 634-7980.

Administrative Law Judge Case Assignments OSAHRC
Administrative Law Judge Case Processing OSAHRC

Applications for Employment OSAHRC
Commission Members Case Processing OSAHRC
Mailing Lists for News Releases, Speeches, Reports OSAHRC
Parties, Correspondence Records OSAHRC
Travel Records OSAHRC

Office of Management and Budget

For information about any OMB system of records, write to the following address, identifying the system of interest: Assistant to the Director for Administration, Office of Management and Budget, Old Executive Office Building, 17th St. & Pennsylvania Ave., NW, Washington, DC 20530, (202) 395-4790.

Library Circulation System
Payroll and Leave Records

Personnel Summary
Private Relief Legislation
Recruiting and Applicant Records
Researcher Request File
Staff Directory Card
Staff Parking Application File
Staff Travel Records
Veterans Education and Training Load Model

Office of the Special Representative for Trade Negotiations

For information on any files maintained by this office, write to the following address, identifying the file of interest: Executive Officer, Office of the Special Representative for Trade Negotiations, 1800 G St., NW, Washington, DC 20506, (202) 395-5123.

Applicants for Employment STR
Correspondence File STR
Payroll Records STR

Overseas Private Investment Corporation

CONDUCT AND DISCIPLINE OPIC

All employees of the corporation against whom disciplinary action has been taken or is being taken, or who have filed a grievance or an appeal in connection with a disciplinary action initiated by the corporation.

Director of Personnel and Administration, Overseas Private Investment Corporation, 1129 20th St., NW, Washington, DC 20527, (202) 632-3858.

SECURITY VIOLATIONS OPIC

Officers and employees of the corporation who have committed a security violation.

Director of Personnel and Administration, Overseas Private Investment Corporation, 1129 20th St., NW, Washington, DC 20527, (202) 632-3858.

Additional Files

Following is a list of the remaining files maintained by OPIC. For information concerning any file, contact:

Corporate Secretary, Overseas Private Investment Corporation, 1129 20th St., NW, Washington, DC 20527, (202) 632-1839.

Applicants (General) OPIC
Applicants (General Counsel) OPIC
Attendance and Leave Records OPIC
Awards OPIC
Biographies of Key Employees and Board Members OPIC
Compensation OPIC
Conflicts of Interest OPIC
Directors (Current) OPIC
Directors (Former) OPIC
Employee Health and Life Insurance OPIC
Employment (Excepted Positions) OPIC
Evaluations OPIC
Photographs OPIC
Placement of Handicapped Individuals OPIC
Position Classification OPIC
Recruitment OPIC
Retirement OPIC
Security and Investigations OPIC
Travel Advances OPIC
Travel Obligations OPIC

Office of Telecommunications Policy

The Office of Telecommunications Policy, at the White House, and the Office of Telecommunication, at the Department of Commerce, were merged in 1978 into the National Telecommunications and Information Administration. The new agency is under the Department of Commerce, although it still serves the White House as well.

For information concerning any files maintained by either agency, write to the following address, identifying the files of interest: Administrator, National Telecommunications and Information Administration, 1800 G St., NW, Washington, DC 20504, (202) 377–1800.

Bioeffects Project Resumes OTP
Congressional Relations System OTP

Contractor Record System OTP
Employee Reports of Financial Interests and
  Employment OTP
General Personnel Records (Official Personnel Folder
  and Records Related Thereto) OTP
Inventory Control of Property OTP
Library Circulation Control Records OTP
Military Personnel System OTP
Payroll/Personnel System OTP
Personnel Applicant Records OTP
Travel Payment System OTP

Panama Canal Company

APPEALS, GRIEVANCES, COMPLAINTS, AND ASSISTANCE RECORDS, PCC-CZG/CZPB-2

Applicants for federal employment and current and former federal employees in the Canal Zone who have appealed a qualification or rating or who have registered complaints or made requests for assistance on any phase of the operations of the board and the central employment office.

Executive Officer, Canal Zone Civilian Personnel Policy Coordinating Board, APO Miami 34011.

ARREST RECORD FILE, PCC-CZG/CAPL-13

All individuals who have been arrested, fingerprinted, photographed for violations of law; persons required to appear in magistrate's court for traffic violations.

Chief, Police Division, APO Miami 34011.

CARDEX FILE—CONTRABAND VIOLATIONS
PCC-CZG/CACU-6

Persons reported to be involved, or suspected of being, involved in activities which are violations of Canal Zone regulations governing the importation, purchase, use, or transfer of goods or services obtained through Canal Zone facilities; including but not limited to unauthorized entry into Canal Zone retail facilities posted against trespassing, transfer of duty-free goods and services into the Republic of Panama without proper Canal Zone customs clearances.

Chief, Customs Division, APO Miami 34011.

CARDEX FILE—SMUGGLING: NARCOTICS:
VIOLATORS OR SUSPECTS AND FUGITIVES,
PCC-CZG/CACU-4

Persons reported to be, or suspected of being, involved in violation of existing laws and statutes pertaining to smuggling, narcotics possession, use, or trafficking; also persons reported to be fugitives from justice.

Chief, Customs Division, APO Miami 34011.

CASE INVESTIGATIONS, PCC-CZG/CAPS-2

Persons involved in, witnesses to, or suspected of activities related to offenses involving narcotics, obscene literature, fraud, prohibited mail matter, rifling of mails, tampering with mailboxes, theft of mail, threatening letters, theft of money orders, theft of postal keys, vandalism of mailboxes, wrong payment of money orders.

Director of Posts, APO Miami 34011.

CASH AUDIT FILES, PCC-CZG/FVGA-1

Panama Canal Company and Canal Zone government collecting agents whose accounts are audited by the General Audit Division.

General Auditor, APO Miami 34011.

CLAIMS FILES, PCC-CZG/FVAK-1

Persons making or filing claims against the Panama Canal Company or the Canal Zone government; and/or persons and companies who are subjects of claims by the Panama Canal Company and/or the Canal Zone government.

Chief, Claims Branch, APO Miami 34011.

COMPLAINTS AGAINST POLICEMEN FILE,
PCC-CZG/CAPL-15

All police personnel about whom written complaints have been submitted by citizens.

Chief, Police Division, APO Miami 34011.

CONVICT FILES, PCC-CZG/CAPL-4

All persons who have been sentenced and have served any length of time in the Canal Zone Penitentiary.

Chief, Police Division, APO Miami 34011.

CUSTOMS FUGITIVE RECORDS, PCC-CZG/CACU-3

Fugitives.

Chief, Customs Division, APO Miami 34011.

DETECTIVE CONFIDENTIAL FILES, PCC-CZG/CAPL-3

Persons who are or have been subjects of police investigations; persons who have made official complaints to the police, who have been reported to the police on official complaints, persons involved in pending criminal investigations, and persons involved in incidents of police interest.

Chief, Police Division, APO Miami 34011.

DRIVER'S LICENSE INVESTIGATORY FILE, PCC-CZG/CALS-7

All persons who have had their Canal Zone license or privilege to operate motor vehicles in the Canal Zone revoked, suspended, or cancelled, or who have a medical problem related to driving.

Chief, License Section, APO Miami 34011.

DRIVER'S LICENSE REVOCATION LISTS, PCC-CZG/CAPL-20

All persons who have had their driving privileges revoked in the Canal Zone.

Chief, Police Division, APO Miami 34011.

EMBEZZLEMENTS, BURGLARIES, AND CASH SHORTAGES, PCC-CZG/FVAC-1

Panama Canal Company and Canal Zone government employees under investigation for embezzlements, burglaries, and cash shortages.

Chief, Agents Accounts Branch, Accounting Division, APO Miami 34011.

EQUAL EMPLOYMENT OPPORTUNITY COUNSELING AND INVESTIGATION FILES PCC-CZG/GVEO-2

Employees and applicants for employment who complain of discrimination based on race, color, sex, age, religion, or national origin.

Director of Equal Employment Opportunity, APO Miami 34011.

FINGERPRINT FILE, PCC-CZG/CAPL-7

All persons having been fingerprinted by, or whose prints have been provided to, the Canal Zone police in the process of authorized law enforcement activities in the Canal Zone.

Chief, Police Division, Box M, APO Miami 34011.

GRIEVANCES AND APPEALS RECORDS, PCC-CZG/PR-4

Current and former employees of the Canal Zone government or the Panama Canal Company who have filed a grievance, appealed a disciplinary action to the agency or an adverse action to the agency or to the Civil Service Commission, or submitted a position classification appeal to the agency or the Canal Zone Board of Appeals.

Personnel Director, Panama Canal Company, APO Miami 34011.

HOUSING COMPLAINTS FILE, PCC-CZG/SC-2

Occupants of Panama Canal Company quarters whose cases have been referred to the Quarters Retention Committee.

Administrative Services Officer, Supply and Community Service Bureau, APO Miami 34011.

IMMIGRATION DETENTION ORDERS, PCC-CZG/CACU-12

Stowaways, deserters, crew members, and passengers in violation of Canal Zone immigration regulations.

Chief, Customs Division, APO Miami 34011.

IMMIGRATION AND NATURALIZATION SERVICE LOOKOUT BOOK, PCC-CZG/CACU-2

Individuals suspected of, involved in, or convicted of various offenses such as drug abuse or smuggling.

Chief, Customs Division, APO Miami 34011.

LAW ENFORCEMENT CASE REPORT FILES, PCC-CZG/CAPL-1

Persons who are or have been subjects of police investigations, including persons who have, or are alleged to have, committed crimes, persons witnessing or reporting criminal activities, missing persons, and persons filing official complaints about the conduct of other persons when such conduct is not a violation of law.

Chief, Police Division, APO Miami 34011.

MASTER NAME FILE, PCC-CZG/CAPL-10

Persons who have been arrested, reported offenses to the police, been involved in an incident coming to the attention of the Canal Zone police, been reported missing, or who have outstanding warrants.

Chief, Police Division, APO Miami 34011.

PENDING DETECTIVE INVESTIGATION RECORDS, PCC-CZG/CAPL-8

Offenders, alleged offenders, witnesses, victims, investigating officers, and informants who are subjects of or involved in cases pending investigation by the detective unit, of the Canal Zone police.

Chief, Police Division, APO Miami 34011.

POLICE HEADQUARTERS CONFIDENTIAL FILE, PCC-CZG/CAPL-2

Persons who are or have been subjects of police investigations, including persons who have or are alleged to have been involved in incidents of police interest, and persons witnessing or reporting activities of interest to the police.

Chief, Police Division, APO Miami 34011.

POLICE PHOTO FILES, PCC-CZG/CAPL-6

All persons who have been arrested, booked, and photographed by the Canal Zone police.

Chief, Police Division, APO Miami 34011.

POOR RISK/DELINQUENT CITATION/WARRANT FILE, PCC-CZG/CAPL-19

All persons who have failed to honor their written promises to appear and pay in court for traffic citations received, and/or are being sought on outstanding warrants.

Chief, Police Division, APO Miami 34011.

PRESENTENCE AND PRE-PAROLE INVESTIGATION REPORTS, PCC-CZG/CAPR-2

All persons convicted of crimes who have been referred to the probation office for investigation.

Probation and Parole Officer, APO Miami 34011.

PRISONER PROPERTY RECORD, PCC-CZG/CAPL-18

Persons whose personal property is held or seized by the police at the time of arrest or incarceration.

Chief, Police Division, APO Miami 34011.

PRISONER RECORDS CARDS, PCC-CZG/CAPL-5

All persons who have been arrested by the Canal Zone police.

Chief, Police Division, APO Miami 34011.

REFUGEE RECORDS, PCC-CZG/SC-4

Persons granted temporary refuge in the Canal Zone because of civil disturbance or natural disaster or because they are seeking political asylum.

Assistant Chief, Community Services Division, APO Miami 34011.

STATE DEPARTMENT VISA LOOKOUT BOOK, PCC-CZG/CACU-1

Aliens subject to investigation or denial of entry into the United States.

Chief, Customs Division, APO Miami 34011.

YOUTH UNIT DRUG ABUSE FILE, PCC-CZG/CAPL-11

All juveniles who have appeared before the Canal Zone Drug Abuse Board.

Chief, Police Division, APO Miami 34011.

YOUTH UNIT NAME INDEX FILE, PCC-CZG/CAPL-12

Juveniles who have been the subjects of Canal Zone police division juvenile reports, arrest reports, missing persons reports, etc.

Chief, Police Division, APO Miami 34011.

Additional Files

Following is a list of the remaining files maintained by the Panama Canal Company. For information concerning any file, contact: Executive Secretary of the Canal Zone, APO Miami 34011.

Accounts Payable Disbursement Records, PCC-CZG/FVAC-8
Accounts Receivable Records, PCC-CZG/FVAC-2
Admeasurer Examination File, PCC-CZG/MRPA-1
Advance Authorizations to Enter the Canal Zone, PCC-CZG/ADRM-2
Applications for Importation, PCC-CZG/CACU-8
Automatic Data Processing and Retrieval Systems, PCC-CZG/FVDP-1
Biographical Data, PCC-CZG/GVPR-1
Biographical Data Cards, PCC-CZG/ISO-5
Biographical Data Files, PCC-CZG/ISO-6
Canal Zone Awards and Service Contracts Control Records, PCC-CZG/FVAC-7
Canal Zone Board of Registration for Architects and Professional Engineers Directory, PCC-CZG/BRAE-2
Canal Zone Board of Registration for Architects and Professional Engineers Reference Files, PCC-CZG/BRAE-1
Canal Zone Immigration Station Admission Records, PCC-CZG/CACU-11
Canal Zone Library Registration Record, PCC-CZG/CALM-1
Canal Zone Vehicle Registration Listings, PCC-CAG/CAPL-17
Card Index System, PCC-CZG/ISO-3
Cardex File—Vehicle Exporters, PCC-CZG/CACU-5
Cash Collection Agents and Subagents, PCC-CZG/FVAC-6
Cash Register Receipt Shortages, PCC-CZG/FVGA-2

Civil and Amateur Radio Operator and Station License Files, PCC-CZG/CALS-4

Civil Defense and Natural Disaster Records, PCC-CZG/EPCD-1

Confidential Sources and Contracts, PCC-CZG/ISO-2

Contractor Employee Payroll Records, PCC-CZG/ECCN-2

Delegation of Authority for Procurement, PCC-CZG/GVAC-5

Disability Relief, Retirement, and Group Supplementary Life Insurance Records, PCC-CZG/PR-1

Employee Application for Outside Employment, PCC-CZG/ADGS-2

Employee Benefits Records, PCC-CZG/PR-2

Employee/Dependent Photo—Identification Card Applications, PCC-CZG/CALS-1

Employees' and Dependents' Travel Orders, PCC-CZG/ADTR-1

Ethyl Alcohol Certificates of Purchase, PCC-CZG/SC-5

Expert and Consultant Records, PCC-CZG/SC-3

Fishing Pass Application File, PCC-CZG/CALS-3

Freedom of Information Act Requests for Records, PCC-CZG/ADRM-4

General Files of the Canal Agencies, PCC-CZG/ADRM-1

Health, Medical, Dental, and Veterinary Records Systems, PCC-CZG/HL-1

Hire-A-Kid Program File, PCC-CZG/GVYA-1

Housing Files, PCC-CZG/SC-1

Hunting Permit Application File, PCC-CZG/CALS-2

Incentive Awards Program Files, PCC-CZG/FVXI-1 Index of Contractor Employees, PCC-CZG/ISO-4

Industrial Accident Prevention Supervisor/Unit Awards File, PCC-CZG/SF-1

Informant Name File, PCC-CZG/CAPL-9

Injury Compensation Payroll Records, PCC-CZG/FVAP-3

Inmate Trust Fund File, PCC-CZG/CAPL-14

Internal Revenue Service Notice of Levy Files, PCC-CZG/FVTR-2

Land License Record, PCC-CZG/CALS-5

Mail Covers, PCC-CZG/CAPS-1

Marine Accident Reference Cards, PCC-CZG/MRTO-1

Marine License Files, PCC-CZG/MRBLI-1

Marriage License Records, PCC-CZG/CALS-9

Medical Administration System—Exempt, PCC-CZG/HL-2

Medical Administration System—Nonexempt, PCC-CZG/HL-3

Merit System Recruiting, Examining, and Placement Records, PCC-CZG/CZPB-1

Minority Group Designator (MGD) Records, PCC-CZG/PR-11

Motor Vehicle and Motorboat Registration and Operator's License Files, PCC-CZG/CALS-8

News Media Representatives, PCC-CZG/IO-2

Office of the Secretary Operating Unit Personnel Files, PCC-CZG/WO-2

Official Permits to Have or Carry Firearms, PCC-CZG/CALS-11

Operating Unit Employment Inquiry Files, PCC-CZG/OPR-2

Operating Unit Personnel Records, PCC-CZG/OPR-1

Panama Canal Company Board of Directors, PCC-CZG/WO-1

Panama Canal Company Board of Directors Biographical and Correspondence Files, PCC-CZG/EPS-1

Payroll Deductions, PCC-CZG/FVAP/AC-4

Payroll Master File for Panama Canal Company and Canal Zone Government Employees, PCC-CZG/FVAP-1

Payroll System for Vessel Employees, PCC-CZG/FVAP-2

Personal Data Records, PCC-CZG/PR-3

Personnel Investigation Records, PCC-CZG/CZPB-3

Personnel Security Files, PCC-CZG/ISO-1

Philatelic Program, PCC-CZG/CAPS-5

Plumbing and Welding License Files, PCC-CZG/ECCN-1

Post Office Boxholder Records, PCC-CZG/CAPS-4

Postal Claims and Inquiries, PCC-CZG/CAPS-6

Privacy Act Requests Records, PCC-CZG/ADRM-3

Probation and Parole Unit Child Custody Reports, PCC-CZG/CAPR-1

Prohibitory Orders Against Sending Pandering Advertisement in the Mails, PCC-CZG/CAPS-3

Protocol Unit Operational Files, PCC-CZG/GVPR-2

Purchase Authority Cards, PCC-CZG/ADGS-1

Quarterly Report of Employee Union Dues Deductions, PCC-CZG/GVLR-1

Recruiting and Placement Records, PCC-CZG/PR-5

Runners, Peddlers, and Solicitors—Application and License Files, PCC-CZG/CALS-10

Seamen's Locator List, PCC-CZG/CACU-7

Statements of Employment and Financial Interest, PCC-CZG/GE-2

Student Record System, PCC-CZG/CASC-1

Suspension of Check-Cashing Privileges Files, PCC-CZG/FVTR-3

Systems of Records Noticed by the U.S. Civil Service Commission and Applicable to the Panama Canal Company and the Canal Zone Government. (General Personnel Records; Retirement, Life Insurance, and Health Benefits Records)

Telephone Exchange Director, PCC-CZG/ECLE-1

Termination of Employment Actions Records, PCC-CZG/FVTR-1

Traffic Accident Reports, PCC-CZG/CAPL-16

Training and Employee Development Records, PCC-CZG/PR-6

Trust Fund Records, PCC-CZG/FVAC-3

20/30/40 Year Safety Key Awards Files, PCC-CZG/SF-2

Unnegotiated Checks Over One Year Old, PCC-CZG/FVAC-9

U.S. Army Element, Canal Zone Government Military Administration System, PCC-CZG/MIL-1

U.S. Government Vehicle Operator's Identification and Material Handling Card Application Files, PCC-CZG/CALS-6

U.S. Immigration and Naturalization Service, U.S. Citizenship Certificate Application and Appointment Records, PCC-CZG/CACU-10

Vehicle Registration for RP-Series License Plates, PCC-CZG/CACU-9

Vessel Employee Records, PCC-CZG/TTWT-1

Visa Records, PCC-CZG/GE-1 (STATE-39)

Vital Installation Access File, PCC-CZG/CACP-1

Pennsylvania Avenue Development Corporation

For information about any PADC system of records, write to the named official at the following address, identifying the system of interest: Pennsylvania Avenue Development Corporation, 425 13th St., NW, Washington, DC 20004.

EQUAL EMPLOYMENT OPPORTUNITY COMPLIANCE AND COMPLAINT FILES, PADC

Individuals filing equal employment opportunity complaints with the corporation.

General Counsel, (202) 566-1078.

General Financial Records PADC
General Personnel Files (Copies of OPF-CSC) PADC
Job Applications PADC
Payroll Records PADC
Time and Attendance Records PADC

Pension Benefit Guaranty Corporation

To obtain information about any PBGC system of records, write to the following address, identifying the system of interest: Director, Office of Communications, Pension Benefit Guaranty Corporation, P.O. Box 7119, Washington, DC 20044, (202) 254-4817.

Correspondence Between PBGC and Persons Outside PBGC, PBGC

Disbursements PBGC
Employee Payroll and Leave and Attendance Records PBGC
Employee Travel Records PBGC
Personnel Records PBGC
Plan Participant and Beneficiary Data PBGC

Postal Rate Commission

OFFICIAL PERSONNEL FILES PRC

Employees.

Chief Administrative Office, 2000 L St., NW, Washington, DC 20268, (202) 254-3880.

Request for information should contain: Individual's name, Social Security account number, date of birth, last agency employed with dates, and return addresses.

Privacy Protection Study Commission

For information concerning any file maintained by the Privacy Protection Study Commission, write to the following address, identifying the file of interest: Public Information Officer, Privacy Protection Study Commission, Suite 424, 2120 L St., NW, Washington, DC 20506, (202) 333-0670.

Commission Member and Staff Personnel Records PPSC
Letters of Contact with the Commission PPSC

President's Commission on White House Fellowships

WHITE HOUSE FELLOWSHIPS RECORDS, PCWHF

Applicants for White House Fellowships, speakers for the White House Fellows education program and spouses of White House Fellows.

Administrative Officer, President's Commission on White House Fellowships, Room 1308, 1900 E St., NW, Washington, DC 20415, (202) 653-6263.

Railroad Retirement Board

DISCLOSURE OF INFORMATION FILES RRB

Railroad employees, railroad retirement annuitants, and other individuals with some creditable railroad employment on whose records a request for information, in the form of a subpoena or otherwise, has been received by the board.

General Counsel, U.S. Railroad Retirement Board, 844 Rush St., Chicago, IL 60611, (312) 751-4935.

FILES ON CONCLUDED LITIGATION RRB

Railroad employees, retired railroad employees, and individuals with some creditable railroad service who are involved in litigation in which the Railroad Retirement Board has some interest as a party or otherwise.

General Counsel, U.S. Railroad Retirement Board, 844 Rush St., Chicago, IL 60611, (312) 751-4935.

NEGOTIATED GRIEVANCE FILE RRB

Railroad Retirement Board employees who have filed a grievance under negotiated grievance procedures.

Director of Personnel, U.S. Railroad Retirement Board, 844 Rush St., Chicago, IL 60611, (312) 751-4570.

Additional Files

Following is a list of the remaining files maintained by this board. For information concerning any files, contact: Chief Executive Officer, U.S. Railroad Retirement Board, 844 Rush St., Chicago, IL 60611, (312) 751-4930.

Appeal Decisions from Initial Denials for Benefits under the Provisions of the Railroad Retirement Act or Railroad Unemployment Insurance Act RRB

Applications for Unemployment Benefits and Placement Service under the Railroad Unemployment Insurance Act RRB

Covered Abandoned Railroads RRB

Current Year Wage Study File RRB

Employee Personnel Management Files RRB

Employee Promotion Evaluation File RRB

Four Percent Wage History of Railroad Workers RRB

Freedom of Information Act Register RRB

Health Insurance and Supplementary Medical Insurance Enrollment and Premium Payment System (MEDICARE) RRB

Legal Opinion Files RRB

Master File of Railroad Employees' Creditable Compensation RRB

Medical Examiner's Index RRB

Medical Records on Railroad Retirement Board Employees RRB

MEDICARE, Part B (Supplementary Medical Insurance) Payment System—Contracted to the Travelers Insurance Company RRB

Microfiche of Estimated Annuity, Total Compensation and Residual Amount File RRB

One Percent Historical File of Railroad Unemployment and Sickness Beneficiaries RRB

Payroll Record System RRB

Protest and Appeals under the Railroad Unemployment Insurance Act RRB

Railroad Employees' Cumulative Gross Earnings Master File RRB

Railroad Employees' Registration File RRB

Railroad Retirement Board—Social Security Administration Financial Interchange System RRB

Railroad Retirement, Survivor, and Pensioner Benefit System RRB

Railroad Retirement Tax Reconciliation System RRB

Railroad Unemployment and Sickness Insurance Benefit System RRB

Research Master Record for Lump Sum and Residual Awards under the Railroad Retirement ACT RRB

Research Master Record for Retired Railroad Employees and Their Dependents RRB

Research Master Record for Survivor Beneficiaries under the Railroad Retirement Act RRB

Social Security Administration Summary Earnings File RRB

Social Security Benefit Vouchering System RRB

Travel and Miscellaneous Voucher Examining System RRB

Unemployment Insurance Record File RRB

Renegotiation Board

PAYROLL AND TIME AND ATTENDANCE RECORDS

Current and former employees of the Renegotiation Board.

Director, Office of Administration, Renegotiation Board, 2000 M St., NW, Washington, DC 20446, (202) 456–6220.

Securities and Exchange Commission

For information about any SEC system of records, write to the following address, identifying the system of interest: Public Reference Section, Securities and Exchange Commission, 1100 L St., NW, Washington, DC 20249, (202) 523-5506.

ADMINISTRATIVE AUDIT SYSTEM SEC

All individuals, companies, or other agencies indebted to or due an indebtedness from the SEC.

ADMINISTRATIVE AND LITIGATION RELEASE SYSTEM SEC

Persons who have been named as respondents of defendants in administrative, civil, or criminal proceedings involving allegations of violations of the federal securities laws or related statutes.

ADMINISTRATIVE PROCEEDINGS SEC

Individual respondents, witnesses, attorneys, and others involved in administrative proceedings instituted by the commission.

ADMINISTRATIVE PROCEEDINGS RECORD CARDS SEC

Persons involved in administrative proceedings instituted by the commission.

APPLICATIONS FOR RELIEF FROM DISQUALIFICATION FILED UNDER THE SECURITIES ACT OF 1933 AND THE COMMISSION'S RULES OF PRACTICE SEC

Attorneys, accountants, and other professionals seeking relief from SEC orders suspending or barring them from appearing or practicing before the SEC, or imposing some other sanction or requirements under the commission's rules of practice and information concerning officers, directors, principal shareholders, promoters, partners, underwriters, and other persons associated with the registrant who are seeking to vacate or modify a disqualification imposed by the commission.

COMPLAINT PROCESSING SYSTEM (CMP) SEC

Members of the public and others making complaints to the commission against broker-dealers and others who are subject to the commission's jurisdiction.

DEPENDENT INDEX SEC

Persons involved in legal actions with the SEC or in which violations of the federal securities laws are alleged.

DIVISION OF CORPORATE REGULATION BANKRUPTCY ACT RECORDS SEC

Attorneys for debtors, trustees, attorneys for trustees, United States district court judges, and United States bankruptcy judges.

DIVISION OF ENFORCEMENT INVESTIGATIVE WORKING FILES SEC

Individuals, corporations, partnerships, and other entities that engage in activities which may involve violations of the federal securities laws or the rules of securities self-regulatory organizations; investors or other individuals who became involved in commission investigations.

DIVISION OF ENFORCEMENT LIAISON WORKING FILES SEC

Persons who have been involved in activities which violated or may have violated federal, state, or foreign laws relating to transactions in securities, the conduct of a securities business or investment advisory activities, and banking or other financial activities.

EQUAL EMPLOYMENT OPPORTUNITY COMPLAINTS SEC

Employees making equal employment opportunity complaints and employees involved in the investigation of such complaints.

GENERAL CORRESPONDENCE FILES SEC

Persons who write to the commission seeking information, registering complaints, or just making known their views.

HEARINGS, PROCEEDINGS AND STUDIES SEC

Persons who testify, submit statements, or otherwise participate in commission hearings or proceedings such as commission rate hearings and hearings held in connection with the Institutional Investor Study.

INVESTIGATIONS AND ACTIONS INDEX SYSTEM SEC

Persons against whom the SEC has authorized an investigation or enforcement action.

INVESTIGATORY FILES SEC

Defendants, respondents, witnesses, and other individuals involved in investigations and enforcement actions instituted by the SEC.

INVESTOR SERVICE COMPLAINT INDEX SEC

Persons registering complaints with the SEC.

LITIGATION FILES (CIVIL AND CRIMINAL) SEC

Individuals involved in civil and criminal actions.

MINUTES REGARDING ACTION TAKEN BY THE COMMISSION SEC

Individuals who are the subject of official action taken by the SEC, including individuals who are named defendants or respondents in civil actions or administrative proceedings brought by the commission.

NAME-RELATIONSHIP INDEX SYSTEM (NRS) SEC

Principals and other individuals listed in filings by corporate issuers of securities; principals and other individuals listed in applications for registrations and amendments thereto filed by broker-dealers and investment advisers; individuals who are required to file ownership reports as corporate insiders; individuals, including defendants, respondents, and

witnesses named in investigations and enforcement actions relating to securities violations; individuals on the organized crime list established by the Department of Justice.

OFFICE OF GENERAL COUNSEL WORK FILES SEC

Persons who are subjects of SEC investigations, persons involved in litigation with the SEC, persons involved in administrative proceedings, persons involved in litigation of interest to the SEC, persons communicating with the SEC, SEC personnel against whom complaints have been lodged by others.

OFFICE OF OPINIONS AND REVIEW WORKING FILES SEC

Individuals who were or are respondents in administrative proceedings instituted by the commission.

SECURITIES VIOLATIONS RECORDS AND BULLETIN SEC

Persons involved in actions for violations of foreign, federal, or state securities laws or the rules of securities self-regulatory organizations.

SUBJECT FILE INDEX SEC

Persons who make general inquiries of the commission or who complain of matters under the commission's jurisdiction.

ATLANTA REGIONAL OFFICE GENERAL INDEX OF FILES SEC

Individuals on whom records are maintained in this system are generally from within the region covered by this office and are from one or more of the following categories: Actual and prospective purchasers and sellers of securities; registered investment advisers and associated persons who have been named in any notice, application, questionnaire, report, or document submitted to the commission or its staff pursuant to the federal securities or bankruptcy laws; persons who were or are actual or prospective subjects of investigation in connection with possible violations of federal securities laws; defendants, respondents, or other parties in administrative, civil, and criminal proceedings involving alleged violations of federal securities laws or involving the application of federal bankruptcy laws; persons who have communicated with the SEC or its staff concerning any person within one or more of the foregoing categories.

ATLANTA REGIONAL OFFICE INVESTIGATIVE FILES SEC

Individuals who are involved in investigations into possible violations of the federal securities laws' including broker-dealers, investment advisers, and investment companies.

BOSTON REGIONAL OFFICE
INVESTIGATION INDEX FILE SEC

Individuals who are subjects of complaints, or investigations or who were witnesses called in connection with investigations.

BOSTON REGIONAL OFFICE
INVESTIGATIVE FILES SEC

Individuals who are involved in investigations into possible violations of the federal securities laws.

CHICAGO REGIONAL OFFICE
INDEX CARDS SEC

Individuals who are associated with registered broker-dealers and investment advisers and individuals who have been named defendants or respondents in administrative, civil, or criminal cases.

CHICAGO REGIONAL OFFICE
INVESTIGATIVE FILES SEC

Individuals who are involved in investigations into possible violations of the federal securities laws.

CLEVELAND BRANCH OFFICE
BROKER-DEALER FILES SEC

Broker-dealers registered with the commission pursuant to the Securities Exchange Act of 1934 and persons associated with such broker-dealers located in Ohio and assigned to the Cleveland branch office for inspection by the Chicago regional office; broker-dealers against whom complaints have been filed or about whom inquiries have been made; open broker-dealer complaint file containing complaints against broker-dealers which are being processed and not yet resolved.

CLEVELAND BRANCH OFFICE
INDEX CARDS SEC

Individuals against whom the commission has taken enforcement action, i.e., civil or administrative, or who were defendants in criminal cases in which the commission has an interest; individuals making complaints or seeking information from the staff; individuals involved in investigations conducted by the staff; individuals about whom information was received from other federal, state, local, or foreign regulatory or law enforcement authorities or securities self-regulatory organizations.

CLEVELAND BRANCH OFFICE
INVESTIGATORY FILES SEC

Individuals who are involved in investigations into possible violations of the federal securities laws, including issuers, broker-dealers, investment advisers, and investment companies.

CLEVELAND BRANCH OFFICE INVESTMENT
ADVISER FILES SEC

Investment advisers registered with the commission pursuant to the Investment Advisers Act of 1940 and persons associated with such investment advisers who are located in Ohio and assigned to the Cleveland branch office for inspection by the Chicago regional office and investment advisers against whom complaints have been filed or of whom inquiries have been made.

DENVER REGIONAL OFFICE INVESTIGATIVE
FILES SEC

Individuals who are involved in investigations into possible violations of the federal securities laws.

DENVER REGIONAL OFFICE AND
SALT LAKE BRANCH OFFICE CROSS REFERENCE
INDEX CARDS SEC

Individuals included in the index who are named in filings made with the Denver regional office under Regulations A and F, and Rule 240 under the Securities Act of 1933; broker-dealer registration statements; individuals who are subjects of investigations and who are connected with subjects of investigations; defendants in litigation files; respondents in administrative proceeding files; informants, investors, and witnesses.

DETROIT BRANCH OFFICE BROKER-DEALER
FILES SEC

Broker-dealers registered with the commission pursuant to the Securities Exchange Act of 1934, located in Michigan and northern Ohio, or elsewhere, assigned to the Detroit branch office for inspection by the Chicago regional office, and persons associated with such broker-dealers, as well as broker-dealers against whom complaints have been filed or of whom inquiries have been made.

DETROIT BRANCH OFFICE INDEX CARDS SEC

Individuals against whom a case has been opened, or who are subjects of an investigation or inquiry not yet formally opened.

DETROIT BRANCH OFFICE INVESTIGATORY
FILES SEC

Individuals who are involved in investigations into possible violations of the federal securities laws, including issuers, broker-dealers, investment advisers, and investment companies.

DETROIT BRANCH OFFICE INVESTMENT
ADVISER FILES SEC

Investment advisers registered with the commission pursuant to the Investment Advisers Act of 1940, located in Michigan and assigned to the Detroit branch office for inspection by the Chicago regional office, and persons associated with such investment advisers and investment advisers against whom complaints have been filed or of whom inquiries have been made.

FORT WORTH REGIONAL OFFICE AND HOUSTON BRANCH OFFICE GENERAL INDICES SEC

Individuals involved in investigations and enforcement actions taken by the SEC and other law enforcement authorities and individuals who are affiliated with issuers filing notifications pursuant to Regulation A under the Securities Act of 1933.

FORT WORTH REGIONAL OFFICE INVESTIGATIVE FILES SEC

Individuals who are involved in investigations into possible violations of the federal securities laws.

LOS ANGELES REGIONAL OFFICE INVESTIGATIVE FILES SEC

Individuals who are involved in investigations into possible violations of the federal securities laws including broker-dealers, investment advisers, and investment companies.

MIAMI BRANCH OFFICE GENERAL INDEX OF FILES SEC

Individuals on whom records are maintained in this system are generally from within the region covered by this office and from one or more of the following categories: Actual and prospective purchasers and sellers of securities; registered investment advisers and associated persons who have been named in any notice, application, questionnaire, report, or other document submitted to the commission or its staff pursuant to the federal securities or bankruptcy laws; persons who were or are actual or prospective subjects of investigation in connection with possible violations of federal securities laws; defendants, respondents, or other parties in administrative, civil, and criminal proceedings involving the application of federal securities laws; persons who have communicated with the SEC or its staff concerning any person within one or more of the foregoing categories.

MIAMI BRANCH OFFICE INVESTIGATIVE FILES SEC

Individuals who are involved in investigations into possible violations of the federal securities laws.

NEW YORK REGIONAL OFFICE INDEX OF COMPLAINTS SEC

Registered broker-dealers and persons associated with such broker-dealers.

NEW YORK REGIONAL OFFICE INVESTIGATIVE FILES SEC

Individuals who are involved in investigations into possible violations of the federal securities laws.

NEW YORK REGIONAL OFFICE MASTER CARD INDEX SEC

Records are maintained on registered broker-dealers and investment advisers and defendants, respondents, and witnesses in enforcement actions; also included is information on persons writing for information to register complaints, or for other purposes.

PHILADELPHIA BRANCH OFFICE INVESTIGATIVE FILES SEC

Individuals who are involved in investigations into possible violations of the federal securities laws.

ST. LOUIS BRANCH OFFICE, INQUIRY, COMPLAINT, AND GENERAL REFERENCE FILES SEC

Individuals who request information from or provide information to this office; individuals complaining about other entities or individuals registered with or otherwise required to comply with the provisions of the federal securities laws; individuals who have been the subject of an enforcement proceeding by the commission, by other federal, foreign, state, or local governmental authorities or securities self-regulatory organizations.

ST. LOUIS BRANCH OFFICE INVESTIGATIVE FILES SEC

Individuals who are involved in investigations into possible violations of the federal securities laws, including broker-dealers, investment advisers, and investment companies.

SALT LAKE CITY BRANCH OFFICE INVESTIGATIVE FILES SEC

Individuals who are involved in investigations into possible violations of the federal securities laws.

SAN FRANCISCO BRANCH OFFICE INVESTIGATIVE FILES SEC

Individuals who are involved in investigations into possible violations of the federal securities laws including but not limited to broker-dealers, investment advisers, investment companies, corporations, officers, and directors.

SEATTLE REGIONAL OFFICE MASTER CARD INDEX AND RELATED REGULATORY, INVESTIGATORY, AND LEGAL FILES SYSTEM (MCI SYSTEM) SEC

Individuals on whom records are maintained in this system are generally from within the region covered by this office and are from one or more of the following categories: Actual and prospective purchasers and sellers of securities; registered investment advisers and associated persons who have been named in any notice, application, questionnaire, report, or other document submitted to the commission or its staff pursuant to the federal securities or bankruptcy laws; persons who were or are actual or prospective subjects of investigation in connection with possible violations of federal securities laws; defendants, respondents or other parties in administrative, civil, and criminal proceedings involving the application of federal securities laws; persons who have communicated with the SEC or its staff concerning any person within one or more of the foregoing categories.

WASHINGTON REGIONAL OFFICE INVESTIGATORY FILES SEC

Persons under investigation or otherwise involved in an investigation as witnesses, informants, or in other capacities.

WASHINGTON REGIONAL OFFICE AND PHILADELPHIA BRANCH OFFICE, ADMINISTRATIVE PROCEEDINGS FILES SEC

Persons who are respondents in administrative proceedings and other persons involved in administrative proceedings including witnesses and attorneys.

WASHINGTON REGIONAL OFFICE AND PHILADELPHIA BRANCH OFFICE LITIGATION FILES SEC

Individuals who are defendants in commission injunctive actions and other persons involved in such proceedings including witnesses and attorneys.

Additional Files

Following is a list of the remaining files maintained by the SEC. Anyone interested in obtaining information from any of these files should contact the Securities and Exchange Commission, 1100 L St., NW, Washington, DC 20249.

Acquistion, Tender Offer, and Solicitation Records Filed under the Securities Exchange Act of 1934 SEC

Administrative Law Judge Assignments and Dispositions of Administrative Proceedings SEC

Applications for Registration/Exemption under the Securities Exchange Act of 1934, Investment Advisers Act of 1940, and Investment Company Act of 1940 SEC

Comments on Commission and Securities Self-Regulatory Organization Rules Changes SEC

Correspondence Files Pertaining to Registered Broker-Dealers SEC

Correspondence Files Pertaining to Registered Investment Companies SEC

Denver Regional Office Regulation A Control Cards SEC

Division of Corporation Finance Branch Working Files SEC

Division of Corporation Finance Index for Filings on Schedule 13D and Filings under Regulations A and B SEC

Division of Enforcement Preliminary Market Surveillance Inquiries SEC

Division of Investment Management Regulation Correspondence and Memoranda Files SEC

Employee Photograph File SEC

Employees Current Card File SEC

Executive/Congressional Personnel Referrals SEC

Freedom of Information Act Requests SEC

Los Angeles Regional Office Broker-Dealer Files SEC

Los Angeles Regional Office Investment Adviser Files SEC

Mailing Address Labels (MAL) SEC

Manpower Reporting System (MPR) SEC

New York Regional Office Regulation A Work File SEC

No-Action and Interpretative Letters SEC

Notification of Exemption from Registration under the Securities Act of 1933, SEC

Office of the Chief Accountant Working Files SEC

Office of Personnel Code of Conduct and Employee Performance Files SEC

Office of Personnel Employee Listings SEC

Office of Personnel Employment and Staffing Files SEC

Office of Personnel Position Classification Files SEC

Office of Personnel Training Files SEC

Office of Public Information Records SEC

Ownership Reports and Insider Trading Transaction Records Filed under the Securities Exchange Act of 1934, Public Utility Holding Company Act of 1935, and Investment Company Act of 1940 SEC

Pay and Leave System SEC

Periodic Reports Filed under the Securities Act of 1933, Securities Exchange Act of 1934, Public Utility Holding Company Act of 1935, Investment Company Act of 1940, and Investment Advisers Act of 1940 SEC

Personnel Security Files SEC

Proposed Sale of Securities Records Filed under the Securities Act of 1933 SEC

Proxy Soliciting Material Filed under the Securities Exchange Act of 1934, Public Utility Holding Company Act of 1935, and Investment Company Act of 1940 SEC

Public Utility Regulation Branch Files SEC

Registration Statements Filed Pursuant to Provisions of the Securities Act of 1933, Securities Exchange Act of 1934, Public Utility Holding Company Act of 1935, and Investment Company Act of 1940 SEC

Rule 2(e) of the Commission's Rules of Practice—Appearing or Practicing before the Commission SEC

San Francisco Branch Office Regulation A Files SEC

SECO Files SEC

Staff Transfer and Promotion Records SEC

Selective Service System

To obtain information about any Selective Service System of records, write to the following address, identifying the system of interest. Address correspondence to the office or official noted in the system description: Director, Selective Service System, 1724 F St., NW, Washington, DC 20435, (202) 724-0424.

GENERAL COUNSEL VIOLATOR RECORDS SSS

Alleged violators of the Military Selective Service Act (50 U.S.C. App. 451 et seq.). Request for information should contain: Individual's name, date of birth, Selective Service number, and mailing address to which the reply should be mailed.

REGISTRANT PROCESSING RECORDS SSS

Registrants of the Selective Service System; nonregistrants of the Selective Service System who presented themselves for registration late, after suspension of registration April 1, 1975, and prior to implementation of annual registration; nonregistrants who entered active service in the armed forces of the United States prior to their requirement to register; nonregistrants who are suspected of violation of the Military Selective Service Act. Individual's local board. The State Director of the individual's residence at the time he or she registered. Request for information should contain: In-dividual's name, Selective Service number or date of birth if Selective Service number is not known, and mailing address to which the reply should be mailed.

VIOLATOR INVENTORY MONITORING SYSTEM (VIMS) SSS

Alleged violators of the Military Selective Service Act (50 U.S.C. App. 451 et seq.) General Counsel. Request for information should contain: Individual's name, date of birth, Selective Service number, and return address.

Additional Files

Following is a list of the remaining files maintained by the SSS. Anyone interested in obtaining information from any of these files should contact the Selective Service System, 1724 F St., NW, Washington, DC 20435.

General Files SSS (a subsidiary of registrant-processing
   records)
Master Pay Record SSS
Reconciliation Service Records SSS
Registrant Information Bank (RIB) Records SSS
Reserve and National Guard Personnel Records SSS
Uncompensated Personnel Records SSS

Small Business Administration

For information about any SBA system of records, contact the appropriate official at the following address: Small Business Administration, 1441 L St., NW, Washington, DC 20416, (202) 653-6600.

EEO COMPLAINT CASES

Employees who have filed a complaint regarding discrimination in employment.

Privacy Act officer.

EEO PRE-COMPLAINT COUNSELING

Employees who have requested counseling regarding discrimination in employment.

Privacy Act officer, regional directors, district directors, and branch managers.

GRIEVANCES AND PERSONNEL PRACTICES APPEALS

Employees who have filed grievances under union grievances procedures or personnel practices appeals procedures.

Privacy Act officer, regional directors, and district directors.

LITIGATION AND CLAIMS FILES

All disaster home loan recipients and other individuals who are parties to lawsuits or claims involving the SBA.

TORT CLAIMS

Government employees and certain other individuals involved in accidents.

Privacy Act officer.

Additional Files

Following is a list of the remaining files maintained by the SBA. Anyone interested in obtaining information from any of these files should contact the Small Business Administration, 1441 L St., NW, Washington, DC 20416.

Accountable Property File
Advisory Council File
Applicant Representative Files
Appraisers List
Auctioneers List
Audit Reports
Automated Personnel History
Bankruptcy Filings in South Carolina
Boards of Survey
Borrower Insurance Files
Career Counseling Files
Chamber of Commerce Members
Collateral
Collection Files
Combined Federal Campaign
Commercial Toll Calls
Completion Certificate Control Lists
Congressional Hearing Files
Delinquent Loans
Designations of Cashiers
Disaster Relief Act Printout
Disbursements
Employee Awards
Employee Biographical Files
Employee Bond Participation Files
Employee Counseling Program
Employee Evaluation and Supervision Files
Employee Identification Card Files
Employee Suggestions
Employment Applications

Exit Interviews
Finance and Investment Career Program
Government Drivers' Licenses and Use of Vehicles
Hurricane Agnes Disaster Files
Inquiries and Correspondence
Legal Work Files on Personnel Problems
Lessees of Federally Owned Land on Rivers in Illinois
Loan Accounting
Loan Activity Reports
Loan Case File
Loan Closings
Loan Master Files
Loans in Liquidation, Charged-Off or Paid-In-Full
Management Assistance Resource Files
Minority Groups
Modifications in Loan Accounting
Non-Career Employees
Notaries Public
Occupational Injuries
Official Travel Files
Outside Employment Files
Payroll Files
Personnel Benefits Files

Personnel Card Index Files
Personnel Organization Roster
Personnel Security Files
Portfolio Reviews
Potential Spanish-Surnamed Applicants
Power of Attorney Files
Problem Loan Work Files
Red Cross Blood Program
Reports on Minority Employment
SCORE Master Files
Security and Investigations Files
Security and Investigations Referrals
Settlement and Compromise
Small Business Person Awards
Standards of Conduct Files
Transfer of Loan Records
UCC Refiling and Financial Statements Due
Union Membership
Unofficial Personnel Files
Upward Mobility Files
Virginia Attorneys
Work Progress Reports

Tennessee Valley Authority

DISCRIMINATION COMPLAINT FILE TVA

Employees or applicants who have received counseling or filed complaints of discrimination based on race, color, religion, sex, national origin, or age.

Director of Equal Employment Opportunity, Tennessee Valley Authority, 315 New Spankle Building, Knoxville, TN 37902, (615) 632-2515.

EMPLOYEE ALLEGED MISCONDUCT INVESTIGATORY FILES TVA

Employees or former employees about whom a complaint of misconduct during employment has been made.

General Counsel, Tennessee Valley Authority, 315 New Spankle Building, Knoxville, TN 37902, (615) 632-2241.

GRIEVANCE RECORDS TVA

Employees and former employees who have formally appealed to TVA for adjustment of their grievances.

Director of Personnel, Tennessee Valley Authority, 315 New Spankle Building, Knoxville, TN 37902, (615) 632-3341.

LAND BETWEEN THE LAKES REGISTER OF LAW VIOLATIONS TVA

Persons cited or arrested for violation of state or federal law at Land Between The Lakes.

Chief, Administrative and Protective Services, Land Between The Lakes, Tennessee Valley Authority, Golden Pond, KY 42231, (615) 632-2734.

Additional Files

Following is a list of the remaining files maintained by the TVA. For information concerning any files contact: Director, Tennessee Valley Authority, 315 New Spankle Building, Knoxville, TN 37902, (615) 632-2531.

Apprentice Training Record System TVA
Consultant and Personal Service Contractor Records TVA
Cooperative Training Program for Construction
    Craftsmen TVA
Demonstration Farm Records TVA
Employee Accident Information System TVA
Employee Accounts Receivable TVA
Employee Statements of Employment and Financial
    Interests TVA
Employee Supplementary Vacancy Announcement
    Records TVA
Employee Travel Advance Records TVA
Employment Applicant File TVA
Land Between The Lakes Register of Hunter
    Applications TVA
Management Appraisal Records TVA
Medical Record System TVA
OEDC Quality Assurance Personnel Records TVA
Payroll Records TVA
Personnel Files TVA
Prospective Condemnation Witness File TVA
Questionnaire—Farms in Vicinity of Proposed Nuclear
    Power Plant TVA
Radiation Dosimetry Personnel Monitoring Records TVA
Reforestation, Erosion Control, and Planation Case
    History Record TVA
Rehabilitation and Career Counseling Records TVA
Retirement System Records TVA
Test Demonstration Farm Records TVA
Wildland Owner Survey Records TVA

United States Arms Control and Disarmament Agency

For information concerning any United States Arms Control and Disarmament Agency system of records, contact the Privacy Officer, U.S. Arms Control and Disarmament Agency, Room 5725, 320 21st St., NW, Washington, DC 20451, (202) 632-0760.

Congressional Information and Attitudes Files ACDA
Document Classifer Data Index ACDA
External Contracts (Other Than Small Purchases) ACDA

Freedom of Information Act Requests ACDA
Official Personnel Records ACDA
Pending Personnel Files ACDA
Privacy Act Requests File ACDA
Security Records ACDA
Statements by Principals During the Strategic Arms Limitation Talks, Mutual Balanced Force Reduction Negotiations, and the Standing Consultative Committee ACDA
Top Secret Document Control File ACDA

Civil Service Commission

APPEALS, GRIEVANCES, AND COMPLAINTS RECORDS CSC

Applicants for federal employment, current and former federal employees, agencies, and annuitants who appeal a determination made by an official of an agency or the Civil Service Commission to the Civil Service Commission, a board established to adjudicate appeals, or an agency.

- Appeal control index card or petitioned case file; Chairman, Appeal Review Board, U.S. Civil Service Commission, 1900 E St., NW, Washington, DC 20415, (202) 632-4480.

- Adverse actions appeal records; Director, Federal Employee Appeals Authority, U.S. Civil Service Commission, 1900 E St., NW, Washington, DC 20415, (202) 245-3063.

- Classification appeals to the commission, performance rating appeals, and complaints records; Director, Bureau of Personnel Management Evaluation, U.S. Civil Service Commission, 1900 E St., NW, Washington, DC 20415, (202) 632-4408.

- Agency adverse action appeals records initiated prior to September 9, 1974, classification appeals in agencies, equal employment opportunity complaint files, and grievances records; personnel officer or designated official, local agency installation.

LITIGATION AND POLITICAL ACTIVITY (HATCH ACT) RECORDS CSC

Persons who file civil actions against the Civil Service Commission and persons covered by the Hatch Act who have had alleged complaints filed against them.

General Counsel, U.S. Civil Service Commission, 1900 E St., NW, Washington, DC 20415, (202) 632-4632.

Additional Files

Following is a list of the remaining files maintained by the CSC. For information concerning any file, contact: Director, Civil Service Commission, 1900 E St., NW, Washington, DC 20415, (202) 566-1212.

Civil Service Retirement Records CSC
Confidential Employment and Financial Interest Statements CSC
Defense Mobilization Emergency Cadre Records CSC
Executive Assignment and Inventory Records CSC
Federal Executive Development Program Records CSC
General Personnel Records CSC
Motor Vehicle Operator and Accident Report Records CSC
Personnel Investigations Records CSC
Personnel Research Test Validation Records CSC
Recruiting, Examining, and Placement Records CSC

United States Information Agency

For information about any USIA system of records, write to the following address, identifying the system of interest: Assistant Director (USIA), Public Information, 1750 Pennsylvania Ave., NW, Washington, DC 20547, (202) 724-9646.

EMPLOYEE RELATIONS FILES IPT/USIA

Employees who have filed informal grievances or appeals on job classification action or position audits; individuals or employees affected by a work force; or element reorganization employees who have requested restoration of forfeited leave; individuals for whom special disciplinary actions are in process.

EQUAL EMPLOYMENT OPPORTUNITY COMPLAINT FILES IEO/USIA

Any aggrieved employee or applicant for employment with USIA who believes he or she has been discriminated against because of race, color, religion, sex, national origin, and/or age, and who has consulted with an equal employment opportunity counselor of the agency or a member of the equal employment opportunity staff about the matter.

LEGAL FILES IGC/USIA

Individuals who have filed grievances or discrimination complaints; employees separated or considered for separation for cause; officers selected out; individuals taking legal action against the agency or its employees; tort claimants and accident victims; employees and related persons for whom legislative action is sought; personal property loss claimants; employees and applicants raising legal issues concerning rights or benefits.

Additional Files

Following is a list of the remaining files maintained by the USIA. For information concerning any file, contact: Assistant Director (USIA), Public Information, 1750 Pennsylvania Ave., NW, Washington, DC 20547, (202) 724-9646.

Americans Residing in Foreign Countries, USIA
Artists and Speakers INA/USIA
Bidders Mailing List Applications IOA/C/USIA
Contract Talent and Employee Recruitment Files IMV/USIA
Contract Talent Vendor Files IBS/USIA
Cultural and Centers Coordination Division Recruitment Files ICS/USIA
Director's Secretariat Staff Files I/USIA
Employee Administrative Files IBS/USIA
Employee Awards, Health Programs, Retirement and Out-Placement Records IPT/USIA
Employee Identification Card and Photograph File IOS/USIA
Employee Merit Promotion File IPT/USIA
Employee Payroll and Retirement System IOA/F/USIA
Employee's Confidential Statement of Employment and Financial Interests IGC/USIA
Employee Training Files IPT/USIA
Equal Employment Opportunity General Files IEO/USIA
Foreign Service Ranking and Promotion Files IPT/USIA
General Counsel's Congressional Correspondence IGC/USIA
Locator Cards IOA/S/USIA
Master Employee Records IPT/USIA
Non-Official Personnel Files USIA
Overseas Personnel Files and Records USIA
Personnel Security and Integrity Record IOS/USIA

Press Service Contributors IPS/USIA
Press Service Photographer File IPS/USIA
Printout of Minority Group Designator (MGD) Data System IEO/USIA
Recruitment, Contractor, and Vendor File IOR/USIA
Recruitment Records IGC/USIA

Recruitment Records IPT/USIA
Senior Officer and Prominent Employee Information Files I/R/USIA
Speaker File IAA/USIA
Speaker File IEA/USIA
Speaker Name Files ICS/USIA

United States International Trade Commission

For information about any USITC system of records, write to the following address, identifying the system of interest: Director, Office of Personnel and Management Systems, U.S. International Trade Commission, 701 E St., NW, Washington, DC 20436, (202) 523-0182.

Budgetary and Payroll-Related Records USITC
Employment and Financial Disclosure Records USITC
Time and Attendance Records USITC

United States Postal Service

All headquarters entries below are at the following address: U.S. Postal Service, 475 L'Enfant Plaza West, SW, Washington, DC 20260.

CONTRACT EMPLOYEE DISCRIMINATION COMPLAINTS/INVESTIGATIONS

Employees of contractors.

APMG, Employee Relations Department, Headquarters, (202) 245-4034.

Request for information should contain: firm employed by, and approximate date of filing complaint.

EQUAL EMPLOYMENT OPPORTUNITY—EEO DISCRIMINATION COMPLAINT INVESTIGATIONS

Current and former employees, applicants for positions within USPS, and third-party complainants.

EEO officers at the region or headquarters level, (202) 245-4712.

Request for information should contain: Complainant name, postal location, region, file number, and year.

FRAUD AND FALSE REPRESENTATION RECORDS— CONSUMER PROTECTION CASE RECORDS

Respondents in proceedings initiated pursuant to 39 U.S.C. subsection 3005; names of attorneys representing parties; assigned postal inspectors; and promoter of scheme.

Assistant General Counsel, Consumer Protection Office, Law Department, Headquarters, (202) 245-4385.

Request for information should contain: Individual's name, name by which respondent in proceeding may have been designated; approximate time period in which proceedings may have been initiated.

FRAUD AND FALSE REPRESENTATION RECORDS—PROHIBITORY ORDER

Persons requesting prohibitory orders, the mailers against whom such orders are issued.

Assistant General Counsel, Consumer Protection Office, Law Department, Headquarters, (202) 245-4385.

INQUIRIES AND COMPLAINTS—CORRESPONDENCE FILES OF THE POSTMASTER GENERAL

Employees and Postal Service customers who have corresponded with the Office of the Postmaster General.

Postmaster General, Headquarters, (202) 245-5225.

INQUIRIES AND COMPLAINTS—GOVERNMENT OFFICIALS' INQUIRY SYSTEM

Miscellaneous grouping of employees, former employees, applicants for employment, contractors, lessors, and customers who have written to nonpostal government officials.

APMG, Government Relations Department, Headquarters.

Request for information should contain: Individual's name, the name of the government official to whom the letter was written, nature of the inquiry, and the approximate date.

INQUIRIES AND COMPLAINTS—INQUIRY FOR LOSS OR RIFLING OF MAIL MATTER

Customers who have lost mail or had their mail rifled.

Request for information should contain: Individual's name and address, the addressee's name and address, date of mailing, place of mailing, and contents.

INQUIRIES AND COMPLAINTS—PATRONS' COMPLAINT RECORDS

Customers who have initiated complaints against the postal service.

Address inquiries to the same facility to which complaint was made.

INSPECTION REQUIREMENTS—INVESTIGATIVE FILE SYSTEM

Persons related to investigations, including subject of investigations, complainants, informants, and witnesses.

Chief Postal Inspector, Headquarters, (202) 245-5445.

INSPECTION REQUIREMENTS—MAIL COVER PROGRAM

Individuals on whom a mail cover has been duly authorized to obtain information in the interest of (1) protecting the national security, (2) locating a fugitive, and (3) obtaining evidence of the commission or attempted commission of a crime which is punishable by imprisonment for a term exceeding one year.

Chief Postal Inspector, Headquarters, (202) 245-5445.

PERSONNEL RECORDS—EMPLOYEE DISCIPLINE, GRIEVANCE, AND APPEALS RECORDS

Nonbargaining unit employees in the Postal Service (PS), Postal Management Salary (PMS), Postal Executive Salary (PES) (except officers) and Fourth-Class Salary (FCS) Schedules, who have completed six months of continuous service in the Postal Service or a minimum of twelve months of combined service, without break of a workday, in positions in the same line of work in the Civil Service and the Postal Service, unless any part of such service was pursuant to a temporary appointment in the competitive service with a definite time limitation.

Field employees must submit a written request to the head of the field installation where the action was initiated. They may also request permission to listen to or record tape recordings of hearings. (This must be done in the presence of a postal official.) They must identify themselves to the satisfaction of officials authorized to approve the request.

TORT CLAIMS—TORT CLAIMS RECORDS

Persons involved in accidents as a result of postal operations or who allege money damages under the provisions of the Federal Tort Claims Act.

Head of facility where claim was filed.

Request for information should contain: Individual's name, data, and place of occurrence.

Additional Files

Following is a list of the remaining files maintained by the Postal Service. For information concerning any file, contact: Postmaster General, U.S. Postal Service, 475 L'Enfant Plaza West, SW, Washington, DC 20260, (202) 245-5225.

Children's Act Contest
Collection and Delivery Records—Address Change and Mail Forwarding Records
Collection and Delivery Records—Boxholder Records
Collection and Delivery Records—Carrier Drive-Out Agreements
Collection and Delivery Records—City Carrier Route Records
Collection and Delivery Records—Delivery of Mail Through Agents
Collection and Delivery Records—Mailbox Irregularities
Collection and Delivery Records—Rural Carrier Routes
Communications (Public Relations)—Biographical Summaries of Management Personnel for Press Release
Communications (Public Relations)—School Mailing Lists
Customer Programs—Memo to Mailers Address File
Customer Programs—Sexually Oriented Advertisements
Employee Bicentennial Awards List
Equal Employment Opportunity—Equal Employment Opportunity Staff Selection Records
Finance Records—Accounts Receivable File Maintenance
Finance Records—Employee Travel Records (Accounts Payable)
Finance Records—Uniform Allowance Program
Freedom of Information Appeals System
Non-Mail Services—Food Coupon Program Records
Non-Mail Services—Passport Application Records
Office Administration—Carpool Coordination/Parking Records System
Office Administration—Marketing Memo
Office Administration—Pre-Paid Pass Program— Massachusetts Bay Transit Authority (MBTA)
Office Administration—Response to General Services Administration (GSA) Basic Order Agreement (BOA) Solicitations
Personal Property Management—Accountable Property Records
Personnel—Personnel Research and Test Validation Records
Personnel Records—Blood Bank Record System
Personnel Records—Contract Employee Assignment Records
Personnel Records—Contractor Employee Fingerprint Records
Personnel Records—Employee Accident Records
Personnel Records—Employee Job Bidding System
Personnel Records—Employee Suggestion Control
Personnel Records—Employment and Financial Interest Records
Personnel Records—General Personnel Folders (Official Personnel Folder and Records Related Thereto)
Personnel Records—Master Minority File Records

Personnel Records–Medical Records
Personnel Records–Performance Awards System Records
Personnel Records–Personnel Investigations Records
Personnel Records–Postmaster Selection Program Records
Personnel Records–Program for Alcoholic Recovery (PAR)
Personnel Records–Safe Driver Award Records
Personnel Records–Skills Bank (Human Resources Records)
Personnel Records–Vehicle Maintenance and Operators
  Records
Personnel–Recruiting, Examining, Training, and
  Placement Records
Philately–Ben Franklin, Stamp Club Sponsors Records
Philately–Elementary School Teacher Records File
Philately–Philatelic Automatic Distribution Service
Postage–Postage Refund Records
Postage–Postal Meter Records

Records and Information Management Records–
  Information Disclosure Accounting Records
  (Freedom of Information Act)
Records and Information Management Records–
  Information Disclosure Accounting Records
  (Privacy Act) (Proposed System)
Records and Information Management Records–
  Privacy Act Appeals System
Special Mail Services–Registered Mail Inquiry for Delivery
  and/or Application for Indemnity, USPS
Special Mail Services–Request for Payment of Postal
  Insurance (Claim) Records
Statistical (Cost) Systems–Automatic Data Processing
  Workload Reporting System Records
Statistical (Cost) Systems–In-Office
  Cost System Records

United States Railway Association

For information about any USRA system of records, write to the following address, identifying the system of interest: Vice President for Administration, U.S. Railway Association, 2111 2nd St., SW, Washington, DC 20595, (202) 755-4052.

Congressional Reference System
Employment Application File
Employment and Financial Interest Records
Library Records System
Payroll
Personnel Records
Railroads in Reorganization Employee Information System

Veterans Administration

CLAIMANT LEGAL PRECEDENT FILES VA

VA claimants whose entitlement to benefits involves legal questions which have been or are to be answered by Office of the General Counsel.

Assistant General Counsel (024), VA Central Office, Washington, DC 20420, (202) 389-2479.

CLAIMANT PRIVATE RELIEF LEGISLATIVE NAME FILES VA

Claimants on behalf of whom private relief bills are introduced or proposed for introduction in Congress.

Assistant General Counsel (024), VA Central Office, Washington, DC 20420, (202) 389-2479.

EMPLOYEE UNFAIR LABOR PRACTICE CHARGES AND COMPLAINTS, NEGOTIATED AGREEMENT GRIEVANCES AND ARBITRATIONS VA

VA employees or labor union representatives who have filed, in the name of the VA employee, unfair labor practice charges or complaints and negotiated agreement grievances.

VA station personnel officer.

Request for information should contain: Individual's name, Social Security account number, and the date and nature of proceeding involved.

EMPLOYEES AND OTHERS ALLEGEDLY INVOLVED IN VIOLATIONS OR IRREGULARITIES CONCERNING LAWS, REGULATIONS, ETC. PERTINENT TO VA, REPORTS OF INVESTIGATIONS, VA

Employees and others who conduct official business with VA.

Director, Investigation and Security Service (071), VA Central Office, Washington, DC 20420, (202) 389-3093.

LITIGANT NAME FILES VA

Individual litigants in cases brought by or against the government and affecting the Veterans Administration.

Assistant General Counsel (024), VA Central Office, Washington, DC 20420, (202) 389-2479.

VETERANS, EMPLOYEES AND CITIZENS HEALTH CARE FACILITY INVESTIGATION RECORDS VA

Veterans, employees, and private citizens who have been injured as a result of accident or assault; veterans who have died as a result of violence or accident, such as suicide, homicide, reaction to anesthesia or drugs, assault, transfusion accident, blood incompatibility, error in treatment, neglect of patient, fire, firearms, explosion, etc.; employees and private citizens who have died as a result of violence or accident; veterans who have left the health care facility without authorization; veterans, employees, and private citizens who have alleged the loss of personal property, funds, or valuables; veterans and private citizens who have alleged abuse by members of the health care facility staff; employees who have alleged discrimination, abuse, or threats of violence by other employees, veterans, and private citizens; veterans, employees, or private citizens who have been involved in the sale of illegal drugs or alcohol within the health care facility; veterans, employees, and private citizens who have been accused of stealing from other individuals or from the VA health care facility; employees who have been accused of improper and unethical conduct; veterans, employees, and private citizens who have willfully or accidentally destroyed or damaged federal property.

Submit a written request or apply in person to the appropriate VA health care facility.

Request for information should contain identification of the incident involved and date of the incident, as well as individual's name and return address.

Additional Files

Following is a list of the remaining files maintained by the VA. For information concerning any file, contact: Director, VA Central Office, 810 Vermont Avenue, Washington, DC 20420, (202) 393-4120.

Accredited Representatives and Claim Agents Records VA

Applicants for Physician, Dentist and Nurse Positions VA

Armed Forces Separations (DD-214) One-Percent Sample VA

Blood Donor File VA

Department of Medicine and Surgery Engineering Employee Management Information Records VA

Employee Health Unit and Dispensary Records VA

Employee Reporting System for Project Administration and Control (Data Processing Centers) VA

Individual Requests for Information from Appellate Records VA

Individuals Submitting Invoices/Vouchers for Payment VA

Individuals Utilized on a Fee Basis (Consultants, Attendees, and Others) or on a Without-Compensation Basis in the Department of Medicine and Surgery, Personnel Records VA

Inpatient Discharge Records VA

Loan Guaranty Program Fee Personnel (Appraisers, Compliance Inspectors, Management Brokers) and Program Participants (Builders, Lenders, Developers, and Real Estate Sales Brokers) Records VA

Management Personnel Inventory VA

Missing Veterans File VA

Motor Vehicle Operator Accident Records VA

Outpatient Staff and Fee Reporting Records VA

Patient and Employee Infectious Disease Records VA

Patient Fee Basis Medical and Pharmacy Records VA

Patient Medical Records VA

Patient Summary Records VA

Patient Treatment File VA

Personnel and Accounting Pay System VA

Personnel Registration Under Controlled Substance Act VA

Physician, Dentist and Supervisory Nurse Professional Standards Board Action File VA

Rejected Applicant for Medical Care Records VA

Representative of National Service Organization Certification Records, VA

Veteran, Fabricator, and Employee Prosthetic Records VA

Veteran, Patient, Employee, and Volunteer Research and Development Project Records VA

Veteran, Survivor, and Dependent Automated Prescription Processing Records VA

Veterans Admitted to VA Hospitals for Care of Cancer During Period 1958 to 1963, Central Cancer Registry, VA

Veterans Appellate Records System VA

Veterans and Armed Forces Personnel U.S. Government In-Force Life Insurance Records VA

Veterans Assistance Discharge System VA

Veterans, Beneficiaries, and Attorneys U.S. Government Insurance Award Records VA

Veterans and Beneficiaries Guardianship Records VA

Veterans and Beneficiary Identification and Records Locator System VA

Veterans Claim Number Registers VA

Veterans (Deceased) Headstone or Marker Records VA

Veterans, Dependents, Beneficiaries and Armed Forces Personnel Education and Rehabilitation Records VA

Veterans, Dependents, and Beneficiaries Compensation and Pension Records VA

Veterans and Dependents Inactive Award Account Records VA

Veterans and Dependents (Living and Deceased) National Cemetery Burial, Headstone, or Marker, and Gravesite Reservation Correspondence and Inquiry File VA

Veterans and Dependents National Cemetery Gravesite Reservation Records VA

Veterans and Dependents National Cemetery Interment Records VA

Veterans First Admitted to VA Hospitals for Care of Spinal Cord Injury in Periods January 1, 1946 to September 30, 1955 and October 1, 1955 to September 30, 1965, Spinal Cord Injury Study File VA

Veterans Index Records VA

Veterans Mortgage Life Insurance VA

Veterans and Other VA Beneficiaries who have Responded to VA Sample Surveys VA

Veteran's Spouse or Dependent Civilian Health and Medical Records VA

Veterans, Spouses, Widows(ers), Armed Forces Personnel, Transferee Owners, and Other Applicants for Home, Condominium, and Mobile Home Loan Records and Paraplegic Grant Applicants Records VA

Volunteer Service Records VA

Water Resources Council

All requests for information concerning the systems of records identified below should be addressed to the Administrative Officer, U.S. Water Resources Council, 2120 L St., NW, Washington, DC 20037, (202) 254-6448.

Confidential Statements of Employment and Financial Interests WRC
General Financial Records, WRC
Payroll Records WRC
U.S. Water Resources Council Mailing Lists WRC

State and Local Governments

State Privacy Laws

If you are concerned about what personal files, if any, a state might have generated on you, you must be aware of one important fact: The Privacy Act of 1974 pertains only to federal agencies and contractors who engage in business with the federal government. Each state determines its own privacy laws, and some states currently have no privacy laws to protect an individual's right of access to state-held files. In states that have no privacy laws, you are given access to your own file at the discretion of the agency involved. Those states with privacy laws still deny access to those files exempted by statute or which contain information that might be detrimental to the "public good."

Most states keep records permanently, although the information may be transferred to microfilm after seven years. There may also be a fee charged for copies of a file or at the time of the request, whether or not copies are made.

You should make your request either in person or in writing and should be prepared to offer some proof of identity. Your request should be made to the state department or agency concerned. If the agency is not known, you may contact the office of the governor in this state for assistance. Those states that have a central agency or commission to process privacy requests are noted in the following alphabetical listing of the states and their major departments.

ALABAMA

Office of the Governor, State Capitol, Montgomery, AL 36130, (205) 832-3511.

For information concerning any files maintained by the state of Alabama, contact the department or agency concerned or the office of the governor at the above address. Alabama has no privacy law; information is released at the discretion of each department.

Major State Departments
Alabama Development Office
Alcoholic Beverage Control Board
Attorney General
Board of Corrections
Department of Agriculture and Industry
Department of Banking
Department of Conservation and Natural Resources
Department of Education
Department of Finance
Department of Highways
Department of Insurance
Department of Mental Health
Department of the Military
Department of Pensions and Security
Department of Public Health
Department of Public Safety
Department of Public Service
Department of Revenue
Secretary of State
State Auditor
State Docks Department
State Treasurer

Request for information should contain: Your name, address, and a description of the file requested.

ALASKA

Office of the Governor, State Capitol, Juneau, AK, 99811, (907) 465-3500.

For information concerning any files maintained by the state of Alaska, contact the department or agency concerned or the office of the governor at the above address.

Major State Departments
Department of Administration

Department of Commerce and Economic Development
Department of Community and Regional Affairs
Department of Education
Department of Environmental Conservation
Department of Fish and Game
Department of Labor
Department of Law
Department of Military Affairs
Department of Natural Resources
Department of Public Safety
Department of Public Works
Department of Revenue
Department of Social Services
Department of Transportation and Public Facilities

Request for information should contain: Your name, address, and a description of the file requested.

ARIZONA

Office of the Governor, State House, Phoenix, AZ 85007, (602) 255-4900.

For information concerning any files maintained by the state of Arizona, contact the department or agency concerned or the office of the governor at the above address.

Major State Departments
Banking Department
Department of Administration
Department of Corrections
Department of Economic Security
Department of Education
Department of Emergency and Military Affairs
Department of Health Service
Department of Law
Department of Public Safety
Department of Revenue
Department of Transportation
Insurance Department
Land Department
Parks Department

Request for information should include: Your name, address, and a description of the file requested.

ARKANSAS

Office of the Governor, State Capitol, Little Rock, AR 72201, (501) 371-2345.

For information concerning any files maintained by the state of Arkansas, contact the department or agency concerned or the office of the governor at the above address.

Major State Departments
Bank Department

Commerce Department
Criminal Justice and Highway Safety
Department of Correction
Department of Economic Development
Department of Energy
Department of Finance and Administration
Department of Higher Education
Department of Human Services
Department of Local Services
Department of Natural and Cultural Heritage
Department of Parks and Tourism
Department of Public Safety
Employment Security Division
Highway and Transportation Commission
Insurance Department
Labor Department
Securities Department
Worker's Compensation Commission

Request for information should include: Your name, address, and a description of the file requested.

CALIFORNIA

Office of the Governor, State Capitol, Sacramento, CA 95814, (916) 445-2843.

For information concerning any files maintained by the state of California, contact: Manager, Office of Information Practices, 801 Capitol Mall, Sacramento, California 95814.

Request for information should contain: Your name, address, department concerned, and a description of the file requested.

COLORADO

Office of the Governor, State Capitol, Denver, CO 80203, (303) 839-2471.

For information concerning any files maintained by the state of Colorado, contact the department or agency concerned or the office of the Governor at the above address.

Major State Departments
Department of Administration
Department of Agriculture
Department of Corrections
Department of Education
Department of Health
Department of Higher Education
Department of Highways
Department of Institutions
Department of Labor and Employment
Department of Law
Department of Local Affairs
Department of Military Affairs
Department of Natural Resources

Department of Personnel
Department of Regulatory Agencies
Department of Revenue
Department of Social Services
Department of State
Department of Treasury
Office of Planning and Budgeting

Request for information should contain: Your name, address, and a description of the file requested.

CONNECTICUT

Office of the Governor, State Capitol, Hartford, CT 06115, (203) 566-4840.

For information concerning any files maintained by the state of Connecticut, contact the department or agency concerned or the office of the governor at the above address.

Major State Departments
Connecticut Board of Education
Department of Administrative Services
Department on Aging
Department of Agriculture
Department of Business Regulation
Department of Children and Youth Services
Department of Consumer Protection
Department of Corrections
Department of Economic Development
Department of Environmental Protection
Department of Health Services
Department of Housing
Department of Human Resources
Department of Income Maintenance
Department of Labor
Department of Mental Health
Department of Mental Retardation
Department of Motor Vehicles
Department of Public Safety
Department of Revenue Services
Department of Transportation
Office of Policy and Management

Request for information should include: Your name, address, and a description of the file requested.

DELAWARE

Office of the Governor, Legislative Hall, Dover, DE 19901, (302) 678-4101.

For information concerning any files maintained by the state of Delaware, contact the department or agency concerned or the office of the governor at the above address.

Major State Departments
Department of Administrative Services

Department of Agriculture
Department of Community Affairs
Department of Corrections
Department of Finance
Department of Health and Social Services
Department of Labor
Department of Natural Resources and Environmental
    Protection
Department of Public Safety
Department of State
Department of Transportation

Request for information should contain: Your name, address, and a description of the file requested.

DISTRICT OF COLUMBIA

Office of the Mayor, District Office, Washington, DC 20004, (202) 727-6319.

For information concerning any files maintained by the District of Columbia, contact the office of the mayor at the above address.

Request for information should include: Your name, address, and a description of the file requested.

FLORIDA

Office of the Governor, State Capitol, Tallahassee, FL 32304, (904) 488-1234.

For information concerning any files maintained by the state of Florida, contact the department or agency concerned or the office of the governor at the above address.

Major State Departments
Department of Administration
Department of Agriculture and Consumer Service
Department of Banking and Finance
Department of Business Regulation
Department of Citrus
Department of Commerce
Department of Community Affairs
Department of Corrections
Department of Education
Department of Environmental Regulation
Department of General Services
Department of Highway Safety and Motor Vehicles
Department of Insurance
Department of Law Enforcement
Department of Natural Resources
Department of Professional and Occupational Regulation
Department of Revenue
Department of Transportation

Request for information should contain: Your name, address, and a description of the file requested.

GEORGIA

Office of the Governor, State Capitol, Atlanta, GA 30334, (404) 656-1776.

For information concerning any files maintained by the state of Georgia, contact the department or agency concerned or the office of the governor at the above address.

Major State Departments
Department of Administrative Service
Department of Agriculture
Department of Audits and Accounts
Department of Banking and Finance
Department of Community Affairs
Department of Defense
Department of Education
Department of Human Resources
Department of Industry and Trade
Department of Labor
Department of Law
Department of Medical Assistance
Department of Natural Resources
Department of Offender Rehabilitation
Department of Public Safety
Department of Revenue
Department of Transportation
Department of Veteran's Service

Request for information should contain: Your name, address, and a description of the file requested.

HAWAII

Office of the Governor, State Capitol, Honolulu, HI 96813, (808) 548-5420.

For information concerning any file maintained by the state of Hawaii, contact the department or agency concerned or the office of the governor at the above address.

Major State Departments
Attorney General
Department of Accounts and General Services
Department of Agriculture
Department of Budget and Finance
Department of Education
Department of Health
Department of the Judiciary
Department of Labor
Department of Land and Natural Resources
Department of Personnel Services
Department of Planning and Economic Development
Department of Regulatory Agencies
Department of Social Services and Housing
Department of Taxation
Department of Transportation

Request for information should contain: Your name, address, and a description of the file requested.

IDAHO

Office of the Governor, State Capitol, Boise, ID 83720, (208) 384-2100.

For information concerning any files maintained by the state of Idaho, contact the department or agency concerned or the office of the governor at the above address.

Major State Departments
Attorney General
Department of Administration
Department of Agriculture
Department of Correction
Department of Employment
Department of Finance
Department of Fish and Game
Department of Health and Welfare
Department of Insurance
Department of Labor and Industrial Services
Department of Land
Department of Law Enforcement
Department of Parks and Recreation
Department of Revenue and Taxation
Department of Transportation
Department of Water Resources
Industrial Commission
Secretary of State
State Treasurer
Superintendent of Public Instruction

Request for information should include: Your name, address, and a description of the file requested.

INDIANA

Office of the Governor, State Capitol, Indianapolis, IN 46204, (317) 232-4567.

For information concerning any files maintained by the state of Indiana, contact the department or agency concerned or the office of the governor at the above address.

Major State Departments
Commission on Tax and Financing Policy
Department of Administration
Department of Commerce
Department of Corrections
Department of Financial Institutions
Department of Mental Health
Department of Natural Resources
Department of Public Welfare
Division of Labor
Economic Development Authority
Employment Security Division
Environmental Management Board
Highway Commission
Insurance Department

Interdepartmental Board for the Coordination of
  Human Services Program
State Board of Education
State Board of Health
State Police Department

Request for information should include: Your name, address, and a description of the file requested.

ILLINOIS

Office of the Governor, State Capitol, Springfield, IL 62706, (217) 782-6830.

For information concerning any files maintained by the state of Illinois, contact the department or agency concerned or the office of the governor at the above address.

Major State Departments
Attorney General
Comptroller
Capitol Development Board
Department of Administrative Services
Department of Agriculture
Department of Children and Family Services
Department of Conservation
Department of Corrections
Department of Insurance
Department of Labor
Department of Mental Health
Department of Military and Naval Affairs
Department of Mines and Minerals
Department of Public Aid
Department of Public Health
Department of Registration and Education
Department of Transportation
Environmental Protection Agency
State Board of Education
State Police

Request for information should contain: Your name, address, and a description of the file requested.

IOWA

Office of the Governor, State Capitol, Des Moines, IA 50319, (515) 281-5211.

For information concerning any files maintained by the state of Iowa, contact the department or agency concerned, or the office of the governor at the above address. A citizens' privacy task force is currently being created.

Major State Departments
Bureau of Labor
Commerce Commission
Commissioner of Insurance
Department of Banking

Department of Environmental Quality
Department of General Services
Department of Health
Department of Job Services
Department of Public Instruction
Department of Public Safety
Department of Revenue
Department of Social Services
Department of Soil Conservation
Department of Transportation
Development Commission
Natural Resources Council
Office for Planning and Programming

Request for information should contain: Your name, address, and a description of the file requested.

KANSAS

Office of the Governor, State Capitol, Topeka, KS 66612, (913) 296-3232.

For information concerning any files maintained by the state of Kansas, contact the department or agency concerned or the office of the governor at the above address.

Major State Departments
Attorney General
Commissioner of Insurance
Department of Administration
Department on Aging
Department of Corrections
Department of Economic Development
Department of Education
Department of Health and Environment
Department of Human Resources
Department of Judicial Administration
Department of Revenue
Department of Social and Rehabilitative Services
Department of Transportation

Request for information should contain: Your name, address, and a description of the file requested.

KENTUCKY

Office of the Governor, State Capitol, Frankfort, KY 40601, (502) 564-2611.

For information concerning any files maintained by the state of Kentucky, contact the department or agency concerned or the office of the governor at the above address.

Major State Departments
Department of Energy
Department of Finance
Department for Human Resources
Department of Justice

Department for Natural Resources and
 Environmental Protection
Department of Transportation
Development Cabinet
Education and the Arts Cabinet
Public Protection and Regulation Cabinet

Request for information should be made to the custodian
of the records for the agency concerned and should contain:
Your name, address, and a description of the file requested.

LOUISIANA

Office of the Governor, State Capitol, P.O. Box 44004,
Baton Rouge, LA 70804, (504) 342-7015.

For information concerning any files maintained by the state
of Louisiana, contact the department or agency concerned
or the office of the governor at the above address.

Major State Departments
Department of Agriculture
Department of Commerce
Department of Corrections
Department of Culture, Recreation, and Tourism
Department of Education
Department of Elections and Registration
Department of Insurance
Department of Justice
Department of Labor
Department of Natural Resources
Department of Public Safety
Department of Public Service
Department of Revenue and Taxation
Department of State Civil Service
Department of Transportation and Development
Department of Urban and Community Affairs
Department of Wildlife and Fisheries
Secretary of State
Secretary of the Treasury

Request for information should contain: Your name, address, and a description of the file requested.

MAINE

Office of the Governor, State House, Augusta, ME 04330,
(207) 289-3531.

For information concerning any files maintained by the state
of Maine, contact the department or agency concerned or
the office of the governor at the above address.

Major State Departments
Department of Agriculture
Department of Business Regulation
Department of Conservation
Department of Defense and Veterans Services

Department of Educational and Cultural Services
Department of Environmental Protection
Department of Finance and Administration
Department of Human Services
Department of Indian Affairs
Department of Inland Fisheries and Wildlife
Department of Marine Resources
Department of Mental Health and Corrections
Department of Public Safety
Department of Transportation
Manpower Affairs

Request for information should contain: Your name, address, and a description of the file requested.

MARYLAND

Office of the Governor, State House, Annapolis, MD 21404,
(301) 269-3591.

For information concerning any files maintained by the state
of Maryland, contact the department or agency concerned
or the office of the governor at the above address.

Major State Departments
Department of Agriculture
Department of Budget and Fiscal Planning
Department of Economic and Community Development
Department of General Services
Department of Health and Mental Hygiene
Department of Human Resources
Department of Licensing and Regulation
Department of Natural Resources
Department of Personnel
Department of Public Safety and Correctional Services
Department of State Planning
Department of Transportation

Request for information should include: Your name, address, and a description of the file requested.

MASSACHUSETTS

Office of the Governor, State House, Boston, MA 02133,
(617) 727-3600.

For information concerning any files maintained by the state
of Massachusetts, contact: The Division of Public Records,
Office of the Secretary of State, One Ashburton Place, Room
1703, Boston, MA 02128.

Request for information should contain: Your name, address, department concerned, and a description of the file
requested.

MICHIGAN

Office of the Governor, State Capitol, Lansing, MI 48903,
(517) 373-3400.

For information concerning any files maintained by the state of Michigan, contact the department or agency concerned or the office of the governor at the above address.

Major State Departments
Attorney General
Department of Agriculture
Department of Civil Rights
Department of Commerce
Department of Corrections
Department of Labor
Department of Licensing and Regulation
Department of Management and Budget
Department of Mental Health
Department of Military Affairs
Department of Natural Resources
Department of Social Services
Department of State
Department of Transportation
Department of State Police
Department of the Treasury

Request for information should contain: Your name, address, and a description of the file requested.

MINNESOTA

Office of the Governor, State Capitol, St. Paul, MN 55155, (612) 296-3391.

For information concerning any files maintained by the state of Minnesota, contact the department or agency concerned or the office of the governor at the above address.

Major State Departments
Attorney General
Department of Administration
Department of Agriculture
Department of Cable Communications
Department of Commerce
Department of Correctional Security
Department of Economic Development
Department of Education
Department of Energy
Department of Health
Department of Housing Finance
Department of Human Rights
Department of Human Services
Department of Labor and Industry
Department of Natural Resources
Department of Personnel
Department of Pollution Control
Department of Public Safety
Department of Public Service
Department of Public Welfare
Department of Revenue
Department of State Planning
Department of Transportation

Department of Vocational Technical Education
Secretary of State

Request for information should contain: Your name, address, and a description of the file requested.

MISSISSIPPI

Office of the Governor, State Capitol, Jackson, MS 39205, (601) 354-7575.

For information concerning any files maintained by the state of Mississippi, contact the department or agency concerned or the office of the governor at the above address.

Major State Departments
Attorney General
Department of Corrections
Department of Education
Department of Health
Department of Insurance
Department of Public Safety
Department of Workman's Compensation
Employment Security Commission
Tax Commission

Request for information should include: Your name, address, and a description of the file requested.

MONTANA

Office of the Governor, State Capitol, Helena, MT 59601, (406) 449-3111.

For information concerning any files maintained by the state of Montana, contact the department or agency concerned or the office of the governor at the above address.

Major State Agencies
Department of Administration
Department of Agriculture
Department of Business Regulation
Department of Community Affairs
Department of Education
Department of Fish, Wildlife, and Parks
Department of Health and Environmental Services
Department of Highways
Department of Institutions
Department of Justice
Department of Labor and Industry
Department of Livestock
Department of Military Affairs
Department of Natural Resources and Conservation
Department of Professional and Occupational Licensing
Department of Public Service Regulations
Department of Revenue
Department of Social and Rehabilitative Services
Department of State Lands

Request for information should contain: Your name, address, and a description of the file requested.

MISSOURI

Office of the Governor, State Capitol, Jefferson City, MO 65101, (314) 751-3222.

For information concerning any files maintained by the state of Missouri, contact the department or agency concerned or the office of the governor at the above address.

Major State Departments
Department of Agriculture
Department of Conservation
Department of Consumer Affairs
Department Elementary and Secondary Education
Department of Higher Education
Department of Highways
Department of Labor and Industrial Relations
Department of Mental Health
Department of Natural Resources
Department of Public Safety
Department of Revenue
Department of Social Services
Department of Transport
Office of Administration

Request for information should be addressed to the Custodian of Documents and should contain: Your name, address, and a description of the file requested.

NEBRASKA

Office of the Governor, State Capitol, Lincoln, NE 68509, (402) 471-2244.

For information concerning any files maintained by the state of Nebraska, contact the department or agency concerned or the office of the governor at the above address.

Major State Departments
Attorney General
Auditor
Department of Administrative Services
Department of Agriculture
Department of Banking and Finance
Department of Correctional Services
Department of Economic Development
Department of Health
Department of Institutions
Department of Insurance
Department of Labor
Department of Motor Vehicles
Department of Public Welfare
Department of Roads
Department of Water Resources
Secretary of State

Secretary of the Treasury
State Board of Education

Request for information should contain: Your name, address, and a description of the file requested.

NEVADA

Office of the Governor, State Capitol, Carson City, NV 89710, (702) 885-5670.

For information concerning any files maintained by the state of Nevada, contact the department or agency concerned or the office of the governor at the above address.

Major State Departments
Adjutant General
Attorney General
Comptroller
Department of Administration
Department of Agriculture
Department of Civil Defense
Department of Colorado River Resources
Department of Commerce
Department of Community Services
Department of Comprehensive Employment and Training
Department of Conservation
Department of Economic Development
Department of Education
Department of Employment Security
Department of Energy
Department of Finance
Department of General Services
Department of Human Resources
Department of Law Enforcement Assistance
Department of Water and Natural Resources

Request for information should contain: Your name, address and a description of the file requested.

NEW HAMPSHIRE

Office of the Governor, State House, Concord, NH 03301, (603) 271-2121.

For information concerning any files maintained by the state of New Hampshire, contact the department or agency concerned or the office of the governor at the above address.

Major State Departments
Attorney General
Commissioner of Public Works and Highways
Department of Administration and Control
Department of Agriculture
Department of Education
Department of Employment Security
Department of Health and Welfare
Department of Labor

Department of Resources and Economic Development
Department of Revenue Administration
Department of Safety
Insurance Department

Request for information should contain: Your name, address, and a description of the file requested.

NEW JERSEY

Office of the Governor, State House, Trenton, NJ 08625, (609) 292-6000.

For information concerning any files maintained by the state of New Jersey, contact the department or agency concerned or the office of the governor at the above address.

Major State Departments
Department of Agriculture
Department of Banking
Department of Civil Service
Department of Community Affairs
Department of Corrections
Department of Education
Department of Environmental Protection
Department of Health
Department of Higher Education
Department of Human Service
Department of Insurance
Department of the Judiciary
Department of Labor and Industry
Department of Law and Public Safety
Department of the Public Advocate
Department of Transportation

Request for information should contain: Your name, address, and a description of the file requested.

NEW MEXICO

Office of the Governor, State Capitol, Santa Fe, NM 87503, (505) 827-2221.

For information concerning any files maintained by the state of New Mexico, contact the department or agency concerned or the office of the governor at the above address. New Mexico has no privacy law; information is released at the discretion of each department.

Major State Departments
Attorney General
Department of Agriculture
Department of Commerce and Industry
Department of Criminal Justice
Department of Finance and Administration
Department of Health and Environment
Department of Highways
Department of Human Services

Department of Natural Resources
Department of Taxation and Revenue
Department of Transportation
Secretary of State

Request for information should contain: Your name, address, and a description of the file requested.

NEW YORK

Office of the Governor, State Capitol, Albany, NY 12224, (518) 474-8390.

For information concerning any file maintained by the state of New York, contact the department or agency concerned or the Committee on Public Access to Records, Department of State, Albany, NY 12231.

Major State Departments
Banking Department
Department of Agriculture and Markets
Department of Audit and Control
Department of Civil Service
Department of Commerce
Department of Correctional Services
Department of Environmental Conservation
Department of Health
Department of Labor
Department of Law
Department of Mental Hygiene
Department of Motor Vehicles
Department of Social Services
Department of State
Department of Taxation and Finance
Department of Transportation
Education Department
Insurance Department

Request for information should contain: Your name, address, and a description of the file requested.

NORTH CAROLINA

Office of the Governor, State Capitol, Raleigh, NC 27611, (919) 733-5811.

For information concerning any files maintained by the state of North Carolina, contact the department or agency concerned or the office of the governor at the above address.

Major State Departments
Department of Administration
Department of Agriculture
Department of Commerce
Department of Corrections
Department of Crime Control and Public Safety
Department of Cultural Resources
Department of Education

Department of Human Resources
Department of Insurance
Department of Justice
Department of Labor
Department of Natural Resources and
    Community Development
Department of Transportation
Secretary of State
State Treasurer

Request for information should contain: Your name, address, and a description of the file requested.

NORTH DAKOTA

Office of the Governor, State Capitol, Bismarck, ND 58505, (701) 224-2200.

For information concerning any files maintained by the state of North Dakota, contact the department or agency concerned or the office of the governor at the above address.

Major State Departments
Attorney General
Department of Accounts and Purchases
Department of Agriculture
Department of Banking and Financial Institutions
Department of Business and Industrial Development
Department of Game and Fish
Department of Health
Department of Highways
Department of Insurance
Department of Labor
Department of Land
Department of Motor Vehicles
Department of Public Instruction
Department of Vocational Education
Tax Department
Workers' Compensation Bureau

Request for information should contain: Your name, address, and a description of the files requested.

OHIO

Office of the Governor, State House, Columbus, OH 43215, (614) 466-3526.

For information concerning any files maintained by the state of Ohio, contact the department or agency concerned or the office of the governor at the above address.

Major State Departments
Adjutant General
Board of Tax Appeals
Bureau of Employment Service
Bureau of Motor Vehicles
Commission on Aging

Department of Agriculture
Department of Commerce
Department of Economic and Community Development
Department of Energy
Department of Health
Department of Highway Safety
Department of Industrial Relations
Department of Insurance
Department of Mental Health and Mental Retardation
Department of Natural Resources
Department of Personnel
Department of Rehabilitation and Corrections
Department of Taxation
Department of Transportation
Department of Welfare
Department of Worker's Compensation
Environmental Protection Authority
Highway Patrol
Industrial Commission
Office of Budget and Management
Youth Commission

Request for information should include: Your name, address, and a description of the file requested.

OKLAHOMA

Office of the Governor, State Capitol, Oklahoma City, OK 73105, (405) 521-2342.

For information concerning any files maintained by the state of Oklahoma, contact the department or agency concerned or the office of the governor at the above address.

Major State Departments
Attorney General
Department of Agriculture
Department of Corrections
Department of Education
Department of Energy
Department of Health
Department of Industrial Development
Department of Labor
Department of Taxation
Department of Tourism
Department of Transportation
Department of Welfare

Request for information should contain: Your name, address, and a description of the file requested.

OREGON

Office of the Governor, State Capitol, Salem, OR 97310, (503) 378-3100.

For information concerning any files maintained by the state of Oregon, contact the department or agency concerned or the office of the governor at the above address.

Major State Departments
Administration and Support Services
Bureau of Labor
Department of Commerce
Department of Education
Department of Human Resources
Department of Justice
Department of Revenue
Department of State
Department of Veteran's Affairs
Environment and Natural Resource Program
Public Safety Program
Secretary of State
Transportation Program
Treasurer of State

Request for information should include: Your name, address, and a description of the file requested.

PENNSYLVANIA

Office of the Governor, State Capitol, Harrisburg, PA 17120, (717) 787-2500.

For information concerning any file maintained by the state of Pennsylvania, contact the department or agency concerned or the office of the governor at the above address.

Major State Departments
Adjutant General
Attorney General
Department on Aging
Department of Agriculture
Department of Banking
Department of Budget Administration
Department of Commerce
Department of Community Affairs
Department of Education
Department of Environmental Resources
Department of General Services
Department of Health
Department of Insurance
Department of Labor and Industry
Department of Public Welfare
Department of Revenue
Department of Transportation
State Police

Request for information should be made to the records access officer of the agency concerned and should contain: Your name, address, and a description of the file requested.

RHODE ISLAND

Office of the Governor, State House, Providence, RI 02903, (401) 277-2397.

For information concerning any files maintained by the state of Rhode Island, contact the department or agency concerned or the office of the governor at the above address.

Major State Departments
Department of Administration
Department of Business Regulation
Department of Children and Families
Department of Community Affairs
Department of Corrections
Department of Economic Developments
Department of Elderly Affairs
Department of Employment Security
Department of Environmental Management
Department of Labor
Department of Mental Health, Retardation, and Hospitals
Department of Social and Rehabilitative Services

Request for information should contain: Your name, address, and a descripton of the file requested.

SOUTH CAROLINA

Office of the Governor, State House, Columbia, SC 29211, (803) 758-3261.

For information concerning any files maintained by the state of South Carolina, contact the department or agency concerned or the office of the governor.

Major State Departments
Attorney General
Commission on Human Affairs
Court Administration
Department of Agriculture
Department of Consumer Affairs
Department of Corrections
Department of Education
Department of Health and Environmental Control
Department of Labor
Department of Mental Health
Department of Mental Retardation
Department of Social Services
Department of Veterans' Affairs
Department of Youth Services
Division of General Services
Division of Law Enforcement
Employment Security Commission
Energy Management Office
Highway Department
Insurance Department
Secretary of State
Tax Commission
Vocational Rehabilitation Department

Request for information should contain: Your name, address, and a description of the files requested.

SOUTH DAKOTA

Office of the Governor, State Capitol, Pierre, SD 57501, (605) 773-3212.

For information concerning any files maintained by the state of South Dakota, contact the department or agency concerned or the office of the governor at the above address.

Major State Departments
Attorney General
Bureau of Administration
Bureau of Finance and Management
Department of Agriculture
Department of Commerce
Department of Economic and Tourism Development
Department of Educational and Cultural Affairs
Department of Environmental Protection
Department of Game, Fish and Parks
Department of Health
Department of Labor
Department of Military and Veterans Affairs
Department of Public Safety
Department of Revenue
Department of School and Public Lands
Department of Social Services
Department of Transportation
Department of Vocational Rehabilitation
Department of Motor Vehicles
Department of Transportation
Department of Wildlife
Equal Rights Commission
Gaming Control Commission
Indian Affairs Commission
Industrial Commission
Planning Coordinator
Public Service Commission
Secretary of State
Treasurer

Request for information should include: Your name, address, and a description of the file requested.

TENNESSEE

Office of the Governor, State Capitol, Nashville, TN 37219, (615) 741-2001.

For information concerning any files maintained by the state of Tennessee, contact the department or agency concerned or the office of the governor at the above address.

Major State Departments
Department of Agriculture
Department of Banking
Department of Conservation
Department of Corrections
Department of Economic and Community Development

Department of Education
Department of Employment Security
Department of Finance and Administration
Department of General Services
Department of Human Services
Department of Insurance
Department of Labor
Department of Mental Health and Mental Retardation
Department of the Military
Department of Personnel
Department of Public Health
Department of Revenue
Department of Safety
Department of Transportation
Department of Tourist Development
Department of Veterans' Affairs
Department of Urban and Federal Affairs

Request for information should include: Your name, address, and a description of the file requested.

TEXAS

Office of the Governor, State Capitol, Austin, TX 78771, (512) 475-4101.

For information concerning any files maintained by the state of Texas, contact the department or agency concerned or the office of the governor at the above address.

Major State Departments
Attorney General
Board of Control
Comptroller of Public Accounts
Department of Agriculture
General Land Office
Parks and Wildlife Department
Secretary of State
State Board of Insurance
State Department of Highways and Public Transportation
Texas Department of Community Affairs
Texas Department of Human Resources

Request for information should contain: Your name, address, and a description of the file requested.

UTAH

Office of the Governor, State Capitol, Salt Lake City, UT 84114, (801) 533-5231.

For information concerning any files maintained by the state of Utah, contact: Utah State Archivist and Records Administrator, State Capitol, Salt Lake City, UT 84114.

Request for information should contain: Your name, address, department concerned, and a description of the file requested.

VERMONT

Office of the Governor, State House, Montpelier, VT 05602, (802) 828-3333.

For information concerning any files maintained by the state of Vermont, contact the department or agency concerned or the office of the governor at the above address.

Major State Departments
Attorney General
Department of Agriculture
Department of Banking and Insurance
Department of Budget and Management
Department of Corrections
Department of Economic Development
Department of Education
Department of Fish and Game
Department of Finance
Department of Forests and Parks
Department of Health
Department of Highways
Department of Housing and Community Affairs
Department of Labor and Industry
Department of Mental Health
Department of Motor Vehicles
Department of Personnel
Department of Public Safety
Department of Public Service

Request for information should include: Your name, address, and a description of the file requested.

VIRGINIA

Office of the Governor, State Capitol, Richmond, VA 23219, (804) 786-2211.

For information concerning any files maintained by the state of Virginia, contact the department or agency concerned or the office of the governor at the above address.

Major State Departments
Department of Administration
Department of Commerce
Department of Education
Department of Health and Welfare
Department of Natural Resources
Department of Public Safety
Department of Transportation and Highways

Request for information should contain: Your name, address, and a description of the file requested.

WASHINGTON

Office of the Governor, State Capitol, Olympia, WA 98504, (206) 753-6780.

For information concerning any files maintained by the state of Washington, contact the department or agency concerned or the office of the governor at the above address.

Major State Departments
Department of Agriculture
Department of Commerce and Economic Development
Department of Ecology
Department of Emergency Services
Department of Employment Security
Department of Fisheries
Department of General Administration
Department of Labor and Industry
Department of Motor Vehicles
Department of Natural Resources
Department of Personnel
Department of Programs, Planning, and Fiscal Management
Department of Revenue
Department of Social Services
Military Department
Planning and Community Affairs Agency
State Patrol

Request for information should contain: Your name, address, and a description of the file requested.

WEST VIRGINIA

Office of the Governor, State Capitol, Charleston, WV 25305, (304) 348-2000.

For information concerning any files maintained by the state of West Virginia, contact the department or agency concerned or the office of the governor at the above address.

Major State Departments
Attorney General
Commission on Mental Retardation
Department of Agriculture
Department of Banking
Department of Corrections
Department of Education
Department of Employment Security
Department of Health
Department of Highways
Department of Mines
Department of Motor Vehicles
Department of Natural Resources
Department of Public Safety
Department of Rehabilitation
Department of Social Welfare
Department of Welfare
Economic and Community Development
Finance and Administration
Military Department
Tax Department
Treasury Department

Request for information should contain: Your name, address, and a description of the file requested.

WISCONSIN

Office of the Governor, State Capitol, Madison, WI 53702, (608) 226-1212.

For information concerning any files maintained by the state of Wisconsin, contact the department or agency concerned or the office of the governor at the above address.

Major State Departments
Department of Administration
Department of Agriculture, Trade, and
    Consumer Protection
Department of Business Development
Department of Employment Relations
Department of Health and Social Services
Department of Industry, Labor, and Human Relations
Department of Justice
Department of Local Affairs and Development
Department of Military Affairs
Department of Natural Resources
Department of Public Instruction
Department of Regulations and Licensing
Department of Revenue
Department of Transportation
Department of Veteran's Affairs
Public Service Commission

Request for information should contain: Your name, address, and a description of the file requested.

WYOMING

Office of the Governor, State Capitol, Cheyenne, WY 82002, (307) 777-7434.

For information concerning any files maintained by the state of Wyoming, contact the department or agency concerned or the office of the governor at the above address.

Major State Departments
Attorney General
Board of Charities and Reform
Department of Administration and Physical Control
Department of Agriculture
Department of Education
Department of Environmental Quality
Department of Health and Social Services
Department of Highways
Department of Occupational Health and Safety
Department of Public Service
Department of Revenue and Taxation
Department of Workman's Compensation
Employment Security Commission
Game and Fish Commission
State Auditor
State Examiner

Request for information should contain: Your name, address, and a description of the file requested.

Local Governments

For information concerning files maintained by local governments, you should contact the section of government which you feel may have information about you. Whether such information is released depends on existing local and state laws.

Requests for information may be in writing or in person and should contain: Individual's name, address, proof of identity, and a description of the file requested.

Consumers and Privacy

Consumer Policy

As a consumer you must be aware that there are few laws to protect your privacy in the marketplace. *Federal and state privacy laws cover only those businesses with which the government contracts; these businesses must use the same standards for recordkeeping as does the federal government or the state government involved.* There are federal laws to protect the privacy of the consumer in the areas of credit and credit bureaus and in educational recordkeeping. But for the most part, the private sector is its own watchdog and the consumer is at the mercy of the industry.

Credit Bureaus

The Fair Credit Reporting Act of 1971 guarantees certain consumer rights in the reporting of credit information about consumers to credit grantors. You are guaranteed the right of access to all information in your credit file and the sources of information. You must also be told the names of those who have received employment reports within the past two years and the names of all others who have received credit reports about you within the past six months.

You have the right to make corrections in your file or at least to make a written statement contradicting information in your file. Adverse information in all files is purged after seven years or after the expiration of the statute of limitations, except in the case of bankruptcies, which remain in the file for ten years.

Other than you, only businesses or individuals with legitimate business needs may obtain a credit report. Only those governmental agencies that propose to extend credit or a license to a consumer may have access to the consumer's credit report.

Credit Report

Credit reports are released to individuals, business firms which have a contract with the credit bureau, credit-granting governmental agencies, and others by your permission.

For a credit bureau record, contact the nearest credit bureau.

Your request should be in writing (the credit bureau may require that a specific form be filled out) and should contain: your name, address, and Social Security number. Note: After the form is filed, information may either be mailed to you or released to you over the telephone.

Educational Reports

Students are protected by the Buckley Amendment of 1974 (officially termed the Educational Rights and Privacy Act). This law guarantees students and their parents the right of access to school records.

Students must grant permission for other educational institutions, possible employers, or governmental agencies to gain access to their files. One result of the Buckley Amendment has been to reduce the validity of recommendations and evaluations by professors and teachers who fear lawsuits based upon their remarks. So in order to encourage honesty in recommendations, you may voluntarily seal portions of your student files to your own access. Having once waived this right of access to a certain portion of your file, you may not change your mind to try to see any past records, but you may remove the waiver on future records.

PUBLIC AND PRIVATE ELEMENTARY AND SECONDARY SCHOOL RECORDS

Records are released to student, parents, guardians, others (by permission of student) and some governmental agencies.

Your request for information should be in writing and should contain: Student's name, address, and if not currently a student, dates of attendance.

RECORDS OF PUBLIC AND PRIVATE INSTITUTIONS OF HIGHER EDUCATION

Records are released to student, parents or guardian of dependent children, others (by permission of student) and some governmental agencies.

Your request for information should be in writing and should contain: Student's name, address, and, if not currently a student, dates of attendance.

Insurance Records

Insurance records are covered by the Fair Credit Reporting Act of 1971. Insurance companies make use of credit information available from credit bureaus, when considering applications for coverage.

In the case of life or health insurance, you must grant permission for your doctor to release medical records to your insurance company. Once that information is released, however, it may end up in the computer of the Medical Information Bureau (MIB), where it is available to the subscribers of that company.

You have the right to see your file which is maintained at MIB, but you should be aware that at least some of the errors could be a result of information supplied by your physician. The files at MIB are automatically purged of information which is seven years old.

In the case of automobile insurance, most insurance companies rely on the state's department of motor vehicles for information or an individual's driving record. In turn, the insurance companies may report claims to the department of motor vehicles so that the information may be added to your file. In this case, you might do well to request a copy of your motor vehicle record before you contact your insurance company.

Homeowners insurance relies on the word of the consumer; there is no central pool for information on individuals who have or want homeowners insurance. The insurance company may or may not request the names of previous insurors, but the insurance company may check your general credit rating. If you are denied insurance of any kind, you must be told the reason for denial and the names and addresses of any companies or individuals who provided negative information.

LIFE AND HEALTH INSURANCE

Records are released to you, other insurance companies that subscribe to the Medical Information Bureau if your insurance company is also a subscriber, and others by your permission.

Your request for information should be either in writing to the company involved, or to MIB, 35 Mason St., Greenwich, CT 06830. Request should contain: Your name, address, and insurance company involved.

AUTOMOBILE INSURANCE

Records are released to you and, in most states, anyone else who pays the fee for a copy of your motor vehicle record.

Your request for information should be made to the company involved or the state motor vehicle agency.

HOMEOWNERS INSURANCE

Records are released to you and others by your permission.

Your request for information should be made to the local insurance agent or company involved.

Medical Records

Of all records, medical records and the individual's right of access to them have the least uniformity. The courts have ruled that medical records are the private property of the physician; however, you have the right to some of the information in your file, especially information concerning an ongoing illness and the treatment of that illness. Physicians and hospitals may not refuse to release information for the sole purpose of avoiding a malpractice suit.

You may request that your files be released to you, to another doctor or hospital, or to an insurance company. Most doctors and hospitals require that the request be in writing. Some doctors and hospitals may be reluctant to release a file directly to you, fearing you might not understand the technical nature of the information involved. Mental health institutions and psychiatrists and psychologists, in particular, may refuse access to you but will transfer your records to another hospital or psychiatrist. Because of the confidentiality of the doctor-patient relationship, the courts are denied access to medical records except in cases specified by law or in cases where access is "for the public welfare."

Medical records are kept permanently by physicians and hospitals, but they may be microfilmed to reduce the file space needed. Hospitals may charge a fee for reproducing a file.

Technology has made recordkeeping in all areas a simpler task. Computers today have assumed much of the load of keeping, updating, and correcting records. But with progress has come the problem of access. By using computers, companies, hospitals, doctors and the overall number of people who have access to your private files—just in the course of normal work—has increased. Every additional person who handles information becomes a possible leak, a possible error-producer. Only your careful surveillance can assure that the information in your files is correct. In many cases, you may not even know of an error until you are denied credit, or insurance, or admittance to a school.

HOSPITAL RECORDS

Records are released to the patient, and to doctors, insurance companies, and attorneys with the patient's permission—subject to subpoena by court. For any hospital records, contact the records department of the hospital concerned.

Your request for information should be in writing and should contain: Your name and address, patient number, if known, and date of hospitalization. Note: Some hospitals do not release files directly to you but require your physician to review the file with you.

MEDICAL AND DENTAL RECORDS

Records are released to patient, doctors, insurance companies, and attornies with the patient's permission. For any medical records, contact the physician or dentist concerned.

Your request for information should be in writing and should contain: Your name and address, and, if not a current patient, the date of last services rendered. Note: Some states recognize medical records as the property of the physician and therefore the physician may release information at his own discretion.

PSYCHOLOGICAL AND MENTAL HEALTH RECORDS

Records are released to the patient, and to doctors, and attorneys with the patient's permission. For any medical records, contact the physician, psychologist, or counselor concerned.

Your request for information should be in writing and should contain: Your name and address, and, if not a current patient, the date of last services rendered. Note: These records are of a highly confidential nature, and, for the welfare of the patient, the physician or counselor involved may refuse to release the records, even to another physician.